Memoirs of the Life, Character, and Ministry of William Dawson
by James Everett

Memoirs of the life, character, and ministry of William Dawson

James Everett

EXTRACTS FROM REVIEWS

OF

DAWSON'S MEMOIRS.

———

" The subject of these memoirs was a celebrated Local Preacher among the Wesleyans, and was, in several respects, an extraordinary man. Possessing great physical energy and superior native genius, he was also distinguished by deep and unblemished piety, burning zeal, unwearied activity, disinterested labours, and extensive usefulness. Mr. Everett has produced an interesting and instructive piece of biography. It abounds with incident, anecdote, and graphic sketches." The PATRIOT, March 17, 1842.

" It abounds with amusing anecdotes, dialogues, and repartees, and contains some passages on which all who wish to study human nature in its variety of aspects may meditate with advantage." BAPTIST MAGAZINE, April, 1842.

" There has just issued from the press a highly interesting life of the late Mr. Dawson, a man of great originality, and one of the most popular preachers in modern times. In him were combined perhaps, more of the fervour of Baxter and the imagination of Bunyan than can be found in any other minister. The work is perfectly *Dawsonian,* as much so as Boswell's life of Dr. Johnson is *Johnsonian.* You see the man in private—in social life—in the pulpit and on the platform, and all so correctly represented, that all those who were acquainted with the original, were his name entirely omitted, would at once exclaim this is Mr. Dawson, for this is his *image and superscription."* BRISTOL MERCURY, March 19, 1842.

" The volume contains some homely wisdom, and original traits of manners, with abundant evidence of the piety of its subject." TAIT'S EDINBURGH MAGAZINE, April, 1842.

a

"Mr. Everett has earned for himself an established reputation for this class of writings by his 'Memoirs of Daniel Isaac,' his 'Wall's End Miner,' and his 'Village Blacksmith.' The latter work especially brought out his talent for delineation, and fixed him on the pinnacle of biographical fame. The peculiarly captivating style which marks Mr. Everett's former works, distinguishes also the present volume; and though examples of involved, of obscure, and of cramped composition might be picked out, they seem to serve as foils to the general beauty of our author's diction, in which there is an air and a spirit that throw a charm over the whole. The perpetual bubbling up of classical poetry and other literary allusions, intermingled with striking and appropriate metaphor, cannot fail to delight the reader of taste, and to afford an exquisite gratification to the mind previously familiar with general literature. If we were disposed to find fault at all, it would be on the ground of too great a profusion in the use of similes; but even this, we have no doubt, will be more acceptable than otherwise to a numerous class of readers; and were that not the case, what are a few minor defects in the midst of so many excellences? It is not every writer of memoirs that *possesses* the tact for catching the *distinctive features* of a character, and so presenting to his readers an actual portrait of the individual subject of his pen: but no one can read the works of Mr. Everett without perceiving that this necessary talent is possessed by him in a high degree, and that he strikes off a likeness true to nature, yet robed in such drapery as only a brilliant imagination could paint, and a discriminating judgment adjust. Such is 'Everett's Life of Dawson.' The book is not a *mere* collection of facts and incidents; it is an *exhibition of character*, in which facts and incidents are abundantly introduced as the faithful colouring and true filling up of an ably drawn outline. Those who knew Mr. D., will know his picture. Those who knew him not, and who love to study *real character*, will feel themselves not a little obliged to our author for the manner in which he has performed the task assigned him, of bringing such a specimen of humanity under public review through the medium of the press."—NOTTINGHAM MERCURY, April 1, 1842.

"This is the biography of an eminent Methodist,—of which system it was Mr. Dawson's great object to make his life a perfect exemplification." ATHENÆUM, March, 26, 1842.

In the Press, and speedily will be Published,

A VOLUME OF LETTERS,

SELECTED FROM THE CORRESPONDENCE OF

MR. W. DAWSON.

N. & P. Holl fc.

I am yours affectionately

W Dawson

London, Published by Mess. Hamilton, Adams & C.º Paternoster Row, 1842.

Published by Mess. Hamilton Adams & C. Paternoster Row.

MEMOIRS

OF THE

LIFE, CHARACTER, AND MINISTRY,

OF

WILLIAM DAWSON,

LATE OF BARNBOW, NEAR LEEDS.

BY

JAMES EVERETT,

AUTHOR OF "THE VILLAGE BLACKSMITH," "THE WALL'S END MINER,"
"THE POLEMIC DIVINE," &c., &c.

"Narrow is that man's soul, which the good of himself, or of his own relations and friends can fill: but he, who, with a benevolence, warm as the heat of the sun, and diffusive as its light, takes in all mankind, and is sincerely glad to see poverty, whether in friend or foe, relieved, and worth cherished, makes the merit of all the good that is done in the world his own, by the complacency which he takes in seeing or hearing it done."—ANON.

"HE WAS A BURNING AND A SHINING LIGHT."—John v. 35.

FIFTH THOUSAND.

LONDON:
PUBLISHED BY HAMILTON, ADAMS, AND CO.,
PATERNOSTER-ROW.

1842.

365.

PREFACE.

———

As to personal history, many of the more prominent facts recorded in these Memoirs, were communicated to the biographer by the subject himself, either directly, in the way of information, or incidently, in the course of general conversation.   Partly through the accumulation of these facts—which a friendship of nearly twenty eight years continuance might naturally be expected to produce, but still more because of the high value fixed upon moral, religious, and intellectual character, a purpose was formed, in the event of the writer being the survivor, of furnishing a simple narrative of the life of his friend.   This design being reserved to himself, he was not a little surprised, soon after the decease of the beloved subject, to be waited upon by the executors,— Messrs. Charles Smith and Edward Phillips, of Leeds, requesting him to undertake the Memoir of their long endeared and venerated friend; stating, at the same

a 2

time, that the family united in the request. Something providential appearing in this coalescence of intention, arrangements were immediately made to enter upon the work. The executors, with promptitude and kindness, placed the papers of Mr. Dawson in the hands of the writer ; and, combining with his own collections whatever was available for the purpose of biography, he proceeded with all possible care and despatch, to furnish the following pages ; which, under these circumstances, are presented to the public, not only with the sanction of the family, but under the authority of the executors.

Though the writer had a valuable collection of Letters in hand, obligingly furnished by different friends, he studiously avoided the introduction of them into the Life ; first, because they would have swelled it to an inconvenient size ; secondly, he was anxious to introduce as much incident as possible ; and thirdly, he foresaw that the Letters themselves would form an excellent volume——running chronologically arranged by the side of the Life, as a kind of companion,——leaving it optional with the reader to take one or both, as inclination or circumstances might lead.

In each of the biographies in which the writer has been engaged, it has been a maxim with him to be *honest*—to give both sides. He has never been either afraid or ashamed to look human nature in the face, so far as simple *character* has been concerned—apart from vice—whether in its strength or weakness, its eccentricities or its regularities ; nor has he ever tried to make a man *what*, in reality, he was *not*,—so that when his friends and neighbours have seen him in print, they have been unable to recognize him—having been made so much *better* than he actually was. Religion requires no deception ; and happily for the biographer, he undertook a subject that could sustain a scrutiny, — a subject as open as the day,—and, for sincerity, as transparent as the light. That subject the biographer commits to the world, with an ardent wish, that the virtues embodied there, may be exhibited both by himself and his readers.

JAMES EVERETT.

YORK, Feb. 12th, 1842.

ADVERTISEMENT

To the Second Edition.

——————

THOUGH it was the study of the biographer to render the present Memoir as acceptable and useful as possible, agreeably to the materials he possessed, and he was aware of the hold his subject maintained on the respect and affection of a large portion of the religious public, he could not but be surprised on finding the impression—comprising between two and three thousand copies, sold in the space of twelve days, with demands, in consequence of orders uncompleted, for a second edition. While he traces this up to its legitimate cause—to his *subject*, it would argue equal insensibility and ingratitude, to manifest any feeling beside that of a pleasurable one, in adverting to the favourable manner in which the work has been noticed in several of the public journals. Where a suggestion has been offered in the spirit and character of fair criticism, it has not only been freely and gratefully received, but readily acted upon;

when otherwise, reasons have been assigned for adhering to any previously established position or advanced opinion.

A few homely, as well as cheerful incidents and expressions, are retained in the present edition, for the very same reason that they were originally introduced,—as "part and parcel" of the man, who was as remote from the scholar, the courtier, and the droll, as he was from vulgarity, asceticism, and gloom. The biographer affirms much, when he declares he *felt* his subject; but he never, while prosecuting his task, lost sight of Mr. Dawson as he *was*,—though sometimes at the risk of being charged with a want of more refined taste by the more fastidious. He was aware, that persons of sense and candour, would no more renounce their claim to such attributes, by denouncing a book as bad for a few defects, and by confounding plainness with vulgarity, than an agriculturist could be brought to pronounce a field of wheat to be a field of tares, because of a few stray weeds in the centre, or in the more immediate neighbourhood of the fence. Wholesale opinions often proceed from the ignorant and malevolent.

The writer may observe here, what, perhaps, might have been more properly stated before,—that he has been liberal in his use of the literary productions of others; but he is not apprehensive that many of his readers will fall into the mistake of the good old man, who, on reading a work interlarded with quotations from other authors, replied, on being asked his opinion of the work,—"It is very good; but the hero of the tale is surrounded with a number of persons he knew nothing about;" thus confounding the writers adverted to with the persons with whom the subject of the Memoir associated. The biographer would remark on this subject, that whenever a thought occurred to him, which he either found more satisfactorily expressed, or more happily illustrated, or which at all confirmed his own previously formed opinions, in the writings of others, he consulted as much the gratification of his readers as his own, in its insertion;— being happy, at the same time, to find his own sentiments confirmed by persons possessing an authority with the public, to which he himself can assert no claim.

Some weak people, when a writer is tolerably free in conversational remarks, can conceive of no other plan—the one of course which they would propose to themselves, than that of retiring to his study at the close of each successive day, and entering into a Diary the various conversations he may have heard, in the various circles in which he may have moved; and they have not only dropped a cautionary remark to others, but have observed an impenetrable silence themselves; lest their own manifold wisdom should be surreptitiously recorded for the benefit of posterity. But they are few indeed who stand out from their fellows, and who, by common consent, are deemed men of more than ordinary pretensions to observation, and that would either tempt an amateur in this way, or pay for the trouble of following; and only a few of the more choice sayings of even these ought to be placed on permanent record. A man capable of Boswellising, will rarely leave his company in debt, as far as he himself is concerned; and will generally take a Johnson for his subject. Others, in common-place life, among whom the timid objectors are often to be found, and who are the most ready to adopt the language of the Scotch poet,—"A chiel's among you taking notes," have generally least occasion of alarm on their own account,—having formed a much more exalted notion of themselves, and of the importance of their "sayings and doings," than the writers referred to are apt to entertain. Men who are the most in danger of being Boswellised, are often the least suspicious;—being always at home with themselves and with others, which renders them more natural and easy in their manners, and more cheerful, graceful, varied, and bold in their conversation. It is a painful situation for a man to be placed in, to be ready to speak and to act, and no one at hand to write. Persons who speak for print, are often disappointed;—and the disappointment is remembered long after it ceases to be distressingly painful.—J. E.

York, April, 28th, 1842.

CONTENTS.

CHAPTER I.

CHAPTER II.

CHAPTER III.

CHAPTER IV.

CHAPTER V.

CHAPTER VI.

CHAPTER VII.

CHAPTER VIII.

CHAPTER IX.

CHAPTER X.

CHAPTER XI.

CHAPTER XII.

CHAPTER XIII.

CHAPTER XIV.

CHAPTER XV.

CHAPTER XVI.

MEMOIRS

of

WILLIAM DAWSON.

CHAPTER I.

PERSONAL religion cannot appear otherwise than glorious in a Christian minister, dissevered from all secular employment, and exclusively consecrated to the service of the sanctuary. Under such circumstances, he is, in scripture phraseology, "as the sun when he

A

goeth forth in his might ; " unaccompanied by a single
cloud, and mounting up his shining way, amid the
pure azure of heaven, till he attain his meridian height
and glory. The same amount of piety in a man
mixed up with the bustle and business of life, is in
danger of having a portion of its real worth imperceptibly abstracted from it, in consequence of the
association ; whereas, the real glory of the latter tran-
scends that of the former, by reason of his coming
out of a feast, a place of trust, with its untold
thousands, a mercantile transaction—out of *the world,*
in short,—as pure as from the temple of God, with its
means of grace. Such a man was WILLIAM DAWSON,
the subject of these Memoirs, whose honour as a man,
and whose character as a Christian, stood not only
unimpeached, but were the subjects of glowing eulogy ;
being deservedly classed with those "that buy, as
though they possessed not," and that "use this world,
as not abusing it."

The grandfather of William was colliery agent to
Lord Irvine, of Temple Newsam ; and one of the
brothers of his grandfather was land and colliery
agent to Sir Rowland Winn, Bart., of Nostal Priory,
near Wakefield, about the time that the celebrated
John Nelson was employed as a stone-mason, in the
re-erection of the family mansion.

The name of William's father was Luke Dawson,
and his mother's maiden name was Ann Pease. She
was distinguished for great strength of mind, a shrewd
insight into business transactions, combined with considerable foresight—being capable of diving into remote conclusions from present appearances ; added
to which—possessing the fear of God, she was a

woman of sterling integrity. Being in the habit of visiting Leeds occasionally, and of comparing the past with the present, she sometimes amused her children with the change ;—telling them, that she recollected to have seen grass growing in Briggate, after attaining the age of womanhood. Her husband, the father of William, acted as steward to Sir Thomas Gascoigne, one of the descendants of the ancient family of Gascoigne, of Gawthorpe ; the baronetage of which became extinct on the death of the late Sir Thomas, when Richard Oliver, Esq., of Parlington, succeeded him in his estates ; and, in compliance with his will, assumed the name of Gascoigne. The office of Mr. Luke Dawson was to superintend the colliery department, which office he sustained for a period of twenty-one years, when death put an end to his labours. He died Aug. 5, 1791, in the fifty-first year of his age, leaving a widow who reached her "three-score years and ten." His comparatively premature removal from this transitory state, was not remarkable, he having been, in the language of the subject of these pages to the biographer, "but a sickly man. " One circumstance, in addition to the fact of his office having terminated only with his life, goes to prove, that he had not only the respect, but the fullest confidence of his master. In a case of some difficulty, when a party appealed to Sir Thomas, whose decision would have been final, and to give which would have been attended with no impropriety, he replied, "Gentlemen, I shall not decide, till I have first seen Luke Dawson, and consulted him on the subject."

Mrs. Dawson bore ten children to her husband. Two, who were twins, died soon after they were born ; another—a boy, quitted life at the age of one year and three quarters; and a fourth—a girl, was called hence when verging on her second year; the other six reached maturity, one of whom—a sister, who was married, died in London; and four of the remaining five, two brothers and two sisters, survived the subject of these pages.

William was the oldest child, and was born March 30th, 1773, at Garforth, a small parish town, three miles from Aberford, and seven from Leeds, in the county of York. The other children were born at Barnbow,* a short distance from Garforth, whither his parents went to reside while he was yet a child in the arms. The house at Barnbow being then in the course of erection, William was sent to Whitkirk, little more than two miles distant, to reside with his grandfather and grandmother on the paternal side, with whom he continued for a period of nearly five years. One circumstance connected with infancy may be noticed, as it had an influence upon his opinions in mature life. During the first half-year of his existence, he was feeble and sickly, and cried both night and day; so much so, that his father and all the domestics, with the exception of his mother, wished—for his own sake —supposing that his life would be one of debility and suffering, that the Lord would call him hence. To this almost incessant crying, he afterwards attributed the strength of his lungs; and certainly, if there is any truth in the remark, that strength is acquired by exercise, his opinion was correct. When able to run abroad, he had a little play-fellow, of the name of William Arthur, of whom he was passionately fond.

---

* The population of Garforth, according to the census of 1831, amounted to 731 persons. The townships of Barnbow, Morwick, and Scholes, contained a population of 764; the first comprising 273, and the two latter 491.

His namesake having taken the small-pox, he was cautioned against visiting the house. Heedless of the injunction, and insensible of the danger, he proceeded to the abode of the little invalid. His absence soon awakened suspicion at home; and those who were sent in pursuit of him, found him with the sick boy, into whose bed he had crept unperceived by the family. There, in his child-like way, and with a warmth of feeling creditable to riper age, he was consoling him under his affliction. This is a fine instance of what is denominated the "intelligence of affection," which is carried on by the eye only, and which, while it exists in the heart, is often falsified by the tongue, through the refinements of society. The eye of little Dawson saw the plague-spot of that disease of childhood upon his companion of "sports and pastimes;"—his heart was smitten with a tenderness of which he knew not the name;—he clasped the contagion to his bosom, and bore it away to his own couch; where he lay, like his play-fellow, the subject of tender domestic solicitude. Both of the invalids, however, soon recovered, and were as soon beheld sporting on the village green; shewing to the separate families by what fine-spun threads the affections are drawn together,—threads as fine as those spun from the bowels of the spider, and yet so strong, as to bid defiance to disease and death in mature age.

The house of old Mr. Dawson adjoining the burial-ground belonging to the Established Church, the two boys were often found gambolling among the tombs, —a ground, which, next to a place of worship, should be held sacred, but which is too often thoughtlessly passed over by both old and young, and not sufficiently fenced by the proper authorities. The subject of these Memoirs having been taught to read, and having strolled into the church one day, while the sexton was engaged in the discharge of some of his duties, proposed to his companion "a game," as it was termed, "at parson and clerk,"—selecting for himself the more dignified character of the former, and assigning to his fellow the more humble office of the latter. Accordingly, Dawson, who could in many instances mimic to the life, entered the reading-desk, opened the Bible, whose unwieldy size required all the physical energy he possessed to unfold its pages, announced the book, and, with an audible voice, read a chapter, occasionally bending his eye upon his less dignified companion in the clerk's place below, which he was the better able to effect, in consequence of having elevated his person by something which he had found at hand adapted to the purpose. This led his mother pleasantly to remark, in after life, when his ministerial labours were adverted to—"He was born a preacher."

On the death of his grandfather, he returned to his parents at Barnbow, where he resided till within three or four years of his own demise. He accompanied his father and mother to Kippax, about three miles distant, where they sat under the ministry of the Rev. Miles Atkinson, afterwards of Leeds ; *—a man of evangelical sentiment and Christian character, both of which, in all probability, led Mr. and Mrs. Dawson to prefer Kippax to their own parish church at Barwick. This is the more likely, as the latter—had they not, like the children of the "elect lady," known and

---

* It is to this excellent man, that Mr. Wesley refers in his Journal, May 2, 1779, having been requested by him to preach in his church.—Works, Vol. IV. p. 151.

walked in the "truth," presented—especially in unfavourable weather, greater inducements to flesh and
blood, than the former, requiring a journey of only two
miles instead of six. William heard Mr. Atkinson during
a period of four years, but observed to the biographer,
that he was unable to comprehend what was advanced,
and was consequently not properly impressed by it ;
a circumstance, perhaps—as the ministry was strictly
evangelical, though not peculiarly striking,—more to be
attributed to the carelessness of the hearer, than to any
want of perspicuity in the matter, or seriousness in the
demeanour of the preacher.

After this, when in his ninth year, he sat under
the ministry of the Rev. W. Richardson, who officiated in the same church. Mr. Richardson was more
adapted to his genius ; for dealing occasionally in strong
expressions, not unfrequently spiced with the quaint-
nesses of the preceding age, he at once caught and
fixed the attention of his young auditor, whose mind,
like the opening bud, was gradually expanding to the
solar rays of instruction. One of these peculiar forms
of expression he carried with him through life, sometimes employing it to good purpose : "I love," said
Mr. Richardson, when speaking of persons acting with
a "single eye,"—"I love those *one-eyed* Christians." *

With such aid in the pulpit, Mrs. Dawson, to whom

* Mr. Richardson afterwards removed to the city of York, where he exercised
the ministerial office 30 years, having been in the ministry 50 in all. On his
decease was published, " The Faithful Minister, Israel's best Defence. A
Sermon preached at St. Michael-le-Belfry, York, May 27th, 1821, in consequence of the death of the Rev. W. Richardson, Minister of that Church.
By the Rev. J. Graham, Rector of St. Saviour, and St. Mary, Bishop-hill,
sen., and Domestic Chaplain to the Rt. Hon. Earl Bathurst. " 8vo. pp. 33.
It appears from Mr. Graham's account of Mr. Richardson, that he was no
ordinary man ; his perception being acute and discriminating—his memory

William looked up as his priestess, and who was anxious to promote the religious welfare of her children, was greatly assisted in her domestic appeals to the conscience. Though she had no vices to preserve in check, no acts of immorality to condemn, yet she knew, that personal religion was not of spontaneous growth,—that human nature would no more send forth its shoots of piety, without culture and grace, than a naturally unfruitful soil will yield golden crops without care, seed, manure, and tillage; of which she had a striking example in a portion of the land tenanted by her husband. While Mr. Dawson, therefore, was engaged with his farm and his stewardship, Mrs. Dawson took upon herself the momentous charge of the children, as to religion and morals. For this, she was not only religiously disposed, but admirably fitted; and, as in the order of Providence, she was destined to be left with them, while some of them were yet young, she acquired by it a commanding influence through life, which was the more important as age advanced. In order deeply to impress William's mind, together with the hearts of the other children, as they rose under her training hand, she prayed with them, read the Holy Scriptures to them, and enforced many of her remarks by select portions from the "PRACTICE OF PIETY." Two paragraphs of the latter, William observed to the writer,

accurate and tenacious—his judgment sound — his reading extensive—his learning solid and useful—his discourses, at the same time, being enriched with maxims of substantial, practical wisdom—and his conversation eminently engaging and improving. As to personal religion, his devotion is stated to have had the character of strength rather than warmth, being seated in the mind rather than in the passions. He was the staunch friend of Bible, Missionary, and other valuable institutions, and was considered the "FATHER" of the Sunday Schools belonging to the Established Church, in the city of York.

late in life, fastened their contents upon his mind; further stating, that he often wept and prayed over them,—adding, in his expressive way,—" Many a time have I thumbed them since."

"Drelincourt on Death," and "Flavel on the Soul," were also books which he read in early life, and which seriously impressed him with the awful realities of an invisible world. But there was one book, he re-marked, when speaking of his juvenile days, the exact title of which had passed from the memory, but whose purport seemed to be the vast importance of religion, professing to solve the momentous ques-tion—Shall I be Lost or Saved? which made the deepest impression upon his mind. The book, he stated, was afterwards either lost or destroyed; and as religion rose in importance in his esteem, he felt the more anxious to procure a copy; but, in the whole of his search, he was never able to meet with anything capable of satisfying his mind with the fact of it being an impression of the same work. It did not occur to the biographer, till sometime after the con-versation took place, that it might possibly have been a copy of "The Great Concern; or, a Summary Account of the Fear of God, and Keeping his Com-mandments, by Samuel Wright, D.D.," a third edition of which was published in London, in 1733, and was a likely book to find its way into a family where the "Practice of Piety" was so highly esteemed. But whatever might be the work, he observed at the same time with deep and sweet emotion,—as though all other oracles spoke through one, and as if every ray of light from other sources flashed upon his spirit through the same medium—"I owe much to

A 2

my MOTHER!"—a subject on which he was always tender, and under which, whenever he touched it, an audience has sighed and wept like a child weeping before its parent; and has been as much subdued into softness, as the maddened spirit of Saul was toned down to subordination and quiet, when the fingers of the Hebrew bard swept across the strings of the Jewish harp. Oh, yes! the kindest lessons are those which a mother teaches, as the most touching and solemn warnings are those which issue from her heart and from her lips, when she warns away her child from danger: and William Dawson was one who, though he stood in awe of his mother, never ceased to love her, whether in youth or in age; and the biographer himself, with silverlings now sprinkling his head, still recollects, while writing, with a gushing heart, and eyes swimming in tears, a mother's love,—a mother who descended into "the valley of the shadow of death," with many endearing recollections, at the advanced age of between eighty and ninety.

The subject of these Memoirs seems to have had much more of the mother than the father, both with regard to physical energies and to intellectuality. He possessed, with the exception of the first half-year of his life, a sound, healthy, constitution,—was remarkable for muscular strength, as soon as he was able to exercise it, —and manifested, as age crept on, amazing vivacity, with occasional corruscations of genius. His grandmother, adverting to his general health, his readiness for his meals, and the cheerfulness with which he seemed to partake of the bounties of providence, used to say, "Child, thou hast a crop for all kinds of corn." With some of these proverbial expressions, whose sense was full, and whose alliteration rhymed to the ear, he would occasionally amuse the writer.

His first school-master, on leaving Whitkirk, was Joseph Cromack, of Barwick. The school-room in which he was taught, adjoined the church-yard, and stood on the site of the present erection. Here, but slender progress was made in learning. Joseph seems to have wanted some of the pre-requisites for his situation, and to have been only less pedantic than another master of the ferula, to whom William referred one day to the writer, of the name of John B., who kept a school at Scholes. He humorously represented John as a wholesale reader of one of the largest Leeds papers—commencing with the first advertisement on the first page, and systematically proceeding with every word to the imprint at the close. Adverting to some effects which were advertised for sale, but not being conversant with the several items, John observed to a villager, who was not quite so profoundly learned as himself—"The whole, I suppose, will be *devil-oped* on the day of sale."

His next tutor was the Rev. W. Hodgson, curate of Garforth, who taught a school at Barwick. This gentleman, being defective in Christian conduct, often neglected his pupils ; the consequence was, that young Dawson was next sent to Mr. Ephraim Sanderson, of Aberford, who kept a large academy in that place ; and who, exclusive of day scholars, had sometimes as many as forty boarders. The distance was three miles from Barnbow, and thither our tyro proceeded daily. There he made the greatest progress in learning, and finished his education ; often, at a subsequent period, when capable of forming a judgment, complimenting his master for his conduct and abilities. Zimmerman speaks of learned men, who are ignorant of nothing, saving their own ignorance. Mr. Sanderson was not of this class, and it is a happy circumstance that Dawson's close at school was much more propitious than its beginning.

Owing to the religious instruction received at home, William was the better prepared to profit under the ministry of the Rev. Thomas Dikes, who officiated as curate at Barwick-in-Elmet, for a period of two years, prior to his final residence in Hull. Under that gentleman's ministry he received his first deep and permanent awakenings, subsequent to those produced under domestic tutorage. Not only was he favoured with his ministry, but with his counsel in social life, as well as with his epistolary correspondence; the latter of which was not only expressive of high esteem, but a deep anxiety on the part of Mr. Dikes to promote his best interests. Among other helps to piety, Mr. Dikes put Doddridge's "Rise and Progress of Religion in the Soul," into his hand. He was sitting in the barn one day, when John Batty, one of his father's servants, who was also the subject of serious impressions, found him poring over its pages. On going into the house, he was asked by his master whether he had seen William anywhere; to which he replied in the affirmative. He was next asked what he was engaged in, when he returned—"reading." Having seen him in deep distress, and being afraid lest it should be a book that would increase it, and so, in the language of Festus, set him "beside himself," his parents were anxious to know its character, and also to secure possession of it, without exercising force or severity.

When John returned to the barn, he informed William of what had passed; saying, by way of apology, "What could I do? I was obliged to speak the truth!" William replied. "You did right." This book he generally concealed on what was called the wall-plate of the granary; and to the granary, or some other private place, he used to retire, when he wished to read without interruption. He appears to have derived unusual benefit from it; for on Friday, July 25th, 1790, he wrote an extract from it, embracing nearly two folio pages, and headed,—"A Solemn Surrender to Almighty God;" to which he appended, opposite the date,—"solemnly performed this day."

His solicitude for deliverance from spiritual bondage increasing, he naturally sought for relief in the use of the ordinances of God; and it was agreed, that he should receive the sacrament of the Lord's Supper at the hands of Mr. Dikes, in connexion with John Batty, who, by this time, had grown up into a kind of band-mate for him. The minds of both were impressed with sacred awe,—vows, promises, and protestations were made,—and the "Week's Preparation" was not only seriously read, but its directions were rigidly observed. Though the day of liberty was still in hazy twilight, his ardour for salvation was considerably increased by the solemnity of the occasion. All was anxiety within; the spirit was struggling to be free; and the very solicitude experienced, was so strained and overbent, that it seemed to break and prove a hinderance to itself; like a body of water, which, in consequence of its own super-abundance and onward force, is prevented from finding a ready issue through the straitened sluice. He was unable to give full expression to his feelings ; and hence, sat brooding over his inward wretchedness.

During the residence of Mr. Dikes at Barwick, a church was in the course of erection for him at Hull, to which place he finally removed ; and in which place he was living, in mellow age, and crowned with honour, when the subject of these pages had finished his course. Mr. Dikes, in early life, was particularly distinguished for his zeal; and though William Dawson did not enter into Christian liberty till some time after he left for Hull, yet he "took," as he expressed himself to the biographer, "the mould of" his "religious character from him," which was then beginning to unfold itself in its various lineaments and features.

Though he was not at all superstitious, and used to state, in reference to dreams, that only one in a hundred might possibly be improved ; yet, there was one about this period, the effects of which he was never able——nor did he wish, to shake off. He dreamed one night, that he saw two roads, the one broad and the other narrow,——that multitudes were crowding the former, where they were dancing along in tumultuous joy, favoured with everything capable of gratifying the heart, fascinating the eye, enchanting the ear, and regaling the taste,——and that the other was nearly without a traveller.   Various inducements were held out to him, to take the broad way, all of which he declined ; and turning to John Batty, whom he thought he saw standing at the entrance with himself, he said, "We'll take the narrow path, John ; it will do for us ; we shall be less incommoded in it."   They pursued the line some distance, in agreeable companion- ship with each other, when he awoke.   Though only a vision of the night, it haunted him like a spectre by day ;—his young spiritual feelings, his vivid imagination, his pulpit monitor, his training at home, and above all, his Bible, in which he read also of a *broad* and a *narrow* way, enabled him to decipher the whole ; —it induced a spirit of fear and of caution, lest he should incline, even in purpose, to the left, in which direction the broad path lay ;—and meeting his early, and then old friend, a short time before his dissolution, who was thus one of the principal personages in this midnight drama, he exclaimed, with a fine flow of feeling, as if he had just been throwing the eye along the line of road they had actually travelled, and seen all the dangers they had separately escaped,— " Bless God, friend Batty, we are in the narrow way yet !" Can any one doubt, that " God, in a dream, in a vision of the night, when deep sleep falleth upon men, in slumbering upon the bed;"—can any one doubt, that God " then openeth the ears of men, and sealeth their instruction ? "

A young man, of the name of Samuel Settle, servant of Mr. Miles Jackson, of Hillam Mill, spoke to William on the subject of personal religion, and told him for his encouragement, that he himself enjoyed an assurance of the favour of God. This was like a light unexpectedly springing up in a dark place ; and the subject of these Memoirs kept his eye as steadily fixed upon it, till he was led to the Saviour, as did the " wise men " on the portentous " star," that finally guided their steps to Bethlehem, where they beheld the same object, only in an infant form—" the young child with Mary his mother," and where they " fell down, and worshipped him." Samuel was William's

guiding star. The latter had read of Christian assurance, and had heard what he deemed something
like it, urged from the pulpit; but he had been led
to contemplate it as the privilege only of a highly
favoured few—of saints of the first order, and rather
to be beheld in prospect—approaching nearer and nearer
to it, till just on the verge of the grave, than to be
enjoyed at present : and till now, he had never conversed with any one who experienced the blessing. This
anticipated experience is but too common with many.
If death were the *journey* instead of the *end* of it,
then such anticipations might be cherished. But who
would feed a lamp with oil, when the wick has reached
its end, and the flame is about to expire! The blessing
is as necessary for the spirit's sustenance on the *way*
to heaven, as at the *close* of it ; the manna was even
more essential to the Israelites on their march through
the wilderness, than when in sight of the promised
land, at the latter of which periods it ceased to descend.

The " sense of assurance," as enjoyed by Samuel,
dwelt on the mind of young Dawson, like the preceding dream, by night and by day. Samuel was looked
upon by him in the light of a superhuman being;
and he was in the habit of speaking on this—to him
mysterious subject, to John Batty, while at the plough,
and when otherwise engaged in the work of the farm
—" wondering in himself," like Peter in another case,
"at that which was come to pass." The distress of
mind which he had for some time experienced, rendered relief desirable, and for this he sought : but now
he knew how to give it a name,—saw a living example
of it in humble life, in one about his own age, and in
one respecting whose piety and character he entertained

the highest opinion. This increased his earnestness for the blessing, and he embraced every opportunity that presented itself of conversing with Samuel, and of corresponding with him, on the all absorbing subject. On leaving church, they often slipped notes into the hands of each other ; and thus, for some time, enjoyed the advantages of Christian fellowship. It is interesting to look at the outset of this youthful trio ;——John Batty, a servant in the house of one of his companions ; ——Samuel Settle, with his little bed in a part of the mill ;——and William Dawson, looking no higher than the plough ! How different their station and effects upon society, through life !——John Batty becomes a respectable farmer, quietly and unostentatiously settling down at Throstle Nest, a short distance from Barwick, where he was acting, as he had long done, in the capacity of a class-leader, on the death of William ——shining like a fixed star ; and where, to return to the former allusion, he was likely to end his days, saying with Job,——" I shall die in my nest ! " Samuel Settle is sent to college, chiefly through the instrumentality of the Rev. John Graham, leaving the noise of the mill for the calm of the study, and exchanging his powdered costume for the more stately and sombre drapery of a clergyman of the Established Church, in one of whose pulpits he was officiating at Salisbury, at the same period,——modestly pursuing his course, in beauty and in serenity, like the moon in the heavens ! William Dawson, on the other hand, is like a blazing sun, but with comet-like course, astonishing, entrancing, and fixing the gaze of the multitude ! And yet, without the grace of God, not one of these young men would, in all probability, have been known beyond their own homesteads, or, at furthest, beyond their own immediate vicinity !

William still continued to "groan, being bur- thened" with a sense of his moral wretchedness.   The Rev. Thomas Dikes, adverting to this, in a letter to the Rev. William Dawson, nephew of the subject of these Memoirs, dated Hull, July 30, 1841, observes ; "When I entered upon my ministry,"—referring to Barwick-in-Elmet,—"William Dawson was one of my parishioners, and regularly attended Church.   Then it was, I believe, he received his first religious impressions. He was wont to call upon me, and open his mind very freely.   His convictions of sin were deep and pungent. He was deeply sensible of the corruptions of his own heart, and felt how unable he was to deliver himself from the body of sin and death.   The foundation of his religion was laid in deep humility.   It was this that led him to diligent prayer, to steadfast faith in Christ, and to seek for that influence of divine grace by which he might serve God in righteousness and true holiness. His attendance on religious worship was regular, his behaviour devout ; and I shall never forget the marked attention he paid to the discourses from the pulpit. His walk and conversation were unblameable, and his whole deportment was serious,—yet, softened by that cheerfulness which, I believe, rendered him through life, an agreeable companion to those with whom he associated.   Soon after I became acquainted with Mr. Dawson, I left my curacy.   Mr. Graham, of York, succeeded me ; and his ministry, I am persuaded, was made a great blessing to Mr. D."   This is an inter- esting reminiscence of a venerable clergyman, upwards of eighty years of age, throwing his mind back upon a period of half a century, and bringing from the recesses of that mind the state and character of one of his parishioners; and excellent indeed must the character have been, to have left an impression so indelible on the mind of the pastor; nor is it less complimentary to the pastor himself, that he should have rendered himself so familiar with the state, not only of the sheep, but of the lambs of his flock. Mr. Dikes adds; "I am sorry I cannot contribute my quota to the life of one who did so much to promote the glory of God, and the benefit of his fellow men." Here, of course, he refers to his removal from Barwick, when personal intercourse ceased, and with it, personal observation. But the reminiscence itself, so far as early character goes, is an excellent condensed history.

The Rev. John Graham entered upon the duties of the parish, as curate, some time in the year 1790; under whose enlightened ministry, William—as anticipated by Mr. Dikes, received great advantage. But though the subject of these Memoirs considered himself a member of the Established Church, to which he was strongly attached, both by principle and gratitude; yet he had, from boyhood, been in the habit of attending the prayer-meetings among the Wesleyans, and of hearing the local preachers in the afternoon of the Lord's day, but without any intention or disposition to unite himself to the body. During the successive labours of Messrs. Dikes and Graham at Barwick, his attachment to the Establishment was still more strongly marked: the former minister influencing his heart by fervent zeal, the latter maintaining his authority over his intellect by superior talent. The two combined, not only nailed him to the door-posts of God's house, but exer-

cised a beneficial influence on his character in after life :
and a spirit at once so ardent, and a genius so exuberant, required the more sedate training of the clergy of
the Established Church, to moderate the strength of the
one, and prune the luxuriant shoots of the other. In
having two such guides, just at the turning point of life,
when one false step might have changed the whole face
of his character, and so have fixed his destiny for ever—
he may be considered as having been highly favoured.

Not having yet received a sense of the divine favour,
and having but little society adjacent to his own home-
stead, with the exception of the family and John Batty,
William was often the subject of more than ordinary
depression of spirit, which is not unfrequently the case
with persons who are a good deal thrown upon their
own resources. On one of these occasions, he went
into the fields—not like Isaac at eventide to meditate,
but more in the spirit of Jeremiah, to pour forth his
notes of sorrow. The sun, it would seem from his own
account to the biographer, was up in the heavens, the
fields were gay with flowers and rich in verdure, the
birds were warbling out their varied strains; everything
around him instinct with life, seemed happy, and, in his
own language, "all appeared striving to contribute to
his happiness." But no consolation could be derived
from either the reflections of his mind, or the objects—
animate and inanimate—around him. At length he
went behind a hedge, and while sweeter songsters left
him unmoved, one of the less beautiful and more
diminutive of the feathered tribe caught his eye, as it
hopped from twig to twig, uttering its monotonous but
cheerful note of—"chirup, chirup." This, by a sudden turn of thought, was instantly transformed by the

fertile imagination of the melancholy wanderer into—
"cheer-up,—cheer-up,—cheer-up," which, even in its
abbreviated form, presented no great dissimilarity to the
ear. He said within himself,—"Here is a little bird
happy, and I—and I—possessed of an immortal spirit
—born for heaven—cared for by a watchful providence
—fed, sheltered, protected, redeemed—with salvation
within reach—and the very heaven for which I was
born, offered—am yet unhappy!" This circumstance,
though not less important in its nature than the case
recorded by the Hebrew bard, who contrasted his
suspended privileges with those of the " sparrow" and
the " swallow," one of which had " found an house,"
and the other "a nest," contiguous to the spot around
which the good man ever delights to hover—the "altars
of the Lord of Hosts,"—led to a train of serious reflection, which issued in serenity of mind ; and he could
not but adore the goodness of God,—humbled and
prostrated before Him, without whose permission a
sparrow cannot fall to the ground,—in thus employing
so minute and unimportant a creature, to be the instrument of such a reversed state of feeling,—from that
of deep overshadowing gloom, to the tranquillity and
cheerfulness of a summer evening.* This, however,
was but a foretaste of what was in reversion, for as yet

---

* The influence of external objects upon the mind, and the aspects in which
they are viewed, in certain moods and states, is strikingly illustrated by
Cambo, a negro in one of the Southren States of America, who was desired
to give an account of his conversion, and who proceeded thus : " While in
my own country, (Guinea,) me had no knowledge of the being of a God ; me
thought me should die like the beasts. After me was brought to America,
and sold as a slave, as me and another servant of the name of Bess were
working in the field, me began to sing one of my old country songs, ' It is
time to go home ;' when Bess say to me, ' Cambo, why you sing so for?' Me
say, ' Me no sick, me no sorry ; why me no sing?' Bess say, ' You better

he had not experienced the assurance to which his friend Settle had attained. It encouraged him, in the mean time, in the midst of further despondings, and inspired him with a hope, that the day of complete deliverance was not remote.

His father dying when he was only between eighteen and nineteen years of age, he succeeded him in the stewardship over the collieries of Sir Thomas Gascoigne, and became in his turn, and at this early period of life, the father of the family. With the stewardship was still connected the farm, consisting of about one hundred and fifty acres, some of the land of which, as already hinted, was exceedingly poor. To this his brother chiefly attended; and on its produce the family were principally dependant. Though he was now, in a certain sense, a master, yet, such was his reverence for his mother, that she bore the rule, while he attended to the provision of the family; thus presenting a fine example of filial obedience.

Mr. Graham had not been long at Barwick, before the subject of these Memoirs was enabled to lay hold on Christ by faith, and to rejoice in a sense of sin forgiven. This took place some time in the year 1791, in the church at Barwick, while Mr. Graham was administering the sacrament of the Lord's Supper, and just as he was uttering, " The body of our Lord Jesus Christ, which was given for thee, preserve thy soul

---

pray to your blessed Lord and Massa, to have mercy on your soul.' Me look round, me look up, me see no one to pray to; but the words sound in my ears, ' Better pray to your Lord and Massa !' Bye and bye me feel bad—sun shine sorry—birds sing sorry—land look sorry—but Cambo sorrier than them all. Then me cry out, ' Mercy, mercy, Lord! on poor Cambo !'—Bye and bye, water come in my eyes, and glad come in my heart. Then sun look glad—woods look glad—birds sing glad—land look glad, but poor Cambo gladder than them all. Me love my Massa some; me want to love him more."

and body unto everlasting life. Take and eat this in remembrance that Christ died for thee, and feed on him in thy heart by faith with thanksgiving." Than this, scarcely anything could have been more appropriate :—the seeking *sinner* was at the *table* of the Lord—in immediate contact with the *cross*—the *bread* was shadowed forth, which alone could impart life to the soul, and satisfy its cravings—an exhortation was given to the exercise of *faith*—the sentence of *death* was felt within—the death of the *Saviour* was exhibited for the *life* of the *transgressor*—and all this for THEE—yea, for THEE! He was overwhelmed with a sense of the mercy of God in Jesus Christ, and had the love of God shed abroad in his heart by the Holy Ghost given unto him.

It was not long before his new situation became a source of temptation ; it afforded him but few moments of leisure, and his tender conscience vibrated in the case of the coal measures used by the men, between justice to his master, and honesty to the purchaser —being unwilling to give the one any unfair advantage over the other. To this there seems to be a reference in the following letter to him from his old pastor, the Rev. Thomas Dikes, dated Hull, Nov. 21, 1791.

"DEAR SIR.—We must recollect, that we are not yet in heaven. This world is a wilderness, in which we must not expect rest and peace. Our Saviour Christ went through a great variety of afflictions, when he was upon earth : if the Head suffered so much, no wonder that the members should likewise suffer. Prosperity hardens the heart ; adversity softens it. The natural impetuosity of our temper will but ill brook subjection to God ; we must not be surprised, therefore, if the Almighty puts us into the furnace of affliction, that he may bring down the insolence of our pride, and make us submit to his yoke. 'Whom the Lord loveth, he chasteneth.'

"I am not sufficiently acquainted with the business in which you are engaged, to give you any directions respecting the proper discharge of it. I think your father was careful in seeing that the men gave full measure, which is certainly a duty you owe to the public. And I need not say, that you never can be too earnest in your endeavours to support your mother and family. Think no pain, no labour ill bestowed, if you can advance their interest. Be not slothful in business, but fervent in spirit, serving the Lord. Idleness lays us open to Satan's assaults. When he finds us unemployed, he will usually take care that we shall not be long without employment. But in the midst of your worldly business, find time for prayer and meditation. Dread a dull uniformity in religion worse than death; for when the mind falls into a dead, stupid frame, and is excited by no hopes, nor alarmed by any fears, then a total falling away from God is much to be feared. Let not a view of your sins discourage you from coming to Christ, for he is willing to save you, and is the author of eternal life to all that believe. Make him the beginning and end of all your religion. And remember, that eternal life will be the reward, through grace, of all who shall continue steadfast to the end. Be thou faithful unto death, and thou shalt have a crown of life. My kind regards to Mr. Graham. Yours, sincerely,

"In great haste,—THOMAS DIKES." *

* This is the manner in which the name is spelt in the letter; latterly it has been spelt Dykes.

CHAPTER II.

Commences a Diary.—Essays.—Letter from the Rev. T. Dikes.—Select religious Meetings.—Labours of the Rev. J. Graham.—Rev. T. Galland.— W. Dawson begins to exhort.—Attends the Religious services of the Wesleyans. — Hears the Rev. S. Bradburn.—Monarchy.—Prays in public.—Early Compositions.—The fall of man.—Sojourners.—The Scriptures.—The Apocalypse.— Reading. — Books. — Attempts to court the Muse. — Rev. R. Hemington. — W. Dawson becomes more public in his character.—"Grime Cabin."—Renewal of Covenant.—The Rev. Joseph Benson.—S. Settle sent to Magdalen College, Cambridge.—Reserve.—Sincerity.

In the spring of 1792, he commenced a Diary, which, though occasionally referring to graver matters, seems to have been chiefly intended for secular purposes, including the engagements of the day, the state of the weather, price of grain, &c. A few brief extracts, without following each successive day, as distinctly marked, will be sufficient to shew, not only its design and character, but also, that if there had been the least temptation to self-indulgence, his native energies and general activity would never have allowed such indulgence a moment's quarter,—ever acting, from nature and from habit, on the advice of Mr. Dikes,—and concluding "no pains, no labour ill

B

bestowed," to "advance the interest of the family."
"Mond. Ap. 14, A.B. *   Sowing in the morning.
Forenoon, in Broom Close."   "Tuesd. 15.   At Leeds.
Sold 8 lds., at 20s. 6d."   "Frid. 18.   Good-Friday.
At the *sacrament*."   "Tuesd. 22.   With Mr. P.
At Garforth in the evening."   "Mond. May 28.   Till
ten o'clock at the Colliery.   Then to B. C. [home,
Barnbow Car.]   Went to the *Society*."   "Tuesd. 29.
At Leeds, with Wheat.   At 14s. 3d."   "Wed. 30.
At Colliery."   "Thur. 31.   At do."   "Frid. June 1.
At Colliery.   Measured by Hole.   22 yds.   Mr. Porter
let the road to throw out, at 7s. per acre, four yds.
wide."   "Mond. 4.   Forenoon at Colliery, and after-
noon at Roundhay for G. S."   "Tuesd. 5.   At Colliery,
removing the gin to the sinking pit.   Mr. Emerson's
pasture at the bottom of the wood."   "Friday 8.
Rainy day.   No work."   "Sat. 9.   At the Colliery.
Balanced with Lun, &c., for sinking the pit in Mr.
Cotton's close."   "Thursd. 14.   Winnowing in the
forenoon.   Afternoon at the Colliery."   "Wed. 20.
At Colliery in the forenoon.   Afternoon at Mrs. Dawson's funeral."   "Thursd. 22.   At Colliery forenoon.
Afternoon at Boroughbridge fair."   "Sat. 23.   At
Boroughbridge till nine o'clock.   Bought 20 Wethers
at 16s. 3d., and 7 Gimmers at 13s. 6d.   At Colliery
in the afternoon."   "Tuesd. 26.   At Leeds."   "Wed.
27.   At Colliery.   Then washed sheep."   "Mond.
July 2.   At Colliery.   After, clipping sheep."   "Mond.
16.   At Colliery.   Begun to mow at Col.   Also
clover at home."   "Wed. August 2.   At Garforth
moor, putting up a beam."   "Mond. 6.   At Colliery

---

* "A. B.," is the abbreviation of—*At Barnbow*, as "A. C.," in the Diary,
sometimes stands for—*At the Colliery*.

in the morning. Stacking hay at home. Hay-making in the afternoon." "Frid. 10. At Colliery. James Hunsworth broke his leg in the top pit." "Sat 11. At Colliery. Mr. P. turned off J. Hunsworth, G. Scholes, and J. Dawson." "Sep. Wed. 5. At Colliery. Collins began to shear in Quarry close." "Mon. 10. At Colliery in the morning. Afternoon, making a stack upon Little Holme. A very high wind." "Tuesd. 11. Stacking oats, and at Col." "Thursd. 13. At C. forenoon. Leading corn in the afternoon. A strong wind." "Sat. 26. At Col. A very rainy week." "Tuesd. 25. At Leeds with corn and wool. S. C. at 19s. wool 11s. 9d." "Mond. Oct. 1. At Aberford fair. Sold a horse for twenty guineas." "Mond. 8. At Colliery till nine o'clock. Begun to sow." "Tuesd. 15. At Leeds. After, at Wm. Waits' funeral." "Mond. 29. At. Col. Coals raised 6d. per cwt." "Sat. Nov. 3. At Col. Settled with the colliers at 10½ per dozen, near end at 15d. per yd. Engine end 11d. per doz. Broad at 18d. per yd." "Mond. 5. At Aberford Statute the colliers stuck out." "Mond. Dec. 3. At the engine, taking pumps out." "Sund. 9. At Whitchurch in the forenoon. Afternoon at Barwick." "Mond. 17. At Garforth moor sinking. Begun to sink a deep pit at the engine end."

In this Diary, the Sabbath is distinguished with from two to four capital letters, in red ink, one involved within another, with some of the graceful curves of the writer, exceedingly difficult to decipher : mostly B. C., as if Barwick Church were intended, and sometimes the S. dexterously worked into them, as if the Sacrament were included.

Among his papers, are three essays, in his hand-
writing, dated 1792; one on "Christ's Love," another
entitled, "A Soliloquy," and the third founded on
Mark xiii. 37, "What I say unto you, I say unto all,
Watch." The last of these was begun in "June,"
and was enlarged "Decr. 1793." The first is desultory and common-place,—displaying more of piety
than ability. The second exhibits equal piety, but
more mind, and greater condensation. In the third,
he indulges a little in metaphor, and shews symptoms
of the future man. It is easily perceived in each,
that JESUS is not only "the brightness of the Father's
glory," but the object of the writer's love, and the
subject matter of his musings.

Mr. Graham had now been settled sometime at
Barwick; but though the subject of these Memoirs
had excellent help in him, he still availed himself of
the privilege of corresponding with Mr. Dikes, in
cases of depression, when placed in difficult situations,
or disturbed with the plague of his heart. He received another letter from that gentleman, bearing
date, "Hull, Feb. 2, 1793;" directed for "Mr. Will.
Dawson, Barnbow Carr, near Barwick, to be left at Mr.
Butterfield's, Horse and Trumpet, Cross Parish, Leeds."

"DEAR SIR,—I received your last latter, dated the
28th January. I shall be glad to give you any advice,
that might tend to comfort you, or to render your
progress more easy in the way of godliness. I feel
a regard for the Barwick people, among whom I
laboured two years, though not with the success I
could have wished. It is God, however, who must
give the increase. But I need not be large in my
admonitions to you, because you have an excellent

minister, whom you may consult as occasion requires ; and I advise you often to speak freely to him, and to lay open the state of your mind.   Such conferences will be attended with unspeakable benefit to yourself.

" Respecting your temporal circumstances, I shall not say much.   Read the xi chapter of the Epistle to the Hebrews.   Think of the things which are eternal.   It will soon be of little consequence whether you were high or low, rich or poor.   The proper way to get rid of anxious disquietude is, to furnish the mind with better thoughts.   Think much of Christ and the heavenly kingdom, to which you are hastening ; and you will find, that earthly things will seem less than nothing and vanity.

" Respecting spirituals.—You grow, I trust, in a knowledge of the evil nature that dwells within you. The more you know of indwelling sin, the more you will love Christ, who delivereth us both from its curse and power.   Hence, you will likewise grow in humility ; and he who groweth in humility, groweth in grace.

"But you must not think, that you are destitute of the grace of God, because you see greater iniquity in your heart than you have been wont to see.   The same evil, yea more abundant evil, was there before, —only your mind was darkened by sin, and you saw it not.   The depth of corruption, which is in the heart, can only be discovered by the grace of God's Spirit.   I trust you hate and loathe sin, and strive to be delivered from it.   This is a good evidence in your favour ; and you may conclude, that he who has begun a good work in you, will carry it on to the day of the Lord.   Believe, therefore, in Christ, and don't think you must stay till you are better, before you believe in him: but go to him, just as you are. Deliver yourself day by day into his hands, to be saved, sanctified, and governed. Keep up an intercourse with him in your soul, and seek grace out of his fulness for the supply of your daily necessities. Thus, in time, you will be enabled to adorn the doctrine of God your Saviour, by a holy life and conversation. Don't be always poring over your own heart, but look more at Christ the Son of God, who died for sinners.   Yours sincerely,

"THOMAS DIKES."

Mr. Graham preached regularly forenoon and afternoon on the Lord's day; and in the evening of that day, expounded in the school-room, adjoining the church; generally selecting a whole chapter, or particular sections, as the ground-work of his remarks. He held also a select meeting on the Thursday evening, which at first assembled in his own house, and afterwards in a private dwelling. Of this meeting, William Dawson was a member; and here the devout feelings of the heart were not only cherished, but the opening powers of the mind were brought into fuller exercise. Of Mr. Graham, he always spoke affectionately and respectfully, and often with deep feeling; stating, that of all the lecturers on entire chapters of the Bible, he was the most lucid, connected, comprehensive, interesting, and impressive, he ever heard.*　In this meeting, particularly in the absence of Mr Graham, during the vacation of school, or when otherwise called from home, William read a

* When naming this circumstance to the biographer, he added,—" Next to Mr. Graham, I am partial to Mr. Galland, who was sometime under Mr. Graham's tuition, at York, and who probably—seeing this excellence in the

portion of Scripture, and offered a passing remark upon it ; or, as he playfully observed, in the language of an illiterate man, whom he sometimes quoted, and who was in the habit of ignorantly substituting one word for another—" *expunged* a little." Here also, he often prayed, but never at this early period, in any public meeting, without a printed form. His remarks were at first rather sententious, and shewed great ripeness of judgment, combined with occasional flashes of genius.

His multifarious engagements had no influence upon him, in diminishing his efforts to increase in personal piety, or in damping his ardour in seeking the salvation of his neighbours. He continued to fill the chair left vacant by Mr. Graham, during the recess of the school—prayed—exhorted—and occasionally mingled with the members of the Wesleyan Society, both as a hearer and in their prayer-meetings. Adverting to the devotional meetings of the latter, when narrating, in friendly conversation with the biographer, the history of early days, he remarked,—" A shy, dry, reserved old class-leader, turned to me one Sunday afternoon, on being disappointed of a preacher, and said, ' Willy, go to prayer.' I refused, and felt indignant at the request. Though I could listen to others, while praying, yet I could not think of engaging officially in prayer myself, in a place unconnected with the Established Church. After this,

master, ventured upon it as a pupil. His *expositions* are superior to his *sermons*. In the former he excels. On having a vacant forenoon, or on my work for the Sabbath lying in that direction, I have gone frequently into Leeds on purpose to hear him expound the lessons for the day. To me, it was always a high treat, when he was in the Leeds circuit. I know no man equal to him as a lecturer in the Connexion."

I went to church as usual, but felt no freedom in the service. This led to serious self-examination; and I asked myself, why I should refuse to pray, when requested? It occurred to me, that either *pride* or *shame* must have been the cause, and that neither of these were fit companions for a professor of religion in a place of worship." This was sound reasoning, and rendered him much less repulsive at a subsequent period.

Mingling occasionally, as has been intimated, with the Wesleyans, and having heard of the fame of the Rev. Samuel Bradburn as an orator, who was announced to preach in the chapel in which the Rev. Edward Parsons officiated, he decided on visiting Leeds. This was during the Conference of 1793. His prejudices, he remarked to the writer, were exceedingly strong at this time in favour of the Established Church; and up to this period—with the exception of the Wesleyan local preachers, he could scarcely bear to hear a person preach without a gown. This predilection in favour of the clerical costume was met on the present occasion, in consequence of the preacher being habited in the vestment usually worn by Mr. Parsons; and apart from his oratorical powers, Mr. Bradburn's noble, commanding figure, powdered hair, and advanced age, at once fixed his eye and captivated his heart. His subject was the Kingly Office of Christ; and being at the period of those feverish heats occasioned by Paine's "Age of Reason" and "Rights of Man," when man himself was running riot, and preparing his way for the severest denunciations and heaviest penalties of all law, civil and religious, he availed himself of the spirit and opinions of the times—a work for which he was well qualified, for the purpose of shewing the advantages of a monarchical, over all other forms of government,—never losing sight of the subject in hand, but directing the attention of his auditory to the kingdom of Christ. Though the British government is unquestionably mixed, and therefore properly denominated by some writers, a limited monarchy, the preacher could at once shew the admirable balance of power in the very circumstance of its being formed by a combination of the three regular species of government, —the monarchy residing in the King, the aristocracy, in the House of Peers, and the republic, as represented by the House of Commons. The kingly office of Christ, at all events, was grateful to one who had submitted to his laws; and the preacher's denunciations against scepticism and insubordination, could not be otherwise than satisfactory to a member of the Church of England.

Mr. Bradburn, on giving out the last hymn, inclined his person over the front of the pulpit, and looking to the precentor, who had either not pleased him, or preferring it for some private reason, said, "I will give out the two last verses myself;" which were,

> " The government of earth and seas
> Upon his shoulders shall be laid ;
> His wide dominions shall increase,
> And honours to his name be paid.
> " Jesus, the holy child, shall sit,
> High on his father David's throne ;
> Shall crush his foes beneath his feet,
> And reign to ages yet unknown."*

These verses, the subject of these pages had never heard before; and yet, from the bare recital of them by the preacher, he recollected them ever afterwards. His memory was naturally tenacious, and was considerably improved afterwards by habit. This specimen

* Watts' Hymns, Book I. Hymn 13.

B 2

of simple, free, powerful, and impassioned oratory, which he had in Mr. Bradburn, gave him a more favourable opinion of the Wesleyan preachers, and a more kindly bearing towards the body : and certainly, if in oratory, the greatest art is to hide art,—*Artis est celare artem,*—the speaker in question, with all his other accomplishments, had this in perfection.

It was not long before the old class-leader among the Wesleyans, somewhat oddly portrayed already, " stuck the hymn-book in his face," to employ the subject's own words, while attending a prayer-meeting, saying unceremoniously, "Here, give out a hymn, and go to prayer." He did so ; and after this, occasionally assisted in the prayer-meetings. He was, however, according to his own statement, much ashamed of himself, saying, that he "made but poorly out." The truth is, that there was more of the publican in the present exercise, as there was more of the pharisee in his former refusal. But still, it was the pharisee in momentary practice, rather than in confirmed sentiment, and had no baneful influence on his general feelings and character.

He continued to exhort in the private meetings, and also to exercise his pen. Some of his compositions were in all probability the ground-work of his addresses. Though he did not formally announce a text, yet select passages of Scripture appear to have been very often the subject of serious reflection, and to these he occasionally adverted,—avoiding, at the same time, the formality of a sermon, with its divisions and subdivisions. A few of these pieces, written at this period, may be noticed, as it is interesting to trace the openings of such a mind, and to become acquainted with the subjects upon which it was employed. The first is dated, "Feb. 1794," and is founded on Rom. iii. 23, 24; the second, "March," and has for its base 1 Chron. xxix. 15; the third, "March 29," the day before the twenty-first anniversary of his birth-day, and evidently intended for its celebration; the fourth, "May," in which he launches forth into the Apocalypse, xix. 11— 13; and the fifth, "July 30," entitled, "A Meditation on the glorious Attributes of God." The mind, in each case, appears active, and becomes more and more expanded. He manifests considerable native vigour, and puts forth a bolder pinion for flight than heretofore. The facts of the fall and restoration of man, in the first paper, are assumed rather than proved, —illustrated rather than defended. He is, in thought, what a person is in actual vision, who is introduced into a region where but few things are familiar, and to whom most are new and interesting, and who is not disposed to discredit the testimony of his senses. With slender biblical helps, he seems to look upon Scripture as the best interpreter of Scripture,—has all the marks of sincerity in his pursuit of truth—and is zealous in its propagation. Though loose, and a stranger to correct composition, yet improvement is perceptible; the essentials of religion are steadily maintained, and his vocabulary is gradually enlarging. His disposition to indulge in *contrast*, in which he afterwards often excelled, is apparent. After describing the first pair in paradise, and the sudden reverse on their expulsion, he observes,—"It is not within the power of the imagination to depict their feelings and their state :—Yesterday, dwelling in the sunshine of God's smiling countenance, —to-day, terrified beneath the dark cloud of his avenging wrath !—Yesterday, the place in which they resided, brought forth fruit in abundance,—to-day, they are not only blighted with the curse of God themselves, but the very earth is cursed for their sake!—Yesterday, the garden brought forth fruit of itself,—to-day, they are doomed to labour for their bread by the sweat of their brow, and when they have exerted themselves to the utmost, the ground yields but a scanty supply in comparison with that of Eden!" Directing his attention to the scheme of human redemption, he remarks,—" Without this, we must have been inevitably lost,—lost beyond the power of man or angel to recover us. But now, the way is plain to all that believe. There is a gate, which stands open, though a strait one. There is a market, with an abundant supply of provision, in which we may buy without money and without price. There is a well at which we may constantly drink and be satisfied. Yes, though Adam brought death upon his posterity, and though such is the cohesive quality of sin,—constantly clogging and retarding the soul in its ascension to heaven in prayer, and holy meditation,—yet Jesus, who beheld the weight of wrath from above ready to fall upon us, and the depths, the unfathomable depths of misery to which man was exposed, has come to his rescue."

His second paper furnishes a good deal of the picturesque. Man is represented as passing through a wilderness, and a parallel is run between the journeyings of the Israelites from Egypt to the promised land, and the Christian on his route to heaven. Thoughts appear to teem upon him, and words are frequently omitted in his haste to transmit them to paper. An extract will shew the man. " *We are strangers before thee, and sojourners, as were all our fathers: our days on earth are as a shadow, and there is none abiding.* We are only tenants of this earthly tabernacle, and know not how soon we may be served with an ejectment. What is there in a wilderness to divert a traveller whose heart is set upon home? What can a person wish to have in such a dreary situation? Can he wish to stay, and take up his portion here, without thinking of going to his resting place? Would he prefer to dwell among dragons, and exposed to dangers? Does he conclude he has not a home to go to? that there is no city, whose maker and builder is God? . . . . Travellers, and especially those on foot, ought to carry as small a burthen as possible. They should do the work their situation requires, and return to their destined place with the utmost despatch. . . . . Think not that almost leaving the world will do. If we but almost leave the world, we cannot be altogether Christians. . . . . Look to thyself, O my soul, and see how matters stand with thee. Is this world a stranger to thee? Are thy affections set on things above? Art thou looking for, and hastening to the day of God? Art thou running the race set before thee, looking unto Jesus? Dost thou keep the glory of the Sun of Righteousness in thine eye? Art thou, eagle-like, mounting towards the meridian splendour which emanates from his countenance? Dost thou, like Abraham, take thy wife—thine heart, and forsake thy habitation, and travel towards that good land that God has promised to every believer in Jesus? Dost thou erect an altar in every place on the road, where thou art likely to stop a little, and offer the incense of the merits of thy faithful

Intercessor to a merciful prayer-hearing God? Dost
thou constantly apply to him for strength to enable
thee to run so as to obtain? Dost thou ascend to the
top of Pisgah, and, with the perspective glass of faith,
look into the land to which thou art travelling?" In
this way, many of his papers—though they commence
with others, terminate in a close application to himself; thus shewing a mind, not only rigid in its scru-
tinies upon itself, but intent in its pursuit of the "one
thing needful."

The piece dated, "March 29," comprises some
eulogistic remarks on the word of God, and an exhortation to himself to become more familiar with
its contents. He thus soliloquizes: "Consult thou,
O my soul, the word that will make thee wise to
salvation. It will not deceive thee, if thou lookest
properly into it. There thou wilt find the deformity
of man in its proper light; and there also, thou wilt
perceive the blessedness of the bleeding Jesus set off,
but not without a lustre. Look, I say, into this
mirror. Some females spend no small portion of
their fleeting time in gazing upon themselves in gilded
mediums—mediums washed with silver. But these
only represent the outward form and features. The
Word of God goes into greater niceties: it goes through
the walls of both skin and bone, and gives to a man a
true section of himself; it exhibits the magazine of
sin; it throws light upon the cage of unclean birds
—screaming like owls, and unable to bear the lustre
of so glorious an object. O my soul, do not thou
forget to look constantly at thyself in this glass. Thou
art in a world where dust and dirt, where moral filth
may be contracted, and if thou lookest not at thyself

here, thou wilt have many spots upon thy garments —so many, that the true followers of the Redeemer, will conclude thee to be either slovenly or indolent. Look, then, more and more to thyself. Follow not the man who sits in the seat of the scorner. Strain not thine eyes in looking at thy neighbour—trying to discover some flaw in his conduct. Do not be too ready to observe the slips or stumblings of fellow-travellers, unless it be to increase thine own watchfulness. On perceiving a fault in another, instantly turn the eye inward, and thou wilt perhaps find, that if thou excellest him in this, he has other qualifications superior to thine, and that, in other matters, thou art inferior to him. Yes, my soul, look to thyself. Time is passing, posting, flying—going at a rate beyond the power of man to compute; and ere the morning watch shall arrive, the angel may have uttered the irrevocable decree, 'Time with thee shall be no longer.' Twenty-one years will then have elapsed, and gone to give in their accounts; and thou canst form some idea of what is placed against thee. If God were to give the bill to thee, demanding payment at thine own hand,—threatening to cast thee into prison, till thou shouldest discharge it, what would become of thee? Couldst thou give a receipt in thine own legal righteousness, and would it be deemed good coin for cancelling thy contracted debt? Alas! no; thy best will be found but base metal when tried in God's furnace. Christ alone can pay all demands. He has fulfilled all righteousness,—has magnified the law and made it honourable. Examine thyself closely, O my soul, in this important matter, and see, whether or not, Jesus is thy Friend in the court of heaven. Look to him,—follow—cry—cling—live to him. Read his Word. See there, what is offered to thee in that exchequer! It is to thee an inexhaustible fund;—a land-mark to direct thy course, and to prevent thee from splitting on the rocks of open sin; a candle put into thy hand, to save thee from tumbling over the precipice of ignorance and error, into the pit of eternal perdition! He that despises this word, and takes it not as his guide, is intoxicated with the liquor of blind, natural reason's brewing; and unless he is roused by some powerful hand, he will continue drunk, till seized by God's bailiff, and cast into outer darkness.—O thou sovereign Disposer of all things, look upon me, and bless me yet more and more, in everything calculated to promote the power of true religion in my breast! Wean me from everything opposed to thy will! Stablish me in every good word and work! Fix within me a principle, which will never be reconciled to sin; and grant that I may be a child of Jesus, ever walking worthy of my Christian profession!" This extract is the longer, as it exhibits the inward workings of the soul.

There is less reference to his religious state in the article on the Apocalypse, xix. 11—13, penned in the month of "May." The "white horse" here, may not improbably have ultimately led the way to his famous sermon, entitled,—"Death on the pale horse." There is great wildness in this piece; much more of fancy than of judgment; and no wonder;—for wiser men than he have often betrayed their folly in attempting to guess out the meaning of the more abstruse parts of the Apocalyptic vision; and certainly, with the exception of the Song of Solomon, there is not a more hazardous book to descant upon, than the one in question, for persons susceptible of lively impressions, of a vivid imagination, and of infantile religious experience. All the way through, our juvenile expositor seems struggling with his subject,—desirous of mastering it, but is evidently mastered by it. But as he makes a more liberal use of his imagination, than of sober reason, we are checked in our remarks by the observation of a popular writer, who states, that "in criticism, to combat a simile, is no more than to fight with a shadow, since a simile is no better than the shadow of an argument."

In the last piece, of "July 30th," "On the Divine Perfections," his reasoning powers begin to unfold themselves; and in one part, he maintains the position, —"That sin would not be sin, if God were not holy; —that iniquity would not meet with punishment, if the punisher were not pure." His knowledge, too, of the Sacred Writings becomes more extensive,— manifesting a readiness in bringing forward the most appropriate texts to establish the points under discussion.

The year 1795, found him equally diligent in business, and fervent in spirit, with the year preceding. Being resolved on becoming better acquainted with the Scriptures of truth, he purchased a copy of Dr. Doddridge's "Family Expositor," March 24th. Here a new vein was opened, and while mining for the sake of enriching his own mind, he was pouring forth on paper, such of his meditations as he hoped would prove beneficial to others, in his oral addresses. In the course of this and the following month, he wrote some papers entitled,— "The Law and the Gospel,"—the "Vanity of the World and Creature

Comforts, ''—''The Love of God in the Soul.'' These are longer, more laboured, and much more correct, than his preceding compositions; and, as usual, are mixed up with appeals to himself, and thus rendered useful as topics for self-examination.

That he might not be entirely ignorant of the world in which he lived—but chiefly, no doubt, for the sake of agricultural and commercial information, he began to subscribe for a newspaper. This kind of reading, however, never became a passion; nor was it ever permitted to occupy the time demanded by other duties.

He was led also, about this time, to read more freely the publications which issued from the press among the Wesleyans, and to pick up, in his perambulations, when at Leeds, selections from their poetry, together with the more didactic portions of their prose. His first purchase in this way, he jocosely observed to the biographer, was ''a threepenny hymn-book.'' He next procured Watts's Psalms and Hymns; then the large hymn-book, or ''Collection of Hymns for the use of the people called Methodists;'' and succeeding these, a copy of the Olney Hymns, which he highly valued. Having hitherto been accustomed to hear and read only such of the Psalms as were ''Done into Metre,'' by Sternhold and Hopkins, by Nahum Tate and Nicholas Brady, these productions opened up an additional source of delight; and such was their influence upon him, that he himself attempted the composition of some hymns, together with other poetic pieces. One of the former, he gave out at a prayer-meeting, subsequent to this period, when Mr. W. E. Miller paid a visit to Leeds and its neighbourhood, previously to his becoming an itinerant preacher,—the hymn itself terminating with — " *Ye must be born again,*" which speaks more for the piety than the ear of the versifier. As he was disposed to be facetious on the occasion of mentioning the circumstance, he was reminded by the writer, of the Rev. S. Wesley's clerk, who, on the return of King William to London, after some of his expeditions, gave out, in Epworth church, "Let us sing, &c., a hymn of my own composing," and was recommended to adopt the same form of announcement, should he be tempted to give out any of his own compositions at any future period. But he was too much dissatisfied with himself on the occasion to which reference is made, to attempt it again; and with few exceptions, after this period, presumed to court the Muse, whose steps he was but indifferently qualified to follow. His versifications, apart from other defects, were too extemporaneous in their character to be good; and ought to be judged, according to the notion of Shenstone, as persons judge of a horse pushed into full speed,—not by the gracefulness of his motion, but the time he requires to finish his course. The measures adopted were "Long," "Common," "Four-eights and two-sixes," "Tens and Elevens;" and the subjects were, "The Christian's Conflict,"—"Love,"—"The Fellowship of Saints,"—"An Address to a Young Friend,"—"Verses on the Death of S. Simpson," &c.

One piece, reserved for distinct notice, is on the "Last Judgment," in blank verse, comprising 422 lines, 20 pages, 4to. It is entitled, — "A literal Description of the Judgment, concluding with the Folly of Sinners, and the Safety of Saints." It appears to

have been re-perused by him at a subsequent period,
when he appended to it,—as if acting on the advice
of Horace, not only in having preserved it, but in
severely criticising its merits, the following opinion;
—"What a poor *semblance* of poetry is here! When
young, how soon are we blinded with the dazzle of
appearances,—blinded when there is but little of the
real or the substantial to support claims to merit!
There may be some *Gospel sparks* shining here and
there; but in poetry, the piece is defective indeed.
Mar. 20, 1806." There is truth in this decision, as
far as poetry of the first order is concerned,—more,
perhaps, than he himself was aware of; but there
is a great deal of the "real," the "substantial," and,
it may be added, of the striking and the powerful
in it, both in thought and expression. To subject
it to the test playfully proposed by Dean Swift, would
be to do it injustice. He advises his readers to "Try
a good poem as they would sound a pipkin," assuring
them, that "if it rings well upon the knuckles, they
may be certain there is no flaw in it;" further re-
marking, that "verse without rhyme is a body without
soul, or a bell without a clapper,—which, in strict-
ness, is no bell, as being neither of use nor delight."
Another critic tells us, that blank verse is merely
poetry to the eye. But what becomes of Milton, if
the only poetry embodied in his "Paradise Lost," is
to be tested by the eye? In the piece in question,
it is but justice to state, that the subject of these
Memoirs far exceeds all his previous efforts, whether
in prose or verse; and that if it had been re-touched
by him twenty years after the first copy was written,
it would have done him no discredit.

He remarks in his Journal, for the same year, June 22, that he had the privilege of hearing the Rev. R. Hemington, at Barwick; and this is noticed here for the purpose of connecting with it another fact. This excellent clergyman was forty-five years vicar of Thorparch, and died Sep. 10, 1820, in the seventieth year of his age. He was at this time in the zenith of his usefulness, preaching not only in the several churches, but in barns and private dwellings. In the course of one of his outgoings, William, who, by this time, had acquired some degree of notoriety as an exhorter, and by taking a leading part in meetings for Christian fellowship, and other religious exercises, was requested by Mr. Hemington, at the close of his sermon, to engage in prayer, with which request he immediately complied. This speaks as much for the established Christian character of the one, as the ardent zeal and condescension of the other; at all events, it is a circumstance of rare occurrence in the service of the Established Church, and bears the Wesleyan aspect of a preacher requesting one of the members of society to engage in prayer after preaching, when a good influence has accompanied the sermon.

Hitherto the colliery accounts had been kept in a place which subjected him to some inconvenience; but Sep. 4th, they were removed to "Grime Cabin." In this place, often called "a shed," upwards of a mile from home, and which has since been converted into a stable, he not only attended to the business of the colliery, but also to that of the church. It was, in fact, both his study and his place of worship. Here he composed the principal part of his sermons; and here also, he met in band with John Batty every

Sabbath day morning, at seven o'clock; when they sung a hymn, prayed, and communed with each other. John by this time having become a Wesleyan, and William, continuing a Churchman,—the one, on quitting the place, proceeded to the public service of the Establishment at Barwick, and the other to hear a Wesleyan preacher at Garforth. Both hearts were right with God, and their separate creeds were correct in the essentials of Christianity; all minor differences, therefore, to employ the language of the author of "The World before the Flood," were "lost, like the prismatic colours, in a ray of pure and perfect light."

On the 14th of this month, he renewed his covenant with God; in which covenant he expresses his wonder that he has not been " cut down with the axe of divine justice," and that God, " with the fan of his holiness, had not blown him, like chaff, into unquenchable fire;" and such were the views he entertained of his impotency, that, without divine aid, he had no more hope of attending to the *"rules"* specified in the covenant engagement, than he could expect to "remove a mountain with a bruised reed." The "rules" penned, and which he resolved to observe, are such only as were likely to occur to a person strictly conscientious, highly devotional in his spirit, ardent in his pursuit of entire sanctification, and anxious to be useful to his fellow-creatures. He charges the whole upon his soul, with the solemnity of a judge exhorting a criminal to prepare for eternity, after having received sentence of death; closing the document with, "Lord, help me! Lord, help me!

' Help I every moment need.'"

It was towards the close of 1795 too, that he, for the

first time, heard the Rev. Joseph Benson, who, at the Conference, had been appointed to the Leeds circuit. Having been announced to preach at Seacroft, William went to hear him. His remarks on the occasion, to the writer, will convey, not only an idea of the preacher, but of his own feelings under the sermon. "His word," said he, "was irresistible. I knew what religion was, and had the evidence of it in my heart. But there was a power in it at Seacroft, to which I had not been accustomed. I wept—wiped off the tear—felt ashamed;—wept, and wept again—struggled with my feelings, and strove to repress them : at length, I said to myself, 'Let it come;' so saying, I laid my head on the front of the gallery, and let the tears *hail* their way to the bottom of the chapel. No man ever took the hold of me that Mr. Benson did ; and his preaching produced the same overwhelming effect, whenever I heard him."

Ere this, his friend and companion, Samuel Settle, had left all secular employment, and gone to college, to prepare for the Christian ministry. As the letters which had passed between them, up to this period, were given up to each other by mutual consent, the following is the first of the second series, from the collegian :—

"Magdn. Col., Cam., Nov. 6, 1795.

"DEAR DAWSON,—Our friendship is now become firm through long continuance, and I should be sorry to be the least occasion of its diminution. Indeed, I hope we have been acquainted too long to suspect each other's sincerity. Besides, it would be exceedingly absurd, after having agreed so long, in travelling the same road, to shew any marks of unkindness, and so give up friendship, now that we are so much nearer our journey's end. I have a letter by me, which I should have sent from Hull; but I thought it was not worth postage. I got to Cambridge, Oct. 31st, and had a very comfortable journey. All the letters which I had of yours, I packed up before I left Cambridge last year, and directed them to be forwarded to you. Thus much I deemed necessary, on account of the uncertainty of our continuance in the present life, and owing to the various changes in human affairs; and I beg it, as a favour from you, that my letters in your possession, may be packed up in the same way, and directed for me. I hope you will have no objection to comply with my request; for it appears reasonable, if I die first, that you should have your own letters returned; and if you die first, that I should have mine returned. One reason for this is, I think we shall be able to make a better use of our own, than other persons, into whose hands they might fall. But, perhaps, we may both die together, and die at the same time; and then it will be of little concern to us, in whose possession the said epistles may be. We shall, in such case, be tuning our harps, and hymning our Redeemer's praises above. Till that period, we must give all diligence to make our calling and election sure. 'Be thou faithful unto death, and I will give thee a crown of life.'

"I wish we could consider our privilege more fully ——that we are heirs of God——joint heirs with Christ ——and that mansions are prepared for us in heaven. I cannot conceive greater anguish, than to see Abraham, Isaac, and Jacob, entering into the kingdom of God, and we ourselves shut out. Perhaps we know a little of this, when we see persons seemingly begin in the spirit, and end in the flesh. It is an awful consideration, to stand knocking at the gate of heaven, and then be compelled to turn our backs upon it, before the porter can have time to open it. Alas, we have often done this ourselves. After much prayer and importunity, we have, for want of patience and perseverance, come from the throne of grace without a blessing. Real religion is a serious matter; it is no trifling work. If we are right, and in earnest, we shall find many misgivings and stings of conscience, when we come to our Beth-els. I cannot say, that I remember you in every prayer with that earnestness I ought; but on occasions, and at particular seasons, I do remember you from the bottom of my heart. It is our happiness, our duty, our privilege, to love one another; it is the fulfilling of the law; it is our greatest worldly comfort. What would this life be, if we were to hate one another? The more we love one another for Christ's sake, the more we resemble God, for 'God is love.' He that dwells in love, dwells in God. With regard to ourselves, our motives to love one another are stronger than with persons who are strangers to each other, because we began to seek God about the same time, and now have almost become surety for each other. I could write a great deal, but I wish to advance that only, which will unite us in heart. Doctrines, and such like things, I omit. Our letters should always be the pictures of our hearts. It is only in this way we can really become acquainted with each other.

"Mr. Graham's meetings will, I trust, be useful. Some will be built up in righteousness; and should others slacken their diligence, let it be our great end

c

and aim to improve every opportunity, for, in due season, we shall reap, if we faint not. Let us look more and more into the cause of backsliding, viz.—our own depravity; and let us constantly repair to the fountain opened for sin and uncleanness. It is only when we are sensible of our own guilt and misery, that the salvation of Christ becomes desirable, and is accepted.

" Give the enclosed to my father, when you see him. Mr. Dikes enquired after you. I hope he will be made useful to many souls in Hull. The harvest is truly great. Let us pray that our nets may be kept whole, that we may not loose the fish. I long to hear from you. Yours. Respects to all friends.—S. SETTLE."

Mr. Settle, in stating that " our letters should always be the pictures of our hearts," appears to be of the opinion of Steele, who observes, that " there is no rule in the world to be made for writing letters, but that of being as near what you speak face to face as you can." Sincerity will always effect this. Real friendship needs no disguise, and religion will not admit of it. Not anything can be more true, than that " a reserved man is in continual conflict with the social part of his nature, and that he even grudges himself the smile into which he is sometimes betrayed." Nor less correct is the language of an English prelate; that " sincerity is like travelling in a plain, beaten road, which commonly brings a man sooner to his journey's end than bye-ways, in which men often loose themselves." Reserve in friendship awakens suspicion, destroys all freedom, and finally produces estrangement.

CHAPTER III.

Letter from Mr. Settle.—Mr. Kilham and his party.—York Assizes.—A religious Diary.—Extracts from it.—W. Dawson formally takes a text.—Besetment.—William Smith—Kindness to the Widow.—Reproof.—Pressed to enter into Holy Orders. —The ELLAND SOCIETY.—The Latin Language.—Difficulties and Cares of Business.—The Rev. J. Graham's testimony in favour of Wm. Dawson.—Slender Remuneration.—Despondency. —Letter from Mr. Settle.

THE salvation of the soul was the "great concern" of life with the subject of these Memoirs. He knew, with one of his favourite authors—Baxter, that it is one thing for a man to take God and heaven for his portion in the heyday of life and health, and another thing to be desirous of it, as a kind of reserve, when he can maintain his grasp of the world no longer ;— one thing to submit to heaven as a more diminutive evil than perdition, and another thing to be anxiously solicitous respecting it as a greater good than earth ; —one thing to lay up treasures and hopes in heaven, and to seek that heaven first, and another thing to be content to accept it in the day of necessity--having first sought and secured the world, finally resigning into the hands of God that only which the lusts of the flesh can spare,—a putrid carcass, a depraved

spirit, the last sighs of an expiring life. If personal
religion consisted only in "bodily exercise," in moving
the lips, in bending the knee, it would be as common
for human beings to step into heaven as to enter
an adjoining house to visit a friend.   But to separate
the thoughts and affections from the world, to draw
forth to open day the graces which adorn the Christian character, to fix each grace on its proper object,
and to hold the respective graces to the work—waxing
stronger and stronger, till every enterprise, every labour
of love prospers in the hand, is a work of no ordinary
difficulty, and will always distinguish the genuine
Christian from the hollow and superficial professor.
All the characteristics of a sound, healthy, religious
state of feeling, were exhibited by William Dawson.

His friend, Mr. Settle, continued to pursue his
studies at College, and the friendship between them
remained unbroken.   The former writes,—

"Jan. 1, 1796, Mag. College.

"DEAR DAWSON,—It is now, at least, six years
since we began to seek salvation by grace, in Christ
Jesus.   I cannot say that my mind is in so forlorn a
condition at present, as it was six years ago ; yet I feel
the depravity of the heart, and that, without watchfulness, it would bring me into captivity.   But God has
promised, that sin shall not have dominion over us.
As yet, I do not seem sufficiently to have considered
the nature of the religion of Christ ; I mean, I have
not looked upon it as properly consisting of two
parts,—Justification and Sanctification.   The former
part has, in general, occupied my attention.   But,
alas, it is but a small thing for us to be justified,—
that is, delivered from wrath.   We want something

more ; we want righteousness—purity—holy affections
—heavenly tempers—a fixed and sure foundation of
holiness wrought in our souls by the Spirit of God ;
that our whole man, and all our conversation may
be seasoned with salt, meet to minister grace to those
that hear us. It is vain, I find, to be continually
forming resolutions to break off this, and the other,
bad habit. It is God alone, that can work in us a
hatred of all sin, and a desire after real holiness.

" When I consider this, my wonder ceases at the
Methodists dwelling so much on the nature of holiness, and purity of heart. I do not say, that they
have not carried their notions too far on this important point of religion. Of this at least, I am
certain, that Christ promises great things to those
who earnestly seek him. The Gospels, and great
part of the Epistles, abound with passages to this
effect. You will be ready to ask, ' Have you turned
Methodist?' My dear friend, I only notice these
things, because I suffer much uneasiness, in consequence of not being washed and cleansed from sin,
as set forth in the Scriptures,—of not having my
habits, tempers, and desires, brought into subjection
to the law of the obedience of Christ. Besides,
when I name the Methodists, I mean and intend
the Old Methodists. I scarcely know what the New
Methodists, so called, are. You will best understand
my meaning by an example. Here is a person
accustomed to acts of theft and injustice. To-day,
he is at court—released from punishment—and
receives his liberty : but he carries with him the
same principle, the same disposition to acts of injustice ; and therefore, falls into his former practices.

I have mentioned this instance to illustrate my own case in minor things. It is God alone, that can write his laws on our corrupt hearts, engrave them on our minds, and enable us sincerely to love and delight in holiness, in heavenly mindedness. What is more common, than continually to hear, from all religious sects and denominations, 'That, in order to enjoy God, we must have something in us of his likeness?' God himself asks, 'How can two walk together, unless they be agreed?' And, indeed, it may be asked, how—in natural things, bodies can be compounded or blended, which are totally averse to union? Apply this. How can we, with all our sinful passions, be united to God, and enjoy fellowship with him—God, who is gloriously holy,—pure beyond all conception? It is said, 'Grow in grace,' &c. Certainly this is a very different thing from a mere speculative knowledge of the doctrine of justification. The one sort of knowledge seems to be finite, the other infinite. The perfections of God are infinite; and it is on this account, as I conceive, that our growth in grace,—our transformation into his image and likeness, will be always progressive, but never entirely complete. This is a subject on which, I pray God, that both you and I may be employed in contemplating for ever!

"What I have penned, would be much more interesting in conversation, as we could then, enter into many particulars, remove doubts, and explain the subject more fully to each other. We live in times of great profaneness, and great gospel privileges. I hope I can heartily join with you, in praying, that God may not visit us with a famine of the word.

The word of God was precious in the days of Samuel. It is now plentiful. Because iniquity abounds, the love of many shall wax cold. But in such times, they should be examples of greater diligence. I hope God will be with you in your meetings, and stand by you in all your persecutions. All that will live godly in Christ Jesus, shall suffer persecution. We have need of being stirred up. When God sees us waxing cold, and growing faint in our minds in religion, he shakes us with tempests, and causes all his billows to pass over our souls. The grace of our Lord Jesus Christ be with your spirit. Amen!—S. SETTLE."

Mr. Settle refers, no doubt, by the "New Methodists," to the party gathering around Mr. Kilham; and not being acquainted with the points in dispute, might see proper to guard his remarks, lest any of the essentials of religion should be involved in the general question. On Mr. Kilham's expulsion from the body, the subject of these Memoirs,—though little versed in Wesleyan politics, was curious enough to step into one of the chapels in Leeds, when he was making some of his statements. He observed to the writer, that he felt little interest in what was said, and was rather disappointed in Mr. Kilham's appearance,—especially his face, which he considered as not at all indicative of intellect. Towards the close of the year, he remarked, a person put Mr. Kilham's "Defence" into his hand. On reading it, he said to himself, "I am incapable of judging of the points at issue for want of fuller information; but with this man, I can have no sympathy; for I perceive his spirit is bad." There is propriety in this; for a man is in nothing so much himself, as in the temper and the character of his passions and affections. If he loses what is Christian and worthy in these, he is as much lost to himself, as when he loses his memory and his understanding. To attempt to defend and support Christian truth in companionship with a bad spirit, is the antinomianism of a polemic; and is the same, as it regards the man himself, as a person professing the sanctification of the spirit in connexion with an immoral life. Reason and free enquiry are the only effectual antidotes of error. Give them full scope, and they will uphold the truth, by bringing false opinions, and all the spurious offspring of ignorance, prejudice, and self-interest, before their terrible tribunal, and subjecting them to the test of close investigation. Error alone requires artificial support, and the malignity of an inquisitor to assert its claims; truth can stand alone, and no more requires a bad spirit to support it, than a Christian requires the presence and actual aid of a demon to enforce his commands. These observations—though arising out of the remark in reference to Mr. Kilham, are intended to apply generally—not to the man, but to the spirit, in whomsoever it may exist.

He attended the spring assizes at York this year; but on what occasion, is not stated. The use, however, which he sometimes made of judge, jury, criminal, and witnesses, in arraigning man before his Maker, as a transgressor of the divine law, is a proof that he permitted few impressive scenes to pass before him without improvement.

Finding that his secular Diary of 1792, which he continued sometime after this period, was scarcely adapted to religious purposes, and that he required something in which to minute the workings of the soul, as well as the toil of the hands and the feet, he commenced another—a day-book for the heart, which he continued for some years, the first entry in which is dated, "April 28, 1796." He commences with—

"Begun this Diary. Rich and adorable Saviour, in whose presence is life, and whose absence is death, look upon this attempt of thy sinful creature. Bless it with thy favour—own it with thy peculiar benediction, —and make me faithful in recording thy dealings with my soul, whether prosperous or adverse; that I may derive benefit from hence, according to my present state and situation, and that seeing thy goodness in times past, I may be led to a fresh application to thee for help, and so by renewed and lively thankfulness for past mercies, and an entire surrender of body, soul, and spirit into thy hands—thou who hast wonderfully conducted me so far—I may rejoice in hope of thy glory, and praise thee with all my powers. And thou, O my soul, may the present intention be useful for the promotion of the best ends, in reference to thee—the furtherance of vital godliness! May it be the means of spurring thee forward to greater attainments,—of quickening thy spiritual speed! only looking at the things behind, with a view to animate thy every faculty, and rouse thy every affection,—pursuing with earnestness and steadiness the prize that is set before thee. Above all, and before all—for he is all and in all; fix thine eye upon Jesus,—look unto Him for grace, for strength, for instruction, for pardon, and to Him as thine exemplar, to enable thee—as a runner ought to do, to lay

c 2

aside every weight, and run with patience the race set before thee, that thou mayest at last receive an incorruptible crown, reserved in heaven for thee!"

In this Diary, the ministry of the Rev. John Graham and that of others, is repeatedly and emphatically adverted to, as highly instructive and religiously impressive, and outlines of several of the sermons are recorded. The Diary, as a whole, forms a kind of window, and the different days of the year, are so many squares of "many-coloured glass," through which the reader is permitted to look into the breast of the penman, as into the interior of a building, and to see the undisguised operations of the "inner man." Without following him through each successive day, or giving the whole of what is penned for the day, a few brief sentences for the month, as in the case of his previous Diary, will be sufficient for every biographical purpose, and will shew the running interest religion sustained in his mind. The separate sentences, abstracted from those with which they are found associated, exhibit every variety of feeling, and would—many of them at least, form useful topics for conversation in a social party. It may be necessary to observe, that though the extracts are grouped together for the *month*, the *dash* is intended to separate the matter belonging to each respective *day*, and to shew by the break, what is to be appropriated to that day by the reader.

APRIL. "Wanderings in prayer.—Saw Barmistone happy in his Saviour.—A sweet hymn sung in the school-room, which was useful to me.—Anxious for a clearer interest in Jesus.—Had some useful conversation with John Warner.—Long for a closer union with Christ.—The corruption of the heart not yet dead.—

Read a letter of Romaine's, in which I saw a glorious sufficiency in Christ, which I pray may be mine.——Have to complain of wandering eyes.——Peevishness, be still!——Christ is all and in all.——Wrote a letter, and was comforted by it.——A sweet refreshing shower.——Oh! what thanks are due to the Saviour for temporal mercies!

MAY. "Cold in the public service of God.——At a prayer-meeting at Barwick.——Heard Mr. Richardson; loud responses; at a loss to know how far they are proper.——Much of the world, and the spirit of the world.——Too expensive in clothes; many are starving; part of the money ought to have been given to the poor. ——Admonished while reading the state of the Laodiceans.——Convinced of the need of candour in all matters of judgment, and hearing both sides of a question with humility.——Preserved from sin; thanks be to God for it!——Grievously forgetful.——Murmur not, my soul, at God's dispensations; thank him! thank him! thank him! ——A peculiar discovery of the deceitfulness of sin.——A happy morning with Jesus, in private prayer.——Pray, my soul, for charity!——Overcome by the enemy, but not abandoned of God.——Lord, purify my diabolical heart! ——Consolation under the ministry of the word.——Still deeply humbled. Mark the foe!——Hard work to pray for a blessing on our endeavours to do good to others, without mixing up our own honour with it.——Steady attention in family prayer.——Profitable conversation with Wm. Smith.——Some have left their religious profession at Barwick, and in the neighbourhood.——Need of wisdom.——Too apt to forget God and myself.——Overtaken with levity.——Heard a useful discourse on industry in temporal things, Prov. vi. 6; another from Mr. Griffin,

on Amos iii. 3.—Cause of self-condemnation.—Too
much formality.—Longing after closer communion with
Jesus.—Meditated and spoke on the descent of the
Holy Ghost on the day of Pentecost, and the effect
produced on ministers and people.—Meekness and candour felt in hearing reports concerning others.—Happy
in having God to go to as a director, protector, and
comforter.—Again overcome with levity ; and my soul
is not heartily weary of it, nor in earnest for its destruction.—The work of the glorious and mysterious Trinity
considered in the salvation of sinners.—Want to live
upon, and in Jesus, more and more.—Much benefited by
a letter.—Abhor equivocation.—Useful conversation with
friend Settle.—Praise God for preservation from sin ;
though the act was not committed, yet the will, it is to
be feared, was there.—Beheld the goodness of God in
the midst of the ravages of a desolating fire.—A delightful time with Wm. Smith.—Read the fifty-fifth chapter
of Isaiah ; a delightful chapter to a hungry soul !—
Spoke upon sin in believers ; and in what sense they
are free from it.—Do not sufficiently carry a savour of
religion about with me.—Betrayed into lightness ; an
evident sign of the want of a deeper impression respecting eternal things.—Awful news from Leeds ; Mr.
Thoresby holding a love-feast, the floor gave way, and
report states twenty killed, and nearly one hundred
wounded.—Nothing short of regeneration will save a
man.—Sometimes fear I am a cheat, a hypocrite, an
Agrippa !—Too little stirred by things acknowledged to
be momentous.—Let my words be few.—Disturbed
with irreligious thoughts.

JUNE. "Still haunted with improper thoughts.—
O my soul! flee and pray! fight and pray!—Pardon

the iniquity of my holy things!—Bless God for a Sabbath!—A most beneficial season at the school-room, under the consideration of Mark vi. 45 to 56; and a sweet hymn at the conclusion.—A sharp temptation.—Conversed and prayed with W. Smith, and not without benefit.—Lukewarmness dreaded.—Coldness in family prayer.—See the necessity of habitual seriousness.—Feel the risings of a corrupt heart.—Always wish to speak to the glory of God.—Very sorry for Peter Porter's imprudence.—Still tormented with P. P's. folly.—Lord, give me wisdom!—Earnestly united in supplication with the minister at the school-room, on the Sabbath evening.—Wrote P. P. a reproof.—Peevishness.—Ready to start aside.—Lord, quench the fire of wrath!—Conversation with Settle.—A sweet discourse on Prov. i. 7.—Cold in private prayer; not sufficiently felt.—Mourn over the folly and vanity of the eye.—Too little of thy presence, blessed Saviour! and yet easy without it.—Quickened in prayer with W. S.—Lament the sin of others.—Heard Mr. Postlewaite in the school-room, on Saul's hypocrisy, and Samuel's honesty.—Prayed for a revival.—A serious discourse by Mr. Thom, on Col. i. 28.—Friend Settle spoke on Matt. v. 13—16.—Melted while meditating.

JULY. "A sweet nearness of soul to Jesus in private prayer.—Carried away with a bad spirit.—Why should God permit such a wretch to speak to him?—Tasted that the Lord is gracious, and yet rather light. How is this?—Oh, that my heart were saved from wandering!—Heard Mr. Thoresby.—Why should I be so light, when I have so much cause to be serious?—Spoke on Psalms lv. 6. Well may a Christian wish to be at rest. In all I do, there seems to be something of pride mixed up with it.—Read Watts on the 'Mind.'—Friday set apart for prayer.—Heard Mr. Graham on the deceitfulness of sin; and had a conversation with him in the evening.—Grieved with the cold state of the society.— Attended William Smith's funeral; peculiar solemnity; Mr. Graham's subject exceedingly serious; a happy account of William's death.—Wish to be meek, charitable, humble.—Overcome with anger.

AUGUST. "Tempted to disbelieve the providence and omnipresence of God.—Tempted to draw back.—Mr. Graham treated on the sacrament; also on self-examination.—Carried away with levity.—Did not stop at sacrament.—Much in the world; may I not be of it!— A blessed Sabbath day.—Still a savour of yesterday's blessedness.—A delightful conversation with J. Rhodes, and a time of refreshing under Mr. Hemington.—Mortify the eye and the heart.—Read 'Alleine's Alarm,' and 'Watts's Death and Heaven.'—Grieved with false shame.—At Leeds. Heard Mr. Atkinson and Mr. Thom; useful sermons; but derive most profit in attending our church at home.—Much tried, and rather peevish.—Levity is the daughter of forgetfulness of God.—Thursday, sweet views of Jesus and heaven; spoke on 2 Cor. i. 3—6; if any benefit, God be praised.—Feel the risings of pride.—Glory be to God, for a blessed Sabbath; a sweet, searching, useful discourse on Agrippa's confession.—Set a watch, O Lord, before my mouth.—Was advised, with others, not to frequent Methodist meetings.—A sad peevish heart. Mr. Graham strongly recommended domestic religion. — Sweet time with Settle in the B. Lord answer our united prayers! —Too great a compliance with the world.—The murmurings of unbelief.—Dread, and pray against lukewarmness.

SEPTEMBER. "A fine shower; God is good to his inheritance.—Felt nearness to God in public prayer. —Heard Mr. Dean on St. Paul's carnal man; and Mr. Graham on keeping the whole Law, and offending in one point.—Dissatisfied state of mind; felt joy in meditating in the evening.—Unbecoming temper.—O levity, thou art one of my sorest plagues!—Longing for a more even walk.—Delightful communion with God in prayer.—Much tried; meekness, gentleness, and love, not sufficiently conspicuous.—Nearness in prayer.—Wanderings.—Delightful discourse from Mr. Graham.—Want more of the salted conversation of the Christian.—Yesterday's discourse still upon my heart with lively force.—Sweet time with H. S.

OCTOBER. "Read Col. Gardiner's Life.—Steady Sabbath in the service of my God; an instructing, convincing, and constraining sermon from Mr. Graham, on Rom. xii. 1.—A constant sense of the presence of God for some time; then came my plague again.—Oh, for greater earnestness!—Partly overcome, and partly overcame. May I render unto God the calves of my lips.—Read our Lord's charge to the church at Ephesus; and also the account to be given of every idle word; and felt condemned.—Steady composure of soul.—Ready submission to the dispensations of Providence.—Some discourses by Mr. Dean and Mr. Graham on the state of the nation.—Poor account of this day.—Wrote a hymn for a society of religious persons.—Much benefited.—A steady frame of mind. —Sweet time at the Lord's table; and useful discourses from Mr. Graham.—Read 'Shower's Time and Eternity.'—Abiding Serenity.—Much troubled with toothache. Oh, how intolerable, if eternity were written upon the pain, when most excruciating!—Disappointments but intended for good.—Haunted with improper thoughts. Lord, cleanse my soul, and pardon all inattention at the means of grace.—Recommended the opening of a little monthly subscription for the purpose of purchasing a few practical authors for the use of the Society.—Oh, the benefit of private prayer!—Wrote a letter to Mr. C. The Lord accompany it with his blessing! —Ministry of the Word irresistibly impressed upon my soul. Enable me, Lord, to follow thy will in all things.—Mr. Graham discoursed on the profanation of the Sabbath, and cautioned the people against feasts on that day.—See clearly that zeal in religion is necessary.

NOVEMBER. "Partook too much of the spirit of the world.—Deeply indebted to God for preserving me from sin.—Read an old author on communion with the Spirit. May I have more of it!—Heard Mr. Graham on the twenty-fifth Psalm, but wandered much in the service. Fix, fix my soul on thee, O Lord!—Want seriousness.—Distant in private prayer. —Oh, the love of God!—Unsteady in soul.—Heard an excellent sermon on the parable of the Prodigal. —Not inclined to the vanities of the world, but the contrary.—Fear not man, my soul, but God.—At Leeds fair. Keep me, O Lord, above the world.— Haunted with uncomfortable imaginations.—Begin with God first in everything.—Condemned for light conversation.—Read 'Baxter's Saint's Rest.'—Sweet are the expectations of the Christian. May I live up to the Christian's privilege.—Oh, may the Gospel never be scandalized by me!—Just ready for my besetment yesterday, but saved. O God, I thank thee!—Oh, for more real godliness.—A searching sermon; found comfort under some parts of it, and condemnation under others; but praise came in the evening.—Distressed at the discovery of so much of the fear of man in me. What is man! Jesus is a great Friend, and I am a great rebel.—Read Baxter again.—Lamented over the much to be lamented evil of peevishness in professors; and saw myself in a poor light.—Not meet to be called a servant of the Lamb.—Heard of Mr. Graham being likely to leave Barwick. How much, O my soul, shouldest thou be engaged in prayer at this season!—Seem to be a compound of levity, pride, self, babbling, and sin. Search me, O Lord! —Thursday. Spoke on Gen. xix. 15, 16. Pressed upon the society to be seriously in earnest. Lord, grant that I may bind no burthens upon others of which I am not willing to bear my share.—Thoughtlessness, self-pleasing, and the risings of pride.—A comfortable, serious frame of soul. May I ever be honest with myself, sincere, and in earnest!—Let nothing rob thee, O my soul, of God.—Wrote B. a letter.—Partly overcome.—Oh, this carelessness!—Heard Mr. V. The Lord help him to deliver truth in a style, plain and easy to be understood!—Read the ' Address to the people called Methodists,' by Pawson and Mather. Brotherly love is wanting among them. —Lightness and peevishness again.—Want always to feel what I say.—Read Baxter.—Reproving sin not sufficiently attended to by me.—Thursday. Enlarged on the necessity of love, and shewed its decays by comparing it with the actings of our first love. Lord, attend the word spoken with thy blessing!—Some outbreakings of light.—Comfortable time in prayer

with H. S.—Satan is not idle.—A wandering heart.
—Heard a person in the afternoon, I suppose from
Bramham. Oh, the astonishing ignorance of that man's
soul! Lord, open his eyes.—Praise the Lord for
spiritual mercies!—Felt unusual liberty in family
prayer.—Joy laid up in store for the believer.

DECEMBER 1. "Thursday. Heard Mr. Graham on
the abuse of spiritual privileges. Had a conversation
with him on the subject of entering into the ministry.
Lord God of heaven direct me in this matter.—
Friday 2. Strong inclination to enter into the church.
This day should have been set apart for prayer on
that important business, but forgetful and overcome.
—Saturday 3. Asked Mr. Porter whether he would
take my brother into my place, if I left? Consented.
Lord help me in this difficult time and work.—Sunday 4. Informed my mother of my intentions. Thy
will be done, O Lord! Leave me not under the
awful curse of my own imaginings. Much harassed
with reasoning on the subject. Refreshed in prayer.
—Monday, 5. Many reasonings on the propriety of
entering into the ministry. Rather haunted with
unbelief.—Tuesday 6. Had a little conversation with
Mr. Atkinson, of Leeds, on the longed for employment. Could not but admire his prudence in not
giving me an immediate answer; still my pride rose.
—Wednesday 7. Unbelief, fear, hope, and faith,
alternately rising in the soul; sometimes thinking it
the greatest folly to aspire after such an office, and
at others, cordially embracing. Jesus, guide me!—
Thursday 8. Still reasoning on entering into holy
orders. After all, praised be God, I can say, Thy
will be done. Mr. Graham dwelt on Jesus sending

his disciples to sea, and Peter walking upon it. Lord, be mine!—Saturday 10. Private prayer, how sweet! Anger ready to rise.—Sunday 11. Bless the Lord, O my soul, for this day! Heard Mr. Graham in the morning on Caleb's spirit, courage, honesty, singularity, faithfulness, &c.; and in the afternoon, on Mary's choice. Received benefit.—Monday 12. Comfort in meditating on the heavenly city.—Wednesday 14. Unbelief. Met with Mr. Graham, when going to Aberford. Delightful conversation with him on entering into the church. Reason to bless God for a kind providence.—Thursday 15. Private prayer the best antidote against unbelief.—Friday 16. Steadiness of soul; much lost for want of it.—Sunday 18. Overcome by my sad besetment, levity. Afterwards found nearness to God in prayer. Oh, the mercy of God, that he should favour such a wretch!—Monday 19. Liberty in family prayer.—Tuesday 20. Received a letter from friend Settle. The Lord attend him with his blessing! Reasoning on the ministry. Unbelief stirs.—Wednesday 21. Still reasoning. Alarmed at the badness of a case.—Thursday 22. Spoke on brotherly love.—Friday 23. Peevishness rising in the soul.—Saturday 24. Fear not, for henceforth thou shalt catch men.—Sunday 25. Praise the Lord for his grace! Lord, I am thine; I am thine. Heard an excellent discourse from Mr. Graham on the Song of Simeon.—Monday 26. Full of reasoning.—Tuesday 27. Desirous of greater earnestness.—Wednesday 28. Doubt whether my brother will do for the colliery. Still reasoning. Again overcome. God be merciful!—Thursday 29. O my soul, cast out from thee every thing that has a tendency to indispose thee for spiritual

things.   Heard Mr. Graham on 'Hitherto hath the
Lord helped us.'   Viewed the general mercies of the
year, and laid down several marks of a growth in grace.
—Friday 30. More earnestness.—Saturday 31. O my
soul, thou art come to the close of the year.   What a
scene of mercy and sin hast thou presented to thy view!
Five times overcome by thy besetment ; and often overcome with unsteadiness, peevishness, forgetfulness, and
ingratitude.   O my soul, be serious ; do be serious!
Had it not been for thee, my Jesus, I should have been
cast down long ago, cast into unquenchable fire ! What
is due to thee, dear Lord ?   What can I give thee ?
What ought I to do for thee ?   What *must* I do for
thee ?   I have nothing meritorious in me.   The good
I have is from thee.   Thou art its author, and must
be its finisher.   Thou art my only plea, my only
advocate, my only sufficient Saviour, to pardon my oft-
repeated offences—offences against gospel light, and
against the dictates of conscience.   Quicken me in
the ways of godliness ; spare me, spare me ; cast me
not down, cast me not off.   Plead for me with thy
Father.   And thou, O my Father in Jesus, deny not
the supplications of thy Son.   He has died for me,
satisfied for me, risen for me, and now intercedes for
me.   Send thy light and truth into my heart.   Pardon
my sins, and seal—seal me thine to the day of
redemption.   Give me the earnest of the prepared rest
of thy people.   Go with me through the next year.
Undertake all my business ; work for me and in me ;
direct into all truth : let eternity be impressed upon
my soul in all its awful nearness.   Go before me in my
going out and coming in.   Be my God and guide even
unto death.   Amen. ''

Here we have in operation all the varied feelings exhibited in the Psalms of David,—hope, fear, joy, sorrow,—inward relentings, and outward—though not gross, wanderings;—a man in the battle-field with self and Satan;—now struggling,—now rising; ever clinging to the cross, and the cross pressing upon him; with a thorough knowledge of human nature,—a correct estimate of the value of true religion,—humbled under a sense of the mercy of God in Jesus Christ,—and desirous, though in the midst of conscious weakness and imperfection, to promote the holiness and happiness of his fellow-creatures. There are a few points, however, in the Diary, which may be adverted to, as they had revived in the recollection of the biographer, associate circumstances not recorded by the pen, but communicated in social discourse.

One of these circumstances refers to July 7th, when the subject of these Memoirs spoke in the school-room, on Psalm lv. 6; "And I said, Oh that I had wings, like a dove, for then would I fly away and be at rest." He observed, that he had prepared some remarks on the text, and that it was the first time he had dared formally to announce the book, chapter, and verse, and read the passage as the ground-work of discourse. On the Thursday evening following, no Bible—to his surprise, was visible. This disconcerted him a little; but was sufficiently intelligible, as to the hint conveyed by it; intimating to him, that though, as a lay-man, he had been permitted to occupy the chair of a regularly ordained minister, he had, in this instance, overstepped the legal and accustomed bounds of his calling—being only allowed, as heretofore, to pray, and give a word of exhortation. The text was exceedingly characteristic.

He had watched the bird in its flight and in its habits, in connection with the dovecot at Barnbow; he was full of tender feeling—full as the dove itself, with its melting, mournful cooings, and which is stated by Pliny to be without gall, to shew the kindness of its nature; while the metaphorical language employed, was calculated to awaken into play his gradually unfolding imaginative powers. Nor was it less indicative of the future preacher, who generally selected such texts as a person only would select, whose heart was teeming with the sympathies of human nature—with the two extremes of the tender and the terrific. He felt poignantly on the occasion; but like the bird to which he referred, which will clasp its wings to its side, and conceal the arrow that is preying on its vitals, he hid the wound he had received, and only noticed it among other incidents, which the lapse of years had deprived of their interest.

He speaks of being "five times overcome," in the course of the year. This is not to be interpreted into so many acts of immorality. He characterizes *levity* as his *besetment*; but he also designates it as his *plague* —and, therefore, *hateful* to him. If it be correct, according to Lavater, that volatility of words is carelessness in actions; then it is equally true, that words are the wings of actions, and may sometimes bear a man into regions not at first contemplated by him. But such was the tenderness of conscience of the subject passing in review before the reader, that what his candour would have interpreted into *cheerfulness* in others, his self-scrutiny was ready to condemn as *levity* in himself. In such cases, the sentiment of Confucius, aided by a little Christian light, is worthy of observation:—"Our greatest glory is not in never falling, but in rising every time we fall." At no period of life, however, would William Dawson's native buoyancy of spirit have allowed him to conduct a conversation with the austere gravity of a funeral oration.

William Smith, whom he frequently visited during his last illness, was a man of deep piety; and he was not forgetful of the widow, when deprived of the presence of the husband. It is to the widow of this excellent man, that he refers in his Diary, Nov. 25th, when recording the happiness experienced in prayer with "H. S.,"—Hannah Smith. She resided at Garforth; and to this poor old woman, unknown to his own family, he took his own dinner, two or three days in the week, and thus ministered to her wants, while he himself practised the duty of self-denial. For a healthy man like himself, with an appetite often whetted to intensity with outdoor exercise, this was no ordinary sacrifice; and was as honourable a tribute to the memory of the dead, as it was creditable as an act of charity to the living. She, in the language of the apostle, was "a widow indeed, and desolate;" and he, in visiting and relieving her, gave full proof that he was possessed of "pure religion." The reader is here reminded of the homely simile of Sir T. Overbury, in reference to charity, who observes, that "a wise riche man is like the backe or stocke of the chimney, and his wealth the fire; he receives it not for his own need, but to reflect the heat to others' good." Though the subject of these pages was far from being rich, yet in the language of another writer, equally quaint with Sir Thomas, "he hath riches sufficient, who hath enough to be charitable." He wrote a short memoir

of her departed husband, who is stated in it to have
been a follower of Jesus upwards of forty years,—to
have filled up his station in life humbly, actively, and
usefully,—to have diffused a steady light by his example,—to have been a great, but a patient sufferer,
towards the close of life,—and to have died in the full
triumph of faith.

For the "Letter of Reproof," to "Peter Porter,"
in June, the subject of these pages was well prepared.
He had written an excellent paper "On Reproving,"
in the month of April in this year, founded on Matt.
xviii. 15 ; expatiating, in his best and most consecutive
style, on the manner in which reproof ought to be
given—the timing of it—how it ought to be received—
and the advantages resulting from it : and if the article,
or any appropriate portion of it, met the eye of Peter,
it might, under God, have operated like the glance of
the Redeemer on his apostolic namesake.

As to the subject of holy orders, it may be observed,
that Mr. Graham, in addition to the specimens afforded
him in the school, as to public speaking, had some of
William's compositions put into his hand, and perceiving them possessed of some merit, he concluded that
God had higher work for him than that in which
he was daily engaged.   Mr. Graham, therefore, in
William's own language to the writer, pleasantly—yet
not without sincerity, asked him whether he was
"disposed to exchange the drab for a black coat?"
On replying in the affirmative, the Rev. interlocutor
told him that he would recommend him to the ELLAND
SOCIETY, of which the Rev. Miles Atkinson, of Leeds,
was a member.   This was a society near Halifax, composed of clergymen, whose object was, to recommend

young men of character and talent, and to furnish them with a preparatory education, to enable them ultimately to discharge the duties incumbent on a clergyman of the Established Church. Mr. Graham, with a view to pave the way to future studies, advised him to procure a Latin Grammar; but like most persons, who permit the teens to pass away before they enter upon the study of the foreign classics, he found it hard work to fix his mind, with any degree of satisfaction, on his task. He felt as if the mind, so to speak, had lost all its waxy properties, and was incapable of taking up the necessary impressions, and as if the memory had lost all its tenacity. One dark, interminable passage seemed to lie before him, without a solitary ray to gild any of the intermediate steps, or a single outlet at the close; and the fact of Mithridates being acquainted with twenty-two different languages, would have required—had it been communicated to him, a stretch of faith beyond what he was capable of exercising. The consequence was, that after a short lapse of time, he returned to Mr. Graham in a fit of despondency, observing, that he could "make nothing of it,"—further adding, in his still more characteristic language, that he was afraid it would "crack his brain." His friend—for such he was, and such he confessed himself to be to the close of life, laboured to encourage him; telling him that the rudiments, whether in art or science, were always the most difficult, because new to the learner —but that the language would become more easy as he advanced. He again applied himself to it, and looked forward with mingled feelings of hope and fear towards the sacred ministry.

D

Mr. Graham was directed by the general educational mode pursued, in recommending him to enter upon the study of the Latin rather than the Greek first: and yet it is not improbable, that if he had been advised to commence with the latter, which is the less difficult language of the two, and of which the Latin language is admitted to be nothing more than a dialect, being capable only, according to some of the best critics, of being thoroughly understood by being traced to Greek roots, he would have had fewer obstacles to surmount; and the acquirement of the one would have encouraged him in the acquisition of the other. Quintilian, who was of this opinion, contended that the Roman youth should be taught Greek before their native tongue: and this sentiment seems to be gaining ground, as appears from a work, entitled, "Greek without a Master; or a practical, theoretical, analytical, and synthetical Course of the Greek Language; intended chiefly for the use of Persons who are studying the Language without a Master. By a Graduate of the London University."

In throwing the mind back upon the extracts from his "Diary" for the year 1792,—and these are only specimens of what is recorded of the labour of the intervening days, omitted by the biographer, they will exhibit to the reader a life of varied employment, both at home and abroad;—a life, not only amounting, in many instances, to hard toil, but attended with the distracting cares of business, and will readily account for any apparent irksomeness as to the Latin tongue,— the subject himself being much more disposed to stretch his weary limbs on the couch, than to take his seat at the bench with "Ruddiman's Rudiments" before him,—early retirement for repose being as much pressed upon him by the calls of labour,—having to start with the lark at day-break each succeeding morning, as urged upon him by the still more imperious demands of nature.

Mr. Graham, like Mr. Dikes, crowned with the snow of years, adverts to those times, in a letter from York, dated July 31, 1841 ; and observes of the subject of these pages,—"During the whole of my residence of five years and a half at Barwick in Elmet, as curate, which terminated with the year 1796, I knew him intimately, and loved and valued him as a brother. His natural vigour and originality of mind —his clear and comprehensive views of Scripture doctrines and duties,—his experimental knowledge of Christ and his salvation, and his solid yet fervent piety, seemed only to require a more regular and extended education to make him, what indeed he became without it, 'a burning and a shining light.' Having occasionally, in my absence from home, conducted for me a sort of cottage lecture, in which his talents and gifts conspicuously displayed themselves, I often expressed to him my wish, that he would enter upon a course of preparation for the ministry in the Church, of which he was then an attached member. But his zealous love for Christ and for souls would not permit him to wait three years in silence and study. My removal to York, and his connection with another denomination of Christians, while they subtracted nothing from our mutual affection and esteem, naturally in a great measure suspended our intercourse ; so that during the interval of forty-four years, though we had occasional interviews, we had no epistolary correspondence.

He is gone to his rest in the presence of his God and Saviour. May my last end be like his!"

To return to the proper period of the subject's personal history, from which we are led by the last sentences of the above extract; between the colliery and the farm—the latter not being entirely left to his brother, the head and the hands were busily employed; neither of them affording a fair remuneration for the labour and expense bestowed. The former, indeed, seems to have been a mere appendage to the latter, which was neither moderate as to rent, nor yet excellent as to soil. On finally quitting the farm, he observed to the agent in the transaction, "I think I might claim some attention, when I add, that neither my father nor myself were equally remunerated for our time and pains, as agents of Sir T. Gascoigne. You will be surprised when I inform you, that my father never had more than 12s. per week, and coals and candles allowed! I had 12s. per week, until 1793, when the wages of the colliers were raised, and then I had 15s. The colliers struck again, about a year or two after this, when another advance took place, and mine was raised to 18s. per week. Thus, my father and myself served the Gascoigne family for a period of nearly forty years, for what I have just stated; and what I may call—a paltry wage.— I have often told you, that for twenty years, I have thrown £20 a year of my own money into the farm; and, except for the last two years, I have not saved a penny for twenty years." This, though partly anticipating the more advanced stage of these Memoirs, shews how this excellent young man was circumstanced in some of his early struggles.

Though he had his joys, he was, as will have been perceived, often the subject of painful feeling. Such was the "hour and power of darkness," that on one occasion, he lost all evidence of his acceptance. As this was not occasioned by any sin of which he had been guilty, it was of course unaccompanied with remorse of conscience. It seemed partly to have arisen from the want of some old experienced guide on the road to heaven, to keep pressing it upon him as a constant, common Christian privilege, and partly from false reasoning. Such, however, was the effect of the simple loss of it, without being able to charge himself with any known sin as its cause, that he was plunged into the deepest distress of mind. He compared himself to Bunyan's Pilgrim, when he lost his "roll," and was no less in earnest to regain his lost peace. At one period, such was his anguish of spirit, that he was tempted to throw himself into a river, as he was walking along its banks. A world was valueless in his esteem, compared with the repossession of his "roll." It was not long, however, before he regained the desire of his heart, and no one knew better than himself how to solace the distressed, or entered with a deeper interest into their feelings and circumstances.

In his dullest moments, he continued to cherish, some time after this, a hope of preaching in the pulpits of the Established Church. This, in all probability, was preserved alive by the success of his friend Settle; one of whose letters is referred to in the Diary, and which is as follows :—

"Cambridge, Dec. 17, 1796.

"DEAR DAWSON,—I have remained a longer time silent than I intended. But I hope you will not

consider my silence a proof of any diminution of
friendship. I still profess a sincere regard for you,
and reflect with much pleasure on our past intercourse
on particular evenings, and in particular places. I
have been busy in attending lectures; but the term
ended yesterday; and now, I must be up to the head
and ears, in reading for the schools. My neglect of
reading in summer has thrown me into deep confusion.
However, there is divine reading which cannot, or at
least ought not to be omitted. But alas, we are
purblind; present objects engage our view, and we
lose sight of that which is invisible. Custom has a
powerful influence on the mind, and we cannot brook
the idea of being exceeded by those whose abilities
are only equal, or perhaps inferior to our own. But
this is a weak argument when placed in competition
with the affairs of the soul. Inferiority is no disgrace,
provided religion be kept in the heart. We ought
to labour for an immortal crown; and I wish it were
my concern in a far greater degree. 'Can a man
walk on hot coals, and not be burnt?' Can I be
among those who are deeply engaged in study, and
who profess to have the same views of religion as
myself, — I say, can I be among them, thus circumstanced, and not be fired with a spirit of emulation?
You see of what spirit I am.

"I have seen in the public papers, Mr. Graham's
preferment. Well, how do you feel? It appears likely
that Mr. Atkinson's son will succeed him. I have
never heard him preach. He is inferior to Mr. Graham
in intellect. But piety is what is chiefly wanted in
a minister, and where we see that, we can bear with
natural weaknesses. I am aware, worldly people despise

weak ministers, and especially when piety is combined
with weakness. But this is a topic upon which we
have already dwelt; and, indeed, there are few subjects, whether moral or religious, on which we have
not frequently conversed.

"Let me have an account of you all. Mr. Graham
named to me a subscription for books. I confess to
you, it appears to me to be a *party subscription*.
When the new curate arrives, I know not how he
will go on with you. Pray, do your sentiments
respecting your present situation fluctuate? Have you
made your choice in reference to the part you intend
to act in life? I shall be glad to hear from you.
Till then, I remain, sincerely yours,—S. SETTLE."

CHAPTER IV.

On the first day of **January, 1797,** he started in the Christian race, as though he had for the first time entered the course. Part of his language is,—"O Eternal King, I have this day dedicated myself to thy service ; determined, through thy strength, to walk henceforth in thy ways with greater stability and conscientiousness—to resist every sin—to have no other lords to rule over me, but to take thee as my portion, my helper, my guide, and my God. Oh, deny not thy helping hand ; receive me into thy favour and protection ; and enable me to separate every idol from my heart,—to sacrifice, not an hour, not a talent, not a faculty to any object, but to live in perfect conformity to thy revealed will. Impart to me an increase of thy love,—strengthen me by thy Spirit in the inward man,

—sanctify my body and soul, my taste, wishes, and desires,—and let this year manifest in my soul, and also to others, that I consider myself a sojourner on earth as all my fathers were. Accept me, O Lord, in thy Son ; strengthen these resolutions ; inspire me with Christian humility and zeal, that neither pride nor cowardice may rule in my soul. Let my courage be regulated by thy restraining and assisting grace, and enable me to adorn my Christian profession, in the promotion of thy glory, and my own everlasting salvation."

The succeeding day was distinguished by the divine blessing ; hence his language on the occasion,—" In a happy frame of mind. The service of God is perfect freedom,—nay, rich enjoyment ! Praise God ! O my soul, thou art not thine own,"

Having profited so much under the ministry of Mr. Benson at Seacroft, he went to hear him in another place on New Year's day, and also on the 4th of the month at Scholes. In the first instance, he wrote, on his return home, a full outline of the sermon, founded on Rom. xii. 1 ; commending it in his Diary, as both " sweet and searching." That at Scholes was on Psalm cxviii. 1—4 ; and the occasion was rendered equally a time of refreshing from the presence of the Lord. These visitations drew him nearer and nearer, and, by almost imperceptible degrees, towards the Wesleyans.

Mr. W. E. Miller, who was like a flame of fire, visited Barwick ; and his name having gone forth as a revivalist, the subject of these Memoirs was induced to hear him also. The scene was new ; he had never been in a meeting of such apparent tumult before, and had entertained scruples respecting the loud responses which accompanied the prayers and preaching of Mr. Richardson, a Wesleyan local preacher. He sat and watched every movement with critical severity ; occasionally darting an ardent, curious, and impassioned glance at the speaker, some of whose sentences and images—rich, though occasionally extravagant, had a magical attraction, and were to him, as has been said of another, as "splendid and graceful as a diamond concealed under the leaves of a rose." Still, he was ill at ease with the vehement bursts of passion, incidental to the outbreak at the close, when Mr. Miller went from seat to seat, praying with, and speaking to the people. Coming to Dawson, he laid his hand upon his head, and said, "Thou wilt do a great deal of good in the church, when thy heart is emptied of pride." It would seem from William's account to the biographer, that Mr. Miller had imputed his apparent inflexibility to pride ; though his not joining in with the work, like a well-disciplined Methodist, was more owing to its novelty, than to any want of devotional feeling.

He proceeded with his Latin exercises, though somewhat beclouded in his prospects of entering the Church. Mr. Atkinson of Leeds, had informed him, that the state of the funds of the ELLAND SOCIETY, had brought the members to the resolution of admitting no more candidates on the books, till they should be warranted to do it, by an increase of subscriptions. To this there is a reference in the following letter from his friend, Mr. Settle :

"January 31, 1797.

"DEAR DAWSON.—I heartily thank you for your last letter. I knew the Society had as many candidates as it was able to maintain. But you know some of us will be weaned soon, and then, I doubt not, that you will be taken on. I am glad that you have made a beginning; it is probable you will some time or other come to an end. However, if you never should be taken on to the books of the Society, a little grammar can do you no harm. Nay, I dare say, that *dominus, domini,* &c., will be of great advantage. There is one comfort, if God want workmen, he will call them; and I confess I feel so little party-spirit, that I care not how or in what manner we are employed, if so be that we are only made useful to the conversion of souls. And if learning be required in a minister of Christ in one party, it is required in all. You need not, then, look upon fagging at the Latin Grammar, as improper. I trust, that you will one day, stand up before a congregation;—a congregation of what kind? Nay, I care not of what kind, if so be that you only preach Christ and him crucified.

" Pray have you seen Mr. Atkinson yourself? or did you make application by Mr. Graham? Does Mr. Graham stand your friend, and does he give you encouragement? He, I suppose, will recommend you to the Society, as he is well acquainted with you, and therefore, knows whether you are a proper person to be admitted. However, do not render yourself uncomfortable; for God can work, and who shall let it? After you have got the verbs, you may then go on with any easy Latin Work, with an English translation. Take care of long and short syllables—for they are very much regarded in Latin. You may get a dictionary of my father; take the best,—for there are two. Do not be in too great a haste. Get well grounded in the first principles. Turner's Exercises will be of use: it will teach you to decline and conjugate, &c. Supposing you should not be very perfect in the rules, you will acquire at least a good many Latin words and phrases, which will be of use when under a master.

"I am very glad of the information you give me respecting my brother. I hope you will make it your business to see him as often as you can make it convenient. God will take it as done to himself. But I need not urge you to this. You know the value of a soul. Pray write soon, and let me know how you go on. I am obliged to leave off. Mr. Atkinson is waiting for this letter. Wishing you all prosperity in body and in soul, in Christ Jesus, I am,

"Yours sincerely and affectionately,

"S. SETTLE."

Mr. Settle again addressed him in the course of a couple of months, under considerable anxiety respecting his brother, whose case is adverted to in the preceding letter.

"Cambridge, April 5, 1797.

"DEAR DAWSON.—I received a letter from my brother Thomas about a fortnight ago. He informs me, that William is very weak, and appears as if he could not be long in this world. He observes, that you have visited him regularly once a week, some time. I acknowledge myself much obliged to you for this kindness, and esteem what you have done for him, as done to myself. There is no saying how God may be pleased to bless your conversation to his soul. I shall be exceedingly glad to hear of his being brought to an acquaintance with himself and with Jesus Christ. You

will do me a favour, if, when you write, you will give
me any particulars respecting him ; for you know, that
both my father and my brother Thomas, will write in
general terms. I suppose he is still living.   Alas, I
am stung with painful feeling, that I did not speak
more freely to him, when I had the opportunity.   But
this is our folly, and our weakness.   We lament when
it is too late ; and what is worse, our past neglect, and
loss of opportunities, seldom make us act with greater
diligence and prudence in future.   I should like to see
him ; but the distance is too great, and travelling is
very expensive.   Besides, what can I do for him ?   He
may continue some time yet, though my brother writes
as if near death.   Please to write in a day or two ;
and, if living, let me know how he is.   To stand at
death's door is an awful situation.   The good and the
bad, the prepared and unprepared, start back when
they think of dying.   Serious men tell us, that we
must often revolve in our minds, the thoughts of death
and judgment, and by that means make them familiar
and common to us.   But if I take away what often
moves me with alarm, I throw off one of the most
powerful restraints against sin ; I mean, if I think of
death and another world in such a careless manner,
they will at length become so familiar to me, as to make
no impression upon the mind.

   " I forwarded my brother William a parcel by Mr.
Atkinson, and sent you a letter at the same time.

   " I assign to you a good deal of work.   But you can
write to me a letter of questions and answers.   How
does Mr. Atkinson go on in preaching ?   Are your
meetings kept up ?   Does he explain a chapter on the
Sunday evenings in the church or school ?   Has he

taken lodgings, or has he engaged a house, at Barwick ?
Have you seen Mr. Graham since he left you, or have
you heard from him?   Does he continue to take
pupils, or has he given them up?   How, if in possession of two or three churches, are they supplied ?
Have you heard anything more of the Ellanders?   Do
you read Latin?   Does young Mr. Atkinson assist you
in the Latin tongue?

"Lately, I have been much engaged in the Schools ;
and am surprised that wise men will regard such
nonsense.   But, the fact is, I am tired of Cambridge
studies ; and I am persuaded, I shall always consider
my time spent in Mathematics, the least beneficial of
any employed in the whole course of my life.   Had I
been engaged in searching the Scriptures, in composing
sermons, and in reading the history of mankind, I
should then have possessed some useful knowledge,
on going forth into the world.   Instead of that, I
shall have spent three or four years in grammar, and
three or four more in again forgetting it.   Such is my
tale.

"This, I forward, by way of Wetherby, that it
may reach you the sooner.   I am afraid lest it should
lie at Leeds till Tuesday.   Yours sincerely,

"S. SETTLE."

This portrait of a college life, at the close of the
letter, and which must either have been written under
momentary depression, or under the longings of a
man to be at the work of converting sinners, was but
little calculated to fascinate the ardent spirit of a
Dawson, breathing after an increase of personal piety,
and more extensive, as well as more immediate usefulness, to the perishing multitude.   An answer to some

of the questions propounded—though not written with that view, may be gleaned from William's Diary for the year.

As to Mr. Atkinson, who succeeded Mr. Graham in the curacy at Barwick, though inferior to his predecessor in some respects, yet his labours are adverted to with respect, and several outlines of his sermons were deemed well worth recording. Mr. Dean, the rector, generally occupied the pulpit in the forenoon of the Lord's day, and Mr. Atkinson in the afternoon. But the evening lecture on that day, appears to have been discontinued.

The Thursday evening meeting was preserved alive on the departure of Mr. Graham, chiefly through the influence and exertions of his helper in the work— the subject of these pages,—who preached regularly the first eight months, without apparent aid, till the month of August, when Mr. Atkinson took a part in the services ; after which, to the close of the year, they occasionally took the work alternately ; and in one instance, December 28, they gave the people in the same service, a double lecture,—Dawson leading the way on the subjects of creation, preservation, and redemption ; and Mr. Atkinson following on the former part of the eighth chapter of the Gospel according to St. Matthew. This is a fine specimen of liberality both on the part of Mr. Atkinson, and his excellent predecessor ; and may serve as a hint for maturing more fully the Pastoral Aid Society, in the Established Church, in the more liberal use of lay-men.

The texts upon which our clerical helper descanted were the following :—Psalm lxxxiv.—Psalm lxxiii. 22. 26 ;—2 Cor. iv. 17 ;—2 Cor. v. 5—11 ;—Heb. xii.

1, 2 ;—1 Cor. ix. 24 ;—Joshua xxiv. 14—25 ;—Isaiah liii. 4, 5 ;—Psalm xc ;—Gal. ii. 20 ;—Psalm lxiii. 3 ; —Psalm xxx. 4, 5 ;—Rev. part of xxi. xxii ;—John xxi ;—Psalm xxvii. 39, 40 ;—John xi. 25, 27 ;—Malachi iii. 16 ;—Rev. xiv ;—Psalm xi ;—Isaiah lxi. 1, 2, 3 ; —Rev. i. 16—20 ;—Heb. xi. 14, 15 ;—Gen. xxii ;— Isaiah xxv. 6—9 ;—Luke ix. 33 ;—Ephesians iii. 14— 21 ;— Philippians iii ;—1 Cor. xv. 55—57 ;—1 John i. If an opinion of the matter is to be formed from the texts selected, it may be presumed to have been such as would interest both the heart and the understanding ; and if the devotional character of most of the texts is to be taken in connexion with his experience, it would be candid to infer—without even an appeal to his Diary, which supports it, that William Dawson was deeply and personally interested in the "one thing needful." In some instances, he engaged in prayer, after Mr. Atkinson preached.

The Sabbath evening services which had been rendered so useful to the piety and instruction of the more devout part of the parishioners, under Mr. Graham, were adverted to with pleasure, while their discontinuance was imbittered by the reflection. In consequence of Mr. Atkinson having taken private lodgings, the Thursday meeting was removed from its accustomed place, which might be one reason why he did not close in with its services at a more early period. It was held in the house of S. Simpson towards the latter part of the year.

Mr. Graham left in January, having informed the society on Thursday, the 12th of that month, that it was the last time he should address them as their curate. He visited Barwick, Thursday, March 2, when he preached to the Society; and also Monday, July 10, when William had an interview with him, and conversed freely with him on the subject of the ministry. The day previously to the last date, he had received a letter from Mr. Dikes. Thursday, August 17. Mr. J. Atkinson informed him, that there was a probability of his entering into the ELLAND SOCIETY; but the scene was once more overshadowed by a cloud; and the latter wrote to his early patron and friend, Mr. Graham, October 20, when the subject seemed to be further set at rest.

Whether William received any assistance from Mr. Atkinson, in acquiring a knowledge of the Latin language, is not stated; but as he frequently notices conversations with him in his Diary, the probability is, that he might receive some incidental, if not formal and systematic aid, not only from him, but also from Mr. Settle, with whom he associated, during the suspension of his studies at college: and that he proceeded in his attempts to acquire a knowledge of the language, is evident from a translation of the Latin into the English, in his Diary of January the 15th.

In addition to his arduous secular avocations,—his regular perusal of the Word of God,—a new sermon for some months successively, for his Thursday auditory, —the public ordinances at Barwick,—visiting the sick, —attending prayer-meetings at Scholes and elsewhere, —writing letters of reproof, advice, and encouragement, he found time for the perusal of "Law's Serious Call," part of Fletcher's Works, of Madely, "Young's Night Thoughts," the "Arminian Magazine," "D. Brainard's Journal," &c.; faithfully recording the effects of the latter upon his mind, and accompanying each letter

with an ardent prayer to God to bless it to its intended
use.   He was deeply imbued in a Christian sense, with
all that is implied in the celebrated saying of Zeuxis,
Pingo eternitati—I paint for eternity, for he evidently
lived for eternity.

How different is such a man from the countryman
portrayed by Bishop Earle, the exuberance of whose
wit is only exceeded by the truth of his pencil!
"A plain country fellow," he observes, with a quaint-
ness peculiar to the times, and not out of place for
rural manners and scenes, "is one that manures his
ground well, but lets himself lie fallow and untilled.
He has reason enough to do his business, and not
enough to be idle or melancholy. His hand guides
the plough, and the plough his thoughts; and his
ditch and landmark are the very mound of his meditations.   He expostulates with his oxen very understand-
ingly, and speaks *gee*, and *ree*, better than English.
His mind is not much distracted with objects; but
if a good fat cow come in his way, he stands dumb
and astonished; and though his haste be never so
great, will fix here half an hour's contemplation. His
religion is a part of his copyhold, which he takes
from his landlord, and refers it wholly to his discretion;
yet if he give him leave, he is a good Christian to
his power, (that is,) comes to church in his best
clothes, and sits there with his neighbours, where he
is capable of only two prayers, for rain and fair
weather.   He apprehends God's blessing only in a
good year, or a fat pasture, and never praises him
but on good ground. Sunday he esteems a day to
make merry in; and thinks music as essential to it,
as evening prayer, where he walks very solemnly after

service, with his hands coupled behind him, and censures the mirth of his parish. He thinks nothing to be vices but pride and ill husbandry, from which he will gravely dissuade the youth, and have some thrifty hob-nail proverbs to clout his discourse. He is a niggard all the week, except only market-day; where, if his corn sell well, he thinks he may get drunk with a good conscience. He is sensible of no calamity but the burning a stack of corn, or the overflowing of a meadow; and thinks Noah's flood the greatest plague that ever was,—not because it drowned the world, but spoiled the grass. For death he is never troubled; and if he get in but his harvest before, let it come when it will, he cares not." This picture drawn by a Yorkshireman,—for the worthy bishop was born in the city of York, 1601, — and possibly the likeness of a Yorkshire farmer taken from life, furnishes, though tolerably charged, a fair description of a sordid, contracted mind. It is here given for the sake of contrast: for there is not a single point in which William Dawson was not at the antipodes. He neither permitted his farm, the vineyard of the Lord, nor "himself to lie fallow and untilled;" but laboured in each department as though each demanded his sole attention and toil, and as if afraid, lest any part of life should be allowed to stagnate.

Added to the abridgment of those meals which he gave to widow Smith, he set apart days for fasting and prayer, and otherwise practised great self-denial. He assisted in the course of the year too, in establishing a society for the benefit of the sick. So attentive was he to the means of grace, that he missed Barwick only twice in the course of the year. Both of these

times were in the depth of winter; and one of them
was when he fell and lamed himself on his way to
the place, and was compelled to return home. Every
opportunity was embraced of hearing Mr. Hemington,
when in the neighbourhood; and he notices having heard
him both at Barwick and Garforth.   Secret and family
prayer and sacramental occasions are often adverted to
in his Diary, as productive of great spiritual good.
There was in the midst of all, the deepest self-abhorrence
and self-abasement ;—severe inward conflicts ;—occasional outbreaks of levity, his constant bane, from
which he would instantly revolt, and again sink into
the dust ;—a resolute cleaving to God ;—a full and
grateful sense of the value of a Saviour ;—and an
almost incessant cry for the *cleansing* influence of the
Holy Spirit ;—exclaiming in the midst of all,—"Oh,
how hard, in the midst of the schemes of life, to
keep the eyes fixed on God! to keep them fixed
there, while up to the ears in worldly employment!"
He often felt the force of the Gaelic proverb, in his
prostrations of spirit, that "If the best man's faults
were written on his forehead, it would make him
pull his hat over his eyes."   But conscious integrity
enabled him to bear up under all his discouragements.

He was now in a state, that while he still had no
wish to unite himself to the Wesleyans, he was unable
to resist the charm which attended many of their
religious meetings.   He heard Messrs. Myles, Pawson,
and Mather, and was much pleased with them ; often
stealing away to a part of the service after attending
his own Thursday evening meeting.   On one of these
occasions, Mr. Mather exhorted his hearers to seek
first the kingdom of God, and his righteousness,—

encouraging them with the declaration, that all other things should be added to them,—stating, in language as homely as that of Bishop Earle, and which was not likely to be lost on a mind constructed like that of the subject of these Memoirs, and by way of shewing the insignificance of everything short of religion—that the *world*, in a somewhat tradesman-like manner of proceeding, would, like pack-thread, be given into the bargain. The Conference being held at Leeds in the course of the year, he availed himself, when at the Tuesday market, of slipping into "Ebenezer chapel," and hearing "an old man on the Prodigal's return." He revisited the centre of attraction on the Sabbath day, August 6th, where he heard four sermons, with which he was much delighted. The preachers were Messrs. Pawson, Bradburn, Griffith, and Dr. Coke.

A fortnight after this,—having heard Mr. Dean, the rector, in the morning, and Mr. Atkinson, the curate, at noon, he went to hear a stranger preach out of doors. The site chosen appears to have been an artificial mound, adjoining Barwick, formerly the seat of the kings of Northumberland, and supposed to have been thrown up by Edwin, one of its brightest ornaments. "The great extent and magnificence of this fortification," says Dr. Whitaker, "which is four furlongs in circumference, and contains an area of more than thirteen acres, sufficiently prove that it has been a royal park." The mount, called Hall Tower Hill, was formerly encompassed by a double trench ; on this mount, the royal mansion in all probability stood, and is the only part that remains. Here the preacher stood, and here Dawson, with the listening crowd, heard the Word of Life; himself declaring, that he "was in a measure enabled to lay hold of the promise." The subject was the prophet's expostulation with Nineveh; and Jonah could not have had a fairer view of that ancient city, than the preacher had of Barwick and its population, over the latter of whom he yearned with bowels of compassion. After this, William,—as though he had caught the spirit, entered upon out-door work himself, and gave out the hymns at the funeral of John Cawood, as the mourners passed from the house to the church-yard.

Though he did not, as will have been perceived, neglect to extend his knowledge by reading, yet he seems, from the native force of his own mind, and the fertility of his imagination, to have thought more than read, and to have employed a considerable portion of his time on new compositions. "A Word to the Persecuted," was one which engaged his pen; written probably with a view to console some of his religious associates under domestic opposition. Another was on the state in which Jesus Christ found man, when he entered upon his divine mission, and the blessings resulting from his obedience and death. In one of his addresses, after looking at man, as described by the sceptic and the moralist, who deny the doctrine of human defection, he closed with—" Here is a brief, but pleasing picture of man; differing, however, from the ugly original; and in this state the Redeemer finds us all. The fallen sons of Adam are swimming on the ocean of their own passions,—riding on the tumultuous billows,—blown onward by the storms raised up by the prince of the power of the air ;—going full sail with the tide,—and, for anything they know to the contrary, may—the next day, nay, this very night, have shot the gulf of eternity. See them! *there* they are,—*there* they ride unconcerned, with their backs to heaven, and their faces towards hell,—striving against conviction, against light, till they force their best Friend to seize them, and in that friend, feel the grasp of an enemy, whom they have compelled to become such by their carelessness and their transgressions." Passages like these, delivered with his usual force and fire, would, however incorrect and uncourteous to the ear of the fastidious critic, fall with tremendous power on the heart of an untutored sinner.

He now let himself out more freely in establishing prayer-meetings, and in attending those already established, in the neighbouring villages ; occasionally giving a word of exhortation. After leaving church one day, in company with his friend John Batty, and being desirous of becoming more extensively useful, he proposed a private meeting for prayer, that both might be guided to the fittest scene of labour. They retired to a wood, and in the bosom of that sylvan scene, poured out their supplications before the Lord ; when they agreed—being most deeply impressed with it, to go to Scholes, where they held a prayer-meeting with the villagers. Samuel Hick, " The Village Blacksmith," was at Scholes on one of these occasions, and requested William to go to prayer. Not aware that he had exercised in this way before among the Wesleyans, the good man took the credit of introducing him to public life, and was sometimes innocently egotistic on the subject. Samuel passed no high encomium on the prayer, and was permitted, undisturbed, to indulge himself in the persuasion, that he had been the honoured instrument of planting him among the Wesleyans.

Soon after this, the subject of these pages wrote two Sermons, one of which was founded on Prov. xxix. 25 —and the other on Isaiah iii. 10. The one on Proverbs, "The fear of man bringeth a snare," was probably occasioned by previous embarrassment, arising from the evil referred to. And this is the more probable, from the reference there is to pride, cowardice, and courage, in his piece on the dedication of himself to God at the commencement of the year, and his prayer to be delivered from the evils of which he stood so much in awe. The good people of Scholes, having heard of his exhortations in the school-room, at Barwick, and also in other places, invited him to give them the benefit of his public labours. He complied with their request, and informed the biographer, that he took the above subject, and addressed them upon it, both with a view to their benefit and his own. He afterwards wrote in pencil, on the MS., "This was the *first* text which I ventured to take publicly." The school-room addresses were not deemed *public* by him, but delivered to a select party of religious friends ; and, in other places, the separate texts around which the mind was permitted to revolve, had never been formally announced. The MS., comprises eight closely written foolscap, 4to pages, and is in his usually neat and small hand. It is headed with, " The causes, character, and folly of the fear of man ; " and was subsequently "delivered at Colton." The latter delivery is dated " June 24, 1798." The composition is distinguished for acuteness, a good knowledge of the human heart, a thorough acquaintance with the trifling yet criminal subterfuges of sinners, when pressed to duty, and a close application of the subject, with a special appeal to the young. The following sentiments will furnish an idea of his style and manner: —" Consider, that the season of affliction is fast hastening to your door. How soon it will be said, 'There is a sick man in the house,' no one knows! Will the best friend you have in the world, who is himself but mortal, be able to give you ease in pain? Can he prevent the disease from growing worse, or impart comfort under it? Can he assuage the still more poignant pangs of conscience—prevent the lightning flashes of reflection,—or settle the storm of misery blowing over the soul, and say, peace, be still! No; perhaps he may have been the cause of the whole. How is he, then, to quench the flame? His presence is the remembrance of your faults. You think, when you see him,—'But for you, I might have been in heaven!'—Oh, then, sit down and count the cost. Review the whole. Weigh things fairly. Set Time against Eternity,— Man, whom you fear, against God; and see which end of the scale will fall, which will rise! You will find, that TEKEL will then be written upon both the character and end of man, and also upon the world. Every thing short of religion will be found wanting, when weighed in the balance of equity.—To you who are young, I especially address myself;—you who are actuated by the fear of man. Your hearts are yet tender; impressions have been made upon them; and persuasion has made them consent to the reasons adduced. You have been under conviction from childhood. The Bible, your own consciences, and the

E

secret suggestions of the Holy Spirit, have all spoken in favour of the majesty, goodness, beauty, and sufficiency of the Lord Jesus Christ. You have in some degree yielded to the influence of gospel truth, and assented to the importance of what you have heard from faithful ministers, when reasoning on righteousness, temperance, and a judgment to come. You have heard and trembled, resolved and feared. When the gospel trumpet, like heavenly music, has sent its echoes through your listening soul, you have been almost persuaded to become Christians; but like too many, who wish they were in heaven, but never prepare for it, your good desires have died in the place where they were formed; you have again mingled with your companions at the close of the sermon,—laughed away your feelings,—and forgotten what manner of persons you were. Think, young friends, upon your state. Do not permit the fear of man to bring you into a snare,—the snare of the devil, which, like a net, will entangle you, and endanger your eternal happiness. Turn your backs upon your former ways and companions. The latter may laugh, may even curse, but you shall bless. Give no ear either to their threatenings or their promises. Jesus loves to see a young Timothy bold and valiant in his cause."

In the sermon on Isaiah iii. 10, he has the merit of more immediately keeping in view the unity of his subject; and the convulsions arising out of the French Revolution, would seem to have influenced his mind in its composition,—fortifying the Christian against the perils of a threatened invasion. There is much more nerve and condensation in it, than in the preceding sermon; being full of a fine mixture of stirring, awakening, powerful, consoling thought, and displaying a great deal of intuitive knowledge, considering the comparatively limited character of his reading. He never attempts to speculate, but goes direct to the work of conversion and edification,—pouring forth the trumpet-clang of alarm upon the ear of the sinner, and warbling out his notes of consolation to the saint, which are felt in the inmost soul, as though a songster of the grove had taken up its residence in the breast. Had it not borne the dates of 1797—8, in his own hand-writing, it would have been mistaken for one of his more matured productions in after life. It is of the same size as the preceding, but is distinguished for greater fire and earnestness, and is evidently more adapted to the character of his genius, and the state of his religious feelings. Without attending to connection, and merely to shew the train of thought indulged, two or three extracts may be made.

"*Say ye.*" This he applies to the prophet, and then to the Christian minister. "Souls," says he, "are at stake! and shall the watchman sleep? Immortal spirits are perishing, and shall the shepherd not sound the alarm, and call for assistance? God speaks! and are ministers to be careless? Christ commands! and shall these disregard what is said? The Holy Ghost strives! and shall we be indolent? Time flies! and are not the stewards of the gospel to improve it? Eternity is at hand! and shall they loiter? The gates of heaven and hell stand open to receive the ruined or the saved! and shall not the minister of Christ warn men to escape the one, and exhort them to enter into the other? Yes, men in

this office, with their eyes open to see the value of
an immortal soul, must, in obedience to the dictates
of their own consciences, and in conformity to the
command of God, speak and spare not: *say ye*, &c."
Speaking of the "righteous," he observes,—"His
estate is 'the pearl of great price;' and, in this, he
has secured to himself that which is of greater value
than the world, were its mountains silver, and its
oceans liquid gold." Glancing at the future state of
the "righteous," he remarks,—"They shall be ac-
quitted and honoured in the great judgment of the
world. The resurrection will deliver their bodies out
of prison; and then, they will lift up their heads,
for their redemption draweth nigh. Suppose we had
a cause in any court of judicature, and that no bill
of indictment could be found,—that no witnesses were
to appear,—and that the judge was known to be our
sworn, constant friend! Should we be afraid, under
such circumstances, to appear in court? Should we
tremble on our approach to the bar? Certainly not.
People would be heard to say,—' It cannot but go
well with them; they have everything in their favour,
and nothing against them.' Such will be the case
with the righteous. Who is he that condemneth? It
is God that justifieth,—Christ that died,—yea rather,
that hath risen again. Then shall they eat of the
fruit of their doings. That which was sown in time
shall be their feast in eternity."

Turning to the more appalling side of the subject,
in connection with the other, he observes:—"The
righteous have a rich inheritance on this side death,
and an invaluable treasury in the book of God. Not
so the ungodly. There are no promises to a hardened

sinner; no comforts for an impenitent rebel. Every leaf, which drops honey on the lips of the believer, is a drawn sword to the wicked,—ready to cut him down; every command, in the performance of which the believer rejoices, stands clothed in terrible armour against the wicked—against those, who, instead of obeying the commandments of God, glory in the breach of them. The threatenings are as a bow bent with fiery darts, and ready to wing their way through the soul of the sinner. The wicked flee, and flee too, when no man pursues them; and God, in their flight, instead of assisting them, will exert the arm of his majesty to hurl them into eternal perdition.— When the sword is commissioned to go through the land, it shall make them tremble; it will affright them to see garments rolled in blood,—themselves expecting the next deadly blow. And oh, from whence are they to have peace? Shall they sing in the fires? Will they have God for a very present help in trouble —a refuge from the storm—a shadow from the heat— a light in darkness—a deliverer out of their distress? —To the righteous, death comes on the kindest errand; he comes as their harbinger to glory,—comes to knock off their chains, and bring them to the liberty of the children of God. Is this the case with the wicked? No; death will be to them the greatest of misfortunes; an unwelcome guest,—a visitant that will bring intelligence to their ears, far worse than the tidings brought to Eli of the defeat of the Israelites, the death of his sons, and the loss of the ark! Then may they say, 'Hast thou found me, O mine enemy? Must I go? Must I leave all that I love, and all I once enjoyed?' Yes, go—go—go you must. The

summons is from God, and death is the bailiff. Oh,
what horrible thoughts rush into the mind at this
moment! What feelings excruciate the heart! How
different the aspect of things! The mask drops from
the face of every former foolery and enchantment!
Every thing appears in its native hideousness and
deformity. The devil, who once lulled them asleep,
now grins in their face, and enhances their misery by
his diabolical injections. The world has left them in
darkness and despair. The flesh trembles through
fear, and swoons at the dreadful apprehensions of
approaching woe. They now open their eyes upon the
truths they once despised; and like Esau, with heart-
sinking disappointment, lift up their voice and cry,
with a great and exceeding cry,—'Woe unto the
wicked, for it shall be ill with him?'—WOE—WOE—
WOE—WOE must be his portion, for God has said it;
God who cannot lie:—Christian ministers are commissioned to say so. But uncomfortable as the pre-
conceived notions of future torment may be in the
present life, they are but an earnest of what is laid
up in store! A drop from the boundless, bottomless
ocean of pain! An atom of the prodigious weight of
WOE that awaits them, on the judgment being set!
—Not a friend in court! Not an answer to the ten
thousand charges brought against them! Infinite
debtors, and not a farthing paid! The Law lays down
its heavy charges, and appeals to the holiness and
justice of Jehovah. The Gospel adds to the long
series, and augments their condemnation. Father,
Son, Holy Ghost, angels and ministers, unite to
condemn! No defence,—no reply! and conscience
seals up the whole! Woe—woe—woe unto the wicked!"

These snatches from the discourse, connected with his energy, and peculiar manner of delivery, would impress the congregation with the fact, that they had no ordinary man before them, and would lead the pious part of his hearers to cherish anticipations of future greatness. A short time after this, being the first time his brother Richard heard him, he took for his text at Scholes, Luke ix. 62. " No man having put his hand to the plough, and looking back, is fit for the kingdom of God." One of his remarks to his rural auditors was, " You all know, that if a man *look back* he will not be able to plough *straight ;* the furrow will have a zig zag appearance ; and unless we continue ' looking unto Jesus,' taking heed to our ways, we cannot obtain a meetness for heaven, and must, therefore, remain *un-fit* for it."

Reference having been made to a letter from Mr. Dikes to him, in the course of the summer, it may here be introduced, to show the intercourse which still subsisted between them.

"Hull, July 14th, 1797.

" DEAR SIR.—I some time since received a letter from you, which I ought to have answered before this period ; but I take the advantage of Mr. Atkinson's return, to say, that it gives me great pleasure to hear of your health and welfare.

"You enjoy many blessings. You have indeed lost one excellent minister ; but another is come to supply his place. You experience no great persecutions ; but can worship God according to the dictates of your own conscience. These are great blessings. May we make a good use of them, and not forfeit them by our ingratitude and abuse of them !

"You complain very much of the evils of your own heart. These evils, I apprehend, you will feel more or less to the end of your days. It is possible; yea I may say, it commonly happens, that in proportion as a person grows in grace, he will see and feel more depravity in his own heart. Not that there really is more evil, but that he has more light to perceive it. Various temptations will occur to call it forth to view; and he will have his eye more upon his own ways. Besides, when we see the holiness of God, the purity of his law, and the true nature of sin, our own corruption will appear great and aggravated. Hence, some persons have been led to suspect, they were more vile than they were, before they knew anything of religion. The truth is, all these evils existed; but they were not known: they lay dormant. While we are eagerly wandering after external pleasures, we remain strangers to ourselves; or, if we do see any evils, we regard them as venial faults, which may be very well passed over.

"You must endeavour to get good views of Christ. He is the Lamb of God, which taketh away the sin of the world. If you were whole, you would not have need of the physician. But amidst all the evils of which you complain, you can have recourse to him. You will find him able to save to the uttermost all them that come to God by him. The more closely you keep to him, the more confidence you place on his atonement, the more peace you will enjoy in your own conscience, and the more strength and power you will find to resist all sin.

"I doubt not, but you will be preserved by the power of God through faith unto salvation. He has certainly begun a good work in you, and he will carry it on to the day of the Lord. I hope your meetings prosper, and that all things succeed well with you. Believe me to remain,

"Yours, very sincerely,—T. DIKES."

Waiving the slender encouragement given to pray for *purity* of heart, in the sentiment—that its "evils will be felt more or less to the end of life," but which, in the mind of the excellent writer, might refer rather to the Christian's *conflict* with evil, than to its *reign ;* there is great propriety in his other remarks, namely, that increasing light produces greater consciousness of the existence of evil, while at the same time, it is no proof of the actual increase of that evil. Thus, a person of a hale, robust constitution, is much more conscious of acute pain just on the tip of the finger, than he is of the health possessed by the whole body at the same moment. Whence is this ? It is not because there is more *pain* than *health.* The pain, though *acute,* is confined to a very *small* part of the *system.* So it is in the divine life. In the struggle between the *flesh* and the *spirit,* the one *lusting* against the other, in the phraseology of Scripture, the *pain* of the *flesh* is much more felt than the *health* of the *spirit.* Not, be it observed, because the Christian, to preserve the phraseology, has *more* of the flesh than the spirit ; for the corruption of the heart is neither perceived nor felt by *corruption,* but by *grace.* The more acute the pain, therefore, the greater the grace, and the less of corrupt nature. Death, even in cases when not violent, is generally painful ; nature will not die without a struggle. But these pains are so many proofs that death is *approaching.* The work

E 2

of conquest is going on ; victory is coming to a point.
The struggle of the *believer,* who is in the enjoyment of pardon, is to get the monster—inbred sin,
whose power is already broken,—fully and finally expelled from the heart ; and the struggle of a person
wholly *sanctified,* is—when the door is closed, vigilantly
to guard every corner and avenue of the sacred temple
against its return.

Doors of usefulness continued to open in different
directions, and in 1798, became next to oppressively
numerous.   His zeal induced him readily to yield to
the promptings of friendship at home, and to the calls
of strangers at a distance, to favour the villages and
hamlets, till then unvisited by him, with a word of
exhortation.   Persons belonging to the Establishment
were not only prepared for such meetings, by such men
as Mr. Hemington, and the Wesleys, but also by Mr.
Ingham, of Aberford, who married Lady Margaret
Hastings, and who was one of the persons that
accompanied Mr. Wesley to Georgia.   This gentleman,
together with his coadjutors and successors, established
the practice of preaching in private houses and in barns,
through the whole of that district ; thus rendering it,
long after his demise, not only easy, but in many cases
acceptable, and even respectable, for a person of piety
and talent, whether in or out of the Established Church,
to instruct the people from behind an old chair, as well
as from the curiously carved pulpit in places more
sacredly devoted to the worship of God.

Colton was the first place at which he preached,
and formally took a text, out of his own parish,—
Scholes, where he had previously taken one, being
considered in it.   He preached in the house of Grace

———the first time. The next time he took his stand on the stone at her door; and subsequently preached on the Common. His subject, on the occasion of his second visit, was the general judgment. Having made some statements in the course of his address, which bore hard on sinners, an old man of the name of Hardwick, standing in the skirt of the congregation, sent his stentorian voice across the heads of the crowd, demanding of the preacher a proof of what he advanced, asking—"How do you know that?" Though possessed of the obstinate courage of the man, who, —*Si succiderit de genu pugnat,* if his legs fail him, fights upon his knees, yet not having been rocked in the storm of out-door preaching, like a Whitfield or a Wesley, his recollection was less at command than his prowess, and his presence of mind failing him, he was dumb for a few seconds before the people. One of his hearers perceiving it, who was a man of some weight of character, immediately encouraged him, by shouting out with a no less audible voice, "Go on, go on;" and perceiving he had the congregation with him, he again rallied, and proceeded with freedom. In this scene of early labour, he afterwards had the happiness of seeing a chapel erected, which he opened in 1832.

His visit to Colton seems to have led the way to the establishment of preaching at Whitkirk, which is in its vicinity. He here preached regularly in the house of Mrs. Dean, a relative of Lady Irvine, who was much attached to him as a preacher, and was in the habit of designating him, "My Willy." He preached the funeral sermon of this excellent lady some years afterwards, at Whitkirk, when a somewhat novel scene was presented to view. The respectability of the deceased, and his own popularity, drew a large concourse of people to the place; the consequence of which was, the auditory had to adjourn from the usual place of preaching to the open air. It was in the evening, and exceedingly dark; but such was the temperature of the atmosphere, though the season was far advanced, that little inconvenience was sustained. That the people might have a faint gleam of his person, as well as hear his voice, a friend suspended a lantern and candle on the bough of a tree, beneath which he stood; and there, in its dim glow—lit up for a different purpose than the lantern employed by Judas, when filled with the execrable purpose of betraying the Saviour, and himself bearing a message unlike that which issued from the lips of the oak-prophets of druidical times,—he proclaimed, like the Baptist in the wilderness, the doctrine of the kingdom. He expatiated likewise on the value of that inward kingdom to the deceased, and the glories of the heaven which she was then enjoying, and which his auditory, on passing through the shades of a deeper night than that which enveloped them, might also enjoy. The whole scene would present to the mind of the hearer a just picture of the Christian's passage "through the valley of the shadow of death," with hope glowing in the midst like the taper over the head of the preacher, accompanied by the voice of the "Great Teacher," cheering him onward, and saying,—"Fear not,—for I am with thee." The scene was admirably adapted to his genius, and to the solemnity of the occasion; and to persons just emerging out of the darkness of nature, and visited with a gleam of gospel light, the whole must have been exceedingly touching. The preacher that could avail himself of every point—that could improve every circumstance; would be sure, while directing the finger to the shaded candle, which rendered him but dimly visible, to encourage the desponding penitent, by telling him, that—

> " The wretch, condemn'd with life to part,
>   Still, still on hope relies,
> And every pang that rends the heart
>   Bids expectation rise :

that—

> " Hope, like the glimmering taper's light,
>   Adorns and cheers his way,
> And still, as darker grows the night,
>   Emits a brighter ray."

In addition to the places already noticed, he preached subsequently in a barn belonging to Robert Moor, of Swillington,—in the house of Mr. Shillitoe, of Little Preston,—before the door of J. Birkenshaw, of Garforth,—at Halton,—and in the house of John Lorriman, of Aberford. He was not satisfied with one service in the day, as will afterwards be seen; nor did he confine himself to the fittest seasons for travelling. After attending public worship at Barwick, he usually sallied forth to the villages at noon; and when not engaged elsewhere, would have returned to assist at the prayer-meeting at Barwick in the evening.

On one occasion, he took up the suitableness of Christ as a Saviour, stating that he was adapted to persons of all ages, and under all circumstances, and run a parallel at the same time, between our Lord and man, in the different stages of human life. Pleased with the idea that flashed upon the mind, and desirous of encouraging all, he observed, that he had passed through the stages of human life for the sake of man ;—that he was capable of sympathizing with him in each ;—that he became a child, for children ;—a youth, for young people ;—a man, for persons in mature life ;—and a labourer,—being the son of a carpenter, for the poor. At the close of the service, a shrewd old man, who was very partial to him, looked at him, and enquired,—"What is to become of me, who am *aged*, if Christ passed through the different stages of human life, to accommodate man from *childhood* to *mature life?*" Dawson turned his head aside, and whispered to a friend,—"I have learned a lesson here." Mackenzie observes,—"If it is dangerous to be convinced, it is dangerous to listen ; for our reason is so much of a machine, that it will not always be able to resist, when the ear is perpetually assailed." True ; and hence the propriety of listening to age, wisdom, and experience. William Dawson felt the force of the remark of his old friend, saw the imperfection of his parallelism, and yielded to the force of conviction.

As he advanced in the work, his zeal became more ardent, and his manner more violent ; so much so, that his mother, after hearing him a few times, observed to him,—"I can do with anything but thy shouting ; it quite distracts my head." Not experiencing any inconvenience from it himself, and therefore, the less sensible of it, he remarked to her on returning from preaching, on one occasion,—"Mother, I have not shouted much to-night!" "Shouted," she replied, "why, child, I never heard thee shout so much before."

CHAPTER V.

His evidence of his personal interest in the atoning sacrifice of Christ, which had often been overshadowed, became brighter and more constant as he proceeded, and as he associated with persons who were themselves in possession of the blessing. He grew less and less disposed also to charge the involuntary stirrings of a depraved nature upon himself with all the force of voluntary transgression, and found that there

was a wide difference between the *pain* produced by
the one, and the *guilt* arising from the other ; being
able, in the former case, to approach the throne of
grace with less of downcast look and feeling, than
in the latter.   He became less disturbed too, on the
subject of satanic suggestions ;   aware that the most
innocent character—as in the case of the immaculate
Jesus, may be tempted, and yet maintain his purity.
But such was the severity of his tests, that a temptation
to sin produced the same abhorrence, and almost the
same amount of painful feeling, as sin itself :   and
though he rarely relaxed in the severity of his judgment, yet his riper experience rendered his decisions
less harassing and painful to himself,—enabling him to
draw a proper line of distinction between the temptations of Satan, and the corruptions of the human heart ;
between a temptation to sin and a participation of its
guilt, by surrendering himself to its power.   His views
and feelings became better adjusted in all matters of
religious experience.   He saw that a temptation might
be presented to the mind, in the way that the eye may
meet an uninvited and unexpected object ;   and that the
mind may as quickly and as innocently turn from the
one, as the eye from the other.   The *impression* may
still be left ;   but it is the Christian's duty to ascertain
whether the impression is one of *pain* or of *pleasure :*
if of pain, then conquest may be fairly anticipated.
The mind, in its wandering and less watchful moments,
may stumble upon what is not altogether profitable or
convenient ;   but even then—without the least *disposi-*
tion towards that which is unlawful, divine grace
instantly interposes its check ;   and the conscience is
left as free from guilt as the man is who *looks* upon a

tree loaded with fruit in his neighbour's orchard, but without the least disposition to *covet*——to look till he loves——to love till he shall put forth the hand to *steal*. The heart of a Christian, like the mind of a wise man, should resemble a mirror, which reflects the object without being sullied by it.

Though never otherwise than decided from the commencement, in his adherence to Christian principle and practice, yet owing to more constant peace, and a stronger assurance of the divine favour, he was enabled to enter with greater freedom into the ministerial work ; while his continued correspondence with his friend, Mr. Settle, seemed to localize his views and feelings to his own neighbourhood, by rendering the discipline of a university less attractive, and holy orders, in the same ratio, less probable and desirable. Mr. S. thus addresses him :—

"Cambridge, Jan. 23, 1798.

"DEAR DAWSON.—After a long silence, I take up my pen to give you a line. I have just taken my degree ; but, I fear, with little or no credit. I shall never make a shining character. Some poor, obscure village will be suitable enough for me. The manner in which the public examination is conducted, were I to describe it, would not be at all interesting to you. It will be sufficient to observe, that I laboured under several disadvantages ; one of the principal of which was slowness, and defective writing ; and the other, too great a fulness in the proofs and demonstration of any particular problem. Besides these, there were others, which I forbear to mention. A maudlin man stands but a poor chance in the senate house. The world, you are aware, is not fond of seeing a religious man honoured; nor can I conceive why a serious man should hunt after reputation in the present life. But as Cambridge professes solely and purely to regard merit, I do not see that it is wrong to complain when any one does not meet with the treatment which his merits deserve. Were you acquainted with the proceedings of the University, I could quickly make it appear to you, that a great deal of unfairness and unjust conduct has been shewn to Magdalen College. Mr. B—r—tt, whom I have often named to you, has, in consequence of this, taken no honour. You are aware, that he was to have been among the three or four first —the place which Mr. Th—p—n was pleased officiously to assign to me; but I have lately had an opportunity of seeing Mr. T., and told him that he lavished his praise with too liberal a hand. He denied the charge; but the evidence was too strong to be evaded. As I am on this subject, I may observe, that persons cannot be too cautious in what they say; for without intention, they may depress, and represent a man as totally insignificant, or elevate him to a rank to which he is not entitled. Mr. T. felt the force of what I said, and acknowledged it to be wrong. You will be ready to exclaim, 'You are full of complaints. Why am I to be troubled with Cambridge affairs?' You are sensible of this, that it is painful to be classed among the first in mathematical merit, and in the end to run the hazard of losing one's degree.

"I expect, should the Bishop not send me back, to get into orders in March. It is supposed, that his grace will have a private ordination in London; and this is the reason why I shall not visit Yorkshire.

"Receive my thanks for your last. The death of

Mrs. Jackson affected me much ; and that of Mary Batty was sooner than I expected. I have not heard anything more of Mr. Graham, and conclude your information incorrect. As to Clifton, I can give you little or no account. Farish tells me, that the people are poor. Let me hear from you soon. Give my respects to Mr. Atkinson, when you see him. I am yours sincerely—and have done with mathematics.

S. SETTLE. "

With all his attachment to the Established Church, several things concurred, like so many small driftings, to bear him out of his original course, and to accelerate the force of the feeling by which he was borne along. His visits to Scholes, Colton, Garforth, Seacroft, Swillington, Little Preston, Aberford, Whitkirk, &c., not only became more frequent, but new places, such as Kippax, Micklefield, Starks, Halton, Stanks, Cross-Gates, &c., were included in his circuit ; making forty-four visits in all in the course of the year, for public addresses, exclusive of prayer-meetings. Some of these places were visited in church hours ; and the church service was omitted by him in consequence. Added to this, he was more frequent in his attendance on the meetings carried on among the Wesleyans, and preached much less on a Thursday evening in connection with Mr. Atkinson—though generally present as a hearer, and sometimes engaging in prayer. He addressed different congregations, in places some miles apart from each other, on the Lord's day, and occasionally preached to the people in the same places in the course of the week ; taking Little Preston in the forenoon, attending church service at Kippax in the afternoon, and preaching at Garforth in the evening.

Having heard a good deal respecting Miss Mary Barritt, who, as a public speaker, was at this time unusually popular, he was induced to go to Sturton Grange to hear her; and availed himself of other opportunities of hearing her in the course of the year, at Whitkirk, Mr. M. Jackson's, of Hillam Mill, and other places. Her subject at Sturton Grange was " Balaam's Wish ;" and he appears to have been favourably impressed with the address, exclaiming—" I thank thee, O Lord, for the least profit which I have received. Let me experience thy full salvation." But he lost, at the close, as at the prayer-meeting at Barwick conducted by Mr. Miller, what he had gained in the beginning ; observing,—" a confused meeting commenced at the conclusion of the sermon, which rather pained my mind." He prayed, however, that God would " lead him right, and keep him right ; " and on his return home, " found unusual liberty in family prayer." Though disposed to exercise candour, the tumultuous meeting at the close, became the topic of conversation the next day, when he was not altogether satisfied with his remarks upon it ; stating, that he " was hurt with what he said ; " adding in his Diary, " it seems better, Lord, that I should say nothing." He was afraid of speaking unadvisedly, and of rooting up the wheat with the tares ; though by no means reconciled to the noise, as is evident from subsequent conversations. The last time he heard Miss B. was at Barwick, on a Wednesday evening, on which occasion his joy appears to have been unmixed ; saying, " Praise the Lord ! found some sweetness in hearing." On this occasion, too, he appears either to have courted, or to have been allured, to a little Wesleyan fellowship ; enjoying the society of

Mr. Blagborne, then stationed on the Leeds circuit, on his return home.

A further advance was made, by stepping from the outer to the inner court of Wesleyan Methodism; having attended three love-feasts,—one at Sturton Grange, July 1st, another at Seacroft, October 7th, and a third at Kippax, November 25th. Mr. Mather preached on the occasion at Sturton Grange, and dwelt chiefly on the love of God. "I found," he remarks, in noticing the circumstance, "a near approach to God. Blessed be the Lord!—Went from thence to Little Preston, full of hope of a gracious time, and was not disappointed. I spoke on the concluding clause of the Apostle's Creed. May the Lord bless the word! I hope, I trust, he will. I wish to leave all self, and simply to go on with the glory of God in full view. Found a warm reception on my return; but praised be the Lord, I found a perfect calm within, and submission to his will." No wonder that his mother, a rigid church-woman, should manifest a little opposition, on seeing him take one step after another—though still unintentional on his part, towards a separation from the Establishment. Mr. Blagborne led the lovefeast in the latter case; and it is probable, that this prepared the way for the intercourse which Dawson had with him, as noticed in the preceding paragraph. Here, however, he was not quite so happy as at Sturton Grange. He complains of "pride," and inferior things occasionally occupying the mind, though he laboured to repel them,—earnestly praying "for more *heart* religion." Without positively affirming it, there is reason to believe that he spoke on the occasion, and that it became a source of temptation to him. It was not the "pride," of which Chapman speaks, which is blind,—making us "eagles in matters that belong to other men," and "beetles in our own:" but that to which Pope refers,—"a consciousness of having done a poor thing, and a shame of hearing it." These two appear to have entered into the composition of the pride of the occasion.

Not only were the Wesleyan preachers followed through the week, but when on a visit to Wetherby and York, he found his way to the religious assemblies of the Methodists, assisting the friends in the former of these places—though a perfect stranger to them, to carry on a prayer-meeting. Whether the Thursday evening Lectures were regularly continued, or whether he found his various engagements interfere with the service, by making so many demands upon his time, is not ascertained; but certain it is, that Barwick was omitted five times on that evening during the twelve months, and only one of those times in consequence of rain. The fact too, of being occasionally under the disagreeable necessity of hearing his old schoolmaster, Mr. H., in the church at Barwick, operated painfully on his mind; observing that not only were "his notions of religion incorrect, but his life was opposed to the ministerial character:" further adding, "what a sad state should I have been in, under such a minister!" But though he had lost his "mainstays" in Messrs. Dikes and Graham, —both of whom he ever remembered with respect and affection,—and a weakening process was going on, of which he was not altogether sensible, he was not without his fears as to the propriety of the steps he was taking, and the real character of the zeal displayed by the Wesleyans. Hence, in his Diary he writes,— " I found my mind in a frame of thanksgiving this morning : " and then, as if afraid lest any of his plans or purposes should at all militate against the hallowed feeling, he directs the heart upward, and pours out his spirit in prayer, requesting the Lord to " Sanctify every faculty of the soul ; not to allow him to misunderstand any feeling; to save him from all enthusiasm, and from confounding the mere effusions of a heated fancy with the comforts of the Holy Ghost ; to give him a discriminating eye, and to enable him to discern Satan as *deformed,* at the very moment that he is *transformed* in all his specious appearances. " Had the works of a late noble author been at this time before the public, this form of expression might have been supposed to have been borrowed from his " DEFORMED TRANSFORMED. " This fear,—though he was frequently called upon to engage in prayer, made him a little shy now and then, of letting himself out too freely. Thus, about the same time, being alive to the practice of calling upon him to exercise, the following entry meets the eye :—" Some men came from Leeds to Barwick, and spoke upon—' This man receiveth sinners. ' I had some reasonings in my mind respecting the propriety of going to prayer, if called upon." He heard Mr. Atkinson, the curate, in the church, in the afternoon of the same day, and went himself to Garforth in the evening, and preached on the " New Birth. " His views, however, respecting Wesleyan doctrine, worship and discipline, became clearer and more enlarged by a continued perusal of the Works of Fletcher, and a close examination of Benson's Defence of the Methodists against the attacks of Tatham, Russell, and others. In the latter case, he exclaims,—"Oh, how hard it is to manage controversy without bitterness!"

His sphere of labour, which was still gradually enlarging, and the slender encouragement given to lay interference and help in the Established Church, may also be considered as contributing no small share to the change which was now drawing to a point ; for in the same proportion as he wandered from the general rules and usages of the church, in calling sinners to repentance—as was the case with the venerable Wesley, belonging to the same community, in the same proportion he entered further and further into the heart of Methodism—a system resulting from the same erratic, but apostolic movements, of the extraordinary man from whom it took its rise.

It is not surprising to find him, considering his religious associates and training, a little at variance both with Methodism and its promoters. Honest Samuel Hick was one of those persons, whose peculiarities he was at first unable to relish, though he could afterwards not only bear with his weaknesses, but duly appreciate his numerous excellences. But though he objected to Samuel, he was no less grieved with himself for the apparent severity of his criticisms upon him ; and hence, revolving on the subject of a Sabbath meeting at Garforth, he observed on the Thursday following, when his sentiments had wound their way back to him from an unexpected quarter, —"I was hurt at some unwary expressions which were dropped respecting some observations made by Samuel

Hick, at Garforth, on Sunday afternoon." He had not only the good sense to know, that extreme severity is not only sure to arm everything against it, and often relaxes into supine neglect, but he carried about with him, a conscience tender of the faults and failings of others.

Still, though he lent occasional, and now more frequent aid, to the Wesleyans, his labours were chiefly directed to the improvement of the members of the Established Church, as his principal friends were yet to be found in that community. He visited its sick not only at Barwick, but at Swillington and elsewhere,—was invited to improve its funeral solemnities, by praying and addressing the people, prior to the removal of the corpse to the place of sepulture,—and sought to advance the spiritual interests of the people, by religious discourse in social life. With the same view, he carried his religion into the "highways and hedges;" and on one occasion, rejoiced in having to record, that he "met with a stranger on the road, who knew something of the divine life," and with whom he had taken sweet counsel. The salvation also of his grandmother, and other friends and relatives, to whom he frequently spoke, and with whom he frequently prayed, was matter of great solicitude with him. Nor were his labours fruitless, either in public or in private. Adverting to the influence of some of his public addresses on different occasions, both upon himself and others, he has the following brief notices :——

"At Stanks in the evening. Spoke on the wisdom, power, faithfulness, and love of Christ. Bless the Lord for a good, spiritual season! Oh, may I ever

F

be moulded to his will! Only let me be thine, O
Lord!

"Spoke on watchfulness at Seacroft. My only end
is the glory of God, and the good of precious souls.

"In the evening at Garforth. Dwelt on the necessity
of the Spirit's influence to change the human heart,
and the equal necessity of that change, in order to
our admission into heaven. May the Lord bless the
means to the hearers! Found a remarkable nearness
to God in prayer at James Watson's. Visited John
Clayton. Oh, may I ever feel the value of souls!—
God is my Father,—Christ is my Redeemer.

"Found God present in the public ordinances.
Gave a serious exhortation to the people at Scholes.

"Thank the Lord for an earnest frame of mind in
the means of grace! Spoke at Whitkirk in the evening
on Gal. iv. 4—6. It was a remarkable season of
refreshment. Praise the Lord!

"Received information respecting some good done
at Colton through my unworthy instrumentality. Praise
the Lord! May he bless the person upon whom the
effects were produced, and render the work permanent!

"Spoke at Garforth on the advantages of early
piety. Heard, in the course of the week, of some
good effects produced on some minds. Ah, where
is the person who has lived thirty years, that has
not had a transient work upon the affections at times!
To God alone I look for a blessing. May none of
my services rise up in judgment against any soul!
—Satan, perhaps, desires to sift me as wheat. May
Jesus pray for me, that my faith fail not!"

The addresses themselves bore strong marks of
originality, and were admirably calculated to rouse

and to fix attention; nor were his communings with himself less calculated to preserve and augment the life of God in his own soul. The latter, as is the case with all who speak from the heart, were mingled with his discourses, and essentially aided him in all his probings and searchings, when employed with the consciences of his hearers. Two or three extracts will shew the character of his thoughts at the time.

SIN. "Reflect upon the momentous concerns of religion in health and strength. Deny thyself. Abandon thy favourite sin. Tear it from the heart, though entwined with its very strings. Carry it to the fire of mortification, as the primitive sorcerers carried their books to the fire to burn them. Sin is a poison; there is something of sweetness in it at the moment of drinking; but oh, when swallowed, what heart-twinges does it produce,—what crampings within, —what a rending of the vitals! Terrible, indeed, will be its effects, if not expelled from the mind. Abhor it in thyself; reprove it in others."

ASSURANCE. "Can we be otherwise than struck with the propriety and necessity of a *sense* of forgiveness, as applied by the Holy Ghost, in the comparison between man as a sinner, and a debtor in a gaol? We can no more suppose, that Jesus Christ would permit a pardoned sinner to live in bondage, than a man would permit a friend to linger out a life in confinement, after he had discharged his debts. Never, never rest, then, without a clear sense of the mercy of God; and, once obtained, continue to walk in the light of his countenance."

DEATH. "Think on a dying hour! Think on that moment, when physicians and friends can do no more for the body, and it lies gasping for breath! The quivering lip hangs feebly down, and the muscles are so unstrung, that they are unable to raise it to its former position. It is sprinkled with a liquid from a feather; but small as it is, it is as refreshing to the body as a slight dew to the earth, during the most parching drought,—though as quickly exhaled. The tongue falters in its delivery, and the attendants are obliged to lay the ear close to the opened mouth to collect the half articulated sentence. When this is the case, what will be the thoughts of the heart? What would be our language to our friends, waiting to close our eyes, and to stretch the lifeless trunk on a plank, if able only in broken accents to utter the feelings of that heart? Should we be disposed to say,—"Take warning of us; we have done too much for Jesus; we have gone further than his commands required; we have spent our breath, our prime, in his service, and for his glory; and now we see our madness, our folly! We see that we might have taken our ease, have indulged in the quiet of home, while drudging for the Son of God!' Ah no! Realize the approaching moment; bring it to the eye—set it before you—let it be imprinted in lively figures upon the imagination."

So graphic were his various descriptions, that he seemed to give reality to everything he touched. "Man," said he, when preaching at Scholes,—"Man, as a sinner, is like a person blindfold, walking upon a bridge without battlements. Instead of going straight along, he has got a turn, and is on his way to the side. Crowds of diseases and accidents are pressing upon him, and may, the next moment, jostle him over into eternity. The folly of delaying repentance to a death-bed, is no less extravagant, than if the same person were to place one foot upon the edge of the bridge, and the other off, beyond the chance of recovery." After proceeding in this way with his picturings and appeals, he suddenly ejaculated at the close, just as the sinner appeared balancing in the "mind's eye" of the auditor, on the perilous edge of some of those bridges thrown across the opening chasms among the Alps,—"Lord, save, or he perishes in the roaring, bottomless ruin below!"

He appears to have met, in some of his perambulations, about this period, with persons of sceptical principles; and one objection urged was,—That religion only tends to nullify the natural appetites of the soul. To this, Dawson replied in the course of the argument, —"Religion certainly *changes* the passions; but that no more proves that the Christian has no enjoyments, than it proves that a man has no stomach, because he does not live upon the same food as an ass." He had penetration sufficient to perceive, not only the different aliments, so to speak, upon which saints and sinners subsisted, but the difference between a *change* effected in anything, and its utter *destruction;* while his simile, by the keen stroke of his wit, not only affected the position maintained, but obliquely reduced his opponents themselves to a somewhat asinine condition.

The number of authors, whose works were read at this period, does not only appear to have been enlarged, but he seems to have been more deeply imbued with the self-denying spirit of Brainard, and the hallowed tone of piety exhibited by Baxter. In reference to the former, he remarks,—"He was a serious man; his life leaves a serious savour on my mind." And in reference to the latter, he gives utterance to a similar sentiment; "A savour of religion remains upon the soul on every perusal of his writings." This had a beneficial influence on his correspondence, conversation, and public addresses; and references to usefulness after this become more frequent. The means of grace were evidently wells of salvation to him, and such was his devotedness of spirit to God, that birth-days —usually seasons of festivity, were converted into fast-days. He speaks of "nearness" in private prayer, —of "freedom" in family exercises,—of Divine assistance in preaching,—closing with, "Jesus died for me."

Numerous as were his blessings, his graces were not a little tried with the "Holy War" carried on in the "City of Man-soul," and with some external exercises he was destined to experience; so that while he found strength sufficient for the day, he was sensible that it was *only* for the day—that there was no stock on hand for any succeeding period. Among other things, he was often tried with his own "spirit," upon which he was always compelled to keep a tight rein. The counting-house was entered by thieves; and although the booty was but slender, he found the circumstances painful in which he stood between the depredators and his master. Some ruthless villain shot a calf, more from malice apparently, than wantonness. The farm was unproductive; which led him to exclaim with deep feeling, though with resignation,—"The Lord seems to be trying us in our temporal circumstances." Various nefarious practices were committed also upon property for which he was partly responsible to his master; and not being able to obtain the least clue to the persons or plans of the agents in the work, he himself—and happy for him that his master had implicit confidence in him, was left for some time, without further means of freedom from blame, than his general vigilance and integrity of character. These, however, were sufficient, and bore him through in triumph. In addition to other things, the "stacks" of coals appear to have been robbed, which rendered it impossible for him to balance his accounts, being short in different instances, and so liable to be exposed to suspicion, when perfectly innocent. The men were allowed a certain quantity of coal weekly, for home consumption. On finding some of the children more frequently at the "pit heap" than the regular allowance would warrant, he followed one boy, with a loaded ass,—but so as not to be perceived by him, to Aberford,—a distance of three miles, where the coals were sold to the inhabitants. Having checked this mode of depredation, he had to combat another. A person who brought the coals from the pit to the "heap," furnished accounts, as to the number of loads, which could never be brought to balance with the quantity sold. Resolved to find out the deception, William went to the blacksmith's shop, where he had a full view of every load delivered. He took no notice of his object to any one; but amused himself with little jobs with the men, together with occasional enlivening conversation. With one waistcoat pocket charged with a number of horse-beans, and the other empty, he slipped a bean from one pocket to the other, as the full wagon passed along the line of road, and was emptied at the "heap."

At the close of the day, he returned to the counting-house, drew out his beans, made an entry of the number, and awaited the man's appearance with his list of loads. On finding the separate lists at variance with each other, he then told the man what he had done, and so exposed his villany. The man,—though not prosecuted, was instantly dismissed; and William, whose character alone had supported him hitherto, had it still more illustriously established by the detections specified.

He was not only disturbed while preaching out of doors, as already noticed, but as a proof that Satan found his interests in danger, in consequence of his zealous efforts to spread the truth, a gentleman of the name of Eamerson, who had considerable influence at Colton and Seacroft, warned his dependants away from hearing him, and accompanied his prohibitions with threatenings of dismissal on a repetition of the offence. In an interview with the gentleman himself, some severe language was employed by him; and William, who was tender of his own Christian character, was afraid lest either his own manner or matter should not have reflected in everything, honour on the cause he espoused,—though without the least design to be uncourteous. Hence his language on the occasion :—" Pardon, O Lord, whatever I might say amiss. Bless, and convert his soul. Keep his malicious speeches from turning to our hurt! " To be mild and respectful under such circumstances, is next to impossible, without the grace of God ; for " there is a time " with individuals, as well as with states, in the language of Burke, " when the hoary head of inveterate abuse will neither draw reverence nor obtain protection."

A considerable portion of public spirit was infused into his soul, in consequence of his public labours. He mixed with society, indulged in an interchange of sentiment and feeling, and acquired information on subjects of national importance. He felt acutely at this time for the disturbed state of Ireland, and no less for the nation, which was threatened with an invasion from the opposite shores. Sir Thomas Gascoigne, in consequence of the menaced state of the country, compelled each of his tenants to find "a man and horse for a troop of cavalry," and Mr. Porter, the head steward, "took down the names of all the colliers, to serve as foot soldiers." The men, soon after this, were ordered by Sir Thomas to proceed to Garforth, when William accompanied them. On such occasions, and especially at the formation of a corps, when men who have everything to learn, and many of whose vicious habits have never been subjected to the severer restraint of military law, there is often much to distress a conscientious mind, and still more of which he finds it impossible to approve. Dawson coupled the Christian with the hero, and made as firm a stand for his God as his king,—resolved to fear the one, while he honoured the other. In acting lawfully, however, in things lawful, he found he gave offence. He bore his honest testimony against every religious and moral impropriety. This brought down upon him the displeasure of his superiors. Referring to this, he observes,—"I have just been informed of Sir Thomas Gascoigne's disapprobation of my conduct at Garforth. What I did, was, I believe, agreeable to the will of the Lord. His will I wish to know in all things ; and my prayer is, that he would assist

F 2

me in everything I undertake." The probability is, from his love to souls, his ardent zeal, and from the last form of expression, that, as Garforth was one of his "preaching places," he *undertook* to give such of the men as might be disposed to listen to him, like honest John Nelson in "olden times," a little wholesome ethical advice, some of them being as little versed in Christian morals, as in military tactics. Whether he had more to do with the foot soldiers, than to attend to different arrangements, is doubtful, as his brother Richard supplied the demands made upon the tenantry, by entering into the cavalry. Nor is it to be supposed, that he acted altogether imprudently in the thing which gave offence; for, as an eminent writer observes,—"If the prudence of reserve and decorum dictates silence in some circumstances, in others, prudence of a higher order may justify us in speaking our thoughts." So it was here. If "prudent men," according to another writer,—Shenstone, "lock up their motives,—letting familiars have a key of their heart, as to their garden," they are not at the same time to place a padlock upon the tongue, when the imperative commands of God are upon them, urged by an enlightened conscience. Dawson's heart dictated these further sentiments on the occasion:—"Into thy hands, O Lord, I commend my soul, body, property, talents, influence, and everything, to be at thy disposal. Oh, give me such a measure of thy love, as will at all times enable me to say, in sweet, passive resignation,—'Thy will be done.'"

He was generally fitted for the exercises of the day by his habits; for when he arose in the morning, he did not only direct the heart to God in prayer, but consulted him also in his Word; and frequently wrote in his Diary the passage, or the sentiment, with which he was most impressed,—thus collecting manna in the morning, like the Israelites in the wilderness, as food for the soul to feed upon through the day. Hence, he writes: "Be steadfast, unmoveable, always abounding in the work of the Lord, forasmuch as ye know that your labour is not in vain in the Lord.' This was one of the first texts that my eye fixed upon this morning. May the Lord enable me to take it into my heart, and to adopt it into every thought, word, and action!" Again, a short time after;—"Rose in a frame of prayer. Praise God! Read God's promise to Moses, — 'My Spirit shall go with thee,' &c. Experienced a Divine unction proceeding from it. O Lord, I rest upon it; and through it, rest upon thee. Let me never do anything to forfeit such blessings!" It is an old proverb—"After the master, is manners." God is the Master of man, the soul is the master of the body. God ought to be served before man, the soul before the body. This truly Christian man, to keep up the allusion, enabled the soul to break its fast at the throne of grace, the first thing in the morning; and he issued from his closet like a giant refreshed with new wine. The day that has a good devotional beginning, has generally a satisfactory close. When the Sun of Righteousness gilds the spirit in the morning, the moon is often found walking in brightness in the evening.

There was a scrupulosity of conscience, however, about him, which, though not at all interfering with the religious exercises of others, was often distressing to himself. "Conscience," observes old Burton, "is a great ledger

book, in which all our offences are written and registered,
and which time reveals to the sense and feeling of the
offender." No man ever turned over the leaves of this
ledger more frequently than William Dawson; and in
no such ledger were more minute entries ever to be
found. The following are a few of those things for
which he empaled himself, and on which he writhed
in agony : viz.——Paying away "a bad shilling," though
perfectly unintentional;——receiving more than he thought
he deserved for certain services, though acknowledging he
would have "allowed others, in the same circumstances,
to have done the same ;"——giving an opinion on men
and things, which, though just, might in some instances
detract from their worth in the esteem of persons not
sufficiently acquainted with them——observing that, " in
free conversation, improper things are apt to slip
out ;"——omitting places, which his zeal prompted him
to visit, but which time, strength, and opportunity,
would scarcely allow;——not practising greater abste-
miousness and self-denial, when further, in some
instances, might have unfitted him for duty ;——smiling
in a place of worship, when the oddity of the expression,
or burlesqued character of the figure, rendered it next to
impossible to repress the feeling ;——employing a sharper
tone in conversation, than what he might suppose
comported with Christian meekness ;——engaging in discourse, which, though harmless, was no more than
harmless——not profitable——saying, on the occasion,
that "such things should not have been introduced,"
and that "we ought rather to forbear lawful things,
than transgress against law ;——inadvertently substituting the word *fortunate* for *providential*, concluding
from the perversion of the term, that he might have

given occasion for a lax view of the government of God
in the world;—allowing himself to lie awake in bed in a
morning, as though feigning sleep, in order to gain
two or three minutes indulgence, when a single call
would have instantly summoned him to the chamber
floor;—a fear of urging upon others what he did not
experience in all its fulness himself;—naming anything, which, though not strictly confidential, and
from the best of motives, might have been as well
withheld;—accusing himself of a shame of the cross,
of the fear of man, or a disposition to indulge, in
his own language, "King Self," in the discharge of
duty, when it appeared to have been a stratagem of
the enemy to check him in his career of usefulness;
—unpleasant reflections, lest he should have become
a partaker of other men's sins, because of his not
having in every instance reproved them, when the
time, occasion, society, and other circumstances, might,
by possibility, have aggravated the case;—and for
indulging in cheerfulness, instead of grave, sober
thought and discourse. Still, though he could not
always stand clear with a scrupulous conscience, he
carried about with him the general "testimony" of
a "good" one: and agreeably to South, "A palsy
may as well shake an oak, or a fever dry up a
fountain, as either of them shake, dry up, or impair
the delight of conscience. For it lies within, it centres
in the heart, it grows into the very substance of the
soul, so that it accompanies a man to his grave; he
never outlives it, and that for this cause only, because
he cannot outlive himself." Here was William Dawson's
safety, in the midst of his distress.

It is rather singular, with so much scrupulosity,—

and his attachment to the formularies, rites, and usages of the Established Church can alone account for it, that he should ever have been induced to stand *sponsor* for a child, which was the case, in the parish church of Whitkirk, May 27, 1798; thus, as in all such sponsorships, taking upon him to answer for the future conduct of the child, solemnly promising to renounce the devil and all his works, to follow a life of piety and virtue; and by this act to lay himself under an indispensable obligation to instruct the said child, and to watch over its conduct. This, when associated with his living and dying a bachelor, gives rise to some rather amusing thoughts. And yet, with him, it was at this time a serious thing; and he chides himself for some inward shrinkings on the occasion, saying, "O Lord, pardon me! I am not half bold enough for thee : I blush at my shame-faced folly."

It may be stated, however, once for all, on the subject of celibacy, and without any feeling of delicacy, that he was not a stranger to the charms of the softer sex—and it would have been a shame if he had! There are intimations of an occasional leaning to the marriage state, in his own hand-writing, and there are facts to support it. But that, agreeably to his own sentiments, "which he considered perfectly lawful in itself, he concluded to be imprudent in him, because of his temporal affairs, and more especially the position in which he stood in reference to his mother and the younger branches of the family." His excellent mother, for whose comfort he could sacrifice any-thing, lived till his habits of "single blessedness" became fixed. After that, with a prudence only equalled by his previous self-denial, he resolved to proceed to the grave unfettered with new connexions and responsibilities ; especially as he had attained a period of life, when he was less able to make provision for those whom—in addition to his brother Thomas, for whom he had to provide, he might leave behind. No man, however, could support a little pleasantry on the subject with a better grace than himself—sometimes styling himself, when others were talking of titles, " *Bachelor of Arts.*" " What," said a friend to him jocosely one day, " I am told you have been disappointed in a love affair ! " He instantly returned, —looking shrewdly, but good-naturedly in the face of the gentleman, who had passed the meridian of life, and who had himself obtained no higher *degree* than bachelor —" That, according to report, is only *one ;* but I am informed, your disappointments have reached the *teens.*" This was as unexpected as the other, for neither of them were aware—though nothing is more common, that *reporters* had been taking notes of their respective cases.

His warmth of feeling, which led to certain external manifestations, and which would have been less conspicuous in a Methodist chapel than in a parish church, attracted the attention of Mr. Atkinson, the curate ; but as it was involuntary on the part of William, he was the less conscious of the habit. It would have been as difficult to stop the bubbling up of a natural spring from the side of a mountain, as to suppress the external expressions of any painful or joyous emotion in him, whether in the social circle, or in a place of worship.

In the course of the same month that he became a

godfather, he received a letter from Mr. Graham, in answer to one of his own ; the only one apparently received from that gentleman, not having any regular "epistolary correspondence," as previously stated, but chiefly personal "interviews," which rendered it the less necessary.

"York, May 2, 1798.

"MY VERY DEAR FRIEND.——Were I not unwilling to fill my letter with apology, and did I not know that I have scarcely a letter to write to a friend that does not need one, I might entreat your forgiveness now for my long neglect in answering your very friendly and agreeable letter. Be assured, my affection for you is not abated, much as my silence may deserve to be construed into neglect. If Barwick is yet dear to me, it is not the soil or the solitude I enjoyed there, that makes it so ; but the few of the Lord's people that live in it. Among them, you, my dear friend, who, while I was present with you, administered most to my comfort, hold the first place in my memory and affections in my absence. I received your letter as a proof and pledge of your sincere regard for me, with real satisfaction—and have resolved, and re-resolved, to gain a few minutes to devote to you, till at last shame, which made me give it up for awhile, has compelled me to realize my resolutions.

" My ministerial responsibility, as well as my private regard, lead me to enquire how the Lord's work goes on in you, and around you. I have no doubt, from the Lord's dealings with you, while I was with you, but that you have learned more and more of his covenant love, wisdom, and goodness, in Christ Jesus. I hope, that as the foundation was laid deep, and attended with sharp conflicts with the pride of reason and the powers of hell—the fruit of righteousness is sown in peace to you ; that you stand rooted and grounded in light and love ; that you find it easier to live by faith, and realize the promises of an unchanging Jehovah.

"Oh, my friend, we trust in a Saviour in whom all fulness dwells ; we serve a master, who can richly repay us ; we follow not cunningly devised fables ; we look for a city which cannot be moved; we have a friend with God, who is touched with the feeling of all our infirmities, and who is able to save us to the very uttermost. Let not our hands hang down; let not our eye of faith quit its mark ; let not our affections languish; let us not sleep as do others, but let us run with patience the race set before us, &c.

"How stands the work of God among you? Does the party meet as before? Do they maintain their former state in numbers, in attention, in fervency of devotion, in brotherly love, in righteousness of conversation? Do they grow in these graces, adorn the doctrine of God their Saviour, and cause the light to shine on those who sit in darkness around them? Are you Mr. Atkinson's *deacon* and helper, as you were mine? Give my best love to them all at your next meeting; and tell them, I often think of them; that it would give me pleasure to see them again, and find them ripening for the great approaching harvest. Request them, in my name, and in the words of the Apostle, that they let their conversation be as becometh the gospel of Christ—that whether I come to see them, or else be absent, I may hear of their affairs ;—that they may *stand fast in one spirit, with one mind, striving together for the faith of the gospel.*

"I was not at Elland the last meeting, nor have I heard any account of their finances, which I fear are not yet extricated from embarrassment. I hope your mind is at ease, in full resignation to the divine will on this point. I should be glad if you could pay me a visit at York ; and give me as much time as you have to spare. You might continue over the Sunday, on your visit. Do come, and soon. I beg my best regards to your mother, sisters, and brothers, and shall be glad to hear that they have all seriously set their faces Zion-wards. My respects to Mr. Atkinson, and believe me to be, with sincere regard,

"Your affectionate servant,—J. GRAHAM."

William, instead of simply tendering Mr. Graham's Christian regards to the "party," namely, the little Christian society at Barwick, connected with the Established Church, read the whole of this truly apostolical epistle to them on the first occasion of their meeting after its reception. This Society lay near the heart of William, of Mr. Graham, and Mr. Settle, the latter of whom was one of its early members, and rarely wrote without an enquiry after its welfare. An allusion to it as well as to the Elland case, which was still in suspense, will be found in the following letter.

"South Clifton, near Newark, Notts., May 12, 1798.

"DEAR DAWSON.—I have just received your letter. The box, in one place or other, had been seven weeks on the road. But 'better late than never.' You have not seen, I dare say, in any of the papers,—The Rev. S. Settle, proposes opening, &c.,—for so and so, upon the easiest, &c.,—for young gentlemen. The situation, &c.—You understand me.

"Some time since, you named a report respecting his grace having taken another living from Mr.——— Is the report correct? Have you seen Mr. Graham lately, or heard anything from him? Pray, how does the meeting go on at Barwick? Does it increase, or does it stand still? You have said nothing in reference to the Ellanders lately. I suppose the subject is set aside. Do you think they will ever call upon you to undertake *hic, hæc, hoc?* Does young Mr. Atkinson ever propose anything, or do you give him any hint on the subject of orders? Have you seen the rector, Mr. Dean, lately; and does he ask you any questions on the matter?—What are you reading—Euclid or Guthrie? Perchance the Methodist Magazine now and then! You see what a number of questions I ask you. There is yet another. Have you heard any talk about Mr. Foster, the new curate, at St. Paul's, Leeds? Does he please, displease, or neither?

"Your father, I hope, was a true prophet. A preacher, of one kind or other, you will one day be, I have little doubt. I have never given you much encouragement in offering yourself to the Ellanders. I have gone the road,—long and dreary, and without a flower to regale the senses; and I have found at the end of it poverty, contempt, and almost universal neglect. However, I make no complaints to any one besides yourself. The first step to usefulness is to be placed beyond the power of want. How Mr. D. could think it possible that a man, a clergyman, one who, though he does not, ought to appear as a gentleman, should be able to live, to keep body and soul together, with the scanty allowance of thirty, or at most, forty pounds a year, argues but little for a knowledge of the world. This is poor encouragement either for a man, like yourself, wishing to enter into the church, or for one, like myself, with one foot already in, and with a desire to continue within its walls. But we may both multiply and magnify complaints to infinity, and be no better. As I expect little favour from the College, I wrote the other day to request a person to take my name off the boards. Young Mr. A. wrote to me, and put the letter into the box. He advised me to look out for cheaper lodgings. But there is not another place where I could lodge at Clifton, either cheaper or dearer.

"I think I have given you some pretty broad hints respecting what I should do, were I in your situation. I have not told you to go and get into the pulpit, and preach among the Methodists; but I have almost told you, to lay aside all thoughts of entering into the Church. But somehow or other, you have never given me your sentiments on that head; and if I were not satisfied in reference to your fidelity, I should hesitate to write to you in so plain and frank a manner. Without flattery, I know that God has favoured you with many good qualifications, and I think it is a pity that any of them should remain dormant. One part of my letter, you state, that you like; and there is one part of yours that I like. You inform me, that you address a word now and then to the Methodists. Why is it only 'now and then?' why is it not as often as possible? You write much about souls perishing, time flying, &c. I think I may retort, and say,—You are halting between two opinions; you are ordered to Nineveh, but you seem resolved to go to Joppa. Apply this.

"Your advice respecting increasing the duty is good. I had put it partially into practice before you wrote. I have also written to Mr. Farish on the subject. He is willing too, that it should be increased occasionally. Respecting catechising, I purpose following Mr. Graham's plan. Would I could execute it only half as well. I purpose, in the course of the summer, to go over some evening in the week, to Hanby, (Shadwell you know,) and for the sake of order, read the evening prayers, and then explain a little, not so much to the children, as to the people. The same is intended to be done at Clifton on Sunday evening.

"Two young men died lately of consumption, both of whom I embraced the opportunity of visiting. One lived within a mile of this place. Him I generally saw daily. It was by mere accident that I heard of him. He did not live in the parish, but had a farm in it. Only part of the town is in the parish. I went to him, and spoke on the miseries of human life, and the cause of them;—all generals, you know. I enquired, whether the clergyman had been to see him. 'O yes,' was the reply, 'and gave him the sacrament.' They had sent for him on purpose. To my no small surprise, the man, as I was taking my leave of him, asked me to pray with him. I returned, 'Yes, by all means.' One of the persons in the house enquired, whether I wished to have a book. I answered, 'No.' After this, I preached the gospel to him, conversed freely with him, and proposed to him various questions. The man, I trust, obtained saving knowledge. He was exceedingly partial to my society, and expressed himself with a good deal of warmth. The other was at Harley, and had a good sense of divine things.

"As it regards myself, I stand much in need of Divine teaching. I want more real life in my soul. My manner of speaking to the people, I fear, is dull, and wants animation. But the minds of my people require to be informed. They ought to understand the Law before the Gospel. God himself first preached the Law to his people, and then the Gospel.

"You perceive I have said nothing about certain particulars ; and yet I expect many from you. Please to tell my father that everything has been received in safety. Pray, write soon.

"Yours, most sincerely,—S. SETTLE."

Of Mr. Foster, William seems to speak favourably in his Diary, having heard him at Barwick. As to the Methodists, it will have been perceived, that Mr. Settle only became more explicit in his remarks, after his correspondent had stated that he occasionally addressed them in public. This was prudent, and shews, that he wished his friend to be guided by the convictions of his own mind ; and the fact of his having laboured among the Methodists, long before he had relinquished all thoughts of going into the Church, and his friends had ceased to interest themselves in the subject, is a proof that everything was the result —not of disappointment, but deep conviction, and sober, careful deliberation. Nor would he, had he not been sincere in all his movements, have ever attempted to prejudice his case with the clergy, by taking a part in the religious assemblies of the Methodists,— and more especially when advised by a clergyman, some years prior to this, not even to associate with them. His silence, too, on the subject of his intentions, of which Mr. Settle complains, shews that he wished to be left to his own reflections, as if afraid of any improper bias from friendly interference. And not anything can be more characteristic of his ardent zeal, than the fact,—while he was furnishing the example at home, of his urging his clerical friend to enlarge the sphere of his usefulness.

The additional shades thrown into the picture of a college life, previously sketched by Mr. Settle, of his struggles and disappointments, are perfectly natural, and what might have been anticipated. He had been engaged in secular employment in early life, and had to enter upon his studies on attaining the age of manhood. Early habits had to be uprooted, and new ones planted in their stead. He was anxious, like all persons of genuine piety, to overstep that part of the path which—though fitting him for it, nevertheless kept him from his grand object—the pulpit. His touching description,—"I have gone the road, —long and dreary, and without a flower to regale the senses," reminds the traveller of the "long and dreary" road across the moors from Sheffield to Hathersage, where all is sterility for a distance of several miles, till he comes on the brow of the hill, leading down to the village, when the lovely vale of Hope suddenly bursts upon the eye, which, in the language of Montgomery to the writer, in reference to the same scene, "lies like a paradise in the lap of desolation." But the heath, the jolting road, and the rocks, which are all in stern contrast with the scene, only add to the enjoyment of it at the close; as the happiness of the collegian would be heightened

when once within the sound of his own "sweet evening
bells," amidst scenes of rural simplicity and beauty,
with the prospect of general usefulness among his
approving and smiling parishioners.   So Mr. Settle
afterwards realized the sweets resulting from his mental
toil ; and it was no small privilege, while on his
journey to the better land, that he had such an ear
as William Dawson's to listen to his sorrows, and
such a breast to sympathize with him under them :
thus requiting him for his song of joy in earlier
times, when all was assurance and peace on the one
hand, and all was despondency on the other.

It was not till the 27th of July, that the subject
of these Memoirs, found it convenient to accept of
Mr. Graham's invitation to York.   He speaks of
experiencing great "nearness to God," as he rode to
the city on the Saturday.   On the Sabbath, he appears
to have been "in the Spirit ; " and what is not a
little expressive of his freedom from all disguise, as to
his partialities and practice, he went to the Methodist
chapel in the morning, where he heard a sermon on
Matt. v. 17—20, under which his heart was filled
with thanksgiving.   He next proceeded to hear the
Rev. W. Richardson, who preached on Ephesians v.
13, 14, and whose voice, manner, and matter, revived
many early recollections.   The public services of the
day were closed by attending on the ministry of Mr.
Graham, who expounded 1 Kings, viii, by which his
visitant was greatly edified.   In his private devotions,
he states, that he "felt a remarkable unction when
reading the cxxxix Psalm."   The next day he had
a conversation with Mr. Graham, on what he terms,
"the Elland business," which seems to have been

the prime object of the visit, and respecting which, his prayer was,—"Direct my steps in thy goings, O Lord. I am thine, do with me as thou wilt."

Some excellent remarks were penned by him in the course of the month, on the duty of "mortification," in things lawful; and evidently applied to himself in a case of some difficulty, in which he displayed the Christian; ending in a further dedication of himself to God.

Additional influences and circumstances, appeared to be bringing him to a decision between Methodism and the pulpit of the Established Church. He found that he had freer scope for the exercise of his talents among the Wesleyans, than he was likely to have in the church in which he had been nurtured; and as the founder of Methodism embodied the doctrines of the Church of England in his writings, and defended them against the attacks of several of the clergy, by an appeal to the Liturgy, Articles, and Homilies, there were the fewer impediments in his way, so far as creed was concerned. In stating that he found fuller scope for his peculiar genius among the Wesleyans, than in the community to which he belonged, is to advance no more than will be admitted by all who knew him; for while he was in the church—violent as was his manner very often, and loud as was his voice, he nevertheless laboured to sober down his native impetuosity into the sedate, systematized manner of the clergy, and so proceeded under partial, and sometimes embarrassing restraint: whereas, on being let loose among a few warm, simple-hearted Methodists, where every man clerked and responded for himself, he sang, he talked, he prayed, and seemed to feel the same

G

difference that is experienced by the bird which exchanges the confinement of the cage for the freedom, the society, and the music of the grove; and that too, as in other cases connected with himself, without fully ascertaining the cause—the whole system being peculiarly adapted to his nature and his genius.   And he had not to go out of the Establishment,—to turn his back upon it, and to enter another community to feel it; but it was while he was yet *in* the one, and before he enjoyed the full fellowship of the other; and therefore, at a time when many of the peculiarities and privileges of both were duly appreciated.

Mr. Atkinson informed him at the close of the Thursday Evening meeting, Oct. 11, that his father wished to see him at Leeds, to speak to him in reference to the Elland Society.   Dawson's language was, "Lord, let thy will be done in all things."   He wrote to his friend Mr. Settle, on the Friday.   On the Saturday morning, he went to Garforth, and there found his other bosom friend, John Batty, with whom he communed; and afterwards visited widow Smith, with whom he prayed.   He received the sacrament at Barwick, in the parish church, on the Sabbath, after the forenoon service, when his heart was filled with "praise," and when he states it to have been "a time in which God shewed his reconciled face."   In the afternoon, he heard Mr. Atkinson; and in the evening, he went to Scholes, where he addressed the people on the "Happiness of heaven," placing it in contrast with the highest happiness to be enjoyed on earth.

Monday, Oct. 15th, there is the following entry in his Diary:—"Dedicated to prayer;—praying that the

Lord would direct my goings in this most trying season. Lord answer. Settle came down."

Here a little additional information may be supplied. Finding his sphere of usefulness gradually enlarging in his own neighbourhood, and having been led, as far as he could perceive, step by step, in the order of Providence, in the work in which he was engaged —for it was perfectly out of the ordinary course of proceeding in the establishment,—he hesitated, and hesitated the more as he found the door so long in opening in reference to the Elland Society, to decide whether he really ought to leave so fair a field of usefulness. He was at the colliery on the Tuesday morning, and so also was John Batty, who was waiting his "*stem*"—a term employed in the neighbourhood, to denote a person waiting his *turn* for a load of coals. The time of waiting happened to be longer than usual, and turning to Batty, William said, "John, this day is to decide whether I am to be a clergyman, or remain as I am." John, who was anxious to bind him to the spot, and win him over to the Wesleyans, proposed a meeting for prayer, when they proceeded to "Grime Cabin," where the colliery accounts were kept. On leisurely going to the place, William observed,—"The best time for thinking with me is, when I have a little leisure, from eleven o'clock in the forenoon to two in the afternoon, which is the middle of the day. These are my best hours; and when these are lost, the best part of the day is lost to me. Now," continued he, "if it were to be decided in my favour, that I should go to college, I should be obliged to remain there three years : these three years would be taken from the best part of my life ; and, as far as

actual labour in the Church of God goes, would be
a mere blank." Whatever complexion this mode of
reasoning might assume to persons who had everything to learn in religion,—who had not yet entered
the field of ministerial toil, and therefore had no *congregations* to leave, but only *one* to look to in the
distance, with Mr. Settle's "long and dreary way"
between, it had its influence upon the subject of these
Memoirs ; and, to a certain extent, prepared the way
for what followed. Unwilling, however, to lean to his
own understanding on the occasion, the twin spirits
entered the counting-house, to plead with God in
fellowship, as William had often sought directions
singly on the subject before. The service was commenced by singing the 429 Hymn, p. 403,* of the
Hymn Book, used among the Methodists, beginning
with—

> " Behold the servant of the Lord !
> I wait thy guiding eye to feel; &c."

than which, scarcely any other in the book could be
found more appropriate : and their voices in those
days were not only powerful and harmonious, but
paired admirably with each other. They then prayed
alternately several times, when the power of God was
felt by each, and the glory of God seemed to fill
the place. It was to them, what the consecrated spot
at Haran was to Jacob—"the house of God," and
"the gate of heaven ;"—and humble as was the shed,
the realities experienced there, seemed—with a slight
transposition of the langage of the poet, to

* The Hymn was composed by Charles Wesley, and originally appeared at the
close of Mr. Wesley's " Farther Appeal," where it is headed "An act of
Devotion."

"Dissolve them into ecstacies,
    And bring all heaven before their eyes."

As they issued from this little sanctuary, like giants refreshed with new wine, or more appropriately, like the priest from behind the veil, where the divine glory had been rendered visible, Dawson exclaimed, "John, I believe I shall have to be a Methodist preacher yet." This was music to the ear of Batty—sweet as the hymn itself which had just been sung in the, "cabin," and made delightful melody in his heart the whole of the day.

William, soon after this, mounted his horse and rode to Leeds, where he had an interview with the Rev. Miles Atkinson, by whom he was informed, that the funds of the Elland Society were still low. This, in connection with previous reasonings, and the impression produced upon his mind by the meeting in the counting-house, seemed to be an indication that the providential cloud was moving in a direction towards the Wesleyan pulpit, rather than that of the Established Church. Mr. Atkinson, however, not to lose his hold of such a valuable man, and still hoping that the funds would soon be replenished, endeavoured, with a view to wed him to the people among whom he had been trained, "to prove," according to the language of William in his Diary, "the superiority of the Church Establishment" over other communities. This, the Rev. gentleman might readily do, so far as his arguments applied to himself, and other regularly ordained ministers : but what applied to himself, would neither satisfy the conscience nor the reason of a man, who was unordained —pressed in spirit, as he believed, by God himself, to preach the gospel, with a "woe" attached to disobedience—who stood alone, as a churchman, in his ministerial character—who could not legally enter a single pulpit in the church to which he belonged —who had congregations in different places, glad to hear him, and benefited by him—the Wesleyans throwing the doors of their private dwellings open for him —the path to holy orders through the medium of the Society proposed to him, intercepted by an apparently insuperable barrier—and at the hazard of having his energies cramped by the next rector that might succeed Mr. Dean, or the next curate that might follow Mr. J. Atkinson.

On leaving Mr. Atkinson, of Leeds, he continued, to employ his own words, "earnest in prayer with God for direction." The next day he went to "Woodhouse, in the afternoon," and was there "till late;" and in the Diary for the same day, Wed. Oct. 17, he adds—"Gave Mr. Graham a denial of entering the Church." Here, his conversations with the biographer, will again supply a few particulars. Mrs. Graham's sister being a resident in Leeds, Mr. Graham was at this time on a visit to the house of his sister-in-law. Having heard that his old parishioner had latterly mingled more freely than usual with the Methodists, and might ultimately unite himself to the body, he resolved, if possible, as one of his early preceptors, and as was natural for him as a clergyman strongly attached to the Established Church, to rescue him from taking a step, which, in his esteem, was so unadvisable. He intimated, that the Methodists, however unintentionally, were increasing the number of Dissenters from the Church of England, and adverted to the dissensions in the body, occasioned by

Mr. Kilham amd others, as offering but indifferent inducements to persons disposed for quiet, to change their religious connexions. Recurring to this interview, the subject in question observed to the writer, "I felt I had gone too far to recede, and employed a strong expression, which not only startled Mr. Graham's sister-in-law, but at which I afterwards trembled myself —I will risk my damnation upon it;" an expression, which, by the way, could only have arisen from a conviction clear and strong, that he was not seeking his own, but was following the leadings of Divine providence. Reflecting on the whole the next day, he entered into his Diary,—"What have I done? O Lord, have I pleased myself, or thee?—thou only knowest. Convince and pardon me, if I have sinned; if not, strengthen and stablish me. Oh, give me not over to mine enemies." He went to the Thursday evening meeting as usual, where he heard Mr. J. Atkinson on Matt. xiii. 47—52; in which the kingdom of heaven is compared to a net cast into the sea: and after Mr. A. had preached, engaged in prayer.

His friend, Mr. Settle, who was in the neighbourhood, preached twice in the church on the following Sabbath, and at Kippax in the course of the week; on each of which occasions, William attended his ministry; and on the evening of the Sabbath—as if honoured with a new commission, took his stand on "Colton Common," and shewed the persons who heard him, how far a person might proceed, and yet only have "a form of godliness"—what the power of godliness was—applying the subject both to professor and profane, and demanding an answer to the question,—"That if persons, who had a mere form, could not gain admission into heaven, how those could expect to inherit it, who were destitute even of that form!"

Though Mr. Settle knew the way in which the Lord had led his friend, and had given him an intelligible hint on the subject of Methodism, yet when it came to a decision, he seemed dissatisfied with him for deciding so peremptorily against holy orders; living in hope, like Mr. Atkinson and others, that a way might still be opened for him to the pulpits of the Established Church, where he might be extensively useful. Mr. Wade advised him to go into the Church, and others were grieved with the result of his interview with Messrs. Atkinson and Graham. Still, unwilling to do anything in haste, and ready to retrace his steps if he had done wrong, he resolved to acquire the best light on the subject he could obtain, and so wrote for advice to the Rev. Joseph Benson. He had heard what could be said on one side of the case; he now wished to know what could be advanced on the other. Mr. Benson wrote as follows :—

"York, Oct. 30, 1798.

"DEAR SIR.—Having been very much engaged ever since I was favoured with your letter, it has not been in my power to pay proper attention to it till now. And even now, having only half an hour to spare here upon a journey I am taking into the North, I shall not be able to return you such an answer as you probably will expect. But if I can suggest any hint which may be a means of casting light upon your path, I shall be glad. Let me observe, first, then, it is matter of very great thankfulness, that so many pious ministers have got into the Church in different parts of the kingdom of late years ; and it is much to be desired that more still should be introduced into it. For, as you justly observe, thousands will hear the gospel in the Church, who will not hear it out of it. Add to this, we are at no loss at all to procure preachers to labour in our Connexion; we have more offering every year than we can take in : but it is not so easy to find persons proper to go into the Church, or to get such as are proper so educated as that they can be admitted. Nevertheless, though I speak thus, I would observe, secondly, it is not in me to determine how far it will be *your* duty to endeavour to get into the Church. Divers circumstances should be taken into consideration, as your inclination and ability to apply yourself to the study of the classics,— how far you can be spared from the calls of your father's family, who, it seems, are partly dependant upon you for support. The loss of five years, which, if you went to the University, would be absolutely necessary to qualify you for orders, is a serious objection which I could not get over, were it not for the prospect of greater usefulness afterwards ; and yet that is doubtful, should it please God to spare your life. Upon the whole, the best advice I can give you is, to remember him who has said, *Acknowledge me in all thy ways, and I will direct thy steps.* If your eye be single to God's glory, and you *sincerely,* *earnestly,* and *believingly* ask his direction, you certainly shall be favoured with it, and shall not be suffered to take a wrong step. Praying that the Lord may make darkness light before you in this business, and guide you continually, I remain your sincere friend and brother,—J. BENSON."

G 2

Had Mr. Benson not given greater satisfaction as
a commentator, in illuminating what otherwise might
appear dark, than he did in removing the difficulties
which pressed upon his enquiring friend, he would
have been less popular than he is ; for in the language
of the subject of these pages to the biographer,—" his
letter just left me where I was." But it is probable,
from the known character of Mr. Benson, that he
felt a delicacy on the subject ; and that he wished to
leave his enquirer to the dictates of his own conscience,
the guidance of his own reason, the counsel of his
friends, and the openings of divine providence. So
William himself concluded. Hence in his Diary it is
remarked, " He leaves it entirely to God and myself:"
and then adds, " once, O Lord, thou madest a way
for me, in a case like the present, when assistance was
not to be found in any other quarter. Suffer me not
to walk in darkness, but to follow thee. Attend me
in all my concerns : and assist me in all things to act
as becometh a Christian."

A few days after this, he received the following note
from Mr. Dikes :—

"Hull, Nov. 5, 1798.

" DEAR SIR.—I lately saw a letter from you to Mr.
Benson. I will take the liberty of giving you my
advice respecting the question you propose to him.
If your family do not require your attention,—if your
entering upon a course of study would be no disadvantage to your mother and sisters, by all means
accept the offer of the Elland Society. Mr. B. tells
me, they—i. e., the Methodists, have more preachers
than they want. As to the time. Why should you
be in such haste ? Neither our Saviour, nor John

the baptist, entered upon their ministry till they were thirty-one. And if persons were not so young, when they entered upon so important an office, it would be better. Only,—if you accept the offer of the Elland Society, you must comply with all their rules, and not preach among the Methodists. Believe me, to remain yours, very sincerely,—T. DIKES.

"P. S.—You must not think all is lost time, which is spent in making preparation for the ministry. I would wish you to pass through the University of Cambridge; it will be a great advantage to you in after life for the work in which you are about to engage."

Mr. Dikes had either not been fully acquainted with the result of William's interview with Messrs. Atkinson and Graham, or some sudden and unexpected change must have taken place, in the improvement of the funds; otherwise, he would not have urged him to "*accept* the *offer* of the Elland Society:" unless it be supposed, that a strong hope was entertained that he would, at no remote period, be admitted as a candidate, and was therefore requested to wait a short time longer. At all events, the "offer" affords additional proof, that his way was now open to holy orders, and that his non-acceptance was the result of the deliberate convictions of his own mind.

In his public addresses, and theological studies, he often felt unspeakable delight,—though he was not without his moments of bondage and depression. The one laboured against the other; and while he was encouraged on the one hand, he was preserved in a state of dependance on the other. Some of his subjects towards the close of the year, appear to have originated in his own experience,—arising from his hopes and fears, his joys and his sorrows ; as the comfort afforded to such as seek the Lord, Ezra viii, 22, —the preciousness of Christ to such as believe, 1 Pet. ii. 7,—the benefits enjoyed by those who are "born again,"—a caution to the lukewarm, taken from the example of the members of the Laodicean church, Rev. iii. 16,—finally, warbling out his "Christmas carol" at Aberford, Dec. 25, on Luke ii. 10. There were several other texts and topics, as appears from his notabilia, on which he dwelt ; but these are expressive of his general state,—making it his constant business to seek the Lord himself, clinging to Jesus, reaping the blessings arising from the change he had experienced, and dreading lukewarmnesss as he dreaded moral evil.

CHAPTER VI.

Wesley's Life.—Reconciliation necessary for a Minister of the Gospel.—People generally moulded by the ministry.—Increasing faith.—Little faith.—Jeremy Taylor.—Extracts from the Diary. —Böhler's advice to Wesley.—Faith to be preached.—Faith in its simplicity.—Examples of it.—Friendship.—Covenant.— Messrs. Graham and Settle.—Advantage of different Christian communities.—Authors and reading.—Sentiments of Dr. John- son and Sir P. Sidney on knowledge.—" Visitation of the sick." —Industry.—Messrs. Settle and Wade.—Mr. Suter.—W. Daw- son supplies the place of the Vicar of Thorparch.—Personal piety and public usefulness.—Self-abasement.—A hoary-headed enquirer after truth.—Watch-nights.—Tries Class-Meeting.— Preaches in the coal-mine.—Dress.—Useless and unseasonable conversation.—Omissions of duty.—Death of the Rector of the parish.—Public business, and rules to be observed in transacting it.—Hard bargains, and love of our neighbour.—Inferior usage. —Contentment.—Presentiment.—Visit of an uncle to Barnbow.— Sermon to young people.—Habit.—Providential deliverance.— Aptitude for improving occasions and events.

THE Life of the venerable Wesley having been put into his hand towards the close of 1798, he began to give it an attentive and serious perusal, at the commencement of 1799. He remarks in reference to it, Jan. 8.—"I read part of Mr. Wesley's Life; and was struck with an observation,—that 'none are proper preachers, who have not the witness of pardon.' This, to me, appears to be a reason, why I should forbear my present mode of proceeding." With this may be coupled another passage in his Diary, for Feb. 1. "I was deeply impressed with 2 Cor. v. 18,—'All things are of God; who hath reconciled us to himself by Jesus Christ, and hath given to us the ministry of reconciliation.' From hence, it seems, that a man must himself be reconciled to God previously to his becoming a minister of the Gospel."

This may be considered as a new era in his Christian experience. The past, in his estimation, seemed to amount to nothing. He appeared to himself to have been satisfying his soul with occasional *comforts* and flashes of *joy*, which were confounded by him with *assurance*, or conscious *pardon*. But others, who knew him, and with his Diary before them—themselves meanwhile conversant with the operations of the Spirit of God upon the heart, would not be inclined thus to view the past. His experience might be deemed *imperfect ;* but still, the work was *genuine* as far as it went. The truth is, that God mostly accommodates his work to the workmen, and the work generally partakes of the character of the ministry. When people sit under a ministry distinguished for dry morality, little else but a decent morality is witnessed. Where a God-fearing, gradual work of grace is insisted upon, without the doctrine of assurance, the people very often live beneath their privilege ; and, instead of rejoicing in God, hang down their heads like bulrushes, as if the religion of Jesus only tended to generate gloom and melancholy. When, on the other hand, *present* pardon—present salvation— the seal and witness of the Spirit are pressed home upon the soul, persons live in the enjoyment of them. Let people *hear* nothing, *expect* nothing, *pray* for nothing, *believe* in nothing in this way, and nothing of the kind is either received or enjoyed. As far as experience is concerned, the religion professed is a mere religion of emptiness. The faith that is not encouraged, is rarely brought into exercise. These remarks are made in the spirit of the sentiment to which the Apostle gives utterance in his first Epistle to the Corinthians,—"Therefore, whether it were I or they, *so we preach, and so ye believed.*" Nor are they less in harmony with the language of the Son of God,—"According to your faith be it unto you." This apostolical doctrine is, in its operation upon the mind, one of the distinguishing features of Methodism. An instantaneous work is believed and urged, and instantaneous pardon is received, accompanied with its internal evidence. Christianity is represented, Rom. vi. 17, under the nature of a *mould* or die, into which its adherents are *cast*, and from which they take the *impression* of its excellence; "ye have obeyed from the heart that form of doctrine which was delivered you." And as is the mould, so will be the figures thrown off—perfect or imperfect, feeble or strong.

The case seems to be this,—the subject of these pages, now *saw* more clearly what, to a considerable extent, he before had *felt*. He began to adopt different *terms*, and to affix either *stronger* or *other meanings* to terms previously employed. He became more in earnest too, for the *direct abiding* witness of the Spirit; had a more correct perception of the nature of *faith*, and was more deeply impressed with the *necessity* of *living* by it. In consequence of not having lived in the constant exercise of faith hitherto, he was often complaining of the "hidings" of God, of "startings of anger," of "earthly desires," of an inclination to "peevishness,"—over the first of which he silently mourned, and against the latter of which he proclaimed incessant war ; but now, it was faith —faith in the beginning, faith in the middle, faith at the close ; the faith in which he found he could alone *stand*—by which he found he could alone *walk* —through which he could alone *overcome ;*—that faith, in short, by which he only could *live*, and so secure, in the smile of his God and Saviour, permanent repose. A want of the constant exercise of faith will as naturally induce doubt, fear, gloom, and consequent dejection, as moral evil will entail its burden of guilt upon the conscience. Hence, the momentous import of that single sentence, uttered by the prophet,—"The just shall live by his faith ;" a sentence iterated and reiterated by the apostle ; — entering into the very spirit of every dispensation of God to man ;—urged upon the ancient Jews, the Romans, the Galatians, and the more modern Hebrews ; * informing the latter, that they were to "LIVE" as their fathers had done, "by *faith ;* "—that faith was as essential to spiritual, as food to natural life,—and that a man could, with as little safety to his comfort and religious being, cease to believe, as he could hope to support existence in the present state without food. Weak faith, like impoverishing diet, preserves the soul in a sickly, languishing state ; strong faith preserves it in vigour. Faith, when weak, endangers

* Hab. ii. 4 ; Rom. i. 17 ; Gal. iii. 11 ; Heb. x. 38.

the life of an apostle, and he feels himself gradually sinking through the yielding waters, in proportion as he ceases to exercise it; whereas faith, when strong, gives courage to the heart, and vigour to the arm of the patriarch, who, in the plenitude of its power, goes forth to the sacrifice of an only son.

It was from his own experience, that he drew many of his subsequent observations, and so far—whatever might be the cost of pain to himself, his exercises were beneficial to others. When speaking of " little faith" afterwards, he exhibited it under the imagery of "A little lad, sitting in a corner, with a blood-shot eye, and a green shade over it." Persons of fastidious taste, would find latitude sufficient here to find fault; but to the spiritually-minded, the right-hearted, the imagery, with the truths couched under it, would afford ground-work for half a dozen dis-courses.—" LITTLE FAITH, " to extend, as well as familiarize the subject, is but a "little lad,"—being comparatively *feeble*, in consequence of not having reached *maturity*;—is found "sitting," instead of being *actively* engaged, and on the alert,—our best divines invariably representing it as an " active principle; "—takes its position in a " corner," instead of going *abroad* to benefit the *public* by its *example*, and to be " seen and read of all men; "—with a " green shade, " *requiring*, instead of *imparting relief;*—" a blood-shot eye," and so *obstructing vision*, by pre-venting the *free* and *full use* of the faculty;—the whole forming a complete contrast to faith in its strength, or,—to pursue the metaphor, faith in its manhood, whose praise is thus chaunted by the bard of Methodism:—

> " Faith lends its realizing light,
>   The clouds disperse, the shadows fly ;
>   Th' Invisible appears in sight,
>   And God is seen by mortal eye. "

And besides,—as already hinted, and as was well attested by the experience of the subject of these Memoirs, "little faith" is more or less in *pain*—perplexed with doubts, and distracted with fears, which was, no doubt, another idea he wished to convey.— Jeremy Taylor, in illustrating faith, takes the case of the Israelites, who were bitten by the serpents ; and shews, to employ his own language, that when even a "blear-eyed" person turned towards the object, and reached it, there was sufficient virtue in the look, in connection with the object so beheld, to save ; though the vision of such a person might be but dim, when compared with the clear, steady, penetrating glance of others. Whatever becomes of the language—and the same apology that will serve the prelate, may be deemed sufficient for William Dawson, —the simile, in both cases, is admirably adapted to illustrate faith in its varied exercises and effects.

Two or three extracts from his Diary, in the course of the year, of different dates, will shew how his mind was absorbed on the subject of faith, and the blessings consequent on its exercise.

"Read some of the experience of Mrs. Rogers. Thy will, O Lord, be done in me, and by me. Let thy mercy preserve and bless my soul. Remove unbelief. Give me faith. Opened on Zech. ix. 9—12, which was made useful to me.

"Much in earnest for strength to *believe*. Frequently opened on different texts in the Evangelists ; such as— 'Thy faith hath saved thee,'—'Only believe,'—'If thou canst believe, all things are possible to him that believeth,' &c. In the afternoon of the same day, I opened on Rom. iii. 25,—'Whom God hath set forth to be a propitiation through faith in his blood, to declare his righteousness for the remission of sins that are past, through the forbearance of God.' Thus, in the death of Christ, by applying faith, God's righteousness is exemplified in the remission of sins that are past, and he can be just, and yet the justifier of him that believeth in Jesus.

"Engaged with the Lord all the day, for the full application of the sense of pardon to my soul. In the evening, when at private prayer, I found a little confidence in the merits of Jesus, by believing in him. This promise is useful to me,—'He that believeth on him is not condemned.' Mr. Fletcher's letters are of service to me, where he shews that believing, and the seal of the Holy Ghost, are two distinct things. But, O Lord, I trust I shall not rest in anything, and especially without this seal,—this earnest of thine,—this pledge of heaven. Never till now did I see so much as is implied in this promise,—'Whatsoever ye shall ask the Father in my name, he will give it you.' Blessed Jesus! I hope this is the beginning of good days. The same day I spoke at Garforth, on—'Believe on the Lord Jesus Christ, and thou shalt be saved.' This is my earnest wish,—a more powerful application of the Holy Ghost to my heart."

In thus preaching faith, while deploring his want of it, and assigning that want as a reason why he should desist from preaching, a person acquainted with the life of Wesley, to which reference has been made, will be led to advert to the following passage, where the latter remarks,— "Immediately it struck my mind, 'Leave off preaching. How can you preach to others, who have not faith yourself?' I asked Böhler whether he thought I should leave it off or not. He answered, 'By no means.' I asked, 'But what can I preach?' He said, 'Preach faith *till* you have it; and then, *because* you have it, you *will* preach it.'" * It is not improbable that Böhler's reply to Wesley was the means of not only preserving Dawson in his work, but of his continuing to preach on the subject of faith. There is one distinction, however, to be preserved in remembrance, —That while Mr. Wesley felt the total absence of justifying faith, William Dawson was only tempted to reason himself out of what he had. He seemed like a person not altogether satisfied with the fruit he had been permitted to taste, and was desirous, if not of entirely rooting up the whole tree, of at least grafting a scion of a different species of apple on the old stock. But he was soon taught to proceed *"from faith to faith,"*— not differing in *kind*, but in *degree*, "by a gradual series," as Mr. Wesley renders the passage, "of still clearer and clearer promises." As the giant Anteus, when wrestling with Hercules, is said to have acquired strength by every fall to the ground; so the faith of Dawson, though occasionally foiled, rose again, and fought more valiantly,—each succeeding conflict yielding greater triumph. †

By repeated conferences with Mr. Thomas Stoner,

* Wesley's Works, Vol. I. p. 86.

†*Simplicity* in all matters of faith, is considered the best guide; and with this, while the poor are instructed, the learned are never offended. A peasant of singular piety, being upon a particular occasion admitted to the presence of the King of Sweden, was asked by him,—" What he considered to be the nature

the father of the Rev. David Stoner, then resident at
Barwick, and Mr. John Warner, together with others,
he became more and more established. Mr. Warner
was at that time in all the strength of his Christian
character, and William Dawson, who could never forget a kindness, was not the man to desert him in
a reverse of circumstances. A false friend has been
very properly compared to the shadow on the dial,—
appearing in clear weather, but vanishing as soon as
it becomes cloudy. The subject of these Memoirs,
on receiving an accession of spiritual strength, never
failed to strengthen the brethren,—to uphold the weak,
and to reclaim the wanderer ; and Mr. Warner was
one who shared in his kind attention.

He entered into solemn covenant with God on the
anniversary of his birth-day, adopting the same form

of true faith ? " The peasant entered fully into the subject, and much to the
king's comfort and satisfaction. When the king was on his death-bed, he had
a return of his fears as to the safety of his soul, and still the same question was
perpetually put to those around him :—" What is real faith ? " The archbishop
of Upsal, who had been sent for, arrived ; and entering the king's bed-chamber,
commenced in a learned, logical manner, a scholastic definition of faith, which
lasted an hour. When he had finished, the king said, with much energy,—
" All this is ingenious, but not comfortable ; it is not what I want. Nothing
but the farmer's faith will do for me. "

A minister, in America, desirous of communicating the notion of faith to a
little boy, took a chair, and placed it some distance from him, when he told
the boy to stand upon it—to fall forward—and he would catch him. The boy
immediately mounted the chair, but did not fall forward as requested. He
wished to obey, but was afraid the minister would fail in catching him. He
however, put one hand on the mantle-piece, thinking to save himself, if not
caught ; but the minister told him, that would not do,—he must trust to him
alone ; adding, that he would surely catch him, provided he would fall forward. The boy immediately summoned all his courage, and fell ; when he was
as quickly caught. The minister then told him, that that was faith, and that
he wished him to go with the same confidence to Jesus Christ. Any child may
comprehend this ; but, alas! the disposition is too often manifested, to lay hold
of some " mantle-piece,"—something in which self is interested, rather than
go direct to the arms of the Saviour.

as the one of Friday, July 25, 1790, saying—"repeated, Saturday, March 30, 1799."

Mr. Graham visited Barwick in the spring, and Mr. Settle in the summer; but no estrangement of spirit was perceptible on either side. William notices his interviews with both, with pleasurable feeling; and with the latter, a regular correspondence was still maintained. They were satisfied with his sincerity in the decision of the preceding year; and though it sundered them in the field of operation, they knew that the great moral waste could only be cultivated and reaped by the different religious communities occupying their different stations and plots, and working their way to the centre, where—on the work being completed, "Harvest home" would be shouted, and the grand "Hallelujah chorus" sung over a once lost, but finally saved world.

He became increasingly attached, in his reading, to the Arminian Magazine, to the writings of Fletcher of Madely, Richard Baxter, Joseph Alleine, and others; and added to them, in the course of the year, those of Rogers, Bishop Newton, Doddridge, Bunyan, Dr. Owen, Ambrose, &c., together with a work on the Success of the Gospel. He was not, as has been stated of another, a labourer in the mines of learning; but more properly an assayer of the metal; one who could test the value of what he read, and then give it currency. His reading was but circumscribed; still, it was good. He seemed instinctively led to some of the most useful works; and as he read chiefly for experimental and practical purposes, he rarely perplexed himself with the more controversial portions of an author's writing. The end which he proposed to himself in reading, preserved him from the error against which others have been cautioned,—of wheeling rubbish to the base of the mountain, without adding to its height, or enlarging its prospect ;—of carrying stones to the architectural pile, and only adding to its bulk, without increasing its strength or its magnificence. The time occupied in reading, was taken in snatches from secular employments ; and as this was compressed into comparatively small compass, he contrived to improve it to the best advantage, by the value of the works that came under his notice. He felt in all its force, what Dr. Johnson with so much judgment has expressed :—"The foundation of knowledge must be laid in reading. General principles must be had from books, which, however, must be brought to the test of real life. In conversation, you never get a system. What is said upon a subject is to be gathered from a hundred people. The parts of a truth, which a man gets thus, are at such a distance from each other, that he never attains to a full view." As a system can only be effectually formed in this way, so that system—when good, will have its corresponding influence on human action ; for, "it is manifest," says Sir P. Sidney, in his more antiquated style, "that all government of action is to be gotten by knowledge, and knowledge best by gathering many knowledges, which is reading."

In obeying the apostolic injunction, "give attendance to reading," he was careful not to permit his attempts to acquire knowledge to trench upon other duties. He knew the liturgy too well to forget "the visitation of the sick ; " and the grace of God had too deep a hold of his heart, to allow him to neglect the kindly office.

A reference has already been made to his diligence and
tenderness in the discharge of this duty; and he was
not without encouragement. "I visited," he remarks,
"a young woman at Scholes. May she know the whole
truth!" Two days after, he adds, in reference to the
same person,—"I am much comforted in the relation
of her triumphant death."

He was in the habit, at this time, of composing a
new sermon every week; and forty of these have turned
up among his papers, dated 1799, together with the
places at which they were preached. Exclusive of short
addresses, seventy-five distinct preaching services are
enumerated in the course of the year. This is the more
remarkable, as he stood nearly alone, not being wholly
either with the Established Church, or with the Wesleyans, though loved and courted by both, and an
attendant on the ministry of each. Among the clergy,
the Rev. Messrs. Atkinson, Hodgson, Foster, Marriott,
Smalpage, Hemington, and King, are noticed this year;
Benson, Pawson, Blagborne, and others, among the
Methodists.

Few were the instances in which he was repulsed, in
the course of public instruction which he was pursuing; and two of these,—which are the only cases that
have come to the knowledge of the biographer, were
not distinguished by anything discreditable to either
party. Some of the friends applied to Mr. Wade of
Sturton Grange, to allow him to preach in his house.
"No;" returned Mr. Wade, with energy and firmness,
"he shall not preach in my house till he is united to
the Methodists." Mr. Wade was ignorant of his inward
struggles, and of the difficulties he had to surmount,
arising from early prejudices and prepossessions. On

the friends at Seacroft requesting Mr. Suter, who preached in the forenoon, to publish for him to occupy the pulpit in the evening, he enquired with some apparent sharpness,—" Who is this Mr. Dawson ? " Further observing,—" He is not regularly acknowledged among us; we know nothing of him." Not being an accredited local-preacher, and the old gentleman being tenacious of rule, he considered himself justified in declining to make the announcement. Yet such was the contrast, in the same place, and about the same time, that when the Rev. R. Hemington, vicar of Thorparch, noticed above, was announced to preach, but prevented from attending, the congregation assembled on the occasion, finding William Dawson present, pressed him to engage in the service, which he readily did, and went through the whole to the satisfaction of the hearers. His own remark in his Diary, in reference to this circumstance is ;—"I was at Seacroft in the evening. Mr. Hemington was expected, but did not come. I spoke to the people. O Lord, let thy good Spirit be found in me, to enable me to rejoice before thee with reverence, and to bear an experimental testimony of thy pardoning grace, in and through Jesus Christ !" He also occupied the pulpit at Scholes, in the absence of Mr. Pawson. Adverting to the extraordinary manner in which he had been led by the providence of God, in early life, as well as his consecration to the Missionary cause at its close, he observed to the writer, after several other remarks,—" I have always considered myself a kind of *nondescript.*"

While the two or three rebuffs just noticed, produced momentary pain, they contributed their quota towards hastening another decision, consequent on that of

H

deciding against holy orders, namely, his becoming an accredited Wesleyan local-preacher. He continued, meanwhile, in the spirit of his work, as the following additional entries in his Diary for the year will shew; and though somewhat similar to extracts already made, they will exhibit his progress in piety.

"At Barwick in the evening. Spoke upon Psalm ciii. 2. Blessed be the Lord, my strength, for a sweet confidential nearness to him in prayer!

"Preached at Micklefield. Praise the Lord! I found him near, and precious. I experienced, as I was going, a sweetness of a peculiar kind, in thus being engaged for God. I spoke on,—'He hath done all things well.' It is still my prayer, that God would reveal himself in my soul more fully—in the full demonstration of the Spirit.

"Had a powerful application of that text,—'How much more shall your heavenly Father give the Holy Spirit to them that ask him?'"

"While at prayer, after dinner, I felt an uncommon influence of God upon the soul; and particularly in reading John xiv. 13—17. In the evening, I spoke at Whitkirk, on our Lord's appearing to Mary Magdalene. Praise the Lord! praise the Lord, for all his benefits! those especially which I obtain while waiting upon him. He is good. Oh, may he attend the poor hints which have been dropped, with his divine blessing!" At the same place again, about a month after, he observes,—

"I was at Whitkirk in the evening, and spoke on Acts xix. 20. Bless the Lord! I think I never remember receiving so much good in my life. Bless the Lord! He is mine,—he is mine. A woman was deeply affected. Oh, may she never rest, till she is completely changed into the Divine image! Blessed Lamb! I wish to be the devil's enemy. O enable me to do much injury to his interests, in thy Name!

"Life and liberty in speaking at Colton, on Prov. xix. 23. I trust my visit will not be in vain.

"Spoke on Isaiah lxii. 6. Solemnly affected in the first prayer. A poor, simple-hearted man stood up in the meeting, and told us what God had done for his soul.

"At Halton. Spoke on Matt. xviii. 3. My prayer is, that God would attend my labours with abundant success to precious souls; and for this, my soul is unusually drawn out.

"In a sweet frame of mind this morning. I hope it will be the opening of a good day. So it proved. At Little Preston in the forenoon; at Robert Moor's at two o'clock; and at Scholes in the evening. Bless the Lord for a finishing blessing! May the Lord hear our prayers for the poor creature that has recently so much dishonoured the gospel, and raise up many in his place! Praise the Lord for a praying frame! Waking in the morning, and going to sleep in the evening in it!

"Blessed be the Lord for a gracious season at Seacroft! A woman was set at liberty from the bonds of sin.

"Oh, may I be moulded, blessed Lord, into thy likeness, so that as thou art the *express image* of thy Father, I may be the *express image* of thee, my Redeemer!"

Notwithstanding his repeated baptisms of the Spirit, such passages as the following, mingling with the preceding, shew, that with the patches of light, there were also some deep shades.

"Appear, O Lord, in my heart, with power! I see and feel my natural depravity. The character of Mary Magdalene was far inferior to mine in sin. Oh, for Mary's sensibility and success!" The succeeding month, he exclaims:—

"God be merciful to me a sinner! Surely, the earth never bore a greater! yet, how little I am affected with it, to what I ought to be! Lord, give me not over to a hard heart, and a reprobate mind!" Again,

"Thou knowest, O Lord, that I would rather die than live in sin. Cleanse me fully! Found sweet relief in, 'Where sin abounded, grace did much more abound.' Praise the Lord! Oh, never, never, never may I, for the twinkling of an eye, indulge the thought of making Christ the minister of sin!" Once more;

"After breakfast, I wrestled with the Lord, with some short intermissions, till noon, for a manifestation of his grace. But he did not appear. Surely it is pride, self, or unbelief, that prevents it. Went to Methley; found some faith to believe; and, the Lord was present to seal his word. In the evening I experienced a calm in my soul. Indwelling evil and fear, seemed to have fled. A quiet resting upon the Lord seemed to be my state, though I cannot say a *lively faith*. Oh, that it may be the preceding stillness for the Lord speaking to my soul! And that this were my experience,—

'Restless, resigned, for this I wait.'"

When thus abased before God, his evidence became bedimned; and he would have implored reconciling grace, like a penitent imploring pardon on first coming to Christ, with an oppressive load of guilt upon the conscience. Thus, "O Lord, thy promises, thy manifestations, all speak thy willingness to communicate thy Spirit to any soul that longs for it. Do I ask amiss? Lord, pardon me! Do I not ask the gifts of thy Spirit, with this one object in view—*thy glory?* Thou knowest self creeps in. Work in me a thorough change—an entire, a new creation: and I protest, in thy presence, and by thy assisting grace, which is ever ready to help, I will not rest without the seal of the Spirit, through faith in Christ Jesus. Thou, O Lord, and thou alone, canst bestow the power to believe. Thou hast given me a will. Let me enter into the liberty of a lively faith in Christ, and out of the bondage of all slavish fear. Let me taste the powers of the world to come. Let the Spirit come in thine own way, and in thine own manner. Thy will be done; only hear my breathings for a present salvation. Bestow a holy sense of thy reconciliation, that I may know, that thou, O Father, for Christ's sake, hast blotted out mine iniquities, and I am accepted in the Beloved. Lord, help helplessness;—a little child, that can only defend itself, and help itself, by weeping! Lord, help me. Let me gather up the crumbs that fall from thy table. Infinite love! let one smile be afforded, that my soul may cease from its own works, and rest in the full and eternal satisfaction of the Redeemer of the whole world!" Like David, he lifted up his heart to the Lord; but he found, as in the weights of a clock, that the spirits might drop suddenly, and with ease, when it required steadiness, strength, and perseverance, to wind them up.

Then again, in his private musings, as well as in his public exercises, to which reference has been made, his soul would reveal itself in smiles, breaking forth like the sun from behind a cloud ; giving utterance to such sentences as these :—"I have a sweet sense of the unsearchable riches of Christ in my soul. Take, oh take, lovely and adorable Lamb, full possession of my breast!" Again,—"Delightful drawings after God. Surely this is the day-star, the dawning of a happy day, when heavenly zeal, burning love, true humility, and every grace of the Spirit shines out with useful splendour on a watching world!"

But whether in cloud or in sunshine, he never lost sight of his own spiritual interests, and the salvation of those around; and the Divine Being knowing his *sincerity*, affixed, in both states, his seal to his ministry. Dwelling, on one occasion, upon "repentance unto faith," and shewing that the one, if followed up, would lead to the other, an old man was deeply impressed with the subject. After preaching, the man of hoary hairs found his way to him, and told him that he had often heard of *repentance*, but that there was something in this "repentance *unto* faith," which he could not understand ; observing,—"You must excuse me asking you for an explanation ; but when you are in the pulpit, you sometimes get above us, and at other times go away to other things, when we want a bit more of what we have just had." Dawson entered into a friendly conversation on the subject, which only gave his auditor a relish for more. Not long after this, he was going to Leeds market, when his horse, somewhat quicker in hearing than himself, started, and seemed disposed to push forward. He had proceeded but a few paces, when he heard a distant pattering noise in the rear, and on suddenly turning round, saw a person posting his way after him on a pony. It was his old friend, who had watched for an opportunity of joining him on his way to the market; and who, on coming up to him, abruptly and unceremoniously accosted him with, —"now for a bit more of this 'repentance *unto* faith.'" Dawson was again as ready to communicate, as his companion was to receive; and unfolding the Scriptures, he "preached unto him Jesus," just as Philip preached to the Ethiopian treasurer, "as they went on their way,"—the discourse continuing till he and his venerable pupil reached Leeds. And in this way, and for these purposes, his society was frequently sought.

Watch-nights were held once a quarter, on a Saturday evening, at Garforth; and these he generally attended, as well as assisted in the service; describing one as a "pentecostal season," in the course of which he "spiritualized the Jewish Jubilee." The love-feasts were also attended as heretofore. Thus, every door was now open to him, and into most he had entered. He had preached in several of the pulpits, exercised in the prayer-meetings, assisted at watch-nights, and had spoken in the love-feasts. But he had not yet passed the Rubicon. Class-meeting, like that inconsiderable stream separating Italy from Cisalpine Gaul, was a boundary over which he had not dared to step; as that would have been—if not to have placed him in a hostile attitude to the Established Church, like Cæsar against the senate and against Pompey,—at least to have recognized his membership in the Wesleyan body. Without any intention, however, to enter as a stated member, and in all probability through the force of persuasion, he at length made a solitary trial of class-meeting, on Sunday, June 9th, in the present year—1799. His

own account of the occasion is exceedingly brief:—
"Hear, O Lord, and answer my poor petitions! Thou
knowest the desires of my soul after thee.—At Scholes
in the evening; spoke on Rev. i. 5, 6. Found but a
slender movement of the affections in my breast.—

'Jesus, I fain would find
Thy zeal for God in me.'

Stayed at the class in the evening. Felt rather better
in my approaches to God." Whatever might have
been the cause, which is not stated, it is certain
that some time elapsed before he again ventured to a
class-meeting. About the same time he has this
remark;—"Heard some reports respecting persons
professing godliness, committing sin. Saw a man who
had been a preacher; and who, it was said, had enlisted
as a soldier. Lord, help me!" These things, though
not occurring in the immediate neighbourhood, might
possibly exercise an improper influence over him, in
preventing a repetition of his attendance. With the
exception of class-meeting, from which he afterwards
derived much benefit, and which he never appears to
have discouraged in others, he manifested the utmost
anxiety for the spiritual prosperity of the several societies, and on one occasion,—the circumstances of the
case demanding it, "wrote an address to the Society at
H,"—probably Halton.

He was no less active below, than above ground.
His office, as steward, sometimes made it necessary for
him to descend into the bowels of the earth, to examine
the workings of the coal mines. He had a dress for
the occasion; and after finishing his survey, he was
often accosted by the colliers on leaving, with—"Come,
give us a word: there are some of your children here,

and they want a bit of bread." This appeal to his ministerial character, 'made by those whom he had "begotten through the Gospel," and who were anxious for the bread of life, was rarely made in vain,—never, indeed, when time and prudence gave their suffrage. And *there*—not in clerical costume, but in his grotesque under-ground habiliments, he addressed the sons of the pit, like so many " spirits in prison," as they squatted around him, with the hue of West Indian slaves,—two or three candles in the midst of the still deeper jet of the mine, held in the hand, or attached by their own tallow to the projecting blocks of coal, rendering the white ring of the eye visible, as it gleamed in the equally penetrating yet benignant glance of the preacher. The biographer can easily conceive the effect of such a preacher, such a place of worship, and such an auditory; having himself embraced the opportunity of preaching to a company of miners, about a quarter of a mile under ground, in a spacious apartment in one of the mines of Cumberland, when led by curiosity into it,—but with this difference—it was less murky,—the whole sparkling like a spacious hall studded with diamonds.

Though necessity was laid upon him to change his attire, when he descended into the earth, he made little or no difference, at this time, between his pulpit costume, and his ordinary dress. As he always gloried in the character of an English *yeoman*, who was qualified to serve on juries, to vote for knights of the shire, and to perform any other act, where the law requires one that is *probus et legalis homo*, so he was partial to his dress, which is thus quaintly described by Fuller:— " The good yeoman, " he observes, " wears russet clothes, but makes golden payment, having time in his

H 2

buttons, but silver in his pockets. If he chance to appear in clothes above his rank, it is to grace some great man with his service, and then he blusheth at his own bravery. Otherwise, he is the sweet landmark, whence foreigners may take aim of the ancient English customs; the gentry more floating after foreign fashions." Notwithstanding the subject of these pages avoided "floating after foreign fashions," and might be considered as a fair and safe "landmark," always habiting himself in a way suited to his station in life, yet it did not quite comport with the views of some of his inferiors in society, and with their notions of the ministerial office, though *lay* in its character. An old man, somewhat facetious in his way, met him in an adjoining wood one day, and touching his breast, said, ——"Put it in,—put it in, and cover it up." Dawson had been preaching in a ruffled shirt, of which he was perfectly unconscious, constituting a part of his ordinary Sabbath dress, and which had as little influence upon his spirit, as the shoes on his feet. But though this soon disappeared, still, all was not agreeable to those who look at "outward and visible signs." While walking, on another occasion, through the fields, on his way to Garforth, in company with John Batty, he took off his neckcloth, and disencumbered it of its "stiffner." John, in a state of surprise, enquired,—"What are you about?" He returned—"Nothing particular;" subjoining rather drily,—"I am only becoming weak to the weak; Mrs. W. has sent me word that I am not to appear again at Garforth with a stiffner in my neckcloth." In this, much more credit was due to the preacher, than to the tongue of the fair hearer.

He was always much more afraid of the spirit, than

the costume of the world; and had to complain of persons, who, on leaving the house of God, entered upon topics irrelevant to the ordinance and the word preached, instead of improving what they had heard; and upbraided himself for not, in every instance, bearing his testimony against it, as well as for not fully delivering his mind in private, on matters of religion, saying, "Oh that I could have said more to——on the important concerns of the soul!" The least omission of duty weighed down his spirits. "I heard a man," he writes, "boast that he was once able to drink a certain quantity of liquor." This same person appears to have become religious, and ought to have been ashamed of giving publicity to the circumstance. Dawson let it pass. But what were his views and feelings afterwards! "O my soul!" said he, when soliloquizing on the subject, "why didst thou not give some reproof? Thou didst wrong in not discharging thy duty. Forgive me, O Lord! I am a sinner. This will not excuse an omission of duty, on another opportunity presenting itself." This is a point of some moment. Persons have been known to dwell on their past sins, when connected with cunning, daring, or skill, more with a feeling of pride, than holy shame; forgetting the odiousness of the act, in the dexterity displayed; when they ought to have wept before God, and blushed before man. He was careful, however, in administering reproof, to award only what was necessary for the occasion; and would have rebuked himself for any defect either in the matter or the manner. Hence his complaint,—"This afternoon I spoke in sadly too strong language. Lord, pity me! I deserve not thy mercy."

On the demise of Mr. Dean, the rector, who quitted

this life, Wednesday, February 6th, of this year, the subject of these Memoirs felt much anxiety respecting a successor; saying,—"O my God, give us a minister who shall preach the whole truth as it is in Jesus!" The new rector, Mr. Hodgson, visited Barwick, on the 6th of March, and preached on the 10th. But William's attendance at the church became less and less frequent, in consequence of his almost incessant labour elsewhere. He attended the sale of Mr. Dean's household effects, but was out of his element. "What advantage," says he, "O my soul, is to be obtained on such public occasions."

His talents, however, were such as to command attention; and he found it impossible to escape from the more chafing parts of public business,—being called upon to engage in valuations, parish meetings, &c. Nor had he a little trouble with the "Income Tax," concerning which he speaks of having received his instructions at Leeds. But into every act between man and man, he took his conscience. Hence some of his cautions :—"Beware of speaking too positively in bargaining." "Guard against an overcharge of liquor. The least degree unfits the soul for communion with God. And this may be the case, when its effects cannot be perceived by man." "Avoid sharpness in conversation." "Never speak disrespectfully of any man." "Flee all self-seeking."

These, and similar maxims, he laboured to carry into effect; and if a bargain seemed hard to the party with whom he was transacting business, though their own deliberate act, while the circumstances in which he was placed, would admit of no alteration, he nevertheless felt acute pain; and instead of boasting of a slight advantage, as is the case with many, whose trumpet is the loudest in transactions the most unjust, especially when the unsuspecting and inexperienced are the prey, he threw his sympathies into the heart of the buyer, as well as poured out his prayers for him,—that the purchase might prove beneficial, and exceed expectation. An example occurs in his Diary, in reference to a person who had taken a lime-kiln, and which he was afraid would prove a hard bargain. The circumstances had all been stated ; but the man ventured upon it ; and though there was no complaint on his part, yet it did not prevent the apprehensions and feelings of the subject of these pages. And this is the very essence of love to our neighbour,—to make his case our own ! Just and liberal, however, as he was, he had not only small wages, as before noticed, but even less wages and fewer privileges than the other book-keepers, in the service of Sir Thomas Gascoigne. But it is no uncommon thing to find the children of this world better paid than the children of light ; nor is it at all marvellous, that a person of superior mind should be found to submit to it, who considers himself in the order of God, and who has been taught to say with the apostle :—" I have learned in whatsoever state I am, therewith to be content." The wheat, too, this year, was " much sprouted." But instead of complaining, he looked upon it as a punishment, saying,—" Thy just judgments, O Lord, are abroad in the earth ; but spare, oh spare thy people ! "

A reference has already been made to his freedom from superstition. But, like many others, he was not a stranger to presentiment. " I am struck with the idea," he observes, " that some trial is hanging over

my head.　If it be not a trial occasioned by, or proceeding from, any fault of my own, the Lord's will be
done !　I have no doubt it will work for good." The
next leaf he notices,—" Richard has taken himself out
of the Barkston-Ash volunteers." He adds,—" Let
thy special providence, O Lord, be over us in all
things !" Though Mr. Richard had sufficient reason
for the step he took, it was calculated to excite the
displeasure of those in command, and might possibly
have worked round painfully upon the family, through
the medium of Sir Thomas Gascoigne.* It is not unreasonable to suppose, that God occasionally permits
these secret forebodings and anticipations to take place,
which, like clouds settling upon the brow of a hill,
overshadow the mind, but which, in thus throwing
their dark shadows over the spirit, prepare and fortify
the individual against the event, as a sudden plunge
into the ocean of sorrow, might terminate in despair :
and this may be admitted, without going to the full
length of the Orientals, in their doctrine of " Khismut."

His uncle William paid a visit to the family in the
course of the year, for whose salvation he had often
prayed ; and as he had to preach at Barwick on the
evening of the Sabbath he was at Barnbow, it is not
improbable, that the uncle might be induced to hear the

* While one of our squadrons was blockading either Brest or Toulon, the
flag-captain had occasion to send for one of the warrant officers, a veteran who
had shewn his undaunted face in some of our severest actions, to receive some
directions on the quarter-deck.　As the ship was just standing off the shore,
and nearly three miles from it, a shot was fired from one of the batteries.　On
seeing the flash, the old seaman clenched his hands, and exclaimed,—" That
is for me! I know it is for me!" The astonished captain had scarcely commenced his rebuke, when the poor fellow's trunk lay bleeding on the planks.
The gun must have had an elevation of twelve degrees or more, so that the
chances of the ball touching anything but the sea were enormous; and the
person destroyed was the only one who even thought about an effect.

nephew.   He spoke on Christ in all things having the pre-eminence; and earnest was the prayer which went from the lip, that "the Lord would change the heart of his uncle by his grace." What a mercy to have one in a family,—if there were no more,—to care for the salvation of the remainder!

From his earliest religious impressions, he had, as occasion has been taken to shew, a tender solicitude for the spiritual welfare of young people. And towards the close of the year, he remarks,—"The propriety of preaching a sermon to young people, at Whitkirk, occurred to me." This was speedily followed up by a discourse to that effect. In addressing parents on the propriety and necessity of inducing early habits of piety, he shewed that habits to which persons were totally averse, might, in process of time, become pleasurable. Here he unexpectedly came down upon a certain portion of his hearers, by an appeal to the use of *tobacco*, in its various forms, and forced a smile from its opposers, at the expense of its advocates. It was one of those illustrations which his congregation could easily comprehend; and it required no great ingenuity to prove, that the habit itself is much more artificial than almost any other in which man can indulge—that there are few more repulsive to natural taste—that it is often acquired with difficulty—and that some who try are unable to acquire it at all. Now, the wonder is, how a habit of only two, or two hundred and fifty years standing, should,—with fewer elements of propagation, exceed all others in the extent of its diffusion. In its extent, it embraces the circumference of the globe. It comprehends every class of people,— from the most savage to the most refined,—and includes

every climate, from Siberia to the equator, and from
the equator to the extreme south.   The Society of
Friends, too, furnishes a fine example of educational
habit. " Habit, or custom," says Robinson, " like a
complex mathematical scheme, flows from a point,
insensibly becomes a line, and unhappily, (in that
which is evil,) it may become a curve :" but it is a
consolation, that it may also become a straight line,—
and that even the crooked may become straight.

In returning home after the public labours of the
Sabbath, over moors, and along deep narrow lanes, he
frequently had to encounter the tempest, driving the
rain, the snow, and the sleet full in the face ; and in
some instances, he found it difficult to pursue his way
in the dark ; yet generally exclaiming at the end of the
journey,—" The Lord has been my preserver and con-
ductor."   On one of these occasions, he was benighted
on a moor ; and being unable to discern the proper
track, he gave himself up to the guidance of divine
providence,—throwing the bridle on the neck of the
horse, and praying for direction, The thunder pealed,
—though in the month of December,—and the lightning only rendered the darkness still more visible.
The next flash struck the stick in his hand, but did no
further injury.   Such was the vividness of each succeeding flash, that the face of the surrounding district
was suddenly lit up, as with a gleam of sunshine,
enabling him,—though as suddenly ceasing,—to guess
his way out of the labyrinth in which he was involved.
Having to preach at Barwick the same evening, he
arrived just as the people were about to disperse.   He
related to them the occasion of the delay, telling them,
with some little improvement of the circumstance, that

it was a sermon sufficient of itself for their further meditation.

There is little doubt that the improvement was a good substitute for the sermon ; for he manifested a considerable aptitude in improving passing events, as well as a readiness to turn public occasions to good account. Thus, at Garforth feast, he took for his text, Isaiah iv. 1, 2, " Ho, every one that thirsteth, come ye to the waters, and he that hath no money ; come ye, buy and eat ; yea, come, buy wine and milk, without money and without price." At the same place, on the occasion of a watch-night, he improved on the shipmaster's address to Jonah, i. 6,—" What meanest thou, O sleeper ? arise, call upon thy God, if so be that God will think upon us, that we perish not."

CHAPTER VII.

The old year.— Time.— The eighteenth century.—Opinions of John-
son and Clarendon.—Disinterested toil.— Usefulness.—Samuel
Hick.— Class-meeting.—Thomas Stoner.—Blessedness of Chris-
tian communion.—Social literary advantages.—Reading and
religious discourse.—Providential choice of lot.— Wit, true and
false.—Study.—Reproof.—HOME religion.—Domestic changes.
—Escape from death.—Murder.—Local preachers.—Pulpit
preparation.—Over exertion.—Progress in piety.—Sinners dis-
turbed in their pleasures by rousing sermons.—Increasing labour.
—Pity to the poor.—Becomes an accredited Local Preacher.—
Wesley, Whitfield, and Cennick's sermons.—Richard Burdsall.
—Enlarged sphere of labour.—Affliction and its fruit.—Meets
the Local Preachers, and attends the Quarter-Meeting.—
Preaches in Leeds.—Rev. S. Bradburn.—Rev. W. Bramwell.—
Sinkings and swellings of heart.—Watchfulness.

WHILE the close of an old year never fails to prostrate the Christian in the dust before God, and to
fill him with adoring gratitude, the commencement of
a new one is rarely without its holy purposes and
protestations. The brief parenthesis between the close
of one century, and the opening of another, is still
more impressive. So it was experienced by William
Dawson, who commenced January 1st, 1800, with a
solemn dedication of himself to God, imploring "special grace," to enable him to do his "perfect and

proper will," entreating at the same time, a "revival of religion in the hearts of those around." Noiseless as are the wings of time, they were all but heard by him on the occasion, and roused him to renewed exertion. He rested his hopes not on the past, but on the future. The eighteenth century had completed its cycle ; but he was aware, that "Time never turns the glass again," to furnish man with an opportunity of going over the ground, in order to improve it. "Time," was to him, "the wise man's treasure,"— "the nurse and breeder of all good :" but he knew, if he could not change the past, by renewed purposes, he could nevertheless make improvements *upon* it ; nor did he fail in this, when defects were detected, though few men had less reason to complain of misspent moments. "Money and time," it is remarked by Dr. Johnson, "are the heaviest burthens of life, and the unhappiest of all mortals are those who have more of either than they know how to use. To set himself free from these incumbrances,—one makes collections of shells, and another searches the world for tulips and carnations." The subject of these Memoirs fixed his mind on things the most momentous ; and finding life exceedingly short, he contrived to press the greatest amount of labour into the smallest possible compass of time ; and this he did under a full conviction of the truth of the sentiments of Clarendon, —"That our precious time is not lent to us to do nothing with, or to be spent upon that which is worse than nothing ; that we shall not be more confounded with anything, than to find that there is a perfect register kept of all that we did in that time ; and that when we have scarce remembered the morrow

what we did yesterday, there is a diary in which
nothing we did is left out, and as much notice taken
when we did nothing at all." Hence his frequent
exclamations, when pressing important truths upon
himself and his hearers, " Let us look at everything
in the light of eternity,—bring everything to bear on
a day of judgment."

In support of the devout resolutions formed, and
as a proof that he was anxious to forward the prosperity of Zion, his sermons in the course of the year
averaged about two each Sabbath,—preaching on some
occasions, when a Sabbath had been omitted, four
sermons on one day,—the places themselves being
some miles apart from each other. Several new places
too, were added to those which had been regularly
visited, as Bramham, Micklefield, Thorparch, Sherburn, Shippin, Lofthouse, Rothwell, Hemsworth, and
Ackworth. For all this toil, the only reward he received, besides that of the approbation of his own
conscience, was an occasional social meal or two with
the friends on the Sabbath ; and even that was regulated by his distance from home. He found his own
horse, paid his own tolls, and supported the whole
of the wear and tear of the road. In this, he had
an admirable example in many of the Local Preachers
among the Wesleyans ; but not being familiar altogether with the system, and being without an example
in his own peculiar situation,—moving alone, to a
certain extent,—his disinterestedness appears the more
conspicuous.

His usefulness kept pace with his sincerity and zeal.
Hence, at Kippax, on a Saturday evening, he observes,
—" This was a season of help, while speaking for

Christ. A woman was remarkably affected. Let it, my Lord, bring her effectually to thee. How far it was right in concluding, the Lord only knows." On another occasion, he remarks,—"John Head has informed me of a person receiving good under my preaching. Praised be the name of the Lord for this! It is the Spirit that quickeneth. A tongue of flesh alone profiteth nothing." Again, when at Saxton, Barkston, and Sherburn, he observes, "I was pleased with the happiness of a young person brought into the liberty of the children of God. Keep her, O Lord, under thy hand; and add many to thy church, who shall be eternally saved." Also at Whitkirk:—"It delighted me to hear the intelligence of J. Harrison's conversion. Praise the Lord, who abundantly pardons all returning sinners!"

The doubt entertained respecting "concluding" at Kippax, seems to have arisen from the fact of the person not having entered into Christian liberty, and the propriety of leaving her in that state, without a continued exercise of faith and prayer on her behalf. He became better disciplined in this work afterwards; but the doubt itself was a favourable symptom.* How far, in the other case, the expression "under," rather than *in* the hand of God, was designed, is not certain; yet it very much resembles one of those happy verbal selections peculiar to himself. The person was *young;* and if, from her native buoyancy,

* He afterwards amused the biographer with a remark of the "Village Blacksmith" in a similar case. "You will not leave the person in distress," said the friends to Samuel, as he was quitting a meeting, on the blessing being pronounced. "Bless you *barns*," he sharply returned, "she will serve as a match to kindle the fire with to-morrow night." Dawson had no such design; and Samuel himself was probably either lacking in faith, or failing in physical strength, when he gave the reply.

she did not require the hand of severity to subdue her spirit, and so "keep her under," she required the constant, gentle training of the vine-dresser, that "under" his "hand"—"under" his tender care, she might bloom in the paradise below.

Though still shy of class-meeting, he found it difficult to steer clear in his frequent associations with the Wesleyans; and accordingly, when preaching at Little Preston in the evening of February 3rd, he enters into his Diary, "Stopped at the class;" subjoining, as though he could not avoid it, and was at a loss to know how far he had acted properly hitherto, in declining it, "The will of the Lord be done!" The other prudential means of grace in the body, such as love-feasts and watch-nights, were enjoyed as usual, remaining in the latter sometimes, when at a distance of some miles from home, till twelve o'clock at night. Thomas Stoner had a meeting too, at Barwick, but whether a fellowship, conversational, or prayer-meeting, is difficult to determine, though it is believed to have been the former. That it was not a class-meeting, is probable from the fact of William first uniting himself formally to the class at Scholes, and the great probability of his joining the one in the house of Thomas Stoner, in consequence of his attachment to him, and the hallowed seasons he enjoyed under his roof.

Being at Seacroft, Thursday June 30, "assisting Mr. Porter with his hay," he states, that he attended "Stringer and England's class;" again adding, "let me do thy will, O Lord!" Having at length decided on becoming a member, he united himself to the Society at Scholes, Thursday, July 3rd; on which occasion, he remarks,—"At Scholes class-meeting for the first time. It is under thy will and blessing, O Lord, I trust, that I should attend there. Let it be for thy glory, and the good of souls." His previous visits were accidental rather than otherwise; now he *formally* entered as a member, and considered it the "first time" of meeting in that character. He subsequently notices the advantage which he received from such Christian fellowship, in the following terms;—August 7. "At Scholes. A season of good from God." August 14. "Great nearness to God. Praise his holy name!" August 21. "In a serious frame, produced by considerations on the shortness of time." September 16. "A partial fast, to intercede with God for his blessing upon the society at Scholes." September 18. "Visited Miss Collingworth. The mind more open. The Lord appeared rather distant at the class towards the commencement, but nearer towards the close." September 25. "A precious season at Scholes!" October 16, "A most profitable meeting, Praise the Lord!" November 6. "Refreshed with a solemn sense of God's presence."

Few men ever entered the Wesleyan Society with greater weight of character, from purer motives, with more matured judgment, or were equally qualified for more immediate and extensive usefulness. And as he had no quarrel with the Established Church—no objection to her creed—and loved her pious ministers, he was not without his regrets. He even venerated her "studious cloisters pale," her "high embowered roof," her "antique pillars;" and although he was going to another "full-voiced quire," and, in process of time, another "pealing organ," yet he was leaving her—

"Storied windows richly dight,
Casting a dim religious light."

But service, ministers, and structures, were to be practically given up, and the face and feet were to be directed towards the ecclesiastical piles less magnificent, and a people comparatively poor, for the sake of a wider field of operation.

One serious disadvantage under which he laboured, was the want of a few friends, who combined with religion a good general course of reading; for whatever may be a man's literary taste, if he be left to toil in the mine alone,—or next to alone, without the sound of other voices, and the operation of other instruments, to cheer him on in his way, as well as superior experience to guide him to the right vein, he will rarely make the progress which he would otherwise make with such helps at hand. As to polished society, the want of this — if such want existed, was amply compensated by his visits of mercy to the huts and homesteads of Hannah Smith, Alice Tillotson, and other aged persons, ripe in religious experience; through whose conversation, together with that of others, he was enabled to cherish the best feelings of his heart; the same having an indirect influence, in the mean time, both upon his reading and his ministry, by leading him chiefly to such theological works as tended to foster genuine piety both in himself and his hearers. These are admirable schools of instruction, when the heart is right with God, and often make up for other disadvantages. There is great truth in the remark, that by reading, we enjoy the dead,—by conversation, the living, —and by contemplation, ourselves; adding, as the result, that reading enriches the memory, conversation polishes the wit, and contemplation improves the judgment. Of these, however, as in the case of faith, hope, and charity, reading is the most important, because it furnishes both the others. In balancing the advantages and disadvantages, the society into which William Dawson was thrown, and which he courted for the sake of its value to his spiritual interests, was, perhaps, the best adapted to his genius. Had he associated with wits, his own would have flashed with the brightest of them ; nor would he have soon become bankrupt for want of stock : but he would have been placed in the most imminent peril of losing his religion. His, however, was not the false wit which consists in puns and quibbles, in anagrams, chronograms, lipograms, and acrostics, but that singular and unavoidable manner of doing or saying anything peculiar and natural to himself only, by which his speech and actions were distinguished from those of other men, and so far impressed with a character of their own ; and which would not have failed to reach all, except those who are placed beyond its "boundaries," and who have been compared to bodies indissoluble by heat,——setting both furnace and crucible at defiance, possessing "minds upon which the rays of fancy may be pointed without effect, and which no fire of sentiment can agitate or exalt." What he lost in intelligence, in some instances, he gained in piety ; and applying himself to his books at home, as he found leisure, and as has hitherto been seen, he was generally on the advance of those around, and never failed to enrich himself by communicating,——it being " more blessed to give than

I

receive." Among other works that engaged his attention about this time, those of Romaine, Walsh, Luther, Manton, &c., may be noticed; and still further to extend his knowledge, he entered into a Subscription Library, distinct from the one referred to in the earlier part of his history. Though he both read and studied hard, he never read to satiety, nor yet studied so "much" as to make it a "weariness to the flesh." Each continued to have its charm; and hence such language as this in his Diary,—"A sweet season, while studying on 'My grace is sufficient for thee!'" The same spirit which was breathed into it, in his closet, was wafted from it, like fragrance, the Sabbath following, when he exclaims,—"The Lord sent home with sweet power, at Seacroft, 'My grace is sufficient for thee.'" His reading and intelligence added to the value of his society, and so held him in increasing request.

Being frequently thrown into irreligious society at Tadcaster, Wetherby, Ripon, Knaresborough, Leeds, and elsewhere, while engaged in business, both on his own account and on that of the colliery, he was often annoyed with the profane conversation of those with whom he came in contact. He notices two cases, two successive days; in the one of which he administered reproof; in the other, for some reason not stated, he condemned himself, so that the ground of omission, must, on mature deliberation, have been deemed insufficient. The first case involves a nice point, which could only be suggested to a mind deeply imbued with the Spirit of God, and a heart—despite of all his upbraidings, distinguished for its tenderness. What else is implied in the following expressions?—"Pardon, O Lord, the sins of my duties! How little, O my soul, didst thou feel in reproving a man? How unlike that which Jesus felt, when he wept over the city of Jerusalem! I say, how unlike—nay, was it not the very reverse?" There is a great deal in timing a reproof, as well as in the manner of its administration. It should never be done when the tempest is up, but when the soul is hushed into repose. Abigail reproved Nabal, not when he was in a state of inebriation, but when the morning light had dawned, and his senses had returned. It is vain to press the seal upon the wax, while it is hard; let it melt, and instantly the impression is perceptible. There is a manner, as well as a time; an oblique way of reproof, which frequently takes off the sharpness of it. Reproof is an excellent parent, but hatred often constitutes a part of its progeny. To prevent the latter, it should always be combined with counsel; and thus, like a sword anointed with balm, should perform at the same moment, the twofold operation of wounding and healing. But even this scarcely entered into the case of Dawson; he wished not only to weep over the sinner, but to feel such an abhorrence of the sin as the sinner ought to have felt himself. It was not an individual case only that often occasioned pain, but public meetings, when he found it difficult to carry out all his desires and designs. Hence he says, "I was at Barwick, settling the accounts for the highways. Here my soul was hurt at not being able to recommend the cause of my Divine Master. Pardon me, O Lord! Justly do I deserve the hidings of thy face."

Having laboured hard in every department, without ever considering it a toil, any uncomfortable feeling which might be experienced, would, by another than himself, have been laid at the door of anxiety for greater good, rather than to neglect of duty; for, like the persevering Roman, he deemed nothing done, while any thing remained undone. In the same way—though the priest of the family for several years, and presenting before it an example of piety and diligence, he seemed to charge every defect upon himself, and feel as though the non-conversion of a member was owing to some negligence of his own. But his very upbraidings here again, were met by the prayers he offered up :—" Lord, have mercy upon me, and help me to walk before my family agreeably to thy will. Make me a HOME CHRISTIAN !"

Several changes took place in the family in the course of the year. His uncle Ingle died, January 10th; his sister Mary married November 17th; and his aunt Mary died December 11th. On the demise of his uncle, he had some thought of entering upon his farm. He sought the advice of Mr. H. Gill on the subject, to whom he had repaired on former occasions, and in whom he could safely confide as a man of experience, prudence, judgment, and piety. Mr. Gill saw no particular objection to it at first, but it was otherwise overruled by Divine providence.

Though death made inroads in some quarters, the good hand of God prevented its ravages in others. "A morning of mercy and judgment," he exclaims; "owing to Mr. Cullingworth's horse running away with the cart, while sister Bessey and brother Tommy were in it. Praise the Lord, that matters were no worse! Lord,

sanctify it to us all!'" While William held the rein,
the horse broke away, and threw him down, when
the wheel of the vehicle passed over his body; on
which he instantly leaped upon his feet, and found
himself happily unhurt. His sister had her foot laid
open, and Thomas fell between the shafts. About
the same period, one of those melancholy deeds was
perpetrated in the neighbourhood, which fill the mind
with horror, whenever they occur, and which greatly
disconcerted his feelings. A gentlemàn of the name of
Medhurst murdered his wife; on which occasion, Dawson poured forth the moanings of his heart on the
impotency and vileness of man. Of such foul deeds,
few have spoken more strongly than Webster :—

> "Other sins only speak, murder shrieks out.
> The element of water moistens the earth,
> But blood flies upwards, and bedews the heavens. "

In consequence of taking a wider sweep of country
than heretofore, he was thrown more frequently in the
way of local-preachers, who were not only anxious to
encourage him, but also occasionally to relieve themselves of an engagement. Messrs. J. Woodcock, T.
Hall, T. Richardson, and others, were among those
who opened his way to new scenes of labour. And
among those at a distance, he became acquainted with
the venerable Robert Spence of York, who preached at
Seacroft, and held a love-feast.

Though he frequently made considerable preparation
for the pulpit, yet he never trammelled himself with
either the plan, or the filling up; or even with the subject, when anything more impressive intervened. Thus,
he observes,—"I was at Whitkirk in the evening, and
spoke on 'Thy kingdom come,' which powerfully struck

my mind, when Mr. Atkinson repeated the sentence in the church, before the sermon in the forenoon."

He sometimes suffered from overstrained speaking, notwithstanding his physical strength, and the admonitions of his mother. He thus bemoans his imprudence : "Heard Mr. Hopkins, at Kippax. In the evening, I spoke. Though in the middle of the discourse I lost sight of God, for which I implore pardon, yet the Lord was precious towards the close. The next day I found some slight effects upon the body. O my soul, let not *self-murder* be charged upon thee. Beware of *suicide*, which may be committed by improper exertions even in a noble and proper employment. Lord, teach me !"

In looking more immediately at his state of religious feeling, in the course of the year, though partially dipped into already, there was the same earnest cry for an increase of faith as in the year preceding, and often the same feeling of destitution ; the clouds occasionally thickening around him, and again breaking out into light and joy. And being no less desirous to keep the "inner," than the "outer man" in view,—the secret springs of action, than the actions themselves,—a few detached extracts may be given. These, as may be expected on such a subject, are more remarkable for depth of feeling, than novelty of expression.

JANUARY. "O God, with reverence I will call thee Father. In thee, O Christ, through grace, I will believe. Pardon, O Lord, my unbelief,—that poison to the life of comfort and love ! I see, I must believe ; Lord, I will believe. Thou art the propitiation for sin. 'I hold thee with a trembling hand, but will not let thee go.' Appear, O Lord, to sin's confusion, and my salvation. Amen.

FEBRUARY. "O Lord, refine my thoughts, words, and actions; baptize me with the Holy Spirit; sanctify me wholly; prevent me from resting upon any thing but thee; take away all props and hindrances. Let thy glory fill my views, that I may pursue nothing else. Give me a more tender regard for souls. Praise the Lord for patience in a particular trial!

MARCH. "Thou art my Father in Christ. But thou wilt shew me greater things than these, if I keep close to thee. Yet, oh, what inward struggles to preserve my confidence,—to keep me from lukewarmness, —to prevent me from resting in divine favours!

"A temptation presented itself. But, praise the Lord, for grace! I see the dispensations of Christ require me to cry,—'Lord, help me.'—A baptism of the Holy Ghost and of fire.—Wrote a few pages on Psalm xxxiv.

"My mind pained, and at a distance from God, through unbelief. Oh, what reasons for thankfulness, that I am not in hell.

APRIL. "This week much shut up in unbelief.— Delivered from fear after reading Luther on the Galatians, especially his short comment on the 'fruit of the Spirit.'

MAY. "Bless the Lord, for a slight taste of mercy and love! Oh, how sweet—how precious!

'A *point* my good, a *drop* my store,
Eager I ask, I pant for more.'

JUNE. "My mind much distracted; but I have obtained some comfort in reading Dr. Owen.

JULY. "O Lord, let me not be given over to mine enemies: nor suffer me to be 'sounding brass, or a tinkling cymbal.' Indisposed to prayer. Lord, quicken me!

"Read part of the Life of Walsh. Oh, what communion with God! I am ashamed of myself. This text kept running through my mind, 'Because I live, ye shall live also.'

"My mind under the happy smile of God's face all day. Oh, appear in my soul more fully, thou 'Hope of glory?' Still happy in the application of some promises which I read yesterday.

AUGUST. "At Mr. Shillitoe's rape-thrashing. Praise God, I got no hurt! So much for preventing grace. At Aberford in the evening. Glory! glory! glory! A precious season! Souls were deeply awakened, and one was enabled to praise the Lord.

"O my Lord, my Jesus, my Saviour, my Father, keep me simple, humble, and holy! A sweet taste of redeeming love.

"Generally above the world; and the mind more solid than it has sometimes been.

"Not so happy. Oh, for simple faith! My sins appear numerous, heinous, and black. Oh, what a wretch! What an object of love and mercy! What but infinite love could have suffered me to live!

"A sweet afternoon indeed to my soul. Oh, may I ever possess the deepest self-abasement and the divinest love!

SEPTEMBER. "At Seacroft in the morning, and found the Lord present. Heard Mr. Barber at noon on the same text I had in the morning. At Scholes in the evening, and found it profitable. While at private prayer, the Lord shewed me such a fulness in Jesus Christ as I never saw before, and my mind closed in with it, to ask of him. Praise the Lord, for such a frame produced by such a sight!

"Much fervour in speaking; but, I fear, a great deal

of it animal. Went to prayer in the kitchen at Whit-kirk, and felt better.

"Oh, how little do I know! How ignorant and weak! 'Weak as helpless infancy!' Make me, my Lord, more weak, that I may fall upon thee for strength! At Aberford. Spent a little time with Mr. Hopkins. On my return home, I felt such a power from God, in the manifestation of himself in Jesus Christ, as I never before experienced. My mind seemed swallowed up in his.

OCTOBER. "A little of yesterday's blessing rested upon my soul.

"Went to pray in a wood. My mind was at first hard, wandering, and distant. On rising, I felt nearer to God.

"At Aberford fair. Afterwards at the christening of John Batty's child. May all I do and *say* be for the glory of God!

"While reading Baxter's Directory, my old sins rose in view. Lord, I see that nothing can remove those painful recollections, but the clear manifestation of thy pardoning love in Christ.

"My mind, from this day to the end of the week, under much insensibility.

"This morning I awoke with some sense of my past sins. I wrestled with the Lord, and asked him to shew me some promise in his Book, which would administer relief. I opened the Bible, and the first text was, 'Neither do I condemn thee; go and sin no more.' The next was, 'If the Son shall make you free; ye shall be free indeed.' Bless the Lord, I claimed the promises. Some reasonings crossed my mind again, while going to Saxton. But these expressions occurred,—'Believe,—Hold fast your shield—Who shall pluck you from his hand?' I heard with profit Richard Burdsall

I 2

of York, at Barkston, in the evening. Praise the Lord, O my soul!

NOVEMBER. "At Seacroft love-feast. Received a letter from Thomas Richardson, which refreshed my soul, containing good news. At Colton in the evening, but much pained at some preparations made by R——k; but was enabled to lay the case at the feet of the Lord.

"Pardon my useless conversation in the forenoon. Made a fresh and solemn covenant with the Lord. May he help me to fulfil it to his glory!

"Heard Mr. Pawson. Felt a touch of divine power, when he cited that text,—'He tasted death for every man.'

"Praise the Lord for this day! I had a glimpse of God's love in giving Christ to be the propitiation for sinners.

"At Barwick. But my soul out of frame. My mind still dark. Lord, shine upon it!

DECEMBER. "The soul is in an easy frame. At Barwick till twelve o'clock. I hope some good was done in the name of the Lord."

The last quotation refers to the service which closed the old year.

His sermons became more and more alarming to the sinner,—more soothing to the penitent,—more cheering to the established Christian,—and, upon the whole, more graphic; the several congregations taking them away with them, and dwelling upon them, both in the mass, and in detail. To sinners especially, his breathings forth were like so many streams of pestilential air upon their artificial enjoyments; his thoughts and images, like so many swarms of locusts, to devour the "fertility and fatness of their laughing fields of pleasure,"—making their past delights odious

to them, and each returning joy, after they had heard
him, just about as effective as falling snow upon a sheet
of water,—

"The snow that falls upon the river,
One moment white—then gone for ever!"

As time advanced, his labours became more arduous;
and although his Diary for 1801, upon which the
reader now enters, presents various omissions, particularly towards the close of the year, yet not less
than one hundred sermons may be enumerated, as
preached in different places. Some of these were of
course preached on the week-day, as usual; and in two
or three instances, he preached four times on the Sabbath,—taking Saxton, Linnerton, Barkston, and Shel-
burn successively. His attendance on the service
of the Established Church became, in consequence,
still less and less frequent, and when *there*, it was
mostly on sacramental occasions; while the Thursday
evening, which was formerly the evening appropriated
to the delivery of his "Cottage Lectures," in company with Messrs. Graham and Atkinson, was devoted
to his class at Scholes. Barwick, however, was not
less endeared to his heart, because of the transfer;
for though the parish school-room was given up, and
his connexion with the curate had ceased, he generally
set apart the Friday evening for the purpose of preaching to the inmates of the workhouse, and to such of
the villagers as might be disposed to attend. In this
labour of love, he was often more than ordinarily
blessed, exclaiming, "Oh, what a time of power from
God at the workhouse!"

The kind of attention which he thus paid to the
spiritual wants of the poor, some of whom were in all

probability unable to reach either church or chapel, is strongly characteristic of his benevolent nature, the impulses of pity in which were not only as sudden as the sound of instruments of music, which obey the touch, but as strong and lasting as the circumstances which called them forth.

Though he had entered the Society, in the summer of the preceding year, it was not till the month of February in the present year—comprising a period of eight months, that he was received as an accredited Wesleyan local-preacher. Messrs. Pawson and Barber were on the Leeds circuit at the time. "They gave me three appointments," said Dawson to the biographer, "leaving it to myself, whether to supply them or not." Why this apparent indifference was manifested, is difficult to determine ; unless it was a fear, owing to his having preached so long in connexion with the Established Church, that he was more inclined to the Church than the Wesleyans. Mr. Pawson had found occasion, in one of his pamphlets, to animadvert on the conduct of some of the clergy towards the Methodists ; and there was, at this time, some sharp shooting on both sides, in the way of controversy. Admitting, however, the spirit of the times to have had no influence on his case, in inducing caution or hesitancy, there could be still less ground for it on the score of talent or piety. Had there been any doubt of the latter, he would not have been admitted upon the plan at all ; and as to the former—talent, they were so fully persuaded of this, that he was never once requested to preach what is ominously denominated a *trial sermon*. He stood No. 22 on the plan, and fulfilled the appointments assigned him with zeal, affection, and integrity. He was planned to three places the first day—Ledstone, Scholes, and Kippax. On the first page of a full outline of a sermon on,—"My sheep hear my voice, and I know them, and they follow me: and I give unto them eternal life; and they shall never perish, neither shall any *man* pluck them out of my hand," John x. 27, 28, is written, "Ledstone and Scholes, Feb. 22, 1801. This was my *first sermon*, when my name, was on the plan; and this was the *first Sabbath* I filled my place as a regular local-preacher—I was never before on the plan." It may be taken for granted, that the same sermon was delivered at both places. On another sermon, on Romans xii. 2, "Be not conformed to this world," &c., written out in full, he entered, "Kippax, Feb. 22, 1801. N. B. This was the first Sabbath on which I preached as a regular accredited local-preacher." In his Diary, of the same date, he writes, "At Ledstone in the morning, and Kippax at noon. Praise the Lord, for a very good time at Kippax. At Scholes in the evening. In a solemn frame of mind."

Such was his popularity even at this stage of his ministry, that he was followed from place to place by the same persons, on the same day. One of the colliers, heedless of the toil of the week, followed him on foot, in the course of the Sabbath, a distance of twenty miles. This was not without its advantages to the preacher; as it led him to diversify his subjects, and so add to his general stock of biblical knowledge.

Up to this period, he had paid but little attention, in the course of his reading, to published sermons; and this was one thing, which, in all probability, independent of his peculiar genius, gave such an air of originality to his discourses. He now read those published by Wesley, Whitfield, and Cennick; and was especially benefited by Mr. Wesley's sermon on "The Witness of the Spirit,"—impressed "with the want of an applied Christ, in reading Mr. Whitfield's sermon on healing the hurt of the daughter of the Lord's people slightly,"—and "quickened by one of Mr. Cennick's on the woman at Jacob's well." He added to his stock this year, the writings of Dr. Goodwin and Matthew Henry; and borrowed the works of others belonging to the old school. Having heard Richard Burdsall of York preach a short time before, and being much struck with the originality both of his matter and manner, he was curious to know something more of him, and so procured the "Memoirs" of his Life, as "written by himself." He was enabled to perceive in the life of this "old veteran," a *fac simile* of some of the leadings of providence, and many of the sacred drawings of God respecting himself, and was not a little relieved by its perusal.

As the year rolled on, his ardour for more extensive usefulness became more intense;—he was found narrating his experience in different love-feasts—preaching occasionally for the travelling preachers—and occupying the pulpits in Leeds, Holbeck, and Hunslet; together with the pulpits and stands of Fenton, Tadcaster, Towton, Dunkeswick, Harewood, Woodside, Eccup, Armley, Wortley, Forge, Allerton, Thorner, Shadwell, Chapeltown, &c., &c.; not omitting *Sturton-Grange*, which he was not permitted before to enter, but which Mr. Wade was now anxious to throw open to him, in order to secure his labours.

In the early part of the year, God was pleased to visit the family with affliction. William was the first upon whom the rod was laid. The stroke was smart, but short. He was no sooner restored, than his sister Sarah was reduced very low, for whose salvation he experienced great anxiety. She was little more than recovered, when his brother Richard was "taken very ill;" himself again, in his own language, experiencing "symptoms of fever;" further observing,—"Let the light of thy countenance, O Lord, shine upon me, and then lay upon me what thou seest good for thine own glory!" Persons who have known little of health, like Watts, Baxter, and others, rarely feel its absence so as to make them unhappy. It is from the remembrance of that which we have lost, that the arrows of affliction are pointed. The subject of these Memoirs had hitherto enjoyed an even flow of health; and although the present affliction did not affect the constitution, he felt severely. But he knew,—to go to his own occupation for a simile, that "As thrashing separates the corn from the chaff, so does affliction purify virtue." A sentimentalist, sitting in his study, and philosophizing on the sufferings of humanity, observes, "Before an affliction is digested, consolation ever comes too soon; and after it is digested, it comes too late: there is but a mark between these two, as fine almost as a hair, for a comforter to take aim at." This is very pretty in theory—somewhat like a piece of frost-work, and might serve the purpose of an irreligious man, just stepping into the room of a spendthrift, stung with remorse at his folly, and putting a purse of gold into his hand; but the Christian must have his consolations both *before* and *after*—aye, and *in* the furnace too.

His indisposition occasioned but a partial interruption of his labours ; and the spirit which he breathed after it, is worthy of notice.

" Praise the Lord! my mind is in a great measure relieved of all painful reflections on my past imperfections, by the contents of—' If any man sin, we have an advocate with the Father,' &c. I was free from distraction, while at church, and had a sweet glimpse of Christ as a Mediator and Intercessor.—Was at Thomas Stoner's at noon. Lord, keep those whom thou hast called by thy grace.—At Bramham in the evening. Praise the Lord for a season of refreshing! Oh, what comfort thrilled through my soul, while singing a few verses from—' The voice of free grace,' &c." A few days after, he remarks,—

" This text is impressed upon my mind, which serves as a shield,—' Look unto me, and be ye saved. ' Bless the Lord for his word!—A precious season at B. Johnson's. "

Every blessing is suspended as by a fibre of the finest silk. So he felt it ; and hence, the day after, he thus pours forth his lamentations :—-' At Leeds ; but lost my shield on my return home. Levity broke out ; and what aggravated it was, I fear it was the fruit of pride or self-complacency. I heard Mr. Barber in the evening at Barwick, and was properly affected with the worship. In private prayer, I smarted for my lightness ; for the Lord appeared not, nor visited my soul. Lord, pardon me !

" Next day, I heard Mr. Barber at Scholes, and was struck, on receiving my society ticket, to find the text upon it, which had been such a blessing,—' Look unto me, and be ye saved. ' — After this, I had a few precious moments with the Lord, in the counting-house."

He now, both as a private member, and as a local preacher, took an interest in everything that concerned the circuit and the connexion. The local-preachers had a meeting in "Wortley chapel," April 22nd; and there, for the first time, he mingled with them, exclaiming on the occasion,—"Bless the Lord for all his mercies!" June 29th, he attended, for the first time, the Quarter Meeting at Leeds. Here he observes,—"I was rather hurt, in giving my vote for a petition for Mr. Bramwell;" afraid, apparently, of any interference with the order of Divine providence; but finally leaving the whole with,—"Thy will be done! Send, Lord, whom thou wilt; only come with them."

His first appearance as a preacher in Leeds, was July 18th, in the old chapel, on a Sunday evening. The Conference commenced the week following, when he attended the religious services connected with it; embracing the opportunity of hearing Messrs. Bradburn, Coke, Benson, J. Wood, Averill, Pipe, &c. Mr. Bradburn preached, as on former occasions, in the chapel occupied by the Rev. E. Parsons. "But it was the last time he appeared there," said Dawson, when relating the circumstance of his having heard him on the occasion, to the biographer; and no wonder. He had preached delightfully; but on coming out of the vestry, when a person was about to assist him off with the gown,—either owing to a contempt of such habiliments, or from some recollection of having been inconvenienced by it in his action in the pulpit, he assumed one of his queer looks—doubled his elbows by his side—clenched his hands before his breast, having taken a

portion of the gown in each,—then suddenly sending forward his elbows, and shooting out his back at the same
moment, rent it from the shoulders downwards, making
an opening sufficient for him to escape by, without the
necessity of seeking egress in the ordinary way.   The
friends felt the insult ; and as to himself, after the mood
was over, he had the full space of time given to him for
repentance, which intervened between the act itself and
the grave.

Towards the close of Conference, the subject of these
pages was at Aberford, Tadcaster, and Towton.   A
travelling preacher was expected at Tadcaster ; but no
one arrived in time for the service, and he was called
upon to exercise.   Not long after, two preachers entered
the chapel, who had lingered behind on purpose to hear.
Neither of them, of course, would preach ; they were
anxious to hear him ; and though he suffered for it,
they were not disappointed.

Messrs. Reece and Bramwell were appointed to the
Leeds circuit, at Conference, in connexion with Mr.
Barber, who had laboured in it the year preceding.
The preaching of Mr. Bramwell was peculiarly adapted
to Dawson's genius, and was made a special blessing
to him, owing, no doubt—like his own, to its alternately
rousing and soothing effects.   Hence,

" I heard Mr. Bramwell.   I thought every bar of
unbelief would give way.

"At Seacroft in the morning, where I heard Mr.
Bramwell.   Saw clearly that nothing but the power of
God can make a preacher useful.   At Armley at noon,
and Wortley at night.   A blessed time at Wortley.
Stopped at Armley all night.   The quarterly meeting
being on the Monday, I proceeded to Leeds.   Found

my mind prepared for a full surrender to God. A profitable day. Much rejoicing (Oct. 4,) at the news of peace. Oh, that our minds were equally affected with the view of peace as offered in Christ!

"Still happy in God! Glory be to his name! Heard Mr. Bramwell."

Speaking of one of Mr. Bramwell's peculiarities as a preacher, he observes :—"I thought the fire of his genius never blazed so brightly, as when he was addressing the sinner. He had a natural talent for poetry, and I have heard him speak, extempore, most striking paragraphs, in a sort of blank verse, for twenty or thirty lines together ; when he seemed to plunge the sinner into the midst of tormenting flames, and we heard him raving out the feelings of his enraged passions in the most horrid soliloquies. I once heard him preach on 2 Thess. i. 7—10, when he displayed ' the terrors of the Lord ' in such a manner, as to make the flesh cringe at the rehearsal." This is a just description of the more terrible character of Mr. Bramwell's ministry. At other times, he was as soft as twilight, and as tender as the mother singing her infant to repose.

Though the subject of these pages had now a good experience in the things of God, as will have been perceived, and was tolerably well versed in the stratagems of Satan, yet, he was often, as in the year preceding, depressed in spirit. He found, that there was no hill without its vale : and we have some of his sinkings and swellings of heart in the following passages from his Diary.

"I feel the uncomfortable approaches of that frame, when I feel nothing but my *want of feeling*. Quicken me, O thou Resurrection and the Life!

"A degree of shame possessed my soul after speaking

at Kippax, because of my unprofitableness and unfitness for the work in which I was engaged; though I felt a sweet taste of the love of God on my return home.

"This week, my mind has been much pained on account of a want of real vital godliness.

"At West Garforth; but overcome with a fit of lightness. Lord, help me!

"I was at home in the forenoon, owing to the great snow (March 15) that fell during the day and night before. Bless the Lord for ever! I, in some measure, relieved my mind to the family. Lord, help me to fulfil my duty in the situation in which I am placed! At Scholes at noon, and Whitkirk at night.

"Alas! at night, I felt, in consequence of some untoward things, a violent start of angry grief, which made me groan. Oh, what must I do? what must I do? Lord, help me! Lord, help me!

"My spirit, at West Garforth, did not sufficiently feel the awful truths I delivered to the people.

"At Seacroft love-feast, I found my mind dry, partly owing, I believe, to a slight prejudice against the leader. Oh, how careful should we be, not to pour that sour evil into the breast of another by whispering!

"Too much shame, and of the fear of man.

"A somewhat clamorous, boasting manner of talking this morning.

"Not properly disposed for prayer this morning. Fruits of bitterness rose in the mind in the forenoon. In the afternoon, conversation wanted its proper savour; and now, at 4 o'clock, I am pained with just heart-aches.

"Blamed myself for allowing a slight spirit of murmuring to rise in the breast.

"Should have been at the workhouse; but let the

rain prevent me. My soul is pained on this account.

"A friend came over, from whom I received no good. I feel condemned for not having warned him more solemnly.

"At Holbeck. A season of temptation at noon; but a blessed time at night.

"Blamed myself for not going to J. Barmiston's funeral."

In this way, he acted the part of a "watchman" over himself, as well as to "the house of Israel;" watching the temper of the mind, the words of the lips, and the general carriage to those around, not only at every point, but every hour of the day; and that too, with the vigilance, rigour, and fidelity of a centinel, whose sole business it is to watch a garrison. Cares, it is admitted, are as innumerable both in kind and degree, as the sands on the sea shore; and the fable, so pleasantly constructed by Hyginus on the subject, shews that man is their proper and almost exclusive prey. But what is applied in another case, will serve here.—"Whenever our neighbour's house is on fire, it cannot be amiss for the engines to play a little on our own. Better to be despised for too anxious apprehensions, than ruined by too confident a security." William Dawson saw the miscarriages of others, and he knew the inclinations, startings, shiftings, and windings of the human heart. He had long manifested the utmost anxiety to be "*put* right," and he was now equally anxious to *keep* so.

The Divine Being, however, did not leave him comfortless; hence, the following gleams of light, and foretastes of heaven.—

"Bless the Lord for his presence at Thomas Stoner's, in the afternoon !

"Experienced some of the droppings of his love into my soul, at Whitkirk, in the evening. Pour the mighty flood !

"A precious season at Linnerton, (on Dike-Side.) Preserve the people, O Lord, humble and simple in thy cause !

"A season of nearness to God, while hearing preaching at Garforth in the morning. At Colton and Scholes afterwards. In a solemn frame all day.

"Between sleeping and waking in bed this morning, these words strongly impressed my mind,—'See all your sins on Jesus laid.' Glory, glory be to God !

"Preached at Ledstone, Kippax, and Scholes. Praise the Lord for a good time at the two latter places !

"Solemnly affected while reading John v. 28, 29.

"Bless the Lord for drawing me to some comfortable verses while at private prayer. Found power and liberty at Sturton. And oh, how sweet at Allerton in the evening, while singing the last hymn !

"A sense of God's presence in private prayer.

"The Lord blessed my soul on opening upon these words,—' Not imputing their trespasses unto them.'

"My mind was much blessed in reading the works of Dr. Goodwin, as published in the 'Christian Library ;' and I seldom, or ever, was more enabled to surrender my all to God.

"Thank the Lord, a precious afternoon ! Religion is no cunningly devised fable.

"Heard Mr. Pawson at Leeds in the morning. Found much of the power of God, while I was preaching at Holbeck in the forenoon. At Leeds love-feast in the afternoon. There, blessed be God, I made a public surrender of myself to him and to his people.

"Attended Barwick church in the forenoon, and heard the rector. Heard John Holmes at Scholes in the afternoon. Returned home and read some of 'Baxter's Saints' Rest' to the family, and went to prayer. Bless the Lord, O my soul! Preached at Barwick in the evening.

"At church, Seacroft, Scholes, and Little Preston. A sweet time at church!—Bless the Lord, I feel the good effects of yesterday."

The omissions previously noticed in his Diary for this year, seem to have been occasioned by discouragements,—some painful feelings and conflicts often preceding them. But in the midst of all, whether in joy or in sorrow, the following sentiments flowed freely from his pen :—"To thee, O Jesus, I willingly yield myself, my all, to serve thine interest when, where, and how thou pleasest. Keep me from evil; support me in trial; and enable me to glorify thee in every thing through which I may have to pass ; and in whatsoever I may be engaged." Adding, in the way of experience, as well as purpose and prayer,—"My soul is not only drawn out *after* God, but I feel some drawings *from* him. This evening, I felt in lying down, a sweetness, a melting of heart, of a peculiar kind. Glory be to God!

> · Take my body, spirit, soul,
> Only thou possess the whole.' ''

CHAPTER VIII.

NOTWITHSTANDING William Dawson's elevation in the sphere in which he moved, he ascended by degrees to the point which he attained; and with the exception of his non-admission to holy orders—which was no discredit either to himself or others, the ladder never once broke beneath him to throw him back, and so render additional ascent laborious. Besides the many rare and curious pieces of " mathematical motion " in the soul, common to all, he had a spring of action within which would never allow him to stand still. Piety and genius were constantly sowing their seeds, and he was as invariably indulged with the honour which springs from them. Whatever may be the truth of the sentiment, when generally applied,— that every man has a portion of rust about him at the beginning, and that in England it accompanies a man to the grave—not even daring to pen a *hic jacet* to speak out for him after his death, William Dawson was an exception. Of his spirit, it might have been said,—

"Strong as necessity, it starts away,
Climbs against wrongs, and brightens into day."

The *ennui*, or wearisomeness of inaction, was unknown to him; and he was so generally approved for piety, talent, and zeal, that Mr. Barber proposed him for the itinerant work, March 29, 1802, at the Leeds quarterly-meeting, when he was unanimously approved by his brethren.

His matter, manner, and Christian spirit, attracting general attention in the societies, led him to take a still more extensive range of country; and not only did he visit places, which to him were new, but greater demands were made upon his labours in the large chapels in Leeds and elsewhere. There was no diminution of attention, with this additional toil, to the wants and interests of his own immediate neighbourhood. He was ready to every good word and work throughout the week; preserving the same anxious solicitude for the welfare of the sick—the poor inmates of the workhouse—and the life of God in the classes; not omitting his accustomed fasts, saying, with the apostle,—"I keep under my body, and bring it into subjection; lest that by any means, when I have preached to others, I myself should be a castaway."

K

He was quickened in this work, and at the same time humbled, by reading Cotton Mather's "Directions to a Candidate for the Ministry."

Though persecution was never rampant and cruel in the district in which he was resident, he was subject, occasionally, to annoyances of a different character from any that have been noticed. While preaching in the house of John Robinson, of Garforth Moor, some young men crept softly to the top of the roof,—the house being low and thatched, and dropped a dead goose down the chimney, whose feathers swept the flue as it descended, and covered the people and the room with soot. On another occasion, the same disturbers placed a large piece of turf on the top of the chimney ; and the good man of the house supposing that the chimney had lost its draught, opened the door and the window, to promote a freer circulation of air. But on finding no alteration, and the soot and smoke rendering the place insupportable, he ascended the roof, and ascertained the cause. These are specimens of the art of war carried on against the peaceable worshippers of God.

A chapel being much wanted at Barwick, and there being no immediate prospect of obtaining ground and materials for one, he earnestly addressed himself to God on the subject ; and observes, that he "dedicated part of a day in prayer, on account of a preaching-house." *

While thus caring for the churches, it was one of the severest years for mental suffering, he had ex-

* This was the name originally given to places of worship among the Wesleyans, by the Church party, and sanctioned by Mr. Wesley.

perienced since the time he first escaped from spiritual bondage. Such expressions as these are employed :— "The devil is determined to ruin my peace, my happiness, my soul. "—"Heavy in heart and mind."—"My soul feels the want of true religion. I am afraid it is too much in the head ; and the reason is, I think, if it were not, there would be greater pleasure and weight in private prayer."—" My spirits are depressed while reflecting on my past life. God raise me up! I would not sin against thee. My heart seems to say,—though I may not wish what is said,—I would rather be in hell without sin, than be in heaven with it. "—" Religion has not been felt this week in its power, in the way I have sometimes experienced it ; and I am dispirited in consequence."—" At private prayer, I am much resisted by the flesh and Satan."— " My soul lies humbled before God. Oh, that it were more so! Let me *die*, O Lord, rather than *live* to grieve thee, or bring the slightest stain upon my soul." —" Lord, am I given up by thee for not doing thy will ? "—" Afraid, lest I should prove a castaway after all ! "—" Nearly in despair. "

The *doubts* entertained of the genuineness of his experience in seasons of depression, are not at all remarkable. A strong prejudice exists in the minds of some people, against that state of the understanding termed doubt ; but a little reflection will soon convince one, that on a subject that admits of strong probabilities on both sides, doubt is as appropriate. a state of mind, as belief or disbelief on others. It has been properly argued, that there are doctrines, propositions, and facts supported and opposed by every degree of evidence, the proper effect of which is, to leave the

mind in an equipoise between two conclusions. In
these cases, either to believe or disbelieve would im-
ply that the understanding was improperly affected.
Doubt, therefore, is the appropriate result from which
there can be no reason either to shrink, or over which
to utter the loud lament. If this is the case in
matters purely speculative, it is still more difficult,
without the direct witness of the Spirit, to arrive at
correct conclusions in things experimental, in moments
of depression, when the light is transmitted, as it
were, through the medium of stained glass, rather
than immediately from the sun ; for the soul, on such
occasions, enclosed within the narrow circle of its own
orbit, feels nothing strongly but what acts within that
circle ; and the present disposition, fear, or desire,
throws its own colouring on surrounding objects.

On these occasions—-feeling so much of his own
imperfection, he could scarcely assume sufficient courage to reprove sin—to enter into the pleasures of
social life,—or proceed in the free and full discharge
of the various duties connected with family religion.
Hence, his personal upbraidings ;—" Hurt in hearing
a man swear, and not reproving. Oh, may I
learn wisdom by experience ! " " I did quite wrong
in stopping so long at Sturton."—" My mind was
remarkably solemnized in reading Baxter's 'Directory.'
I must,—I must speak more to the family. Part of
the day has been devoted to private prayer, to plead
for more of the power of religion. I want it to take
full possession of my soul. Oh, where is the melting
heart ? Where the humility and brokenness of spirit
that ought to possess me ? Give it, thou Prince of
peace ! " He had his siftings also, as on a previous

occasion, on the subject of faith ; but was now as much afraid of the Church as of himself. "I read," he observes, " Mr. Wesley's first Journal. I see I want that faith which raises me still higher into God. Often have I prayed, that I might never become an instrument of bringing into the Church of Christ any deadly evil. But, unless I possess this living faith, I shall either bring an evil into the Church, or myself, or both. Lord, give me this faith !"——As to social intercourse, he was aware, agreeably to the sentiment of an intelligent writer, that, "Company is an extreme provocative to fancy ; and, like a hot-bed, in gardening, is apt to make our imaginations sprout too fast." One of his prayers was, that God would give him "the bridle of inward love, to keep in check, and to sweeten conversation."

In the course of the same month, that he read the last work, he remarks,—"I heard Mr. Barber. Bless the Lord, for an increase of *faith* in the *truth* of his word ! Lord, increase it till I believe myself into the *possession* of the promised blessings. On account of my offences, I look for God's chastening hand. Anything, rather than sin against him !"——To supply any real or imaginary defect at home, as well as to be a constant monitor to himself, he commenced preaching at Barnbow, where he seconded his private, by his public appeals.

He omitted, as in the year preceding, several entries in his journal ; and states, that they were occasioned by his depressed state of feeling : intimating, at the same time, that it was for wise ends, and that reminiscences of the more painful parts of a man's personal history, are useful to those in a public capacity, by way of enabling them to succour such as may be placed in similar circumstances. He obtained considerable relief by reading the Life of Mr. Alexander Mather, and Bunyan's "Grace Abounding;" respecting the latter of which, he remarks, "I perceive, in many instances, a very great similarity between the experience embodied in these pages, and my own. Dear Jesus, I trust I shall yet *see* and *feel* thy great salvation."

He had committed himself to God; and that God who has declared that he will never "forsake," saw what was coming, and took care to wrap the soul up in the garb of humility, before the gale of popular applause was heard, and which he was now beginning to feel. "I have been much haunted with pride and self-complacency," says he, "through the breath of indiscreet praise, wafting like a breeze across the soul. Oh, to be nothing! Oh, to be nothing!" Again. "I preached at Hunslet. My soul was much drawn out after God in prayer, the night before. But in the afternoon and evening, I was much tempted to self-complacency. 'Oh, hide this self from me, that I no more, but Christ in me may live!'" These temptations were but momentary; but his honesty would not suffer them to be passed unnoticed; and it was his safety to find, that they were *but* temptations. Had pride been indigenous to the soul,* he would have

* A critic has been pleased to take exception to this form of expression; and supposes the biographer to have forgotten his "Wesleyan creed." But the truth is, the critic seems to have forgotten his office, by dexterously contriving, in order to make out a case, to shift the subject from the *individual* to the *mass*, and from a *man renewed* by *divine grace*, and deeply *humbled* before God, to *men* in an *unregenerate* state, primed and loaded with every species of moral turpitude; affirming it to be the opinion of the writer, that "pride is *not* indigenous to the soul." To what soul? To a soul *renewed*, or *unrenewed?* The critic wishes his readers to believe the latter. But *pride* is no more indigenous to the " *new*," than *humility* to the " *old man ;*" and the subject of these Memoirs was " renewed in the spirit of" his " mind."

been in the utmost jeopardy, with flattery so near, to hasten its growth. But "pride," which is said to be "as loud a beggar as want, and a great deal more saucy," had no cravings in him. It was not even permitted to take root, much less to throw out its branches to court the sun and the "breeze." To be noticed with esteem, by persons of sense, is often a patent for esteem with those around; then comes flattery at its heels; and in the rear of that again —pride, "the trappings of which men rarely put off, till they who are about them put on their winding-sheet." He knew, that—

> "Humble valleys thrive with their bosoms full
> Of flowers, when hills melt with lightning, and
> The rough anger of the clouds:

that—

> "Heaven's gates are not so highly arched
> As princes' palaces; they that enter there
> Must go upon their knees. "

Though not at all parsimonious in praise himself, when called for, and ready to make selections from the better part of a man's character and performances, when in danger of being undervalued; yet he was careful never to administer the "flattering unction" in the person's presence; and if led, unguardedly, to hazard an unfavourable criticism, he was certain to smart for it afterwards. Thus,—"My mind has been wandering this forenoon. I noticed, perhaps unnecessarily, some innocent improprieties in a preacher's manner of speaking. At all events, my remarks were not to edification. Oh, that my 'speech' may 'be always with grace, seasoned with salt.'" On another occasion; "Gave way to some warmth of temper, in consequence of which some hasty words were spoken, producing

great distance of soul from God. Lord, save me!"
In all cases in which pain seemed to be unnecessarily
inflicted upon another, he was instantly plunged into
the person's circumstances, and was tremblingly alive
all over : for robust as was his figure, and strong as
was his language, he was possessed of exquisite sensibility, and was capable of receiving the most powerful
impressions, whether pleasant or unpleasant, from every
subject that concerned the heart, as well as from every
object that addressed the senses.

The time approached for his acceptance or non-
acceptance, by the Conference, as an itinerant preacher.
Many obstacles of a domestic character stood in the
way ; and the exercise which he had experienced in the
interval, and which seemed to overshadow his Christian
evidence, was the circumstance selected by the disturber
of peace, for annoying him at this critical moment.
The following remarks are found in his Diary.

"Monday, June 28th.——At Leeds, being quarter-
day. Blessed be God, I found my mind in a rising
frame, while a few of the brethren were praying.

"Tues. 29.   Much perplexed in my spirit this
morning, to know how far it is the will of God
that I should be a travelling preacher.   Most wise
and gracious God! over-rule the darkness of my
understanding,——remove remaining unbelief,——and correct self-will in my will and affections!   Let all be
done for thy glory!   Make thy way *plain* before me,
and direct my steps!

"Thursday evening, July 1st.   Disposed for prayer.
One grand objection which appears to me against my
going out to travel is, that I have not at this moment
the *clear* witness of the Spirit.   The apostles were to

be endued with power from on high, *before* they went to preach.

" Friday 2. Set apart for fasting and prayer, that direction may be afforded, and a blessing given, in this important business.

" Saturd. 3. Purchased Mr. Beanland's barn for a preaching-house. Lord, smile!

" Sund. 4. Heard Mr. Reece preach at Bramley in the forenoon. A precious season. I took the pulpit in the afternoon. Not so good a season.

" Mond. 5. Much engaged in mind about travelling, preaching-house, &c.

" Tuesday 6. Went to Leeds. Gave a cool consent to travel. But my mind is touched in a tender part, when I see my mother so much elated at the thought that I shall continue a little longer, on account of the preaching-house. Ah, Lord, how tender a point is this! Look in love upon me, for thy name's sake!

" Thursd. 8. Backward to religious duties. God help me!

" Friday 9. Visited G. Haigh. He seems on the verge of eternity, and under great pressure of pain.

" Sunday 11. At Halton and Colton. Bless the Lord for a measure of liberty at both places!

" Wed. 14. Dismissed my reasonings about travelling, and committed the whole to the Lord. Spent the afternoon with Mr. Reece, and was at Whitkirk in the evening. Praise the Lord for a refreshing season!

" Thursd. 15. Waited upon Sir Thomas Gascoigne, at Parlington, to obtain his acceptance of my brother Richard in my place, as steward of the Colliery."

Though his mother was still opposed to his leaving

K 2

home, it was agreed, at length, that Richard should take his office; and here, his Diary, as to further particulars, leaves the whole blank. But some fragmentary conversations, which he had with the biographer, will supply the omission. He was accepted by the Conference; and his name, in connection with that of Mr. Pilter, stood on the manuscript Stations for Wetherby, near Leeds. The Conference commenced at Bristol, Monday, July 16th. On going to the head steward, on the Saturday evening before, to close his accounts, he found—though everything had assumed the appearance of being amicably settled, that his feelings and expectations had been sported with; the steward coldly stating, that he thought they could do without the services of his brother. Finding that plans had been formed to prevent his brother from entering upon the proposed situation, in order—as it afterwards turned out, to secure it for a relative of the steward's own, Dawson's eye instantly flashed fire, and he said, "Well, then, I'll remain; and you may give me less wages, if you judge proper: this," continued he, "was as great a thunder-clap to the steward, as his statement was to me." He immediately wrote to Mr. Barber, stating that, for the sake of others, he deemed it his duty to relinquish all thoughts of going out to travel; entering into the particulars of the case. What is not a little singular, he met Mr. Bramwell, at Chapeltown, on the 18th of the month, who said to him, in his positive, yet familiar way,—"Billy, I think you ought not to go out to travel; the time has not yet come; you have not done all your work at home:" assigning no reason, but leaving the words to produce their own impression. It may be further

remarked, that though the steward thwarted him
in his designs of itinerating, the steward himself was
afterwards disconcerted in his plans; for the place
which he had in view, on which to settle his relative,
was not only given up, but 30 acres of grass land, which,
though not rich, but serviceable to the farm, was
added to Barnbow in consequence of it; Sir Thomas
observing, to the subject of these Memoirs, "You
shall have the additional land at a rent which shall
not hurt you." So much for integrity and dissimulation. Dawson, through whose "breast of crystal,"
the steward was enabled to read every purpose, reaped
the reward of his sincerity; and the steward, whose
"heart and face were so far asunder, as to hold no
intelligence," was disappointed of his hopes. The
path of dissimulation is not unaptly described by Blair to
be a "perplexing maze. After the first departure
from sincerity, it is not in our power to stop; one
artifice unavoidably leads on to another; till, as the
intricacy of the labyrinth increases, we are left en-
tangled in our own snare." Sir Thomas himself might
not be fully aware of the steward's designs; and,
therefore, might have no intention to counteract them;
but Providence employed him on the occasion to do its
own work, while leaving him in the free exercise of
the will.

William Dawson now dismissed all anxiety from his
mind, respecting any removal from home; and considered himself as fixed in rural life to the end of
his days.

He was at Chapeltown, Oct. 24th, and observes that,
with a mixture of inferior feelings, he felt "a strong
desire for the glory of God." But he adds,—"On my

return home, I found an unusual emptiness of soul."
Two days after he remarks,—"I have been much impressed with an account of the sudden death of one of
my hearers at Chapeltown."

Though he profited greatly by the preaching and
conversation of the other preachers, the return of Mr.
Bramwell to Barwick and its neighbourhood, was especially hailed with joy.   In November, he remarks,—
"Surely the Lord will bless me this day.   Mr. Bramwell is expected at Barwick.   Make bare thine arm, O
Lord, in this place!   At the time of preaching, my
soul was particularly drawn out after God, for a blessing
upon myself and upon the hearers.—We had a meeting
at six o'clock the next morning.   It was a precious season.   Praise the Lord!   Through the remainder of the
week, I experienced unusual power to draw near to
God, and to lay myself at his feet."

On other occasions, painful as the exercises of the
year had been, he could, at intervals, give utterance
to such expressions as these:—"This morning, my
prayers have had wings."—"Uncommon liberty at
Aberford.   It is thy Spirit, O adorable Lord, that
makes the preacher!"—"Inwardly resting upon God.
Oh, how sweet a spirit is passive resignation, grounded
upon the promises! but how much sweeter must
answered expectations be!"—"The Lord is in our
class-meetings!"—"A time of power at Barwick."
—"Made a fresh surrender of myself to the Lord,
at the sacrament."—"Some sweet thrills of melting
mercy!"—"With gratitude, humility, self-abasement,
and self-devotedness, I adore God for his manifested
presence, while preaching at Barwick and Barnbow
Hall."—"Oh, how easy and delightful it is to pray

and preach with divine liberty!"—"A particular manifestation of God. Still, I claim him as my Father reconciled."—"Heard of good being done, through my unworthy services, at Holbeck."

By connecting some of these triumphant bursts with the heart-rendings noticed in the course of the year, his religion will appear to be made up only of contradictions; or, if not of these, one part of his experience at the antipodal point from the other. And yet, they are the contradictions, or opposites, that are found in fellowship with the saints of the highest order. Such sentiments, as the following, are mere paradoxes to the man of the world:—"When I am weak, then am I strong;"—"as deceivers, and yet true,—as unknown, and yet well known,—as dying, and behold, we live,—as sorrowful, yet always rejoicing,—as poor, yet making many rich,—as having nothing, yet possessing all things." Should the Christian be charged with patronizing paradoxes,—in holding forth such expressions, he is entitled to answer with Chrysippus, that they only proceed from his love of truth. He can neither think nor feel like unenlightened men. As he has joys, so he has conflicts, with which the wicked have no power to intermeddle. Music may be in his heart, and he may be ready to burst into song, at the very moment a wicked man is passing him in the street, and pitying him for his sombre views of real life.

We hear the subject of these pages again relieving his soul in imploring accents:—"Bless me, O God, with saving grace in my soul; and make me useful in thy hands in saving sinners! Be this the case, and I care not what I am in temporal circumstances, where I am in life, or how thou art pleased to deal with me!"

An occasion was taken to notice his dress in the preceding chapter, chiefly as to its form ; but he now penetrated a little further.   As he became more dead to the world, he became more cautious not to indulge in any *needless expense ;* that he might have the more to spare for necessary purposes.   His ruffles had been laid aside, for which he innocently stood rebuked ; but he saw that persons might appear plain, and yet be costly in their attire, and that what they gained in conscience by the cut, they might lose by extravagance in the quality.   In one instance, he complains, this year, as he had done in earlier life, of going too high in price for a part of his costume ; stating, that the Christian should be " above unnecessary expenses."   As he strove to steer a medium course in quality, so he knew there was a medium between the fop and the sloven—taking not only the *yeoman*, as previously noticed, but the Christian, into all his considerations.   He had no objection to " the ermine's skin," and to the " silk-worm " becoming the " spinster " of the female, in certain ranks in life, but he had a serious objection to *men*, and especially persons connected with the ministerial office, appearing as " Madame Superbia " is represented, as if constantly " studying the lady's library—The looking-glass." While, however, he loved ease, plainness, and moderation, he shunned coarseness ; persuaded, " that if Tully himself had pronounced one of his orations with a blanket about his shoulders, more people would have laughed at his dress, than would have admired his eloquence."   It is a shrewd remark of a German writer, —that " dress is a table of our contents."

His Diary of 1803, he carried forward to the month

of October ; omitting the two following, and several dates in those preceding. He began, no doubt, to find a sameness in constantly adverting to his joys and his sorrows ; and having the same battles to fight, and the same grace to assist him in his struggles, a record of them seemed less necessary.

On the 7th of January, he "renewed his covenant with God, in the most solemn manner;" and hoped that it would be a "bond never to be broken." In the same month, he was much profited by a visit from Mr. W. E. Miller to Barwick ; and several persons having joined the Society at Scholes, about that time, he exulted to find "most of the lambs" enjoying the full benefit of Christian fellowship ; and also to find, that "Edward Joley's wife had entered into liberty." On the Sabbath day following, he proceeds, —"I preached at Garforth for J. Ible, and heard J. Richards at Barwick. I was at Barwick in the evening. My soul was melted with the Divine presence the whole of the day. P. Smith was deeply affected on account of her lost state, while by herself. On our return from the meeting, we found her in deep distress. The Lord answered prayer on her behalf."

He had been gradually prepared for the more stirring occasions, which often attended the ministry of Messrs. Bramwell and Miller, by the living witnesses that had sprung up under his own preaching, the subjects, sometimes, being unable to repress their feelings during service.

Some additional support from the flourishing state of the Societies, seemed necessary at this time, to enable him to meet, with sanctified feeling, an exercise which affected the family. Feb. 1, he remarks, "I was at Aberford the whole of the day, waiting to take the farm at the advanced rent. I am afraid I talked too much." It would have been marvellous, had he been mute on the occasion, seeing that the farm, with the exception of the grass land added to it, was sufficiently high before. But during the war, many of the landlords injured their estates, by raising the rents, so as to place it beyond the power of the tenant to enrich the land by affording it proper culture. High rents are only calculated to exasperate the restless, and dishearten the obedient : they leave men helpless and hopeless, and accustom them to look upon their best securities from ruin—economy and industry, as perverted for the worst of purposes by those who can be, and who ought to be, the best encouragers of their social interests. Where the grace of God is not present as a corrective, they compel men to exchange love for hatred, confidence for distrust, and submission for resistance. William Dawson, however, took the farm again, resolved, by patient industry, to plod his way through another term ; and for this he was tolerably fitted by exuberant vigour and economical habits.

Two days after, he again visited Aberford, being obliged to be present at the "Coal-feast." But he returned from the feast as from a regular meal ; and not as many do—unfit for either mental or physical labour ; "like lamps choked by a superabundance of oil, or fires extinguished by excessive fuel." On his return, he observes, "I called at Thomas Goodall's, and preached." He was not one of those men of whom Seneca speaks, who divide their lives betwixt an anxious conscience and a nauseated stomach ; and who receive the reward of their intemperance in the diseases it generates. Rising with an appetite, he was sure to secure digestion; and he was as fit for the work of God after, as before the feast. This is a fine example for the drunkard, who is quaintly but pithily said by Swinnocke, "to drown himself in his cups;" and to the glutton, who, with equal force of expression, is said, "to dig his own grave with his teeth."

A little point may be noticed which affected him at the same time, and which may be adverted to for the sake of others. Though he was prudent and cautious, he was not close and suspicious. Christian character inspired him with confidence. But he had to repent of misplaced confidence. "I was hurt," says he, "on hearing that J—— had told what I committed to him as a secret." The thing might have been trivial in itself, and calculated to harm no one. But he looked at the breach of trust. And yet, had he only reflected for a moment, on the frailty of human nature, he would have found, that there is often a proneness to divulge a secret, from the vanity of being entrusted with it. It has been stated with grave humour, but with some mixture of truth, that "Secrets are so seldom kept, that it may be with some reason doubted, whether the quality of retention be so generally bestowed; and whether a secret has not some subtle volatility by which it escapes imperceptibly, at the smallest vent; or some power of fermentation, by which it expands itself, so as to burst the heart that will not give it way." That is a fine sentiment,— "What is mine, even to my life, is her's I love; but the secret of my friend is not mine."

At the close of the same month in which the farm

was raised in rent, Mr. Porter informed him, that
" Sir Thomas Gascoigne intended to set down the
colliery." This of course, affected his stewardship,
and would continue to do so, till either the workings
should be resumed, or another pit should be opened.
"The account," he observes, "was sudden, and produced various thoughts and feelings." He adds, " Lord,
undertake for me and mine." This was probably
occasioned by the advance in wages which took place
at the time.

His labours in the old and new chapels, in Leeds,
became still more frequent, and were not only highly
acceptable, but were rendered a great blessing in the
conversion of souls to God. Hearers and converts,
also, continued to multiply in his own neighbourhood ;
and he himself had become a *leader*, not only at
Scholes, but apparently at Barwick. " Mr. Bramwell
was at Barwick, " he remarks in March ; and proceeds :—" Bless the Lord, for a very crowded house,
—for drawing so many to hear ! Oh, that he would
appear with power and glory in *my classes !* There
is the appearance of an opening work in the neighbourhood. May nothing retard it ! May it be deep,
clear, and effectual ! "

In the same month, he met his uncle William at
Wakefield, to consult him, apparently, respecting the
probable result of his situation, should the colliery
be laid aside. Just after this, on going to Kippax
to preach, he observes,—" The mare fell *under me,*
and *upon me ;* but I was not much worse, except
in my leg which was crushed. Bless the Lord, for
his hand of love, which was over me for good ! "
In the evening, his knee was much swelled at Little

Preston ; and he was compelled, in consequence of it, to rest some time from labour.

On the 29th of the month, on the return of which he was more than usually affected, he enters into his Diary :—"As I call this the last day of this year, (being the day before the anniversary of his birthday,) I desire to be deeply humbled, because of my past imperfections and unprofitableness ; and I wish the feeling to be so strong, as to produce proper and lasting impressions." The next day, he writes :—" In looking *back*, I find much, very much cause for self-abasement. Looking *inward*, I feel the absence of much good, and the presence of much of the evil of human nature. Directing the view *forward*, clouds and darkness appear to be lying on the face of the scene—not knowing what *to do*. My place at the colliery is likely to cease,—the farm is advanced,—and the necessities of the family are great ! What the end will be, is not for me to state. The entrance upon this year of my life is important. Surely it ought to be attended with prayer and self-dedication to God. " So it was distinguished : and he could not but see a providence in his remaining at home, that the family might have the aid of his counsel, and be encouraged by his example and his prayers. His constant prayer, while passing through the cloud, was —" Lord, undertake for me ! "

June 4th, he remarks,—" This day I have to record an affecting providence. My grandmother was found dead in her bed this morning. Pardon, O Lord, any omission of duty in reference to her ! I praise thy name for what thou didst enable me to *do* and to *feel* for her. But after all, forgive omissions." The tender affections, comprehending all the different modifications of love, appeared in him in various forms, and degrees, from the transient good-will which he felt for a common stranger, in matters purely civil, to the fondness with which he watched over the spiritual interests of his own family; and they are never so engaging—as was the case with him, as when they improve the character. This, indeed, is maintained to be their natural tendency, inasmuch as they prevent our attention from being confined to ourselves, and create both an interest in the welfare of others, and also an anxiety to recommend ourselves to their esteem. When the grace of God spiritualizes the whole, then the young Christian becomes a nursing father to the patriarch in years.

One thing which greatly engrossed his attention, was a *new chapel* at Barwick. He had prayed for one; and as events were hastening the fulfilment of his wishes,—and one would scarcely have been ventured on without him, it was converted into another reason in providence for his not going out to travel. April 18th, he states that he went to Fleet Mill, to see whether Mr. Evens would sell a piece of ground for a preaching-house, but did not meet with him at home. Having applied to him in the interim, Mr. E. examined the ground, June 18, and consented to allow him to take as much as was necessary for the purpose, at one shilling per yard. This was matter of praise, as before, the business had been the subject of prayer. Wednesday 21st,—"The chapel," he observes, "was set out, and a part of the foundation dug." The "first stone was laid August 15th;" and he states it to have been "reared Oct. 27th."

In the midst of his joys and anxieties for a place of worship, he had his fears exercised, and manifested deep sympathy with the societies in the case of a partial revolt from the body. July 5, he remarks,— "Important intelligence from Leeds. Mr. Bramwell has departed from the Methodists. Great and un-comfortable, I fear, will be the consequences, if the Lord does not, in mercy, heal the breach. Spare us, good Lord ; and do not permit the spirit of division to rend the hearts of thy people from each other ! Pardon any non-improvement of *union* and *peace ;* and if it be possible, let us not see a house divided against itself; 'but *make* us one in heart and soul, and *keep* us one in thee.' " Such were his musings in his closet. Fifteen years after, when he preached a funeral sermon, occasioned by the death of that excellent man, to thousands of persons in the open air, in Leeds, he adverted to the subject with great tenderness, fidelity, and ingenuity—nicely balancing between the Wesleyan body and his subject, and desirous of giving to each the full weight of their worth. As the sermon was printed and published on the occasion, an extract will shew the delicacy of some of his touches, in handling a subject which involved a difference of opinion.

When adverting to particular traits of character, he observes of his subject, that, "As he was zealous, so he was *jealous* for the honour of his God. His love watched with jealous eye, lest the Lord Jesus should be robbed of his honour, and a rival admitted into the heart of his church. His jealousy suspected that one was insinuating itself among us as a body, and that was THE WORLD ; that a criminal love was openly manifesting itself in a growing conformity to the men, the maxims, and the spirit of the world ; and, as a certain consequence, that there was an increasing deficiency in spirituality of mind, and entire devotedness to God. Now, it is well known that jealousy, which is 'cruel as the grave,' always caricatures and magnifies the object of its suspicions and fears.

"So it was with the prophet Elijah. The revolt of Israel from their allegiance to the true God, and their estrangement from his worship, were viewed with a jealous eye ; and he retired from the hateful scene into a place where his heart could not be torn asunder, by being a witness of the worship of Baal. When the word of the Lord came to him, and said, 'What doest thou here, Elijah?' he answered, 'I have been very jealous for the Lord God of Hosts; for the children of Israel have FORSAKEN THY COVENANT, thrown down thine altars, and slain thy prophets with the sword; and I, even I, only am left; and they seek my life, to take it away.' But the evil was distorted and *magnified ;* and the Lord corrected his error, by informing him, that he had yet left 'seven thousand in Israel, all the knees which had not bowed unto Baal, and every mouth which had not kissed him.'

"So it was with Mr. Bramwell. At a certain period of his pilgrimage, he suspected that the love of the world was dividing our hearts with Christ ; and he could not bear the thought. His imagination took the pencil, to draw the portrait of the hated rival. It rose to a monster before his eyes. It alarmed his fears ; it biassed his judgment ; it influenced his will ; and, in the simplicity and sincerity of his heart, he retired from his circuit. It was at this important crisis, that some of his brethren met with him and enquired, —'What doest thou here, brother?' He might have answered, with great propriety, 'I have been very jealous for the Lord God of Hosts. I fear a criminal love of the world is rivalling Jesus Christ in the heart of his Church ; and, therefore, I thought my best course was to retire, and try what can be done by me in any other way.' But when his brethren softened down the distorted features of the detested object, which his trembling hand, at the instigation of his jealous heart had drawn,—when they took off the deep shades with which he had overcharged its countenance,—when they drew the picture of the monster DIVISION,—when they proved that, in the *present state* of the Methodist body, the evils of a schism and division would be much greater than the evils which he lamented and deplored,—he then saw, in some measure, as they did. Conviction, like a voice behind him, cried out, 'This is the way ; walk ye in it.' He listened. He obeyed. He retraced his steps. He returned to his work ; filled his station with credit to himself, and profit to the Church ; and lived and died in union with his brethren."

CHAPTER IX.

WITH the exception of two or three brief notices, his
religious Diary appears to have terminated with the
year 1803. What chiefly followed from hence, were
minutes of the places he visited, and the texts on
which he preached. Had he indulged in the particu-
larity of Ralph Thoresby of Leeds, in his "Diary,"
or Samuel Pepys in his "Memoirs," he might, with
his observing eye and warm heart, have furnished
many curious, instructive, and moving incidents, while
travelling, as he afterwards did, from one end of the
kingdom to the other.

The chapel which was "reared" at Barwick, October 27th, the year preceding, and in the erection of

which he exulted in being able to state, that "not an accident, as the world employs the term, had happened to any one," was opened by Mr. Thomas Taylor, April 29th, 1804. "This day," he observes, "Mr. Taylor opened the preaching-house, in the presence of a great company of people , and, what is better, under the gracious smile of God, which was sensibly felt by many of his children. We may turn our eyes upon it, and say, 'What hath God wrought!' And with equal astonishment may we look, when we consider by *whom* he has wrought. We dare not impeach the wisdom of the Lord in the choice of such *unworthy* instruments, but adore it as an instance of his unsearchable proceedings, who, in this, as in many other cases, has 'chosen the foolish things of the world to confound the wise,—the weak things of the world to confound the things that are mighty,—*base things*,—and things which are despised,—yea, and things which are not, to bring to nought the things that are!' May the Lord answer prayer *for* it and *in* it, that generations yet unborn may find in it the Lord Jesus Christ!" He further observes,—"The first love-feast was held at Barwick by Mr. Grant, July the 8th. He preached *excellently*. May the Lord follow the means with a lasting blessing to souls!"

Nearly the whole of the trouble connected with the erection devolved upon himself, as to purchases, looking after the builders, joiners, glaziers, painters, &c. ; collecting the monies, and meeting expenses. His "Collecting Book," which has been preserved, is a curiosity, comprising fine specimens of penmanship, exactness, and piety. It is preceded with notices of laying the foundation, rearing, opening the chapel, &c.

L

Then follows, as a kind of title-page,—"June 1803.
'Prosper thou the work of our hands upon us.' Psalm
xc. 17.—'They shall prosper that love Zion.' Psalm
cxxii. 6. June 1804. 'EBENEZER.' 1 Sam. vii. 12.
'Hitherto hath the Lord helped us.' " The next page
is headed with, "An Account of Monies promised and
given, by those who love the prosperity of Zion, towards
the expense of a preaching-house at Barwick." Immediately after this, columns are ruled for double entry,
in pounds, shillings, and pence,—the first three appropriated to monies "promised," the second to monies
"given." The "heading" of each page encloses a
text of Scripture, in the Roman character, as if set in
type, with a view, apparently, immediately to catch the
eye of the persons to whom he presented the book for
donations. The texts selected are ;—"God loveth a
cheerful giver," 2 Cor. ix. 7.—"Freely give," Matt. x.
8.—"Honour the Lord with thy substance," Prov. iii.
9.—"Give, and it shall be given unto you," Luke vi.
38.—"With such sacrifices God is well pleased," Heb.
xiii. 16.—"He which soweth bountifully, shall reap
also bountifully," 2 Cor. ix. 6—"He which soweth
sparingly, shall reap also sparingly," 2 Cor. ix. 6—"I
know thy works, and charity, and service, and faith,"
Rev. ii. 19.—"There is that scattereth, and yet in-
creaseth," Prov. xi. 24.—"Give to every man that
asketh of thee," Luke vi. 30 ; closing with, "Thou
shalt be recompensed at the resurrection of the just,"
Luke xiv. 14. In consequence of taking with him his
—"THUS SAITH THE LORD," he had scarcely a
dozen failures, in the various promises made to him—
some of which might possibly arise from a change of
circumstances ; and in comparatively small sums, from

"Benny Swift's" * *shilling*, to the *five pounds* subscriptions of Mr. Warner, of Garforth,——Mr. Pawson, jun., of Thorner,——Thomas Stoner, of Barwick,——and Mr. Whitehead, of Leeds, he collected, at intervals, from June 1803, to April 18, 1805, the sum of £150. 7s. 9d.

Mr. Taylor, who opened the chapel, had neither fine sense nor exalted sense, so called; but he had what is much more useful,——good, strong, common sense; that of which there is much less in the world than the world is aware. He had no glitter; he despised it; knowing in the language of a wit, that "he who will carry nothing about him but gold, will be every day at a loss for want of readier change." His sermons profited the mass, being within the comprehension of all, and intended to improve the heart, rather than gratify the taste. Mr. Grant, who led the love-feast in the newly erected building, was of a different class. He was an engaging preacher, and was much admired by the subject of these Memoirs, for ease, perspicuity, occasional elegance, and general usefulness. He possessed springs of rhetoric which were rarely dry; and his eloquence, which never failed to plead in companionship with nature, was often irresistible.

This year——1804, the subject of these pages was invited to preach in the Birstal circuit; and being now occasionally selected for special work, he preached a

---

* "Benny Swift," so called, was a poor man, well known in Leeds and its vicinity. He had ingress to the houses of rich and poor—was extensively useful in prayer-meetings—and diligent in visiting the sick. It was towards the approach of the evening of life, when the biographer became acquainted with him; but even then, he was a " *day labourer* " in "doing good." His abilities were slender, but there was great simplicity, cheerfulness, openness, integrity, and industry. He had, in the language of a popular writer, "the stability of the oak, and the flexibility of the osier." He possessed the religion that converts the private christian into a public blessing.

sermon on occasion of the death of Mrs. Wade, of
Sturton Grange, towards its close. The text selected
was, Isai. lvii. 1, 2 ; and being in the *masculine*, might
be deemed a little out of place ; but as he had to expa-
tiate on *character* rather than *sex*, and it was the text
in all probability which most deeply affected his heart,
it became the object of his choice.

In the year 1805, he stood No. 4, on the plan, while
older men were below. This, without making any in-
vidious distinction in reference to talent or popularity,
might have arisen from the length of time he had been
employed in the work,—having been engaged in preaching,—including his labours in the Established Church,
—from twelve to thirteen years. Towards the close of
the year, he preached at Methley, on 1. Sam. xii. 24,
being the day appointed for a general thanksgiving, in
consequence of Lord Nelson's victory at the battle of
Trafalgar.

From 1805 to 1809, his course, though laborious,
was not strongly marked with incident. It was distinguished, however, for increasing piety and usefulness. But as these have been dwelt upon, particularly
his religious experience, by way of shewing the solidity
of the foundation upon which the rising superstructure
of holiness was to be reared, the biographer may now,
with a view to prevent sameness, be more sparing in
his remarks on these topics.

His friends kept dropping into the grave around
him, like leaves strewing the ground in autumn ; and
over these, as over the remains of Mrs. Wade, he
generally had to pronounce the funeral oration. Among
the departed, may be noticed, Ann Smith, S. Thompson, Gabriel Tomlinson, and Mary Clarkson, of Barwick,

—Charles Abbott,—Mr. Barbey, of Swillington,—Mrs. Phillips, of Weeton,—not omitting his old patroness, Mrs. Dean, of Whitkirk, Feb. 4, 1807, whose lantern-light obsequies have already been the subject of remark. Mary Clarkson selected her text on her death-bed, Isaiah lxi. 10,—the others were 2 Tim. iv. 7,—John ix. 4,—Rev. xiv. 13,—Titus iii. 4—8,—Heb. xi. 24—26,—Isaiah xxv. 8 ; and that selected for good old Mrs. Dean, which was a magnificent one for the out-door scene, was Rev. v. 9—14.

Having had occasion to go down to Hull on the business of the colliery, and Mr. Joseph Bradford being stationed there at the time, he was anxious to see and hear him ;—"a man," as he observed to the writer, "who had been on such terms of intimacy with Mr. Wesley." But he was disappointed;—disappointed, he further remarked, both in reference to "matter and expression." This led him to state, with respect to another,—"There was the greatest sameness in Mr. P——, as a preacher, of any of the old preachers I ever heard." With regard to Mr. Bradford, he must either have heard him to disadvantage, or have suffered in consequence of having his expectations raised too high, which is the case with all those who forget that it is "more pleasing to see the smoke brightening into flame, than the flame sinking into smoke." However, being recognized by some one, he had himself, on the same day, to officiate in the same pulpit, in Scott-Street Chapel, which Mr. Bradford had previously occupied. As Mr. John Hill, a merchant in Hull,—a man of general reading, and of a highly cultivated mind, sat in the pulpit behind him, it is probable that Dawson had been engaged to preach in

his stead.   His text was 1 Pet. ii. 1, &c.   Joseph
Agar, Esq., of York, who was present on the occasion,
and who then for the first time had seen him, preserved
a vivid recollection of him as a preacher, when relating
the circumstance to the writer, between thirty and
forty years after, and cherished strong hopes of his
future celebrity.

He had by this time, both as a Christian and a
preacher, acquired what is generally comprehended in
the term—*character*, and that too, in some of its more
striking peculiarities.   "We are," says Helvetius,
"what we are made by the objects that surround us."
This, though not without truth, will serve the purpose
equally of the most refined sceptic, and the brute
system of Robert Owen, which, like a common sewer,
with his doctrine of circumstances, is ready to receive
the vilest filth that is capable of being poured forth
from the most depraved part of human society.   Nevertheless, properly guarded, and in connexion with a
wholesome religious education, it is a fact, as stated
in the "Ethical Questions" of an elegant writer, that
the young pupil is in the habit of taking lessons from
every thing around him, and that his habits and character are forming before he has any consciousness of
his reasoning powers.   But whatever character persons may receive from the circumstances in which they
are first placed, and however wise and benevolent the
superintendance may be, which a proper education
exerts, to give a correct bias to the intellectual and
moral character,—exercising an influence on the improvement and happiness of the mind to the latest
period of existence,—there will be found in the same
school among boys, and in the same neighbourhood

among adults, under the same circumstances and advantages, one who will stand out from all the rest, distinct in character, exclusive of all other attainments. Character, in a moral sense, is defined as that habitual disposition of the soul, that inclines it to do one thing in preference to another of a contrary nature. Duclos, in his reflections upon manners, very judiciously remarks, that the greatest part of the errors and follies in the conduct of mankind, happen because they have not their minds in an equilibrium, as it were, with their characters. Thus Cicero was a great genius, but a weak soul; which is the reason of his being elevated to the highest pinnacle of fame as an orator, although he could never rise above mediocrity as a man. Two things seemed to possess the whole soul of William Dawson,—his own salvation, and the salvation of others. His mind was intent on both; and the disposition which gave rise to character, was vigorously at work at all times, and kept him constantly before the public, in all his native vigour, with—"this one thing I do," imprinted upon every passion of the heart, every sermon from the lips, and every movement in society. He never suffered the disposition to flag which contributed to the formation of character—never allowed himself to undervalue or lose sight of character itself—and preserved a constant recollection of the position in which he stood before the church and the world. These considerations preserved every hallowed feeling in full exercise, and gave a beautiful uniformity to what was at the same time bold, elevated, and commanding,— attracting attention, like a mountainous district, after the eye has for some time reposed upon tamer scenes.

There was another local-preacher on the plan, of the

same name ; and being made of quieter materials than
the subject of these Memoirs, they were distinguished
by the ruder part of the people, when an enquiry was
made as to which of the two should occupy the pulpit,
—not, as in the plan, by their seniority or juniority,
but by their characteristic manner of preaching—giving
to the one the appellation of "sleepy," and to the
other, that of "shouting Billy." The cognomen of
Billy, which could only arise from that low familiarity
which " breeds contempt," and which was too common
even with persons whose sense and education ought to
have taught them better, was never relished by his
mother ; who said,—" he was never called Billy at
home, and I cannot conceive why he should be so distinguished *abroad*." As to his zeal, which gave energy
to voice, matter, and manner, it was not remarkable
that he should be distinguished for loud speaking, as
he continued in the same strain which marked his
earlier pulpit history. Names have great weight, both
with the vulgar and the learned ; but they very often
have beyond their proper signification and applicability
to the persons on whom they are imposed, a tincture of
the character of those who bestow them,—shewing a
disposition to degrade, by lowering the dignity of those
to whom they are applied.

In 1810 and 1811, his circle of admirers was greatly
enlarged ; and he was obliged to yield to pressing
invitations to preach occasional sermons, and make
collections, on behalf of Sunday Schools, chapels involved in debt, at the opening of places of worship,
&c. ; from friends at Batley, Mirfield, Dewsbury, Wakefield, Rotherham, Halifax, and elsewhere. He preached
also at Naburn, in the Kitchen of Mr. Leaf, and in
other places belonging to the York circuit.

His power over the passions, and his tact for improving funeral occasions,—specimens of which he had already abundantly afforded, continued to augment his engagements in this way. In addition to those of his friends noticed in a preceding paragraph, he was called upon to improve the death of John Stead, of Kippax,—Mrs. Batty of Barwick, on Psalms lxxiii. 26,—and of Mr. Ragg of Wetherby, on Matt. xxiv. 45, 46, &c. Of John Stead, he wrote a memoir which was published in the Methodist Magazine, for 1810, p. 321.

He was much pleased and profited at this time, by reading the works of Dr. Bates, and forwarded some admirable extracts to the editor of the above periodical, from the Doctor's sermon on "The Death of Dr. Jacomb," on John xii. 26, for the special benefit of "PREACHERS" of the gospel. These extracts are inserted in the same volume in which the above memoir is found, p. 379; and not only show the kind of mental aliment in which his soul delighted, and which afforded greater pleasure to his intellectual taste than the "savoury meat,' could yield to the palate of the patriarch; but the portrait drawn by Dr. Bates, exhibiting what a minister *ought to be,* is no bad likeness of what William Dawson himself actually *was,*—he having been led to frame his conduct, as a preacher, according to similar instructions, suggested by the word of God, and the impulses of a regenerate heart.

About the same time, his friend Samuel Popplewell, Esq., steward of the Right Hon. Lord Harewood, was passing through deep waters, in consequence of some commercial liabilities to which he had subjected himself, with a view to benefit a part of his family. Mr. Dawson—for thus it is now proper to designate him, from

L 2

the rank he held in society, met Mr. Poppplewell in
Leeds, in the beginning of his troubles; and it was
just such a friend—a man destitute of the sentimental
flights of the novelist, and the sage philosophy of the
mere moralist, that the mental sufferer required; one
capable of the most intimate and cordial coalition of
friendship from the mere instincts of a benevolent
nature, exclusive of religion, and of yielding the respect
and tenderness which man deserves from man. It is
remarked by a writer of celebrity, that "neither the
cold nor the fervid, but characters uniformly warm, are
formed for friendship." So it was here; they were
not "flush heats" from whence his sympathies sprung;
it was a permanent glow. He was one who "kept his
friendship in constant repair." Real friendship has
been represented as a "slow grower," and incapable of
"thriving, unless engrafted upon a stock of known and
reciprocal merit." Whatever may have been the time
of growth in this instance, it was genuine; not that
tormenting and taunting kind of friendship, which tells
a person what he *might* have been, had he followed the
advice given; but that which "weeps with them that
weep." After the usual salutations, Mr. Popplewell
returned to the enquiries made,—"I find my mind as
well as I can expect, considering my situation." Mr.
Dawson replied,—"As far as sympathy can share your
sorrows, I feel deeply concerned for you;" observing,
by way of comment afterwards, that "the soothing
voice of friendship melted his honest heart,—the tear
started in his eye,—and, among other things which he
said, he emphatically remarked,—'Though I do not
know whether I am worth a farthing, yet I should not
so much heed the loss of my property, if I could only

see a satisfactory *end* of the business." In the space of a month subsequent to this, he again saw him, when he again poured the balm of consolation into his wounded spirit. This was work for which he was always in tune,—differing widely from those "sweet instruments hung up in cases, that keep their sounds to themselves." Within the space of about eight months more, he was called upon to preach the funeral sermon of this excellent man, of whom he furnished a memoir for the Methodist Magazine, where it is to be found, Vol. xxxv, p. 941. In that memoir, he gives a characteristic notice of the Rev. Miles Atkinson, under whose ministry Mr. Popplewell had derived much good, and who had manifested great interest in his own welfare. Having first heard him, when he was unable to form an opinion, it is curious to know Mr. Dawson's more matured views. "He preached," he observes, "the plain gospel of Jesus Christ. His appearance was venerable, his voice peculiarly commanding, and his whole manner, both in the desk and the pulpit, was calculated to arrest the attention of his hearers. Such a minister in the Church was a phenomenon in those days, so that his congregations were uncommonly large."

Mr. Dawson's own congregations were now so "uncommonly large," that he was compelled, in many instances, to preach out of doors. As an exception to the general case,—"A prophet is not without honour, save in his own country,"—he was as popular at Barwick, and, apparently, as new at the close, as at the commencement of his ministerial career—embracing, in all, a period of about forty years. Each returning visit to the pulpit was as welcome as the return of an endeared friend, whose absence is regretted, and whose presence is the joy of the circle in which he moves. The faces of the people were all lit up with smiles on his appearance, disclosing the emotions of the heart, like flowers in May unfolding their beauties to the solar heat.   When disappointed of a preacher, he ascended the pulpit,—would stroke his hand over his forehead, —then partially raising it, and modestly peeping as from beneath a veil, would say,—"It is the old face again, friends!" The simple action and expression operated like a charm,—preacher and people were instantly on the sweetest terms of amity with each other; —no one besides himself was wanted,—for he could impart, in his peculiar way, what no one else could give.   His presence and acceptability, however, were sometimes rendered available by the timid and luke-warm, as an excuse for absence; and thus, occasionally, the pulpit labours of others were imposed upon him. Such was the hold he maintained on the public mind, that even in Leeds, when appointed to preach there, some of the most eminent travelling preachers in the connexion, both on ordinary and extraordinary occasions, have met numbers pouring along the streets, to hear him, belonging to the several chapels in which they were appointed to officiate.   The chapels, new and old, were invariably crowded; and the anxiety to hear him, was only equalled by the intense feeling of the people under his effective ministry.

It was in the spring of 1813, when the biographer became acquainted with him.   Their first interview was in the vestry of Armley chapel, near Leeds, Monday, April 19th, on the day of its opening.   The Rev. Richard Watson was then stationed in the Wakefield circuit, and was one of the ministers who officiated on the occasion. Mr. Dawson continued the opening services the Sabbath following, where he rejoiced with the people in the erection,—having often had to preach out of doors before, for want of more ample accommodation. His text was Psalm lxxxvii. 5, 6;—"And of Zion it shall be said, This and that man was born in her; and the Highest himself shall establish her. The Lord shall count, when he writeth up the people, that this man was born there." The writer will never forget the impression his first personal appearance made upon the mind. Mr. Dawson was then in his prime,—stout,—firm,—compact;—not robust;—and his fine forehead was unclouded by the hanging eaves of the thatch-like roof of false hair, which afterwards disfigured it,—escaping, however, by its homeliness, the application of the censure which Milton applies to the ladies,—

————"of outward form
Elaborate, of inward, less exact."

He was seated on a bench, with his body inclined forward,—one elbow on the knee, and the face directed towards the floor,—musing, apparently, on some subject; while the sole of one shoe was grinding the sand beneath it, to the sound of which he was lending partial attention. Just at the moment he was pointed out to the writer, he suddenly raised his head, and shot a glance across the room, from whence a voice issued, which had caught his ear; and it was this, in all probability, that gave additional force to the eye, and so deepened the impression produced. The expression was not so clear as pointed, not so brilliant as quick; equally remote from the diamond, the pellucid stream, or any transparent substance, as from the slow languor that contributes to its beauty,—being attractive, rather than searching, enlivening, rather than lovely. It seemed to give life to the whole form, and to confirm the opinion of those, who believe that the story of Argus implies no more, than that the eye is in every part; that is, as such persons express themselves, every other part would be mutilated, were not its force represented more by the eye than even by itself. This "outward portal," this "common thoroughfare" to the "house within," —to the mind and affections, was a fair introduction to what might be opined of the man; and in no instance, after first acquaintance, did he blight expectation.

Great exertions were making, at this time, by the Baptists, and the agents of the London Missionary Society, on the behalf of the heathen. The Rev. Andrew Fuller,—a man of masculine mind, and originality of thought, preached in the chapel occupied by the Rev. E. Parsons of Leeds, and made a collection in aid of the Baptist Missions. Mr. Dawson heard him, and was much delighted, not only with his matter and unassuming manner, but with the sweet racy feeling that accompanied the word spoken. After Mr. Fuller had elucidated his subject, and expatiated on the great good that had been effected abroad by Dr. Cary and others, he asked, in his energetic way,—"Where will it end?" "In heaven," responded Mr. Dawson, in a tone sufficiently loud to be heard, with his face beaming with pleasurable emotion. This was not the ebullition of that enthusiasm, which, in religion, operates like alchymy in philosophy, but of steady, fervid zeal,— answering to the touch of the preacher, who had bound him, as by a spell, to the all-absorbing subject,—the *conversion* of a WORLD. Ardent zeal was a vein which nature herself had strongly marked on the temper of his mind; and when religion came to its aid, he pursued each divine object, as all inamoratos are admitted to do, whether in art, science, or what else,—with his whole soul. He adverted afterwards, with delighted feeling, to the biographer, to the influence which the subject had upon his mind.

This was an excellent preparation for the first public Missionary Meeting among the Wesleyans, which was held soon after, in the Old Chapel, Leeds. Mr. Wesley had furnished the example in modern times, of weekly, monthly, and quarterly contributions, for the purpose of extending the religion of Christ in the world, and supporting Christian ministers in the work. The excellence of the precedent belongs to St. Paul, who says, " Upon the first day of the week, let every one of you lay by him in store, as God hath prospered him." The weekly contributions of the primitive Church had the benefit of "the saints" for their object; Mr. Wesley's were originally intended to liquidate the general debt at Bristol. The measure was ridiculed for many years; and the preachers were reviled as "roving mendicants," as " men without a local habitation or a name;" and the peculiar mode by which the cause of God was supported among the Wesleyans, insidiously styled " a paltry and unlikely scheme for procuring eleemosynary subscriptions." But in process of time, the views and feelings of a large proportion of the community were changed; for many of the very persons that had previously treated the Wesleyans with such scurrility, began "to perceive such utility in the labours of Itinerants, as to induce them not only so to employ unordained novitiates, around the places of their education, but to recommend, as opportunity might serve, such a practice to fixed pastors." The Wesleyan method, also, of raising money, so much despised before, had, by this period, received the sanction of several of the bishops and nobility of the land, and was resorted to by almost every denomination of Christians,—a decisive proof of the favourable change in public opinion. Bible, Missionary, and Tract Associations, had brought by such means, a vast accession of pecuniary strength to their respective parent establishments. As the plan, in modern times, was purely Wesleyan, and had never been adopted by the Societies as a source of supply to the missionary fund,—as other Christian communities were acting on the example, and opportunities of evangelizing the heathen were on the increase,—and more especially as the missionary cause was losing the personal exertions of Dr. Coke,—it was deemed advisable to convene public meetings, and form associations, for the purpose of raising money to extend the missionary work. Mr. Scarth of Leeds, had repeatedly remarked to Mr. Dawson, before Dr. Coke took his departure for India,—"The missionary cause must be taken out of the Doctor's hands ; it must be made *a public—a common cause.*" This, in Mr. Dawson's view, as expressed to the biographer, was the *germ* of the whole. The Leeds preachers, on taking up the subject, visited the preachers at Bramley, with a view to consult further on the subject ; and all agreed in the propriety, necessity, and practicability of the measure. The fine feelings and gigantic powers of the late Rev. Richard Watson, were instantly brought to bear upon the subject, on being applied to by the Leeds brethren ; and having enlisted him in the cause for which he was so admirably fitted, and which brought him out with redoubled splendour before the public, success, under God, seemed at once ensured. Accordingly, after due deliberation and preparation, with other lay and ministerial accessions, a public meeting was appointed to be held, October 6th, 1813, in the Methodist Old Chapel, Leeds, at two o'clock in the afternoon. *

The occasion was deeply interesting, and fraught with the most important results to mankind. Thomas Thompson, Esq., M.P., after singing and prayer, was called to preside, and opened the proceedings of the meeting. After a speech of some length, distinguished for good sense, and a general attention to missionary operations, he concluded his remarks by observing,— "I will only beg leave, before any other proceeding take place, to request that you will not signify your approbation of the speeches which you may hear from my honoured brethren, by modes of applauding, like those which are practised in theatres, and other places of public amusement. The consideration of the sacred purpose for which we are assembled, will banish from our conduct every expression of our feelings which borders on levity. Whatever may have been the practice of other Christians, on similar occasions, let it be our care that 'all things are done decently and in order.'"

One of the preachers, in social mood, said to Mr. Dawson, previously to the meeting,—"You must take a resolution." All was new ; it was like going an apprenticeship to a new profession. "Me take a resolution!"

* "A Report of the Principal Speeches" delivered on the occasion, was published by James Nichols ; and the Resolutions moved, were published in the Methodist Magazine for 1813, p. 950, under the head of "Religious Intelligence."

he returned; "I know not what to do with it; I shall
be blundering over it, like one of our senators, who had
to take the sacrament, to qualify him for his seat."
This reply, as it was in the freedom of conversation,
excited a little curiosity. "How was that?" It was
replied,—"He was an irreligious man; and being as
ignorant of religion, as he was personally indifferent to
it, he went to church—supposing his appearance within
its walls sufficient—when a female was returning thanks,
and was thus *churched* with her;" repeating, "I shall
be sure to blunder." The disposition to something
like jocularity, was a sufficient intimation that he had
no grave objection to engage in the services of the
occasion. Accordingly, the seventh resolution was
committed to his care, which he moved, and spoke
with great effect. Having caught the fire from the
preceding speakers, he commenced,—

"MR. CHAIRMAN,—I rise with pleasure before you
and this congregation, because I believe that the
grand object of our meeting is under the distinguished
smile of Jehovah. You know, Sir, that the intention
of our assembling here to-day, is, to propose, adopt,
and prosecute the best plans of spreading 'pure and
undefiled religion' to the utmost extent of our abilities.
Noble designs!—Methinks the happiness of surrounding angels is augmented, when they behold
these projects, and the spirit with which we enter
into them. They anticipate the season when these
plans will be executed, when they will have new
melodies to raise over penitent sinners returning to
God.—In my humble opinion, Sir, in what we are now
contemplating, there are two weighty considerations,
which deserve our particular attention. One is,—

That a missionary ministry of the Gospel is under the peculiar approbation of God, and is, in his hand, the grand mean of enlightening a benighted world ; the other—That of all people, the Methodists should be the first to encourage missionary efforts." These positions he established ; took a glance at the divine mission of Jesus Christ to the world—the commission he gave to his disciples, and the energy with which they acted in carrying it into execution—the spirit which was roused at the time of the Reformation—and the efforts to diffuse evangelical truth at subsequent periods.

On the other proposition, viz.—" That of all others, the Methodists should be the first to encourage missionary efforts," he remarked, that, "the reasons for it appeared in the DOCTRINES which they believed, and the PRIVILEGES which they enjoyed." He proceeded, linking himself to all the interests of the body,—

"The doctrines which we believe, bind this duty upon us in an especial manner. You know, Sir, we believe that in the Gospel is provided a full, free, and present salvation from all the moral evils consequent on the fall of Adam. We believe that this salvation is of infinite importance, as being a complete deliverance from infinite evils, and a personal possession of infinite benefits. We believe that wherever the Gospel is faithfully preached, this salvation is within the reach of all. We believe that, as its duties are imposed upon all, its benefits are offered to all. We believe that when ministers preach the Gospel fully, they preach ' Christ in us, the hope of glory, warning every man, and teaching every man in all wisdom,

that they may present every man perfect in Christ
Jesus.' Now these are some of the doctrines which
we believe; and if we act consistently with our principles, we shall not be the least nor the hindmost in
missionary efforts. How highly proper it is that our
conduct should illustrate and harmonize with our creed;
and that we should shew our faith by our works!

"But, Sir, the privileges which we enjoy bring on us
an additional and powerful obligation why we should
be the first in promoting this good work. Is a
missionary ministry of the Gospel under the peculiar
approbation of God? Our regular ministry is truly
of the missionary kind.—Do missionaries make great
sacrifices? So do our ministers.—Do they sacrifice
the pleasures of social enjoyments? Do they leave
father, and mother, and brethren, and sisters, to promote the salvation of souls? So do ours.—Do they
sacrifice all prospects of accumulating wealth? So do
ours.—Do they sacrifice a state and spirit of independence, and enter upon an humble and dependent life?
So do ours. 'Foxes have holes, and the birds of
the air have nests,' to which they claim an exclusive
right, but our ministers have not a place of their own,
where they can lay their heads. We lend them houses;
—we lend them furniture;—and we lend them those
things only for two years, and then they must remove again to another station, and preach the Gospel
to other persons.—Do missionaries many times sacrifice
the sweets of Christian friendship? So do ours. When
a preacher has just got acquainted with some kindred
souls in his circuit, and has begun to repose his
confidence in them, and to taste the delicious gratifica-
tions of their friendship, his two years are expired,

and he is torn away, and sent to some distant part of the country, and perhaps never sees the faces of his friends again, until he meets them in heaven.— Do missionaries engage in arduous duties? So do ours. Almost every night in the week, and generally three times on Sundays, are they engaged in the honourable, but arduous duty of preaching the Gospel ; besides their additional labour in the quarterly examination of the societies.

"In proceeding, Sir, upon this interesting subject, I may, perhaps, wound the generous feelings of my honoured fathers and beloved brethren in the ministry, who are now before me ; but permit me at this time to give vent to my own pleasures, though it be at the expense of theirs. I therefore venture to ask,—Is a missionary ministry under the peculiar approbation of God? With humble gratitude I would answer—So is ours. The best of all is, GOD IS WITH THEM. Stand in the centre of Great Britain, and ask concerning our ministers, 'Have they laboured, or do they labour in vain?' Thousands upon thousands would immediately answer, No. Fly over to the West Indies and ask, 'Have they laboured, or do they labour in vain?' And 15,000 voices answer, No. Stand upon the vast continent of America, and ask once more, 'Have they laboured, or do they labour in vain?' Upwards of 200,000 voices answer, No. But let us concentrate our views and enquiries ; I now look round upon this congregation ; and though we are in the presence of so many of our dear fathers and brethren in the ministry,* I ask you, 'Have

* A considerable number of preachers sat directly before Mr. Dawson, to whom he directed the eyes of the congregation while he was asking this question.

they laboured, or do they labour in vain?' (Here, hundreds of voices interrupted the speaker, and spontaneously spared him the trouble of repeating his negation, by emphatically answering,—'No.')

"I thank you, my friends.—Then, Sir, may I not be permitted to ask—Shall we monopolize the benefits of such a ministry? By the instrumentality of these men, we have received our spiritual eye-sight; and have we received it for no other purpose than to see our poor fellow-creatures going blindfolded to ruin? Is it possible that we can behold such a spectacle, without attempting to relieve them, by sending them the same means by which we got our eyes opened? Surely not. By these men we were directed to the Lord Jesus Christ for salvation, and he has broken our bonds, and snapped our fetters in sunder, and we walk at liberty. And shall we view the poor heathens not only blindfolded, but 'tied and bound with the chain of their sins,' and the grand Deceiver leading them across the stage of life to the 'lake burning with fire and brimstone,' and not strain every nerve to send them ministers to 'proclaim liberty to the captive;' and, under God, to 'turn them from darkness to light, and from the power of Satan unto God?' It cannot be that we can look upon this heart-rending and melancholy scene unmoved!

"Under the ministry of these men, we enjoy 'feasts of fat things, of wines on the lees well refined;' and shall we see our poor heathen brethren famishing with hunger, and not send them one dish of the dainties of the Gospel? It cannot be! Especially, Sir, when we consider that we have a number of young men truly converted, and deeply devoted to

God, who would gladly imitate the angel in the Revelation, and fly through the earth, and 'preach the everlasting Gospel to every nation, and kindred, and tongue, and people.' But they want wings. And shall we deny them pinions, when it is in our power to furnish them with such useful appendages? Surely not! To-day we are met to devise the measures best adapted for attaining this important object; and I trust we shall not meet in vain. If we possess any proper sympathy for our fellow-creatures,—if we feel any powerful sense of our superior obligations to God, we shall neither be the last nor the least in missionary efforts."

Including thanks to the chairman, there were *nineteen* resolutions in all, each with its *mover* and *seconder*. Of the travelling preachers, who had resolutions assigned them, to move or second, only *eight* were *living* in 1841; and of the laymen, about an equal number. The first committee too, of which Mr. Dawson was a member, exhibited the same affecting waste by the ravages of death. Out of *twenty-six* travelling preachers, whose names were upon it, belonging to the Leeds district, only *eleven* were living; and of *forty-eight* laymen, only about *fifteen*. Eternity alone will disclose the full importance of that meeting to the interests of religion in the world. Independent of its influence on other sections of the Christian church, its direct influence on the Wesleyan body has been highly beneficial, in extending the knowledge of the people, in opening up new sources of benevolence, in deepening, elevating, and expanding the piety of the heart, and in employing a number of active agents in the general work of well-doing, who might otherwise have lived in comparative seclusion and ease. *

Than on this occasion, the biographer rarely ever saw Mr. Dawson to greater advantage; not so much for the extraordinary character of his materials, as for the deep tone of piety which he displayed, the sunshine he threw over the meeting,—the spirit which he enkindled in the breasts of those around—the tact which he displayed—and the ease with which he fell into, what afterwards constituted the work of the platform. A missionary spirit was soon excited through the whole Wesleyan Connexion, and invitations poured in upon him thenceforward, not only from newly-instituted societies, but societies as they grew old, some of whose annual meetings he attended for a

* In 1785, the Wesleyans had only three foreign stations—Nova-Scotia, Newfoundland, and Antigua,—5 Missionaries,—and 1408 members on those stations.

In 1813—embracing a period of 28 years, when the Missionary Meetings commenced, they had only 4 Districts in the foreign field, including 22 circuits, upon which were 22 Missionaries, comprising—exclusive of France, Gibraltar, and Ireland, 16,838 members. Seven additional Missionaries were *appointed* at the Conference of 1813, for Asia and South Africa, but had not reached their several destinations. The principal Mission Stations at that period were Sierra-Leone, Nova-Scotia, Newfoundland, and the West Indies.

In 1841—a second period of 28 years, the following " Recapitulation " of a " Summary View," was published as a " Postscript " to the January " Missionary Notices : " " The Society occupies,

Principal Stations, about 256 ;

Missionaries, about 380 ;

Catechists and Salaried Schoolmasters, &c., 322 ;

Assistants and Teachers, not salaried, upwards of 5,600 ;

Printing Establishments, 7 ;

Members or Communicants, 78,504 ;

Attendants on the Ministry, more than 200,000;

In the Schools, Adults and Children, 55,078 ;

Upwards of 20 languages, used by the Missionaries ; into several of which the translation of the Scriptures, and of other useful and instructive books, is in progress.

The Annual Income of the Society amounting to between NINETY and ONE HUNDRED THOUSAND POUNDS! So much for *Missionary Meetings : !*

succession of years. From this period, he advanced in popularity and usefulness, beyond all precedent among his brethren. It was not that kind of reputation which depends upon mere accident, as when the mass of the people are guided by the opinions of their superiors; the few, in such cases, being the keepers of the elevation of others, upon whom the trumpet of applause is bound to attend, and give forth its notes, on a solitary display of talent, or an extra act of benevolence: it was that which arose from his native genius and ardent desire to promote the public good,— sacrificing personal ease, profit, and all private considerations, to promote the grand object. Without this—the public good as a motive, a man is at best but an "inglorious neuter to mankind."

Notwithstanding the chairman's caution to the auditory, self-restraint, seemed next to impossible. Such assemblies are, to a certain extent, in the keeping of the speakers; and to the speakers, rather than the hearers, such cautions should be administered. His style and manner, from the effects produced by them, and which in himself were generally admissible, led the way to certain imitations, and produced a lighter spirit occasionally than what comported with the object of the meetings, and which, so far as others were concerned, it was found necessary to tone down and to check. The evil became the greater, from the circumstance of the imitators being destitute of the weight which he otherwise possessed, and which invariably counterbalanced the flights of fancy in which he was sometimes pleased to indulge.

What was rather extraordinary, on the present occasion, the chairman himself, who was a man of almost

M

stern gravity, was, if not carried away with the excitement, overpowered by the deeper feeling. He had not seen Mr. Dawson before, and remarked to a friend afterwards, that he was frequently drawn to observe him, while the speakers that preceded him were addressing the meeting, and was deeply impressed with his appearance, as being something more than an ordinary character, and especially with the expressions of his face, which every now and then manifested the strongest internal emotions. But when he began to speak, the chairman was apparently under as strong emotions as himself, and towards the close, wept under the affecting appeals which were made to himself and to the assembly.

CHAPTER X.

*Conscience,—a singular Incident.—Tenderness in Preaching.—
The Shepherd personified.—Indirect self-praise.—Revivalists.—
Mistakes in Conversion corrected.—Early Gift in Prayer among
young Converts.—Establishment of Missionary Societies at
York and Wakefield.—Extracts from Speeches.—Mr. Edward
Wade's death.—Selby Missionary Meeting.—Timidity.—Char-
acteristic Remarks.—Conversational Meetings among the Local-
Preachers.—A spiritual Ministry.—Deputation from a distance.
—Death of the Princess Charlotte.—Visit to the North.—A
Dream.—Quarrels from trifling causes. — Fault-finders.—
Prejudice.—Chester and Liverpool meetings.—Dr. Adam Clarke.
—Propriety of bringing acquired knowledge to bear on the
cause of Truth.—Death of the Rev. William Bramwell.—The
Backslider.—Tract Distribution.—Addresses to Children.—
Objections.—The Eternal Sonship.—Authors.*

His ministry, if possible, became more energetic
than heretofore, and was increasingly effective in the
conversion of sinners. Among many other extraordinary effects produced, as to the conviction it carried
to the conscience, one may be here adduced. He was
preaching in the neighbourhood of Leeds, on Daniel v.
27,—"Thou art weighed in the balances, and art found
wanting." A person who travelled the country in the
character of a pedlar, and who was exceedingly partial
to him as a preacher, was one of Mr. Dawson's auditors.

The person referred to, generally carried a stick with him, which answered the double purpose of a walking-stick and a " yard-wand ; " and having been employed pretty freely in the former capacity, it was worn down beyond the point of justice, and procured for him the appellation of "Short Measure." He stood before Mr. Dawson, and being rather noisy in his religious professions, as well as ready with his responses, he manifested signs of approbation, while the scales were being described and adjusted, and different classes of sinners were placed in them, and disposed of agreeably to the test of justice, truth, and mercy,—uttering in a somewhat subdued tone, yet loud enough for those around to hear, at the close of each particular,—" Light weight "—" short again," &c. After taking up the separate characters of the flagrant transgressor of the law of God, the hypocrite, the formalist, &c., Mr. Dawson at length came to such persons as possessed religious light, but little hallowed feeling, and the semblance of much zeal, but who employed false weights and measures. Here, without having adverted in his mind to the case of his noisy auditor, he perceived the muscles of his face working, when the report of "short measure" occurred to him. Resolved, however, to soften no previous expression, and to proceed with an analysis and description of the character in question, he placed the delinquent, in his singularly striking way, in the scale, when instead of the usual response —the man, stricken before him, took his stick—the favourite measure, from under his arm,—raised one foot from the floor,—doubled his knee,—and, taking hold of the offending instrument by both ends, snapped it into two halves, exclaiming, while dashing it to the ground, "Thou shalt do it no more." So true is it,—to employ the language of an eminent minister,—that "no man ever offended his own conscience, but first or last it was revenged upon him for it." Conscience is an equitable and ready judge, when permitted to speak out, and tells a man that he cannot injure another, without receiving the counterstroke,—that he must necessarily wound himself in wronging another. Let conscience be waited upon in all transactions between man and man, and like the fingers of a steady time-piece, it will generally be found to point to the golden rule of equity ; but let it once be tampered with,* and it will soon become "seared as with a hot iron,"—robbed of the integrity in which it was created, nor will it possess light enough to enable him to select the path which leads to heaven.

When the subject led to it, Mr. Dawson, as has been seen, could be as tender, as on other occasions, he was rousing and severe. At the opening of Wortley chapel, near Leeds, he took for his text, Isai. xl. 9—11. He told his hearers, that the text was like a well-toned organ—full, varied, powerful, sweet ; but that it required some one to touch the keys with skill ; and yet, he added,—"a skilful hand, without the breath of heaven will avail nothing." However he himself, he observed, might attempt to handle the instrument, all

* Without entering into the niceties of theological controversy in defence of this sentiment to which a critic has objected, the biographer would refer the objector to Rom. ii. 14, 15, where he will find St Paul maintaining a similar position, and asserting that conscience, although depraved, still sustains the character of a witness and a judge ; "their conscience also bearing witness and their thoughts the meanwhile accusing, or else, excusing one another," which, agreeably to the same apostle, will be the case, till in consequence of tampering and trifling with its monitions, it becomes " seared as with a hot iron." (1 Tim. iv. 2.)

would be in vain, unless the breath of God, "the inspiration of the Almighty," filled the pipes. He believed,
at the same time, that a person like himself, engaged
in agricultural pursuits, and of pastoral habits, could
enter more readily into the meaning of some parts of
the text, than many of his hearers, who had to attend
to the loom, and seldom stirred abroad.   He then
adverted to the eleventh verse,—"He shall feed his
flock like a shepherd ; he shall gather the lambs with
his arm, and carry them in his bosom ; " and depicted,
in fine style, from personal experience, the shepherd
going out into the fields hours after the day had closed,
or hours before day-break, in the cold month of February or March, to visit his flock. The hearers were
then transported in imagination into the rural districts ;
—the heavens, in addition to the darkness of the hour,
sometimes overshadowed with clouds, with a strong
cold vapour floating in the atmosphere,—and at other
times, the stars sparkling in the midst of the dark blue
overhead, with the ground either covered with snow,
hardened by the frost, or slightly crisped under the
feet, with a sharp searching wind.   Under these circumstances, the shepherd was beheld by the "mind's
eye," like a stalking shadow in the midst of the gloom,
—now pausing,—now listening,—pausing and listening
again,—once and again deceived by fancied sounds,—
then hearing the palpitation of his own heart ; proceeding, and halting, and listening, and looking, till a small
white speck appeared a few paces before him.   It was
readily conjectured to be a lamb, only a few hours old,
and nearly frozen to death. The shepherd, moved with
tenderness, as much as by interest, was again represented as stooping down, taking it up,—putting it in

his bosom beneath his upper garment,—carrying it home,—placing it before the fire,—looking upon it with anxious solicitude,—his eye glistening with joy on seeing it stir its limbs,—still more on it raising its head, —and finally transported to behold it, though staggering, upon its feet,—and to hear it bleat. Just at the moment the *bleating* of the lamb seemed to die upon the ear of the congregation, the poor penitent was exhibited, as followed by the mercy of God,—Jesus, the "Great Shepherd of the sheep," pursuing him,— going into the wilderness,—laying hold of him by his Spirit,—bringing him to the fold,—fostering, animating him,—and at length delighted with the voice of prayer,—"bleating in the ear of heaven,—'Mercy,— mercy,—mercy!'"—feeble at first, then waxing stronger and stronger. Here, owing to the manner of working up the subject—imitating, as far as was compatible with the sanctity of the place, the first feeble cries of the returning sinner, which were instantly associated with the first bleatings of the lamb, the subject was overwhelming, and encouraging beyond expression, to seekers of salvation. The Shepherd's ear was represented as ever open to their cry, and his heart as beating with compassion towards them—having a deep interest, at the same time, in the purchase of his own blood.

Though numbers received a sense of sin forgiven under his ministry, he was not in the habit of trumpeting his success from society to society, and from one social party to another, in order to keep up a fever of feeling in his favour, and to attract attention to himself as the principal actor,—saying, in effect,—"Look at me, talk of me, think of me, follow me." Pride is always

the herald of its own fame ; and this is its vice, that it
paints its own virtues and success, and counts its own
numbers, as though no one received good except when
the trumpeter himself was there.   He was no monopolist,
but distributed the success among the different labourers
in the vineyard, and shewed that men might have popular
tact, without much talent.   Listening, one day, to two
or three revivalists, so called,—men of warm hearts,
little thought, and less reading, who were stating that
"so many souls were born of God, in certain meetings
while *they* were present," he observed with considerable
point and emphasis, and perhaps a slight degree of
impatience to administer correction,—"You, and your
friends, talk of such a number being born of God in
your meetings, and you number them as David numbered the people.   No such thing ; they were begotten
of the word, to employ the language of the apostle, by
the ministry of others,—were convinced, and had become penitents.   You are not the men,—your ministry
is not of that cast, to beget souls by the preaching of
the Gospel : I can compare you to nothing but so many
old midwives, calculated to help persons already born
into a little more liberty.   Yours is a very humble
department indeed, and you have but little in which to
glory.   Do not make so much noise ; and never boast of
souls being born under you, that were prepared by
others.   You only entered upon other men's labours ;
and they would have remained unborn for you."   He
found that the case admitted of strong language ; that
the labours of others were not duly appreciated ; and was
anxious that the work of God should speak for itself, in
the *life* of each reformed character, and in the *temper*
of each converted heart ; being persuaded that less

mistake would arise from the *realities* of the one, than the *reports* of the other.

In conformity with these sentiments, a case may be stated, showing his settled views on the subject. Two young men were brought to God in his own neighbourhood, who, the Sabbath after they received liberty, attended a prayer-meeting in a neighbouring village, where they prayed with fluency in public. This was noised abroad as a wonder. Just about the same period, Mr. Dawson, in company with a relative, proceeded to an inn in the vicinity, to meet one of the regular coaches. On entering one of the rooms, to wait the arrival of the coach, they found some persons seated, with whom the conversion of the young men was the subject of marvel, and had been the topic of conversation. Mr. Dawson listened; and being known to some of the party, the discourse was at length directed to him, with a view to elicit an opinion. "God," he observed, "has no still-born children." "True," it was replied, by some one who knew something more of religion than he practised; "but you must admit that conversion, in the case of these persons, was quick work." Mr. Dawson returned;—"It may have been quick in its *crisis*, but slow in its *progress*." Then turning upon the spokesman, and through him upon the others, of whom he had some knowledge, he proceeded,—"Some of you have attended religious meetings for years; you have had convictions, but have refused to yield. Here we find the work *begun*. You have long struggled against God, and I hope the process of conviction will go on. You know what is wrong, and can talk about what is right; the work may be *sudden* at last, and I care not how soon. But how do

M 2

you know what may have been the light, the thoughts, the feelings of these young men? It may be that God had been at work with them for a series of years, and that *now* they may only have yielded to former convictions." While this placed the subject before them in a new light, it served Mr. Dawson's purpose of reaching the conscience. There is another key to the subject, besides that given by Mr. Dawson. " I will pour upon the house of Israel," says the Lord, "and upon the inhabitants of Jerusalem, the spirit of grace and supplication." The Holy Spirit not only animates the affections in prayer, but imparts to the mind something of the *inventive*, both as to thought and expression. " Likewise the Spirit also helpeth our infirmities ; for we know not what we should pray for as we ought : but the Spirit itself maketh intercession for us with groanings that cannot be uttered." Here is both the unutterable groan, and the fluent speech—a *help* to *infirmity ;* and that aid must be effectual, as it is divine in its character. With such a *helper* as the HOLY GHOST, we scarcely need be astonished at the power, the ease, the fluency, and, in some instances, the correctness, with which some new converts, together with poor, uneducated, plain-minded men, pour out their souls in prayer before God. Nor can the gift, in many instances, be accounted for on any other principle than that of the Spirit's influence upon the mind.

Among the numerous missionary meetings in the establishment of which he assisted, those of Wakefield and York may be named; the former, Feb. 7th, and the latter, Mar. 24th, 1814. At Wakefield he shewed, in a speech of great originality and vigour, that the tolerant spirit of the British Government, the peaceable and loyal state of the lower classes of the community, and the commanding attitude of Britain among the nations of the earth, were strong reasons for attempting the conversion of the heathen. He humorously personified the Conventicle Act, as a monster that had made dreadful havoc in former times among good men, but which was afterwards chained by the Toleration Act, and finally put to death by a recent law of the legislature, securing the religious liberties of the country. He then argued, that if Christians enjoyed so much quiet at home, they ought to do much to promote the kingdom of Christ abroad. The "Age of Reason," too, he observed, had passed away, and with it infidelity, blasphemy, insubordination, and civil inquietude. This called for gratitude; and he thought the friends could not shew it better, than by spreading that religion to whose influence they owed so happy a state of society. That great man Mr. Pitt, he remarked, died sighing, "*O my country!*" We too, he intimated, in glancing at the state of affairs, might say, "*O my country!*" but it was with the transport of a fond mother, who clasps her child in her arms, just rescued from danger, and exclaims, "*O my child!*" The effect produced at this moment, is well recollected by the biographer, who was seated near him at the time. He proceeded,—"If God has done so much for our political interests, it is not to inflate our pride, but that he may employ our influence, our example, and our means, in diffusing his truth through the world. Let us, then, send Bibles and Missionaries in every direction. Our ships which carry them, will be like the lights of heaven in their courses. As they make their revolutions round the world, they will reflect the glory of the Sun of Righteousness upon every land they approach."

At York he was much more argumentative : but without attempting to follow him in all his reasonings and details, he observed, that the subject of Christian Missions would bear the closest examination, and that nothing would be lost by the investigation. He then adverted to the state of the heathen world in point of morals ; and shewed that, circumstanced as they were, they had no means of improvement among themselves. He further observed, that the preaching of the gospel was the grand instrument to be employed in the work of evangelizing the world, but regretted to find persons disposed to rob that Gospel of its vital principles, by setting up mere morality as a substitute. "The various miseries of human life," he remarked, "have claims upon us, but they are not superior to those of Christian Missions. Hospitals, almshouses, and public charities, with which York abounds, have claims upon its inhabitants, but their claims are not superior to those of Missions. The Bereans had the Scriptures ; but it was necessary, notwithstanding, that Paul and Silas should go and preach the Gospel to them. In the Bible Society, we see the blushing of an opening dawn ; in the Missionary Society, we see the brightening beams of a glorious sun, portending a glorious day." He concluded, by stating, that York stood one of the first on the list of the Bible Society, and he hoped it would not be the last in missionary exertions.

July the 7th, the day appointed for Thanksgiving for Peace, he preached in Barwick chapel on Psalm cxvii. and lxviii. 5, 6, 7 ; and August 14th, he preached a funeral sermon at Huntington, near York, on occasion of the death of his old friend, Mr. Edward Wade, formerly of Sturton Grange, on Job xix. 25—27. Mr. Wade married, as his second wife, Mrs. Gibson, a relative of the Rev. Walter Sellon, and a lineal descendant of the celebrated John Wickliffe—"the morning star of the Reformation." Mrs. Gibson's son, which she had to her first husband, Walter Sellon Gibson, was brought to God under the ministry of Mr. Dawson, when a boy, at Sturton Grange. After preaching the funeral sermon in a field near the village, Mr. Dawson returned to the city, and preached in New-street chapel to a crowded and deeply affected congregation.

November 16, the biographer had the pleasure of another interview with him, at the formation of the Selby missionary meeting. It was at this meeting the "Village Blacksmith" made his *debut* on the platform. The venerable Walter Griffith was in the chair; and for high wrought feeling, the writer rarely ever witnessed anything equal to it. Materials for speeches were then scarce; and a preceding speaker having occupied the ground, which the biographer intended taking, he found it more difficult to strike out a new track on the platform than in the pulpit. "Friend E——," said Mr. Wild, of Armley, jocularly, on returning home, "take care, when you go to a missionary meeting again, to provide yourself with a double-barrelled gun; if the one does not go off, the other *may*." Mr. Dawson amused himself with this afterwards, when adverting to missionary beginnings.

He himself, however, was not always at home. A person of intellect, having heard of his popularity, observed one day, that he was going to hear him preach, and that he would measure the extent of the mind of his hearers by the sermon he preached. Mr. Dawson heard of this, and having to preach a missionary sermon at D——, was not a little embarrassed in finding the same gentleman putting on a stern front, and seated in a conspicuous part of the chapel. " I felt," said he, " on seeing him, the barometer of my feelings going fast down to rain; but still more so," he continued, "when I saw a platform full of preachers, and a chapel full of emptiness : then, the barometer was fixed for rain." There were several prejudices to surmount, in solitary places, against public meetings. On other than missionary occasions, however, he invariably drew, in the same place, immense congregations. Since then, the missionary cause has flourished in the town and neighbourhood.

In his own remarks on ministers, he was more *characteristic* than *severe ;* and he generally found his way to the leading features of a person's manner. " Such a one," said he, " is like a tailor's goose, *hot* and *heavy*." This was not in the spirit of fault-finding ; for no one could entertain a higher opinion of the fine expansive mind of the preacher, the delightful feeling which pervaded his discourses, and his genuine piety, than himself. The remark was solely applied to manner. Of another, he observed, " when I first heard him preach, he was like the gentle dew to me ; then came the mizzling rain,—next a little more rapid ;—after that, a heavy shower for an hour together ;—at the close of this, the clouds began to collect and darken ;—then succeeded the lightning, when the thunder rolled, and the whole assembly seemed moved." Speaking of the late Rev. Richard Watson one day, and comparing him with another eminent minister, he observed, Mr.—— always reminds me, in his preaching, of a person who writes a beautiful running hand,—neat,—easy—every letter properly formed, with its elegant body and hair stroke —and every word in its proper place. Mr. Watson can write equally as good a hand as he; but then, (imitating the penman by the motion of the hand the while), he throws in the additional *flourishes*, and these, gracefully curving and sweeping around the letters, add to the beauty of the penmanship, and attract greater attention." This comparison embraced the peculiarities of the two men,—Mr. Watson, who combined beauty and genius with judgment; and the other, who had taste and judgment, but was without imagination. Addressing another minister—a strong minded man, and one with whom he was on familiar terms,—" You," said he, " are one of the best taker's of a likeness I ever met with. In drawing the character of a sinner, you do it to the life : but on holding the likeness up to the man, you invariably get him to laugh at himself. " The person referred to has been gathered to his fathers many years; but it was one of those defects to which his ministry was subject, though otherwise distinguished for numerous excellences. "The taste of the public for reading," said he, " in the present day, is like that of sheep put into a new pasture :—no matter how rich and good the grass may be ;—they will run and nibble a bit here—a second bit there—a third elsewhere,—never resting till they have gone round the whole—then, at last, they settle quietly down to one spot, and feed." To a person who sustained the character of a "snarling critic," and who was hazarding some remarks in Mr. Dawson's presence, the latter looked at him, and said, "I passed some geese on Friday evening, on the way to my class, when the old gander stretched out his neck, and hissed at me: you are just like him; for you can do nothing but *hiss*." "Daniel Isaac," said he, in reference to his severity in controversy, "could bite through a nail." "Three things," he observed on another occasion, "distinguished the character of John Wesley,—openness to conviction,—deadness to the world —and attention to the openings of Providence."

A meeting was established by the local-preachers of the Leeds circuit, for "Familiar Conversation." Connected with this was a sermon; and Mr. Dawson being selected to preach on the occasion, delivered a discourse, May 15th, 1815, in the Old Chapel, to a crowded auditory on—"It is the Spirit that quickeneth; the flesh profiteth nothing," John vi. 63. This was just the subject, and the occasion for which he was peculiarly fitted. No man was more anxious to preserve a *living* ministry than himself; and few understood better in what it consisted. There is the same difference between the *spirit* and the *letter*—a *living* and a *dead* ministry, that there is between the execution of a drawn sword in the hand of a person skilled in its use, and one thrown off on canvass by the hand of an artist,—the latter producing as little effect as the sword in the image of George and the Dragon. The word preached without the Spirit, is like the pool of Bethesda without the angel,—the water possessing no virtue till troubled. The letter killeth; it is the Spirit that quickeneth; by which *letter*, is not understood, as Origin would interpret it, the *literal* meaning of the sacred text, and by the *spirit*, the *allegorical* ; nor yet, as some Antinomians would expound it, the former referring to the Old Testament, and the latter to the New ; but the mighty energy of Almighty God, accompanying the word preached, as in the ministry of Peter, when, with the swiftness of lightning, its unconquerable edge penetrated the hearts of three thousand sinners, under one sermon. The word, taken alone, may tickle the ear, and please the fancy ; but without the Spirit, it is like a shell without a kernel, a tree without fruit, a well without water, a body without a soul ; and will lie as harmless on the shelf, and be as passive in the hand of the bookseller as any unheeded volume penned by the Apostolical Fathers. In support of this, on casting the eye around the Christian world, congregations and ministers may be beheld, who have been fixtures from ten to twenty, thirty, forty years, presenting neither diminution nor increase, except by natural births and deaths—without the conversion of a single soul to God, or the exhibition of a solitary reformed rake,—the blind leading the blind, and both falling into the ditch together. Than this—a sapless ministry, and a heartless congregation, there cannot be a heavier curse inflicted upon a town or neighbourhood,—both resembling an old decayed tree—hollow at the heart,—without even the leaf of profession,—with the axe of the woodman laid at the root, and ready to cut it down as a cumberer of the ground ! How different the ministry of the prophets and apostles, before whom even kings turned pale and trembled ! How different the ministry of the Reformers, of the Wesleys, Whitfield, Romaine,

Newton, Venn, Grimshaw, Rowland Hill, and others !
How different the ministry of old Mr. Berridge, with
all his wit and eccentricities, who was visited by a
thousand awakened persons in the course of one year,
and under whose joint ministry, with that of Mr.
Hicks, four thousand persons were converted to God
in the course of the same given period.

These remarks are made, because Mr. Dawson delighted to advert to the successful labours of such men,
and because of the fruitfulness of his own ministry.
The word of God in his mouth was accompanied by
the quickening Spirit. He drew from the Bible, as
from a grand arsenal, the materials that formed the
thunder, which he wielded over unrepenting sinners ;
but he knew, to pursue the metaphor—and therefore making it a subject of earnest prayer, that it
was only the lightning flash of the Spirit that could
wither, blast, and destroy the "man of sin" in the
human soul. He rarely preached, but the occasion
was adverted to either in social converse, in the classes,
or in the love-feasts, as beneficial to either saint or
sinner, or both ; and what ought not to be omitted
in his case—shewing the kind of material in which
he dealt, the conviction produced by his ministry was
deep and lasting. It was not a mere flush of feeling
—a tear—a noise—a gathering—and then a dearth
for others to bewail after he was gone. The per-
manency of the work shewed that GOD was in it—
not *man*.

Instead of his labours being confined to his own,
and the neighbouring circuits and districts, his calls
for special service now extended to the neighbouring
counties. The friends in one of the principal towns

in the kingdom, being about this time disappointed of some of their leading men on a missionary occasion, Mr. Dawson was proposed by a member of the committee, to supply the lack in the emergency. But though fame ran high, yet as he had never visited the place—as only one or two of the less influential members had heard him—as great expectations were raised, and they were not to be realized by the brethren who had been solicited, it was agreed, instead of a letter—for no time was to be lost, that a deputation should be sent forthwith to Leeds and Barnbow. On the arrival of the gentlemen at Leeds, they tried what additional help could be obtained there; but were unable to secure any. They then enquired, with some anxiety, respecting the suitability and the abode of Mr. Dawson. "The very man for you!" was reiterated in different quarters. Thus encouraged, they took a post-chaise, and drove on to Barnbow. On their arrival, they enquired of Mrs. Dawson, to whom they were introduced, for her son. A chaise in the cross road to Barnbow was rather an unusual thing. They soon advertised the old lady, however, of the object of their visit. She told them, that her son was in the fields; but having no boy at hand, and the gentlemen being wishful to go in quest of him themselves, they proceeded in the line directed. The visitants coming up to a person in crossing the fields, who was engaged on the farm, paid their respects to him, and enquired,—"Are you Mr. Dawson, Sir?" An answer in the negative was humbly and respectfully returned; the man adding,—"Master is in a close down there," pointing in the direction which he wished them to go. It was not long before they saw a person

busily engaged in hedging and ditching; and being
pretty near him before they spoke, the humble ditcher
lifted up his head, with the spade in his hand. The
query was again proposed, but with greater certainty
—"It is Mr. Dawson, we presume?" "Yes, gentlemen, my name is Dawson." "We have been deputed
to wait upon you," naming the place and the occasion,
"to request your kindly aid." Mr. Dawson returned,
—"You must be mistaken of your man." "No; it
is no mistake: go, and help you must; we cannot
do without you." Lifting the spade, he struck it
into the earth; and quitting the handle, he said,—
"If it *must* be so, why then, it *shall* be so." Just
at that moment, he put his first and third finger
into his mouth—doubling the second and fourth, and,
drawing a full breath, sent forth a shrill whistle,
that might have been heard a considerable distance
from the place. Instantly, on the sound striking the
ear, a man popped his head over the hedge, a little
further down the field, ready to attend the signal;
thus bringing to the recollection of the reader, the
tales of gone-by days, when the men of some ancient
chief, started from ambush at the sound of the horn,
and suddenly appeared by the side of their master.
Mr. Dawson waived his hand; and the man appearing
on the spot, he said,—"You must go on with this
job—cut in that direction—so low—and it will be a
right depth." So saying, and the servant replying,
"Very well," Mr. Dawson threw his coat over his
arm, proceeded homeward with the gentlemen, where
there was a cold collation provided for them. Before
Mr. Dawson himself partook of it, he went up stairs
—washed—shaved—and, in a few minutes, appeared

at the table, attired in black, with all the respectability of an English squire. They soon entered the chaise; and being in fine health and spirits, Mr. Dawson kept them alive the whole of the way to Leeds with wit and anecdote. They soon found they were in the presence of a man who would lend them efficient help: he proceeded with them, and at the meeting —crowded, and in one of the largest chapels in the Connexion, the whole tide of popular feeling was in his favour. With the paramount claims of religion over all affairs of state, and the surpassing importance attached to the conquest of a world, by means of Christian Missions, when compared with a single conflict between two armies, it can be no degradation to history, to name William Dawson in connection with Cincinnatus; the former brought from his spade and from his ditching, into a large Christian assembly, whose movements were intended to move the world; and the latter informed, while ploughing in his field, that the Roman senate had chosen him to fill the office of Dictator. The ploughman went forth at the bidding of the senate, entered the field that was to be turned up by the ploughshare of war, conquered the Volsci and Æqui, who had besieged his countrymen, and returned, in the space of sixteen days after his appointment, to plough his favourite grounds. No such laurels were won by William Dawson; and there is no disposition to institute a comparison between the two men. The simple act of calling both from the field to posts of honour, in the crowded assembly, renders the one as fit for Christian, as the other for classic story.

Among the several chapels which he opened, from

1814 and upward, was a new one at Knottingley, Sep. 22nd, 1816, and another at Selby, Nov. 19th, 1817, the day in which the Princess Charlotte was interred. His reference to the subject was exceedingly touching; and being almost, if not altogether—all the circumstances considered, without a parallel in English History, it was calculated to awaken all the sensibilities of his nature. Montgomery, in his "ROYAL INFANT," strung his "Harp of Sorrow" on the occasion, with fine Christian feeling:—

> " Yet while we mourn thy flight from earth,
>   Thine was a destiny sublime ;
> Caught up to Paradise in birth,
>   Pluck'd by Eternity from Time.
>
> " The mother knew her offspring dead :
>   Oh ! was it grief, or was it love
> That broke her heart ? The spirit fled
>   To seek her nameless child above.
>
> " Led by his natal star, she trod
>   The path to heaven :—the meeting there,
> And how they stood before their God,
>   The day of judgment shall declare. "

As the biographer domiciled under the same roof with Mr. Dawson, on the occasion, and had the same couch assigned to him, it afforded a fine opportunity, during the more early stage of their acquaintance, of witnessing his habits, and enjoying his conversation.

About the same time, after repeated and pressing invitations, he visited different places in the North, in the counties of Durham and Northumberland. Mr. Reay had long importuned him to visit Carville, and added to letters by post, one journey to Darlington, and another to Barnard Castle, to give him the meeting, and to request him to pay the colliers a visit in the neighbourhood of Newcastle; but his lists of engagements were complete on both occasions. Mr. Reay told him the next journey would be to Barnbow, unless he prevented it by promising a sermon during the first vacancy. They slept in the same room together, at Darlington, in the house of Mr. Dove, afterwards of Leeds. Mr. Dawson, contrary to his general indifference to dreams, as noticed in an earlier part of his history, observed to his companion in the morning, that he had, in the scriptural language of one of our poets, "dreamt a dream"—that he saw a man swaggering past a pit—that he was on the point of falling in—and that he caught hold of him and brought him back again. He added, "I do not like it." Mr. D., a popular local-preacher from another circuit, occupied the pulpit in the afternoon, and Mr. Dawson himself preached in the evening, when he came down like "a rushing mighty wind," in full sweep, both upon saints and sinners. Miners, and others, had travelled from the "Dales" to hear him, some of them a distance of twenty miles on foot, and had twenty more to measure back again after the evening service, having to commence work at the usual hour the next morning. On retiring to their room, Mr. Dawson pleasantly remarked to his companion, "I have had an interpretation of my dream. When I saw Mr. D. in the pulpit, I said to myself, on observing his manner, 'This person will come down either like a *man* or a *mouse.*' Alas! he was in trammels, and came down like the latter. Something within whispered, 'Thou canst do better than that.' The feeling accompanying the sentiment might have endangered my spirit; but I instantly threw myself on God;—He saved me;—he was with me,—and so I escaped the pit dug for me."

This, to say the least, if not to be numbered among pleasing dreams, and as the French would say, *tant gagné*, so much added to the pleasure of life, was devotional in its improvement; and while it added to the safety of his religious character, shews not only nice observation but great delicacy of Christian feeling.

No such interest had been excited in Newcastle, Sunderland, and other places, in the North, by any preacher, except himself, since the days of Messrs. Benson and Bramwell: and the sons of the " Coaly Tyne," as Milton designates the river, were enraptured while listening to him on this and other texts,—" He brought me up also out of a horrible pit, out of the miry clay," &c.

Deep as was the general tone of religious feeling he preserved, it was impossible to be grave in listening to some of his descriptions and comparisons. Two females happening somewhere to imbibe a strong prejudice against each other, in consequence of the one having hazarded a remark upon the dress of the other, and the thing itself,—though exceedingly trivial, affecting others besides themselves, it became a topic of conversation, and was introduced into a party where he was, when from home. This he set aside in a fine vein of satire, mixed up with the ludicrous, and not only shewed the unprofitableness of such discourse, but the imprudence—not to say wickedness, of persons allowing trifles to disturb their peace—suffering, perhaps what was said in pleasantry, to influence the passions, and so stir together the bad feelings of a whole neighbourhood. The Italian proverb may be appropriately applied here—" The mother of mischief is not bigger than a midge's egg." But though the case to which reference was made, would apply to every small matter that kindles a great fire,—"Satire is a sort of glass, wherein beholders generally discover every body's face but their own ;—which is the chief reason for that kind of reception it meets in the world, and that so very few are offended with it." His satire might touch some of the party ; but being in company, it was kicked like a ball from one to another, though it would in all probability settle somewhere after the society had broken up.

In a similar manner, he silenced a fault-finder, whom he met in Leeds, the day after he had occupied one of the pulpits in that town.

Gentleman.—"I had the pleasure of hearing you preach yesterday."

Mr. Dawson.—"I hope you not only heard, but profited ? "

Gent.—"Yes, I did ; but I don't like those prayer-meetings at the close. They destroy all the good previously received."

Mr. D.—"You should have united with the people in them."

Gent.—"I went into the gallery, where I hung over the front, and saw the whole ; but I could get no good ; I lost, indeed, all the benefit I had received under the sermon."

Mr. D.—"It is easy to account for that."

Gent.—"How so ? "

Mr. D.—"You mounted the top of the house ; and, on looking down your neighbour's chimney to see what kind of a *fire* he kept, you got your *eyes* filled with *smoke.* Had you ' entered by the door '—gone into the room—and mingled with the family around the household hearth, *you* would have enjoyed the *benefit*

N

of the *fire* as well as *they*.   Sir, you have got the *smoke* in your eyes."

Prejudice is an equivocal term; and will apply to good opinions deeply rooted in the mind, as well as those that are false and grown into it: but persons not properly affected towards religion, very often enter the maze of error; and having wandered there some time, they often discover to their cost, that they have wandered too long to find their way out.

Mr. Dawson was in Cheshire and Lancashire in the spring of 1818, and attended missionary meetings at Chester and Liverpool, April 20, 21.   It was at the former of these places, that Dr. Adam Clarke first met with him; Messrs. R. Newton, Dawson, and the Doctor being the preachers on the occasion.   Mr. Dawson represented the heathen world under the notion of a field; and the Baptists, Moravians, Calvinists, &c., as engaged in cultivating the great moral waste.   The Doctor was much pleased with the force and ingenuity displayed.   But on travelling between Chester and Liverpool, in a post-chaise, in company with a friend, who had lost a limb, and who, in consequence of the vehicle not being exactly adapted to the bulk of three such personages, aided by its joltings, permitted on first starting,—of course unintentionally, the unfeeling substitute to play off a few rubbers against the Doctor's more sensitive shin,—there was less disposition for free conversation at first, than the social arm-chair would have admitted.   However, as Mr. Dawson observed to the writer, they were soon indulged with some fine gleams of sunshine; and the Doctor adverting to the *cultivators* of the foreign waste in his speech, playfully remarked—shewing, at the same time, his strong general redemption principles,—"If I found a *Calvinistic* field in heaven, I would flee from it, and go to some other." This pleasantry having passed off, the Doctor, in allusion to Mr. Dawson, as an agriculturist, employing his knowledge of husbandry in the service of religion, remarked,—"Mr. John Mason, with whom I was well acquainted, had an extensive knowledge of botany, and Mr. James Kershaw had a good knowledge of medicine; and yet, though plants have their healing virtues, and sin is compared to a disease, I never knew either of these men bring their peculiar knowledge to bear on a single text, or illustrate by it, a single subject : under such circumstances, all was lost. As to myself, I have brought all my knowledge to bear on the illustration of truth. I have no imagination, that I am aware of. My peculiar forte is *investigation*. Give me a subject—for I cannot *create ;* let that subject be proposed : whatever it may be, I can investigate it—(smiling) aye, down to the *black art* ; yes, and I can *elucidate* it too,—bring it out, and make it help truth." Whatever credit the Doctor might *take* to himself in part of this statement, in the freedom of conversation—and he took no more than what would be readily *ceded* to him by those who knew him, he underrated himself in another, for he evidently shewed ingenuity in the *application*, as well as acuteness in the *process*. Adverting to the old preachers again, he observed,—"Talent is as *great* now as it ever was, but it is more *monotonous*—much less *varied*."

In travelling the eighteen miles, the Doctor forgot his shins and his wedgings at least two-thirds of the way, being so much enamoured with the conversation of

his companion : and the next morning accosted Mr.
Newton, who gave them the meeting thus :—" Your
friend Mr. Dawson and myself talked all the way to
Liverpool yesterday evening, and what an astonishing
mind he has got ! He assigned reasons all the way
for everything he had done."

Shortly after this, Mr. Dawson again met with him
in the city of Bristol, when he was much struck with
a statement made by Dr. Clarke, viz.—that he had
examined the religion of the Hindoos, the Mahomedans,
&c., &c., but in all the different religions which had
passed in review before him, CHRISTIANITY was the
only religion that staked its *credit* for *pardon* on *present
belief*.

Mr. Bramwell, the friend of Mr. Dawson, died
suddenly in Woodhouse-Lane, Leeds, August 13, 1818,
as he was leaving the house of a friend. The latter
improved the occasion of his death near the place where
he fell, September 14th, taking for his text, Isaiah lvii.
1, 2. It was calculated, that not less than ten thousand
persons were present on the occasion. In addition
to a sketch of his character in the sermon, which
was published at the time, he entered more largely
into it in a separate article, comprising twenty-six
pages, 12mo., published in the Life of that extraordinary man. Among other conversations which Mr.
Dawson had with the biographer, respecting Mr. B.,
he observed,—" Mr. Bramwell might be classed among
the first men for offering Christ to saints and sinners.
Persons, owing to his sincerity, were more ready to
receive Christ from him than from others ; being
convinced that he himself had made the experiment,
and was in possession of Him." This was not intended

as a reflection upon other Christian ministers, but simply referred to the peculiar "gift of God" possessed by Mr. Bramwell, and exercised so eminently in his ministry.

With his more public engagements, he continued to keep up his "way-side" duties, knowing the blessedness of those who "sow beside all waters." He often either met or overtook a person who was in the service of a miller, on his way to, or from Leeds. The man had been soundly converted to God, and lived in the enjoyment of religion some years; but unfortunately had retraced his steps into the world. He was rarely permitted to pass Mr. Dawson without a word. "Well, John, have you joined the regiment again?" "No, master, not yet," was generally the reply. After having accosted him in this way some time, mingling serious remark with his interrogatories, Mr. Dawson met him full in front one day, and with great emphasis —fixing his eyes upon him like daggers,—said, " I tell thee, John, thou art a deserter from God and truth ; and as such, thou wilt have either to be *whipt* or *shot*," and so left him. This fastened upon his mind ;—and the dread of some heavy personal affliction, together with that of final misery, haunted him wherever he went ; and it was not long after, that Mr. Dawson was overjoyed with the tidings of the poor wanderer being reclaimed.

He was in the habit, also, of scattering religious tracts along the road, when there was a probability of them falling into the hands of passengers. A man seeing him drop one, on one of these occasions, and perceiving, by the keen eye of the distributor, that it was intended for himself, he took it up : but being unable to read, and conscience either smiting him for some misdemeanour, or memory helping him to the recollection of some undischarged debt, he concluded it to be a "*summons ;*" and running after Mr. Dawson, in a state of alarm, he enquired into the reason of his conduct. Mr. D. instantly caught the idea of a summons and improved it to the man's benefit ; and also shewed, in other cases, the advantages arising from a knowledge of letters.

He had a peculiar tact for addressing children ; and was frequently requested to speak to them, when preaching sermons for the benefit of Sunday Schools. After attracting their attention with a play of fancy, alternately indulging in the strange, the beautiful, the great, and the good, he would then have wound his way to their little tricks and sinful propensities. The writer was with him on one of these occasions, and was delighted with the manner in which he accommodated himself to the capacities of the children—becoming a child in simplicity for the sake of children. Having arrested attention, he inclined forward, and fixing his eye upon some of the children, he said, in a half interrogatory and half affirmatory tone, with an expression of tenderness,—" You don't tell lies, do you ? " Several of the little creatures, who had experienced searchings of heart from what had previously been said, and who were anxious to acquit themselves, spontaneously responded, "No ; " one of them adding, in a subdued, yet conscious tone of guilt—" I am sure I do not tell lies." Other questions were answered in a similar way.

Flexible as he was, in accommodating himself to youth and age, to the higher and the lower classes of society, he would never sacrifice truth or character, or suffer his interest in Methodism to be suspected. A gentleman, who had been a Methodist in early life, asked him to step into his house, and take a glass of wine. He no sooner sat down, than the gentleman erected a battery—" I do not like the aristocracy of Methodism." Mr. Dawson, finding where he was, replied,—" That, Sir, is a subject which I never studied : " and, after several remarks, enquired, " Pray, how do you feel as to personal piety ? " The gentleman returned, " I have family prayer." " In that reply," said Mr. Dawson to the writer, " I at once saw the nakedness of the land. Soon after this, out came Mark Robinson's pamphlet, when I said to a friend,—' Why, these are the views of Mr.———, which I have already had to combat in private." An appeal to personal piety, was a weapon which he often wielded with amazing power, when argument failed, and when he suspected the disease to be in the heart rather than in the system opposed.

Few questions agitated either the body, or separate societies, but what he grounded a firm opinion upon, and had his answer at hand, when thrown into circumstances which compelled him to speak. At the time Dr. A. Clarke's view of the Eternal Sonship of Christ was agitated, he acted the part of a moderator ; and in a company where opposite opinions were espoused, he pleasantly broke off the debate, by observing—in allusion to the person of each,—" Dr. Clarke is tall, and Mr. Watson is still taller ; but if the one were placed on the shoulders of the other, the doctrine of the Sonship—such is its profundity, will be found deep enough to drown them both." Then, in reference to the friends of each, he smiled, and said, adopting the proverbial expression—"'Every dog has its day ;' I have had mine, and it has been a very good one ; many have patted me on the back, and stroked my head : in the midst of all I have said —and that is my language now, 'I ask not *life*, but let me *love*.'" He was pleased with the parallel between the *Word* and the *Son*, by the Rev. Abraham Scott, but found fault with another writer, for adopting it as his own in a critique on the subject, without having the ingenuousness to acknowledge the source from whence it was borrowed.

Conversation moving in another direction, Mr. Dawson, among other remarks, observed, " Jeremy Taylor is a charming writer, but not strictly evangelical.— Robert Hall is too severe upon Dr. Owen.—I am less partial to Howe than to Dr. Bates.—Herbert and Quarles are stiff and quaint. Herbert, however, must have been exceedingly popular in his day, which may be inferred from the fact of his being so often quoted." The biographer rejoined,—" good sacred poetry was scarce at that time, which is another reason that may be assigned." On Mr. D. stating, that he was much more partial to " Flavel's Husbandry Spiritualized," than to his " Navigation," the writer returned, that such a predilection might be accounted for on the ground of his own occupation. "Not altogether," said he, " for in the one instance, the writer is improving upon *nature*, in the other, he has to do with *art*.

CHAPTER XI.

*Stage Coach Dialogues.—Retort.—Incognito.—Lord Milton.—
Touching Tale.—Waterloo Conversations.—Matrimony.—Business.—Misers.—Popery.—Socinianism.—People.—Ministers.
—Poetry of Action.—Impotency.—Penitents.—The Worldling.
—The character of Mr. Dawson as a Preacher.—Power of
imagination.—Terrific Imagery.—Candour in hearing.—Selec-
tion of Hymns, and Remarks upon them.—Indiscretion in
singing pieces after sermon.—Death on the pale Horse.—The
secret of successful preaching.—Sermon to Sailors.—Death of
Friends.—Rev. David Stoner.—Different Pulpit methods.—
Mr. Dawson's Class.—False nit.—Bible Meeting at Hull.—
Death of Mr. Dawson's Mother.*

IT was sometimes amusing, but rarely otherwise than
instructive, to listen to him while detailing " Incidents
of Travel," when associated with him in the social
circle.   He was   seated in a " Six Inside " coach
during one of his peregrinations, travelling between
Halifax   and   Leeds,   when   he   heard   the   following
conversation   between   a   gentleman   and   a   lady,   who
sat opposite each other, preceded by a few prefatory
remarks :—

Gentleman.—" You are in the habit, then, of hearing
popular ministers ? "

Lady.—" At Manchester, I am,—not at Halifax."

Gent.—" You have, no doubt, heard Mr.——? "

Lady.—" I have."

N 2

Gent.—" What is your opinion of him ? "

Lady.—" His imagination is like a young colt turned into a field."

Gent.—" Have you heard Mr.——? "

Lady.—" Never."

Gent.—" Mr.——, you will of course have often heard."

Lady.—" Yes, often."

Gent.—" What is your opinion of him ? "

Lady.—" I never got a new thought from him in my life."

Gent.—" Have you heard Dr.——? "

Lady.—" Never."

Gent.—" Have you heard Mr.——? "

Lady.—" Yes."

Gent.—" He is an excellent preacher."

Lady.—" There is too much the appearance of *manufacture* about his sermons."

Gent.—" Have you ever heard Mr. Watson ? "

Lady.—" Yes. He never exhausts a figure. I would go ten miles to hear him any day."

Gent.—" There is a great deal of noise about Mr. Irving. Have you heard him ? "

Lady.—" No ; nor would I go to hear him. He is for destroying the whole language of preaching, and for creating something in its place."

Mr. Dawson was in a large party some time after this, in which one of the gentlemen referred to was present, who sported with a gentleman of wilder imagination than his own, and did not fail to direct attention to the playful fancy of Mr. Dawson. The latter, in the way of pleasant retort, related as much of the above dialogue as comported with the occasion, and was more than usually pointed, when he turned the lady's "colt loose into the field." This prevented the gentleman from ambling at the rate he was proceeding. The person who was partner with Mr. Dawson in the pleasantry, being seated near him, turned round, and said,—"This *colt* has *trodden* upon both of us." Mr. Dawson replied,—"He has not hurt you, I hope?" "No," responded his friend, "for like most young horses turned out to grass, he is without *shoes*."

An *incognita* may be noticed in connection with another journey. He was on one of the Manchester coaches, and seated beside two gentlemen. Passing through Huddersfield, several large placards were perceived posted on the walls, with his name upon them, having been there but a short time before, preaching occasional sermons.

First Gent.—"I have often seen that name posted in different parts of the country, and have heard a great deal about the man : pray, do you know," turning to the person next him, "anything about him?"

Second Gent.—"I heard him preach several years ago, and can recollect the text too ;" naming it.

First Gent.—"Is he a regular preacher among the Methodists?"

Second Gent.—"No ; I am informed he is a farmer, and lives with his mother. He generally goes by the name of the 'Yorkshire Farmer.' But he is a very extraordinary man."

First Gent.—"He will not have such polish, of course, as such men as Mr. Newton ; still he will do very well, I should think, for the lower orders of society."

Mr. Dawson was not a little amused with their remarks, and embedded his chin more deeply in his neckcloth, the more effectually to conceal his features, while the broad brim of his hat threw its shadow over the upper part of his face. He concluded himself rather favourably dealt with, as they had assigned him a post of usefulness among those who most required help—the *poor.* The first gentleman finding that he knew something of Leeds, turned to him, and asked,—

" Are you acquainted with Leeds and its neighbourhood, Sir ?"

Mr. Dawson.—" I am, Sir."

First Gent.—" Do you know the person of whom we have been speaking ?"

Mr. D.—" I do."

First Gent.—" Have you heard him preach ?"

Mr. D.—" I have."

First Gent.—" Let us have your opinion of him."

Mr. D.—" If my opinion is worth anything, I think he is greatly overrated in being supposed to be an ' extraordinary man.' "

Second Gent.—" He is by no means *a learned man :* but in support of what I have said, I adduce, by way of proof, the popular feeling in his favour, and the immense congregations he obtains."

First Gent.—" Had he not extraordinary natural powers, and were he not a good speaker in addition, I cannot conceive how he, as an *illiterate* man, could produce such amazing effects by his preaching."

On arriving at the foot of Stanedge, the outside passengers had to walk : and now, Mr. Dawson began to regret that he had been forced into any part of the conversation, and still more, lest he should be joined by his companions, and cross-examined in walking up the hill. One of them, as has been seen, had been favoured with a half length view of his figure in the pulpit, some years before, and had little more than a half length view of him on the coach. But he knew not how far a closer inspection of himself on the ground, might not reveal the secret. It seemed, however, that his travelling dress, his half-muffled visage, and his more robust form,—having become stouter, preserved his hearer of by-gone days in ignorance. The only point of delicacy with him was, lest, by a disclosure, the two gentlemen should feel a little unpleasant on recollecting the freedom of some of their remarks on the station they had assigned him, and his want of learning. He heard himself, however, freely discussed——for the above is only a specimen of the whole. But he felt most on arriving at Manchester, lest the same eyes should recognize him in the pulpit the next day, and so embarrass both parties, when the mind should be engaged on more important subjects.

In addition to his native worth, fire, and extraordinary powers, the conversation of the gentlemen shewed, that two or three adventitious circumstances contributed to increase public impression in his favour. He was *in* the world, though not *of* it ; and hence, in whatsoever direction the current flowed, the "Yorkshire Farmer" was always floating on the surface. It was next to marvellous, with the irreligious and uneducated, that a man of business, on his farm, and remote from the walks of public life, should be enabled to bring out of his intellectual treasury such an inexhaustible store of "things new and old,"——and one too, so rural often in his appearance,—not being always in black, but sometimes in coloured small clothes—boots with tops, and otherwise plain, though becoming his station,—and, above all, one not entirely devoted to books, and to the work of the ministry.

The present Earl Fitzwilliam, then Lord Milton, was an inside passenger on another occasion. His Lordship, of course, knew nothing of Mr. Dawson, though Mr. Dawson recognized his Lordship, having the advantage which a hearer has over a minister—the one being known, when the other passes unobserved in the crowd. Mr. Dawson made a few passing remarks to draw his Lordship into conversation; but he might with the poet have said,—

"Lo! Silence himself is here!"

Euripides was wont to say,—"Silence is an answer to a wise man." So it would have been to Mr. Dawson; but there were two or three points on which he wished to know the opinion of the statesman; and at length, hitting on one particular subject, his Lordship awoke as from a reverie, kindled into life, and proceeded with the interest he might be supposed to feel in a debate in the senate.

No less interesting, was another little incident which turned up in the course of his various wanderings. He was on his way, as before, into Lancashire; and had two soldiers' wives as coach companions, who were proceeding to join their husbands, belonging to a dragoon regiment. Mr. Dawson had preached in Leeds some short time previously to this, and the conversation of the women soon found its way to himself. "And what did your good man," enquired the one of the other, "think of the great *Billy Dawson* when he heard him?" "Oh, very well," was the reply: "he is such a man! He never heard the like." Mr. Dawson, on hearing this, drew his hat over his eyes—fearing discovery; but was presently satisfied, that his companions were ignorant of his person; and ultimately took a part in the conversation respecting what was said of their husbands, who, it appeared, were members of the Methodist Society. He enquired whether there were many pious men in the regiment, and was answered in the affirmative. One of them turning to the other, said,—"You know, that of all the Methodist soldiers, who were engaged at Waterloo, not one was killed." Mr. Dawson exclaimed, "Indeed!" "Yes, Sir," responded the good woman, "and one of them, Tommy——, no very great horseman, (for he was a tailor), was hemmed in by some French cavalry, when escape seemed impossible; however, nothing daunted, he flourished his sword, spurred his horse onward, crying, —'The sword of the Lord and Gideon for ever!' and dashed through them unhurt." At the close of the journey, some one enquiring whether Mr. Dawson was there, the wondering women discovered that they had been in conversation with "the great Billy Dawson." *

* The biographer, on hearing this tale of Waterloo, recognized as its hero, an old acquaintance, a respectable fishmonger, in the town of Newcastle-upon-Tyne. But there is a slight discrepancy between the good woman's account and his own;—himself not having been a knight of the thimble, and his own excellent wife having been the widow of a Wesleyan, who fell in the battle of Waterloo. The good woman speaking from report, gave the circumstances of the case, of course, as she had heard them. In answer to some queries put by the biographer to the "tailor," so called, the following letter came to hand, dated " Newcastle, Dec. 13th, 1841.

"DEAR SIR.—Don't be afraid at the sight of so large a sheet of paper. I like plenty of room,—that's all. *Question* 1. 'Were you a tailor by trade?' No,—but a stocking-weaver; or more technically, a frame-work knitter. In

A touching tale, in connection with another journey, a few years after, ought not to be lost. Seated beside him on a coach, was a young man, who seemed to be a sailor by his dress. He was full of mirth;—singing —amusing the passengers with anecdotes, and with one piece of wit and drollery after another; and yet so delicate were his strokes, as Mr. Dawson observed to the biographer, that the most refined modesty could not have been offended with them. On a gentleman being named, he stated that he knew him, and had been a student with him at college. The youth was familiar with the Hebrew, and quoted Virgil, in the original, with great readiness. When a poor person came in his way, he invariably dropped something

short, I was a scoundrel from my youth up; and though I tried my hand at many things, I stayed at nothing long: but that was the last thing in which I was employed, when I enlisted. *Question* 2. ' Were any soldiers, united to the Wesleyans, killed?' Yes; one in our troop, James Curtice, my wife's former husband, and several wounded. *Question* 3. ' Did you receive your wounds, &c.?' No. I was just in a charge with the whole brigade; and, by some means, was opposed single-handed to one of the French cuirassiers; and while brandishing swords, he muttered something which I did not understand, and I—thinking I must say something in reply, muttered in my turn,—' The sword of the Lord, and Gideon,' &c. *Question* 4. ' What was the result?' He very wisely turned his horse's head on one side, and rode off; and I as wisely turned my horse's head to the other side, and rode off,—and we have not seen each other since. Now you are ready, perhaps, to propose another question, and ask,—' Pray what became of you?' On perceiving that I had lost time, and that the regiment had left me to settle the question with the French Dragoon, I tried to follow; but in crossing a bad, hollow piece of ground, my horse fell, and before I had well got upon my feet, another of the French Dragoons came up, and *(sans ceremonie)* began to cut at my head, knocked off my helmet, and inflicted several wounds in my head and face. Looking up at him, I saw him in the act of striking another blow at my head, and instantly held up my right hand to protect it, when he cut off my little finger, and half way through the rest. I then threw myself on the ground, with my face downward. One of the lancers rode by, and stabbed me in the back with his lance. I then turned, and lay with my face upward, and a foot soldier stabbed me with his sword as he walked by. Immediately after, another foot-man, with his firelock and bayonet, gave me a terrible plunge, and, while doing into the hand, and treated such of the passengers as were disposed to share his bounty. Mr. Dawson spoke to him on the subject of religion, directing his attention, especially, to that of redemption. He instantly turned it off with—"There is no Redeemer mentioned in the Old Testament." Mr. Dawson reminded him of the passage in Job,—"I know that my Redeemer liveth." The youth immediately quoted the Hebrew, and said it signified an *avenger* as well as a Redeemer; adding, "there is no certainty to which it belongs." After a short discussion, to which he was evidently indisposed, he asked the passengers, whether they would have a song? and elevating his voice, he sung a tune to some lines composed on a boat disaster on the Ouse, at Naburn Lock, about four miles

it with all his might, exclaimed,—'Sacre, nom de Dieu!' No doubt, that would have been the finishing stroke, had not the point of the bayonet caught one of the brass eyes of my coat,—the coat being fastened with hooks and eyes, and prevented its entrance. There I lay, as comfortable as circumstances would allow,—the balls of the British army falling around me, one of which dropped at my feet, and covered me with dirt; so that, what with blood, dirt, and one thing or another, I passed very well for a dead man. I was next plundered of my watch, money, canteen, and haversack. I lay till night,—the British army marching, some near me, and some over me, in pursuit of the French. At length I was picked up by two Prussian soldiers, and laid beside a fire, when one of their surgeons dressed some of my wounds, and left me for the remainder of the night. Next day I received great kindness from an English regiment, just then arrived. An officer gave me a little rum, and one of the privates carried me in a blanket; the latter of whom, as he pushed the blanket under me, repeatedly said,—'Pray to God, comrade. Pray to God, comrade.' It is impossible to convey to you the sensations I experienced on hearing these words. They were like 'Apples of gold' to me. In a day or two more, I was carried to Brussels, and by degrees recovered. If you will take the trouble to look into the Methodist Magazine, for 1816, p. 284, you will there find some lines I wrote in the hospital, beginning with 'Happy the bard by nature made.' It is a somewhat mutilated copy, and had passed through other hands. I hope the above will be satisfactory. If you have any other questions to propose, let me have them. Give my respects to Mrs. E. My wife and Robert unite in love. I conclude by telling you, that my soul prospers. Yours, most affectionately,—THOMAS HASKER."

below the city of York. Mr. Dawson found afterwards,
that he had been educated under Mr. Wellbeloved,
at the Socinian Seminary in that city, had been in
the boat, and had seen his companion carried over
the Lock, and drowned. On coming to the part of
the lines that described the catastrophe, he was sensibly affected, and could proceed no further. Some
time before he reached the end of his journey, he
had squandered away the whole of his money, and
had not wherewith to procure a dinner. A gentleman,
who had been amused with him, proposed to treat
him, but his proud spirit spurned the offer. Mr.
Dawson was provided with a little refreshment in his
pocket, and asked him delicately to partake with
him. He did; and Mr. Dawson was happy in the
opportunity to aid him. In the first case, there was something like part *payment,* for mirth received; in the
second, there was an air of *friendship,* which wound
round the softer feelings. When the gay youth arrived
a short way on the other side of Birmingham, he
became pensive, and was disposed to be silent. Turning
to Mr. Dawson, whom he took for a Wesleyan, he
said,——"My father's house is within eight miles of
this place;—and this night, I shall either be *shut
in* or *shut out :* if *shut* in"—looking at his poor
habiliments, "I shall then have as fine a coat on my
back as a Methodist parson." Mr. Dawson observed,
on relating the circumstance,——"I thought within myself, this poor youth has perhaps broken a mother's
heart, and has either been *sent,* or *run* from home."
The young man added, just as the thought crossed
Mr. Dawson's mind,——"This night will settle all."
About two years afterwards, Mr. Dawson was preaching

at Chapel-Town, near Leeds, when he related part of the anecdote, and employed the expression,—"*Shut in,* or *shut out,*" applying it in his sermon in reference to heaven. After preaching, a lady stepped up to him, and said,—"I am not at liberty to mention names; but the circumstance, character, and family are known to me; and I have the satisfaction of informing you, that the young man was that night *shut in.*"

Mr. Dawson assisted in opening a new chapel at Hunslet, Nov. 20, 1819. He was a close observer of anything that came in his way, and, if capable of improvement, was sure to make it tell either in the pulpit or in social life. This rendered him exceedingly agreeable as a companion; and when he chose to offer remarks, even in the way of criticism, there was nothing of asperity mixed up with them. "The preaching," said he, "of Mr.—— is like the building of Solomon's temple,—without noise; not so much as the sound of a hammer is heard." But he intended something more here than the want of animation; he knew there was symmetry, and even beauty. Some of his more sportive sallies might border upon the extravagant, though still allowable. Stepping into a barber's shop in Leicester, when without his razors, he accosted the man—"If you please, I want your smoothing iron drawn over my face." The man stared, not being able to comprehend his meaning at first; but on seeing the growth of his beard, he perceived what he meant, and soon found his customer on his way to something more tangible and profitable.

It was impossible to be with him any length of time, without being forcibly struck with some points of conversation. He was rarely consecutive, except some special subject was proposed. Seated one day with a few friends, the two subjects of matrimony and business were introduced. "Matrimony," said he, "has two ways leading to it. The one lies straightforward; the lady is beautiful—possesses property—the path is strewed with flowers—all is inviting. The other has inscribed upon it,—'Be not unequally yoked with unbelievers;' but the former is chosen; and the flowers are instantly pointed with thorns. Business has also two ways: the one is,—be rich—here is a good opening—a fine speculation—probable success. The other has affixed to its entrance,—'I have learned, in whatsoever state I am, therewith to be content.' In this case, too, the former is chosen—the bait is swallowed—the way promises success—you follow on —speculate—go over the precipice—and are lost." He further intimated, that a good man had no occasion to walk in darkness, in either case; being persuaded that the providence of God would guide all who sincerely sought direction at his hand. A person in the room, who was high in his profession, and frequently occupied the pulpit, acceded to what Mr. Dawson said in reference to matrimony, though suspicions had been entertained of the purity of his motives in reference to marriage; but on business being named, he was silent, and seemed uncomfortable in his feelings. In the course of half a year, he made a disgraceful failure, and was found to have been acting the villain at the time. "No legacy," says a writer, "is so rich as honesty;" and it may be added, in the language of another, by way of caution, that " he who prorogues the honesty of to-day till to-morrow, will probably prorogue his to-morrows to eternity." To a young friend, who commenced the business of a druggist, in Leeds, with a fair prospect, Mr. Dawson said, on first entering his shop,—"You have got a good shop; I wish you a good trade, a good wife, a good life, and a good end."

Without furnishing the occasion of several of his remarks, or the conversations of others, with which they were often interwoven, a few more may be introduced from the memoranda of the biographer. Of misers, he seemed to entertain the same opinion as Samuel Hick, and gave them no quarter. "Immediately on seeing a placard, for a religious meeting, upon a wall," he observed, "the miser turns away his skin and bones, and says,—'It is money they want.' Admitting it,—what becomes of his own? He is heaping it up, like manure on a dunghill. And what is it worth in his hand? Even a midden will do no good till it is *spread;* so with money. He hoards it up; and his midden of gold will *heat* and *rot,* and will breed *vipers* and *cockatrice* eggs; and these vipers will *sting*—will *coil* round his *heart,* and enwrap his whole form for ever." Popery, as a system, shared the same fate;— "It is a mere *carcass* decorated with the *flowers* of religious ceremonies, having the *form* without the *power.* Socinianism is much worse; for it is a *body* without *blood* and *spirit;* neither possessing the ATONEMENT, nor the influence of the HOLY GHOST." Turning to a medical gentleman seated beside him, he enquired with quiet sarcasm, what he could do in the way of giving life in such a case,—obliquely glancing at the hopeless efforts of Socinian ministers to produce any thing like religious life, when the blood was drained off from the system, and the spirit had fled. Changing the metaphor, in reference to ministers attempting to resuscitate a lifeless form, he observed in the presence of some colliers,—"The private members of the Christian Church are all '*live coals*;' some of them, it is true, are *small*, but heaped together they make a blaze. Ministers, and especially great and good men, are moving '*pillars of fire*,' going before the people." Here, with grace and majesty, he raised his noble well rounded form, and advanced a few paces, turning slowly round, as if every part admitted of the closest inspection, and was intended for use,—suiting the action to what might be conceived of the movements of "the pillar of cloud by day, and the pillar of fire by night," thus presenting the moving column before the camp. The whole was so modulated by his spirit and manner, that it operated on the soul like electricity on matter. It was the poetry of action; and to deny the presence and the power of poetry in deeds and in visible things, is to deny its existence altogether. It is the silent poetry of Nature, which, with its scenes of awe, sublimity, and beauty, steals out the soul with magnetic influence in sympathetic rapture, and bids the poet give it a tongue.

A person complaining of his feeble efforts, and his poverty, was met in the following manner by him;—"You say you are poor, and can do nothing. If you have the grace of God in your heart, you can do something. You shall have the credit of being a farthing candle. Well, a farthing candle can give light. Take it into a dark room, and the inmates will be thankful for it. What, a farthing candle and can do nothing! Yes, you can give light to a beggar. A farthing candle, and can do nothing! Yes, you can set a town on fire. Can do nothing! Yes, you can set a world on fire. Some of the first public speakers were probably lighted by the feeblest taper." He was no less encouraging to the poor in spirit, than ingenious in meeting objections of listlessness. "Christ," said he to a person seeking for mercy, "shall make his enemies, his *footstool*. Not so, the penitent. Thou, poor distressed soul—thou art to come *to* his footstool. *He* will place thee *at* his feet, and thou, in humility, wilt place thyself there. His enemies he will place *under* his feet, he will *tread* them down." With a view to find his way to the better sense of a worldling, by shewing him the absurdity of his conduct, he represented the floor as strewed with new coined sovereigns and old farthings. "A man," said he, "enters the apartment, and is seen anxiously picking up the old copper coins, without either image or superscription ; while those of gold, with both image and superscription, lie neglected. This," continued he, in this burlesqued way, "is a picture of the worldling, who is spending the whole of his time in picking up trifles, while he is neglecting the 'pearl of great price,' 'gold tried in the fire ;' forgetting at the time, that if he were to pick up the sovereigns, he would have the farthings *in* the sovereigns." This imagery was gravely sealed with—"Seek ye first the kingdom of God, and his righteousness, and all these things shall be added unto you ;" and fastened more powerfully than Mr. Mather's "pack-thread," in connexion with the same text. "Let the backslider," said he significantly, "who is unable to stand on his *feet*, get upon his *knees*."

From 1821 to 1824, he was frequently engaged in the Metropolis, Bristol, and the large towns in Cornwall, in the southern, western, and northern counties ; and there were few places of magnitude, with innumerable places of minor note, from which he had not letters of invitation. On one of these occasions, when attending a missionary meeting at Birmingham, an eminent dissenting minister, to whose opinion further reference will be made, went to hear him. Mr. Dawson's text was—" Be it known unto you, therefore, men and brethren, that through this man is preached unto you the forgiveness of sins ; and by him all that believe are justified from all things, from which ye could not be justified by the law of Moses." Service being over, the minister, after a striking exclamation, observed, that he had heard some of the boldest and most original conceptions that he had ever heard uttered, and clothed in language equally remarkable and powerful. The gentleman to whom the observation was made, acceding to the justice of the remark, enquired,—" What would he have been, had he been favoured with an academical education in early life ?" " He would have been spoiled," returned the minister.

The effect of Mr. D's. ministry might have been embodied in a sentiment of his own ;—" If Methodism does not make men into *parsons,* it certainly converts them into *clerks ;* for they are responding 'Amen'—'glory be to God,'—wherever we go." This was the case with his own pulpit exercises, much more than with that of most others. He was irresistible. Preaching on the returning Prodigal, he paused, looked at the door, and shouted out,—after he had depicted him in his wretchedness,—" Yonder he comes, slip-shod! make way— make way—make way there!" Such was the approach to reality, that a considerable part of the congregation turned to the door, some rising on their feet, under the momentary impression that some one was entering the chapel in the state described. In the same sermon, paraphrasing the father's reply to the son that was angry and would not go in, he said,—"Be not offended; surely a *calf* may do for a *prodigal*,—*shoes* for a *prodigal*, —a *ring* and a *robe* for a *prodigal;* but ALL I have is THINE." As to the more striking part, when pointing to the door, similar effects were produced, when referring to the Witch of Endor. His picturings took such hold of the imagination, that, on exclaiming—"Stand by—stand by—there she is," some of the poor people inadvertently directed the eye downward, where his own eye was fixed, and the spot to which he was pointing, as if she were about to rise from beneath their feet, and become visible to the congregation. It was by the force of his own imagination, that he created corresponding images in the minds of his hearers; and many of them seemed abandoned, for the time being, to its power, and to dwell upon the visionary scenes presented,— their feelings varying with the shifting images flitting before them,—either sparkling with beauty, or hideous as spectres.

On one of his visits to the North, when among the colliers, he represented to the imagination of the sinner a pit,—a chain thrown over a windlass,—a weight at one end of the chain;—the other end coiled round the body of a man on his way to the pit;—the windlass whirling round,—the weight increasing in velocity on its way downward,—the man drawing nearer and nearer to the mouth of the pit,—the weight still more and more rapid in its motion;—then shouting out amain, at the moment the head seemed to be whirling with the

o

machinery,—"He is going, he is going,—there is no
stopping him;—he is nearer and nearer,—the final step
is taken,—he dashes over,—disappears,—and the splash
startles the very devils." Here a thrill of horror
seemed to seize the whole assembly. To give effect to
his imagery, the weight was the collective sins of the
sinner,—the chain, the Divine Perfections, all harmon-
izing even in the destruction of the finally impenitent,
—the windlass, the constant whirl of time, to which
"stop" might be cried in vain. Through the fertility
of his imagination, the whole was represented as revolving the reverse way, in the case of the righteous,—good
works, arising from saving faith in Christ, drawing the
Christian more and more from earth, and nearer and
nearer heaven.

Another piece of imagery, equally effective and terrific
in its close, though less rapid in its progress, was
worked up to rouse the conscience of a drunkard, into
whose shop he entered the day after the man had been
indulging in intoxication. "Suppose yourself to be a
servant," said he, "and your master were to come in
the morning, and order you to make a strong chain; on
the following morning he came again, and urged you to
get on with it; and thus, day by day, you were ordered
by your master to the same job. Suppose again, that
while you were working, a person came in and asked
you if you knew what the chain was for; and that you
answered in the negative, adding, that you did not care
so long as you got your wages. But this person tells
you, that he knows it to be a fact, that it is your master's intention to bind you with it in perpetual bondage:
would you, I ask, add another link to it?" The man
answered—"No; and all the money in the world would

not hire me to it." Mr. Dawson then asked him, whether he was not aware that drunkenness was the devil's chain, in which he kept poor sinners in perpetual bondage, and that when they had added the last link, he would chain them in hell for ever. He further observed,—"Whether you know it or not, every drunken frolic is a link added to the chain, and Satan will wrap it round you *red hot.*" This continued to operate upon the conscience of the man for some time,—the thought constantly crossing his mind,—"I am making another link for my chain!" till he relinquished his wicked course of life, when he published his personal history, in "The Tale of the Reformed Drunkard."

Being asked one day, what he thought of the sermon of a preacher from whom little could be brought away either for fireside converse or closet thought, he felt the position in which he was placed, and instantly returned,—"I eat what I can, but pocket nothing;" thus dexterously guarding against any reflection upon the preacher, as well as escaping himself from the charge of being an indifferent hearer. Yet he was sometimes amused with the remarks of persons upon himself. "What," said a poor man, when disappointed of another preacher, "is it you?" "Yes," replied Mr. Dawson, "it is I." "Well," returned the man, intending it for a welcome in his way, "you are better than nobody." Mr. Dawson pleasantly observed,—"I know my place—I am *next* to *nobody.*"

"*Nobody,*" however, as he was here, he was discovered to be *somebody* elsewhere; for in Mr. Baines's "History, Directory, and Gazetteer of the County of York," for 1822, the "Rev. William Dawson, Methodist minister," is the only person noticed in connection with "*Barnbow*, in the parish of Barwick-in-Elmet, wap. of Skyrack;" and noticed too, not barely as the only person worthy of notice in the "townships" of which Barnbow forms a part, but as a *Minister* and a *Reverend*,—no insignificant proof of the general estimation in which he was held for office and character.

His introductory remarks on the hymns which he selected, as well as his observations on particular lines and verses—even in the smallest places of worship, were not only very striking, but just and valuable, and shewed that they had been chosen for his subjects with unusual care.   Two or three cases may be noticed from the many that came under the observation of the biographer.   On giving out the 672nd hymn, he paused when he came to the first and second lines of the second verse,—

> " True, 'tis a strait and thorny road,
>   And mortal spirits tire and faint ; "

and enquired,—" Why do they *tire ?* Is it because it is '*strait* and *thorny ?* ' No—

> ' But they forget the mighty God,
>   That feeds the strength of every saint ; "

thus gliding into the succeeding lines without suffering the congregation to feel any interruption by the break, while he furnished them with a subject for reflection—shewing them that they should "sing with the understanding."

On another public occasion, he announced the 204th hymn, on the 200th page of the large Hymn Book. A number of musical instruments being in use in the service, and each performer evidently bent on attracting attention, he turned suddenly round to the orchestra, on coming to the fifth verse, and with a mixture of holy jealousy for his God, and fear on account of the persons engaged, exhorted them with a rebuking eye, to guard against the evils to which they were exposed;—and then, slowly and gracefully turning to the assembly, he said, in an earnest plaintive tone, and with an expression of pity in his countenance,—"O friends! pray for them—pray for them—for they are in danger!" proceeding with the verse,—

> " Still let us on our guard be found,
> And watch against the power of sound,
>   With sacred jealousy ;
> Lest, haply, sense should damp our zeal,
> And music's charms bewitch and steal
>   Our hearts away from thee. "

In this way, he shewed the depth of his piety,—being anxious to preserve the spirit of public worship in all its simplicity, purity, and power. There was nothing indifferent to him in the worship of God; his eye was fixed on every part, and his heart run out after it in its performance, both as to spirit and manner. Anything light and airy at the close of the service, which is too often the case on special occasions, when the singers wish to shew off, and the organist is disposed to give a specimen of his execution, met with his decided disapprobation. He observed, that "such displays often spoil the effect of a whole sermon." Indiscretion of this kind, is much more hurtful than direct opposition. In the latter case, a man only attacks his enemies, and those to whom he wishes harm ; in the former, he injures indifferently both friends and foes.

Again, in selecting the 190th hymn, page 186,— "Jesus, thy blood and righteousness," &c., on coming

to the last, or 10th verse, he broke off somewhat
abruptly; and with a view to combine *prayer* with
song, of which the lines are susceptible, he remarked,
in addressing the auditory,—"I have often been deeply
impressed with the language of the minister to the
people, in the Communion service; the priest proceeds
saying, 'Lift up your hearts;' the people answer,
'We lift them up unto the Lord.' The priest again
strikes in, 'Let us give thanks unto our Lord God;'
the people respond,—'It is meet and right so to do;'
when the priest closes with,—'It is very meet, right,
and our bounden duty, that we should at all times,
and in all places, give thanks unto thee, O Lord,
holy Father, almighty and everlasting God.'" Then
glancing round the audience, he elevated his voice,
and with amazing energy said,—"'Lift up your hearts;'
—yes, and let the whole congregation repeat,—'We
lift them up unto the Lord,'"—instantly announcing,—

> " Thou God of power, thou God of love,
> Let the whole world thy mercy prove!
> Now let thy word o'er all prevail ;
> Now take the spoils of death and hell. "

The power of sound seemed increased at least two-
fold by the additional number of voices, that had
previously been silent; and twofold in the strength
of those that had taken an interest in the singing.
He had perceived that there was not the power employed, that the multitude warranted; and in thus
testing it, he produced one of the finest bursts of
congregational singing the biograper ever heard. Every
soul seemed suddenly elevated by the power of sacred
song; and dropping on his knees, the feeling was
carried through the whole of the prayer—the people

responding to the various petitions presented to God,
with all the sweet effect produced on a devout auditory
by the emphatic responses at the close of the Litany.
The whole of the Church service being familiar to
him, he occasionally employed different parts of it with
great advantage, both as to argument and acts of devotion.

The 8th verse of the 1st hymn,—"See all your
sins on Jesus laid," produced a similar beneficial
effect on the side of piety. Before announcing it,
he suddenly turned to the Bible, and scanned a few
of the first verses of the sixth chapter of the Apocalypse,
where the expression, "Come, and see," is repeated
on the appearance of the different *horses;* closing by
saying,—"I do not ask you to come and *see* the
preacher, or to hear the voice of thunder; but to
come and see *yourselves,* your *sins,* and your SAVIOUR."
Then, with increased energy, and with a fine extemporaneous intonation of voice,—his eyes sparkling with
pleasure, he proceeded,—"I ask you to come and see
—what?

> " See all your sins on Jesus laid :
> The Lamb of God was slain :
> His soul was once an offering made
> For every soul of man. "

His quick mind had just caught the catch-word,—
"See;" and by a certain association of ideas, at once
turned to a favourite subject, and by one of his sudden
transitions or sallies, gave relief to the length of the
hymn, and produced singular and striking effects. In
many cases, this was purely accidental; but in no
instance did there appear anything like an impertinent
obtrusiveness in his remarks, by permitting one idea,
or one class of ideas, to appear to the exclusion of

others.. He always connected his outbreaks with the subject in hand, and found his way back with the same ease, as if the subject introduced had constituted "part and parcel" of the hymn. Locke would designate such interruption a weakness; and in the midst of less grave subjects, would humorously describe it "as a childishness of the understanding; wherein, during the fit, it plays with, and dandles some insignificant puppet, without any end in view." But such wanderings never excluded Mr. Dawson's subject:—the thoughts were not of the "puppet" kind,—and he invariably kept the most important "end in view."

That he should advert to the Apocalypse in the last instance, is the less remarkable, as it constituted part of a text on which he had preached, and part of which he worked up in a similar way. The text was the one alluded to, Rev. vi. 7, 8.—"And when he had opened the fourth seal, I heard the voice of the fourth beast say,—Come, and see. And I looked, and behold a pale horse; and his name that sat on him was Death, and hell followed with him."

"In the middle of the Apocalypse," observed Mr. Dawson, "there are hieroglyphics, and characters of prophecy, which we do not fully understand; and, in many instances, those hieroglyphical representations which are brought before us, are only what ceremonial observances were to the Jews; they are the shadows of realities which we do not see at present; and we shall only know the import of the shadows, when we see the whole width and breadth of the reality. There are some persons who have a natural talent for explaining these things. They never seem to be at home, but when they are breaking seals, and pouring vials, and blowing trumpets. It is neither my taste nor my talent. A pious clergyman once asked,—'Mr. Dawson, what do you think about the figures in the Revelations?' I answered, I do not think much about them, Sir; nor do I care much about figures; I shall not break seals, pour vials, or blow trumpets—I blow no trumpet but that of salvation to every penitent believer."

With this summary dismissal of the mystic language of the Apocalypse, and the diffuse commentaries of learned divines on the subject, he proceeded in his own original way, to discuss the text; and though some hearers might disrelish his mode of treating the signs and symbols of prophecy, they could not but admire the ingenuity displayed in giving the words a *literal* interpretation. The following extract forms part of the peroration; and will, perhaps, serve to illustrate what was considered by some persons, his "power" in preaching.

"'Come, and see,' then, the awful condition of an unsaved sinner. Open your eyes, sinner, and see it yourself. *There* he is in the broad road of ruin; every step he takes is deeper in sin; every breath he draws, feeds his corruption; every moment takes him farther from heaven, and nearer hell; he is going, and death and hell are after him. The horse and the rider are increasing in speed; they are coming quickly on; they are getting nearer; they are overtaking him. Can you bear the sight? 'Come, and see.' If the rider overtakes that poor sinner, unpardoned and unsaved, and strikes his blow, down he falls, and backward he drops:—hell behind him, and as he falls backward, he looks upward, and shrieks, —'Lost! lost! lost! Time lost! Sabbaths lost! means

o 2

lost! Soul lost! Heaven lost!' Backward he drops; all his sins seem to hang round his neck like so many millstones, as he plunges into the burning abyss. 'Come, and see.' Lord, save him! O my God, save him! 'Come, and see.' Blessed be God! the rider has not overtaken him yet; there is time and space yet for that poor sinner; he may be saved yet,— he has not dropped into hell. 'Come, and see.' The horse and the rider have not overtaken you yet; there is, therefore, an 'accepted time,' there is a 'day of salvation.' 'Come, and see.' There is God the Father, inviting you; God the Father, commanding you; God the Father, swearing he has no pleasure in your death. 'Come, and see.' Christ has come to seek you. He says,—'Come unto me, and I will give you rest.' 'He that believeth in me, shall never die.'"

Death on the pale horse, when Mr. Dawson had freedom, was with him, in speaking, what the same subject was to West with his pencil,—the one being the poetry of painting, and the other, the poetry of preaching. This peroration is a specimen, too, of his more Tarsic manner of treating a subject,—sudden —abrupt—and apparently unpremeditated. *

He was often peculiarly happy in arresting attention in the outset, in this way. A minister who had heard much of him, came some distance to hear him preach, when he was in the North; and not being introduced to him, through some mishap, he entered into conversation with a gentleman, sitting next to

---

* The subject was taken up by old Samuel Ward, of Ipswich, in 1635; and has more recently engaged the attention in a separate treatise, 12 mo., pp. 209, by the Rev. J. Bruce, of Liverpool; but both differ widely from Mr. Dawson.

him, on the properties of Sir Humphry Davy's safety lamp. Mr. Dawson listened to him; and concluded from his dress, manners, and conversation, that he was some colliery agent, residing in the neighbourhood. He was not a little surprised, after the service, to be complimented by this gentleman for his sermon, when he heard him add,—" I wish I could produce the same effect in the pulpit, when I am there." " Ah, Sir, " said Mrs. Reay, the lady of the house, "you must move the hand of Him that moves the world, before you witness these effects." Here lay the " power " of Mr. Dawson, and not barely, or even chiefly, in his manner of handling a subject. Though his remarks were often either awfully solemn, eccentrically original, or movingly natural and pathetic, —the great secret of his success lay in the power which God alone can supply.

The occasion of his first visit to Sunderland, was to preach to the sailors. He was met by Mr. B. Dowell, at Durham, at whose house he was to reside on reaching his destination ; and the next day was taken by him to see the life-boat, &c. Having to preach in the evening, the objects that engaged attention through the day were not lost upon him. Some of the imagery which he employed to rouse the torpid conscience of the sinner was terrific. To accomplish his purpose, he depicted a shipwreck,—the storm raging, —the billows tumultuously roaring,—the wind heaving up its ocean-mountains, and scooping out its vallies,— the vessel on a lee-shore,—the rocks at hand,—the mariners at their " wits end,"—some crying for mercy, —all disposed to aid each other, and to exert themselves to the utmost ;—wives, children, and friends on the shore,

but unable to render them the least assistance ;—one
crying amain, " My brother is lost," another exclaiming, " My father is there;" the vessel at length striking,
—flying in pieces,—the survivors clinging to the wreck,
—and the whole on the point of disappearing.   At the
moment, when all seemed crashing, reeling, roaring,
separating into still smaller fragments, and sinking, he
shouted,—" What is to be done now ?—all is going—
going for ever ! " " What is to be done ! " bawled out
a tar in the midst of the congregation, " why launch
the life-boat." This, with the vivid, bold imagery of the
preacher, produced an extraordinary sensation in the
congregation ; and on the feeling partially subsiding,
Mr. Dawson being in all the majesty of his freedom and
power, turned his eye of terror upon the sinner, and
rolling forth a volume of voice in some of its boldest,
wildest, loudest, and—when suited to the sentiment
and action—tenderest tones, rushed down upon the
previously prepared and awakened feelings, representing
man as lost in the general shipwreck of human nature,
—plunging, on rejecting the only means of salvation
and safety, into the gulf of hell, where every thing was
aggravated by circumstances ; the sufferers, in the one
case, being friendly to each other,—every man meeting
a friend in the vessel, with the additional hope of again
meeting and hailing each other in a future state ; while
in the other case, every lost spirit in perdition would
meet an enemy,—pious friends, father, mother, brother,
and sister seen no more,—the lost soul tost on a
liquid sea of fire—scudding on, and on, and on—the
breath of the Almighty, like an everlasting hurricane,
sweeping across the sea, and blowing up the flames !
After employing this imagery, he took the Bible in his

hand, and in reference to the exclamation of the sailor, said,—"Blessed be God! though there is no life-boat in hell, we have one here!" He then adverted to the Word of Life, which pointed out CHRIST, the *author* and the *way* of life. This was denominated by the sailors, "The Life-Boat Sermon," and was talked of years afterwards.

In 1823, the society at Barwick sustained the loss of two excellent members by death,—the mother of the Rev. David Stoner, and Mrs. Newby; the former Aug. 10th, and the latter Sep. 9th. Brief memoirs of both were forwarded by Mr. Dawson to the Editor of the Wesleyan Magazine, where they appeared in 1824, pp. 140, 209. He wrote also an account of Mrs. Broadbelt of Killinghall, for his friend Mr. Thompson. There were only eleven members in his class at Barnbow at this time, including himself. The Barwick class met a long time in the house of Mrs. Batty.

There were four out of five children, left by Mrs. Stoner, who were found in the way of righteousness. David was the oldest, who was much esteemed by Mr. Dawson, and the more so, as he was brought to God under his ministry. There was another young man of promising talents, who began to preach about the same time with David. Mr. Dawson speaking of them one day, observed, " J——cooks a good dinner, and sets it in order before his guests : but they may either take it or not : if they do not, they may let it alone ; but in such a case, the infant, as well as others, may starve. David, on the other hand, says, ' I'll make you take it : ' he takes the spoon in one hand, and the child by the nose with the other, and pours the contents down the throat. J——*exhibits*, David *preaches*." The eloquence of David Stoner was that which may be compared to a stream that is fed by an abundant spring, and not that, as a writer observes, "which spouts forth a little frothy water on some gaudy day, and remains dry the rest of the year." And yet, though few men equalled him for the uninterrupted tide of eloquence he poured forth in the pulpit, he was exceedingly reserved in social life. Indulging one day his taciturn mood, Mr. Dawson—full of spirit, rallied him on the subject. David, a little tried with it, took up the old proverb,—"Empty casks sound most;" and threw it at Mr. Dawson. "What are full ones good for," returned the latter, "till they are *tapt?*"

The slender number of members in Mr. Dawson's class, as just adverted to, was a source of grief. Mr. Russom, of Tarperly, Cheshire, referring to this period, observes in a letter to the biographer,—"Sixteen years have passed away since myself and two others went to his class at Barwick. 'I had last night,' said Mr. Dawson, 'An impression upon my mind, that God was about doing something for us, and now,'—pointing to us, 'see, here it is—three souls—three souls.—Bless the Lord! Bless the Lord! After enquiring into the state of my mind, and directing me to the 'Lamb of God,' he solemnly put his hands upon my head, and prayed, while raising his eyes to heaven,—'Lord, bless this lad, and make him a blessing!' Subsequently, I was often impressed with his deep humility at class, and once observed to a member,—'Mr. Dawson seems wholly unconscious of his worth to the church.'"

A person meeting with a few religious friends, while Mr. Dawson was present, began to sport his wit, and to state, that when he became serious, he advertised a *sale* of his effects—referring to *sin,* and resolved upon *selling* all off. Mr. Dawson, to put a stop to what might lead to a trifling mode of conversation, on a subject so awfully serious as sin, returned,—" A *buyer* would be wanting for the stuff; the devil would not give a price, for it was his already;—God would have nothing to do with it, for he hates it;—and man needed it not, for he would find he had enough of his own without it." He could relish wit; but not when "reason put in her claim for the one half of it, and extravagance for the other."

Being down at Hull, preaching occasional sermons, the friends of the Bible Society availed themselves of his aid, at one of their meetings. His speech excited great interest, especially when he turned to Mr. Dikes, and acknowledged him as his spiritual father. This revelation to the meeting was the more grateful, because of the esteem in which Mr. Dikes was held, and the members of the Established Church began to look with more respect upon the son in the gospel, for the venerable pastor's sake; and it drew many to a Methodist chapel, who had not been in the habit of entering one before.

His excellent mother died July 9th, 1824, in the 76th year of her age, and was sincerely lamented by the family; but by no one was the stroke so severely felt as by himself, having been at home with her from childhood, and *now,* comparatively alone in the house!

CHAPTER XII.

THE anxiety to obtain the services of Mr. Dawson,
in places which had not been favoured with them,
became more and more intense from 1825 to 1830,
which embraces that portion of his history to which
the reader is now directed : and yet the spirit which
he kindled in the societies that had been so favoured,
rendered it extremely difficult for him to extend his
acquaintance, owing to the friends pressing him to
repeat his visits.   This induced many to apply to

him twelve months before his services were required. He had public engagements now, in a general way, from January to July, as far as his regular work would allow, and also towards the close of the year. "The latter part of July," said he to the writer, "as well as August and October, I reserve to myself; the first, because of the *hay*, the second being the time for cutting the *corn*, and the third for sowing the *seed*." The way in which he accomplished his Herculean toil, may be accounted for partly on the principle laid down in the remarks of a writer of close observation :— "It is an undoubted truth," says he, "that the less one has to do, the less time one has to do it in. One yawns, one procrastinates, one can do it when one will, and, therefore, one seldom does it at all : whereas, those who have a great deal of business, must (to use a vulgar expression), buckle to it; and they always find time enough to do it in." With Mr. Dawson, it was not barely a "*must*" be,—though he was sensible of a "woe be to 'me," if I do it not : but his duty was his delight. He could adopt the language of Ezekiel,—"The Spirit lifted me up." This gave ardour to his love, strength to his faith, and animation to his hope ;—removing from the soul the various weights that clogged it, and adding to it the pinions by which it was borne onward in its flight to heaven ;—being ready, ever and anon, to exclaim, through the fine flow of feeling of which he was the subject, in what might possibly have been proverbial language,—"Or ever I was aware, my soul made me like the chariots of Ammi-nadib."

In one of his excursions to the north at this time, he preached at Carville, near Newcastle. Two persons were passing the chapel, one of them,—a professed deist, said to the other,—"Let us hear what this fellow is bawling about." They went near the doorway, which, as usual, was crowded—the chapel being unequal to the accommodation of the people. After stopping two or three minutes, the other said,—"Come, let us go." "Nay," returned his companion, "I will hear him out." He did "hear him out," and heard to profit; for on the outside of the chapel—the windows and doors being open, the word of God fastened on his conscience; the "strong man armed" was slain; and within a fortnight,—having given every evidence of a divine change, a stone fell from the top of the pit, where he was working, and killed him on the spot! Whether the man was a reader, and entitled to the character of a thinker, or whether his infidel principles arose from the natural enmity of the human heart to God and truth, is of little importance. His principles, or his feelings, or both, preserved him in hostile array against everything sacred: and whether scepticism attempts to rear its own system, or employs its efforts to undermine a better, it is equally fatal to the individual, though not equally easy and pleasant. Hence the truth of the remark, that we may find a thousand engineers, who can sap, undermine, and blow up, with admirable dexterity, for one who can build a fort, or lay the platform of a citadel. The point of interest to contemplate is—that there was hope in the man's death, adding another testimony to the fact, that—

> "The quality of mercy is not strain'd :
> It droppeth as the gentle rain from heaven,
> Upon the place beneath."

Few chapels were now opened, including a considerable extent of country around, to the services of which he was not either pressingly invited, or in a part of which he did not actually engage. It was common, on such occasions, to find his name associated in the same advertisements, in newspapers, and in the posters on the walls, with those of Dr. Clarke, the Revs. R. Watson, R. Newton, and other popular ministers. Among the chapels opened in 1825, Mytholmroyd, in the Todmorden circuit, Cullingworth, Osset, Eastbrook—Bradford, and Brunswick—Leeds, may be noticed.

The last, which was considered the largest chapel in the Wesleyan Connexion at that time,—being 96 feet in length and 72 in width, was opened on Friday, September 9th. The services were resumed on Sunday, September 11th. Its cost was estimated to be about £7900; the collections at the opening, amounted to £853, which was augmented by a few spirited individuals to £1000,—exclusive of previous subscriptions, amounting to nearly £2000. The chapel was calculated to accommodate 3000 persons; and in the genuine spirit of that text of mercy,—"The poor have the gospel preached unto them," *one thousand* free sittings were appropriated to such as were unable to pay for them. Since then, however, it is to be regretted, the number of free seats has been considerably reduced.

Mr. Dawson was visited by a friend on the 10th, the Saturday intervening the services, when he was found busily engaged in marking sheep on his farm. Adverting to his employment, he slyly turned up his eye—his meaning eye, to his friend, who was approaching him, and said,—" I hope to mark some other sheep to-morrow." He did so; for in the afternoon of the Sabbath—during the adjourned services, it was found that he had indeed marked some of the Lord's stray sheep in Brunswick chapel. The honour thus put upon Mr. Dawson, in opening the largest chapel in the Connexion—in his own circuit —he himself a local-preacher—and in a town in which he had preached upwards of twenty years, reminds the biblical student of the honour which God conferred upon David, of whom it is said, "he keepeth the sheep," and who was translated from the sheep-cot to the court of Saul;—of Elisha, "who was ploughing with twelve yoke of oxen, and upon whom Elijah, as he "passed by him, cast his mantle;"—and "of Amos, who," when the spirit of prophecy descended upon him, "was among the herdmen of Tekoa."

One thing annoyed Mr. Dawson here, as in many other places. At the close of the circular announcing the services, it was added,—"The trustees, wishing to accommodate the respectable friends who may attend on the occasion, purpose to reserve the entire gallery of the Brunswick Chapel for their use. To facilitate this, silver will be taken at the foot of the stairs." This was always repulsive to his feelings, and the collectors employed were characterized by him as presenting so many "silver daggers" at the people on their way to the gallery. He associated with the case, the resemblance it bore to persons paying on entering a place of amusement—its apparent opposition to a free gospel, —and the painful manner in which it operated upon the poor. But such were the crowds to hear him, especially in Manchester and other populous places, that the chapel doors were beset with the people long before they were opened for service, the best seats were often occupied by non-contributors, while the most liberal givers were left without. In many instances, the police were obliged to parade before the places of worship, to prevent disturbance among the multitudes who were anxious to hear him, —the baser sort availing themselves of the occasion for the worst of purposes.

Mr. Dawson was not merely popular; nor was the feeling which accompanied his public labours evanescent. There may be popularity without either solid or permanent good,—excitement without a genuine work of God. Popularity is often the mere creature of circumstance, and owes its existence, as well as its continuance, to some external attraction, independent of either extraordinary mental endowments, or exalted piety. Mere excitement is generally confined to the man;—it circumscribes itself within his own sphere of operation, — moves, like his shadow, by his side,—never puts up its appearance, except when he is there,—and leaves all around, save that one spot, blank or dreary. A genuine revival of the work of God, in a town or neighbourhood, is not seen following in the wake of only one person; every chapel is benefited;—every minister of God receives his quota of hearers;—the week-day services are more numerously attended, as well as those appointed for the Sabbath; —the forenoon services are as respectable for number as those in an evening, that have the charm of a prayer-meeting appended to them;—and people are as partial to the *word* of GOD, as to the *prayers* of MAN. Newly-awakened souls— persons hungering and thirsting after righteousness, will not refuse the food because of the less distinguished platter upon which it is served; they will be thankful for the bread of life from any minister of Christ. The ministry that renders people fastidious,—that enamours them merely with the man, to the neglect or contempt of others, is defective in its essentialities. The subtle poison of the Corinthian church is in it. The design of the Christian ministry is to endear God, his house, and his word, to man, and not man to a solitary individual. This was the genuine effect of Mr. Dawson's ministry. Though he was loved and respected, the word of God was loved the better for his services; he did not take the work away with him to the next place; but he left a savour of hallowed feeling behind him, by which ministers and people were benefited after he had quitted the spot. Though he took the torch with him, a number of lamps were left burning by him at the place, which had been kindled at his flame; and he found them more bright on his return. This was the case at Grimsby and other places, where a genuine revival of the work of God broke out, through which whole societies shared in the benefit. The moving of the waters did not subside immediately on his departure, as in the departure of the angel from the pool of Bethesda, and remain a dead calm till his return. The people were left with a relish for the ministry of others, as well as his own. They did not take their ideas of a minister from himself barely,—cherishing the notion that they could receive good from no other;—all others sinking in their esteem in proportion as he himself advanced. He drew them to God, not to himself; and yet, in drawing them to God, he was honoured both of God and man. Here is the difference between sheer popularity and usefulness ; the former follows the man wherever he goes, and moves *only* in his train ; the latter is stationed at the different places : the one has a rambling, gipsy kind of existence ; and the other has its fixed settlement, and erects, if not towns, its congregations and its temples— found years after, as so many monuments of ministerial toil.

He very often had to turn out of the different places of worship, and preach in the open air, to accommodate persons who could not gain access to the chapels ; and the chapels themselves could only be endured, from the intense interest the people felt to hear him. A person came to him at Cullingworth, nearly breathless, wiping the perspiration off his face, and saying, by way of shewing his hardships, and exciting pity,—" I have had to stand all the time ! " " So have I," returned Mr. Dawson, when silence was instantly imposed ;—the person perceiving that Mr. D. had the fatigue of the pulpit added to it. He preached a sermon on occasion of the death of Mrs. Deborah Watson, of Garforth, Dec. 29th, 1825. His text was John iii. 16,—-selected previously by the good woman herself. The selection of texts was rather a usual practice. John Goodall, of Garforth, a collier, who was brought to God under his ministry, while preaching at Little Preston, on Matt. xxvi. 58, requested him to preach his funeral sermon, and to take for his text Galatians vi. 7, 8.

In the course of 1826, he assisted at the opening of chapels at Brotherton, Rochdale, Otley, Longholme, Thorne, York, Mebmerly, Monkwearmouth, Spitalfield—Leeds, Minsten, Shuckerstone, &c. ; and visited

Nottingham, Newark, Sheffield, Doncaster, Newcastle, Shields, Sunderland, Darlington, Halifax, and different places in Lancashire and elsewhere : and it was not uncommon for him to be sowing seed, stacking corn, clipping sheep, &c., on the same day that he was opening chapels and attending missionary meetings,— working "double tides," to employ a nautical phrase, that one thing might not interfere with another, and so bringing "forth his fruit in his season."

While preaching in Albion-street chapel, in one of his visits to York, he took for his text, Ezekiel iii. 17 —19. Towards the close of the sermon, he proposed the question with solemnity and deep feeling,—"Why will you die?" stating, that he would sit down, and give them time for deliberating upon an answer, —taking his seat at the same time in the pulpit, in the midst of death-like silence. The effect would have been ludicrous, had the people not been awed into stillness and sober thought by his previous reasonings and appeals to the conscience. After a short pause, he turned his scrutinizing eye to one side of the gallery, and asked,—"*Why* will you die?" then to the other,—shifting the emphasis on different words, —"Why *will* you die?" next to the front,—"Why will *you* die?" and lastly below,—"Why will you *die?*" With the sound of death still vibrating on the ear, he rose, and in a modulated tone, said, —"What, not an answer! not one capable of assigning a reason for his conduct! Is silence your only reply? Speechless here, and speechless hereafter! At that moment—for it had not occured to him to employ it before, the fact of one of the judges having sentenced a poor wretch to be hung in the city two days before, flashed into his mind; and with the same solemn feeling, he imitated the judge while putting on the "black cap,"—one of his customary actions coming to his aid at the instant, of stroking down his wig on each side with both hands,—pronouncing with firmness and vehemence, that part of the text, "Thou shalt *surely* die." The whole was easy, natural, and contrary to what any one can be supposed to conceive, except those who witnessed it,—deeply impressive.

Though his manner occasionally approached the confines of the ludicrous, and his expressions were sometimes overstrained, there was so much pure nature in the one, and so much meaning in the other, that he generally found an apologist at hand among his auditors. When preaching on Daniel in the lions' den, he drew largely on the pencillings of his imagination, and after depicting the place in all its gloom and horror—the animals in all their power, hunger, and ferocity, he contrasted the whole with the ecstatic frame of mind in which Daniel might be supposed to have been wrapt in the presence of the "angel" of the Lord, while in deep communion with heaven,—finally, representing him as bursting forth into song, till—tamed and charmed by his strains, the lions, under a more powerful spell than the harp of Orpheus, united in the concert, and "growled *bass*" to the *tenor* of his finer and more elevated Hebrew warblings, which were poured into the ear of his angelic companion.

February 29, 1826, his friend John Richardson of Barwick, died, with whom he had often taken "sweet counsel." John, who met in his class, was a rare man, and made a blessed exit. But it could not be said of

P

him as of many, who may say of themselves, in the
affecting language of Sir Walter Raleigh, the night
before he died,—

"The dark and silent grave
* * * * *
Shuts up the story of our days ; "

for Mr. Dawson wrote a memoir of him, which was
published in the Wesleyan Magazine for 1827, p. 721,
and which enables him to speak, though dead—a
sense in which Sir Walter's own "story" still lives,
though the "days" of his life have long been numbered, or "shut up."

Biography had a particular charm in it to Mr.
Dawson. Speaking of the Lives of eminent men, he
observed,—"The Life of Mr. Benson came into my
hand about the same time that I received the Life
of the Rev. Thomas Scott. With the latter, I was
much pleased. I said to myself, 'There is *substance*
here.' A man is best seen in his unstudied *letters*
to his friends. *Diaries* are of little worth, except
for personal use in private, and will only admit of
brief extracts for publication. The sum of the whole
is,"—continued he laughingly, "he got up in the
morning—took his breakfast—sat down to dinner—
drank his tea—took his supper—and went to bed.
The next day is a fac-simile of its predecessor."
There is much truth in this, so far as diaries of
mere experience and domestic life are concerned; and
it shews the change that had passed over him, in
reference to his own. But the Lives of eminent men
were differently viewed, and that for very substantial
reasons; for "Biography," as Burgh observes, "sets
before us the whole character of a person, who has

made himself eminent either by his virtues or his vices—shews us how he came at first to take a right or a wrong turn—the prospects which invited him to aspire to higher degrees of glory, or the delusions which led him from his virtue and his peace ; the circumstances which raised him to true greatness, or the rocks on which he split, and sunk to infamy. And how can we more effectually, or in a more entertaining manner, learn the important lesson, what we ought to pursue, and what to avoid ? "

A death with which Mr. Dawson was more sensibly touched, followed in the course of the same year— that of the Rev. David Stoner, who died at Liverpool, after a short illness, Monday, Oct. 23rd. The mournful intelligence was communicated to Mr. Dawson on the 25th ; and he felt like a father. Mr. Stoner was born near Barwick-in-Elmet, in April, 1794. His parents, who were the intimate friends of Mr. Dawson, taught him what is the good and the right way ; and the Divine Spirit seconded the prayerful instruction communicated, with many drawings from the Father. In the spring of 1806, much fatal sickness, and many sudden deaths, occurred in Barwick ; and, as might be supposed, great alarm prevailed. Among others, who were taken away upon this occasion, was the father of a large family, Thomas Thompson, a collier, who met in Mr. Dawson's class, and whose death was improved by him. His text was Deuteronomy xxxii. 29,—"Oh, that they were wise, that they understood this, that they would consider their latter end ! " Young Stoner was present ; the word entered his heart ; and he was convinced of sin, of righteousness, and of judgment : and at the prayer-meeting which followed the sermon, "he offered up prayers and supplications, with strong crying and tears, unto him that was able to save him from death; and was heard in that he feared." It was a night much to be remembered by him; for he obtained the blessing of conscious acceptance with God. He was then only twelve years of age; and yet he held fast this early beginning of his confidence steadfast unto the end of his life. He was received upon the plan as a local-preacher, when teacher in an academy at Leeds; and during the period of the first plan, it being necessary to call out another preacher for the regular duties of the Leeds circuit, he—though a native, and resident in it, was fixed upon to fill the vacancy. He commenced the itinerant work in 1814, and thus finished in 1826.

The eloquence of David Stoner was, what all true eloquence is described to be—good sense, delivered in a natural and unaffected way, without the artificial ornament of tropes and figures. Our common eloquence, is, with equal propriety, described by Baker, as usually a cheat upon the understanding,—deceiving us with appearances, instead of things, and making us think without reason, while it is only tickling our sense. David Stoner was a modern Apollos,—"An eloquent man, and mighty in the Scriptures;"—overwhelming in the application of divine truth to the understanding and the conscience. A good characteristic memoir of him was drawn up by Dr. M'c Allum—a man, who, like David himself, in the prime of life, and in the glory of his ministerial character, dropped into the tomb the year following. This brief sketch was published in the Wesleyan Methodist Magazine, for 1827,

p. 289. A separate, and more extended memorial of him was published the year subsequent to his death, 12mo., pp. 287, price 4s.; combining with character, "Copious Extracts from his Diary and Epistolary Correspondence." To the preface are affixed the signatures of Mr. Dawson and Mr. Hannah. As a joint production—though highly creditable, it would have probably added to the popularity of the work, if, to Mr. Hannah's good taste, further distinct traces of the sprightly and vigorous mind of Mr. Dawson had been perceptible, to relieve the graver character of the work. It is, however, a volume which young preachers would do well to peruse; and merits, for the sake of its pulpit model, a more extensive circulation.

Mr. Dawson, at the earnest request of the friends in several of the circuits in which Mr. Stoner had travelled, and in places where he was personally known, preached funeral sermons on the occasion of his death; as at Leeds, Huddersfield, Bradford, Birstal, Tadcaster, Barwick, &c.; at the last of which places, his text was 2 Kings, xx. 1; Isaiah xxxviii. 1. At Bradford, where Mr. Stoner had been extensively useful to the church of God, and where he successfully battled, discomfited, and drove the comedians out of the town, Mr. Dawson was unusually moving. In highly impassioned mood, when referring to the ministry of the deceased, he said,—

"When he blew the trumpet of war, hundreds rallied round the banner of the cross, and were ready for the charge of the enemy. Nor was he less successful when he blew the trump of Jubilee,—hundreds going forth at the sound, were crowned with joy and gladness! But look at him now;—look at the coffin and

the corpse;—look, my brethren in the ministry!
There he lies. The trumpet has fallen from his hand.
Speak to him;—say, 'Blow—blow—blow the trumpet
in Zion;—sound an alarm!' but he heeds not. Let
those of us, then, who are in the work, give the
sacred blast. No trumpet ever gave a more certain
sound, than did that of the deceased. How many
will have cause to bless the day they ever heard the
joyful sound from his lips! You, who were in church
fellowship, when he occupied this pulpit, look upon
his coffin and his corpse! He confirmed your faith,
—warned you of danger,—prayed for you,—rejoiced
over you. Many of you were his joy;—now you are
his crown! You were delighted when you saw him,
and still more when you heard him; you went forth
at his bidding, with your loins girt, in the gladness
of your hearts. He placed before you the Saviour,
by whom he himself was saved, and whose example
he imitated. And thou, poor backslider,—roused from
thy lethargy by his voice, but again prostrate in the
encounter, what shall I say to thee? I would take
up his fallen trumpet, and sound an alarm in thine
ear—an alarm both loud and long,—What meanest
thou, O sleeper? Start at once upon thy feet;—
awake to righteousness, and sin not; otherwise the
measure of thy punishment will be great. What do
I read in his Journal? 'If ever a sigh is recorded,
it is when the classes are deserted!' And why, I
ask, did you plant a thorn for his pillow, and make
him sigh in secret, instead of sing a song of praise?
Oh, let his death be your life;—rise—and return to
your first love;—let his happy spirit hear to-night
in heaven, that the prodigal, who has left his Father's

house, is returning to it! And you, O my young friends, I invite you also to look at his coffin! Thirty-two years are set upon the lid, twenty of which were spent in the service of God. Did he, at the close of life, lament that he commenced his religious course so soon? Ah, no. His day was short, but well filled up. His work is done. The trumpet has dropped from his hand."—Then, looking round upon the congregation,—doubling at the same time his hand, and placing it to his mouth, when he quoted, with a full swell of voice, an appropriate passage of Scripture, embodying in it the tidings of salvation to a lost world, he seemed to place his favourite son in the gospel, on the summit of Mount Zion, whence he sent his voice, with the clang of a trumpet, across the "holy city," to rouse its slumbering inhabitants from their sins; asking, while the blast appeared echoing among the "hills round about Jerusalem," and dying in the distance,—"Is there no young man in this congregation, willing to take up the fallen trumpet, and to occupy the station of the deceased in the Church?" accompanying the question with some other pointed interrogatories and remarks,—shewing the need of labourers, to supply the lack of service occasioned by the death of such men as Mr. Stoner.

It is almost impossible to divest the mind of an impression of the ludicrous being mixed up with the solemn occasion, when assuming the tone and character of a person blowing a trumpet; as in his imitation of the judge passing sentence. Yet here, as there, a sacred something was connected with it, which repressed every light feeling, and which produced,—

not omitting the sanctity and solemnity of the occasion, the same effect noticed by Goldsmith, between natural and unnatural speaking, when he observes, that "natural speaking, like sweet wine, runs glibly over the palate, and scarce leaves any taste behind it ; but being high in a part resembles vinegar, which grates upon the taste, and one feels it while he is drinking." This was the critical moment with Mr. Dawson, and between these two points he was sometimes placed in the utmost peril of miscarrying—and did actually occasionally miscarry in the esteem of others than persons of refined taste ; but it operated prejudicially only on a few minds, and to these it was only like a discordant tone in music, preparatory to the richest harmony,—a passing cloud, shading for the moment the disk of the sun, without excluding the surrounding day. Nature, like music, is felt or known by all, and works strangely upon both mind and matter, raising joy or grief, pleasure or pain—giving motion to the blood as well as the spirits—tranquilizing the disturbed thoughts—and even heightening the spirit of devotion itself. But the query is, what part of nature is to be admitted into the pulpit, and what part is to be kept out ; as well as what particular parts harmonize most with each other.

On this occasion, the simple question,—" Is there no young man in this congregation willing to take up the fallen trumpet?" was like a voice from heaven, entering the inmost soul of one lovely youth—Samuel Entwisle, who had been impressed some time with it being his duty to give himself to the work of the ministry, but had resisted the call, till he brought himself into the deepest distress of mind. At that moment, he resolved to yield—took up the trumpet, to pursue the metaphor—began to preach—entered the itinerant work—but soon, like David Stoner, to whom he would have been an admirable successor, sickened,—laid aside the clarion,—and died the death of the righteous. He was the son of the late Rev. Joseph Entwisle, " the beloved disciple " of modern times.

Some of the chapels opened by Mr. Dawson in 1827, were those of Leuthley, Farsley, Henley, Ulleskelf, Kirk Deighton, West Auckland, Farnley, and one in the neighbourhood of Croft ; and among the numerous places in which he preached other occasional sermons, Stockport, Manchester, Salford, Middleton, Ratcliffe Close, Longholme, Keighley, Sheffield, York, Birmingham, Bristol, Bingley, Skipton, Halifax, Wakefield, Bradford, Dewsbury, Pontefract, Snaith, Otley, Stokesley, Darlington, Barnard Castle, Newcastle-on-Tyne, Wall's End, Thirsk, Bawtry, and Ashton-under-Lyne, may be named,

His long tried and excellent friend, Mr. Hugh Gill, died April 27th, this year, aged 74,—forty-eight years of whose life had been consecrated to the service of God. Mr. Dawson wrote a memoir of him, which was inserted in the Wesleyan Magazine for 1828, p. 651. He was one of those men, who never forfeited the reputation of his integrity, and out of whose commercial transactions, the Christian was constantly coming before the eye, like stars, unobtrusively stealing into sight as the evening approaches, and attracting attention, not so much by their sparkling appearance, as by their shining. Mr. Dawson not only penned a memoir of Mr. Gill, but preached his funeral sermon ; as also the funeral sermons of Mrs. Boggitt, Betty Scholes, and Dr. Mc Allum.

P 2

The last was preached at York, July 28; and Mr.
Dawson was probably selected, not so much from any
long established friendship between himself and the
Dr., as from the intimacy which subsisted between the
latter and Mr. Stoner. The biographer knew the Doctor
from boyhood, and was stationed with his excellent
father in the Shields circuit, in 1807, when he came from
Kingswood School, on finishing his education in that
seminary. He even then, manifested unusual powers
of mind ;—quick, yet ·not volatile,—adventurous, yet
possessed of sufficient firmness to be relied upon ;
and could pursue an argument with care, acuteness,
and foresight, without—as is too often the case with
persons of more matured intellectual abilities, suddenly
striking off like the tangent of a circle, and incapable
of being brought back into his orbit by attraction or
gravity. He was usually recollected and guarded. The
same rare combination of sprightliness and solidity
advanced with age ; and had his life been prolonged, he
would have ranked still more eminently among those
men described by Lord Brougham—whom, by the
way, he could imitate to a nicety as a public speaker,
who, by diffusing useful information, by furthering
intellectual refinement, and by promoting moral improvement, "hasten the coming of that bright day,
when the dawn of general knowledge shall chase away
the lazy, lingering mists, even from the base of the
great social pyramid ;" superadded to which, was the
Christian, as well as the philosopher and the scholar,
in which exalted character he shone still more bril-
liantly—even as one of the " stars " in the " right
hand " of Jesus Christ.   His " Remains," preceded
by a Memoir from the classical pen of the Rev.

Jonathan Crowther, deserve a wider circulation than they appear to have had.

The close of the year was distinguished for great excitement among the Wesleyans in Leeds. The main point of dispute was the introduction of an organ into Brunswick chapel; a number of pamphlets, comprising —when bound together, two thick octavo volumes, —were published on the occasion. The agitated state of the Society had been a source of pain to Mr. Dawson for several months; it was brought, however, to a crisis, and " A special District Meeting of Wesleyan Ministers" was held at Leeds on the case, on Tuesday, the 4th of December, 1827, and continued by successive adjournments. Mr. Dawson, in a memorandum made by himself, notices that he was present at the meeting on the 4th, 5th, 6th, and 7th; and appends to the latter date, " The case of Messrs. Sigston and Mallinson examined, and both were expelled."

Several of the ministers and principal friends were assembled in the house of one of the preachers prior to the meeting, when some strong remarks were made. Mr. Dawson observed,—" Hitherto, I have taken part with neither side; and although I cannot justify the dissentients, yet there are some palliations to be offered on their behalf. I put it to you, Mr.——, and, in so doing, I may bear hard upon Mr.——, whether, after the organ question was put in the Quarterly Meeting, and there was an overwhelming majority against it, it was judicious, in such a state of things, to grant permission to the trustees to put one up ? " To this, Mr. Dawson remarked to the biographer,—" Mr.—— was silent." " And now," continued Mr. D., " I turn to Mr.——, and I may bear hard upon him : but would

it not have been better if Mr.—— had avoided the
suspension of ————?   I am aware he acted on the
rule of 1797 ; but that rule had been slumbering for a
period of thirty years ; and that being the case, would
it not, taken in connection with what preceded, have
shewn a disposition to conciliate matters ?   I repeat it,
I do not justify the men : but these circumstances may
be stated as palliatives, in the present stage of the
business." Mr. D. further observed to the writer,—
"Not a word was said in reply."   After a brief pause,
Mr.—— said, "Well, but what is to be done?   The
case is before us, and we must deal with it." "Do
with it," returned Mr. Dawson, "the dissentients have
arrived at that point, that must now compel you to put
them down : there is no peace to be maintained with
them ; and strong measures are necessary to preserve
the healthy part of the society, by separating it from the
infected."   So far he closed in with ulterior measures,
—not as *desirable* in every instance, but as *necessary*.

During this struggle, Mr. Baines of Leeds, manifested anything but candour and fairness towards the
Wesleyan Methodists,—throwing open the columns of
the Mercury to the dissentients, and narrowing the
door, as far as possible, as to the admission of papers
in defence of the opposite party.   Mr. Dawson felt
this, not only on the ground of justice, but on the
score of friendship,—Mrs. Baines, when Miss Talbot,
having been a frequent visitor at Barnbow, and Mr.
Baines himself having received personal kindnesses
from members of the Methodist body.   He addressed,
therefore, a letter to him, through the medium of the
Leeds Intelligencer of December 18th, 1828, signed
"A METHODIST," in which the reader will find a

repetition of the comparison of a "snarling critic" to a gander, and of which the following is a copy:—

"SIR,—In the last fifteen months, the disposition of deep-rooted enmity which you have evinced against the Methodist system, and the Methodist ministers, has given me considerable pain. This, in my apprehension, has been as obvious as the light of day. It has always appeared to afford you real pleasure to insert any paragraph sent from any person, or collected from any quarter, which had a tendency to lessen the system of Methodism in the public estimation. When the unhappy disputes began about the Brunswick chapel organ, paragraph after paragraph appeared in the most interesting column of your paper, the direct tendency of which was, to embitter and inflame the spirit of your readers, and those paragraphs inserted 'without money and without price.'——But, as I have been informed, when Mr. Grindrod sent his communication, then it must be paid for as an advertisement! And pray, Sir, in what particulars have the Methodists injured you? Look over the list of the subscribers to your paper, and will you not find scores of persons who honour that list with their names, who are Methodists? But, Mr. B., review the past;—and 'look to the rock from whence ye were hewn, and the hole of the pit whence ye were digged;' and I ask, who was the gentleman that lent you a hundred pounds, to begin that business with, in which you have succeeded so well? Was he not a Methodist? And, after all this, though at times you appear covered with a cloak of candour, yet, under it, you hide a dagger, with which, at every convenient opportunity, you aim a deadly blow under the fifth rib. Ungenerous

—ungrateful man! Do the Methodists deserve this at your hands? Let any man of sober reason look at your last week's paper, and see the way you have treated the Rev. T. Galland; and can any one conclude that this is the conduct of a *friend?* Impossible! Whatever may be the merits or demerits of his speech, I shall not now decide. But he spoke like an honest man, faithful to his convictions. Has he been answered like a man? If his arguments are weak, they are the more easily refuted. If they are strong, do you suppose that low banter and ridicule will make them fly like chaff before the wind? Pray, Sir, what have your doggerel rhymes and lines upon Mr. G., to do with his cool reasonings upon the Catholic Question? Surely, nothing. Answer his reasonings like a *man of reason*, and not like a *goose;* who, when a gentleman walks steadily on, runs and *hisses* at him, and returns to her flock, and informs them what a victory she has got, and flutters and cackles most triumphantly! I would advise you, Sir, not to indulge and manifest such perverseness to the Methodist system and the Methodist ministers; as I think they do not merit it from you: and, therefore, how far it is proper in our friends to support such a paper, I will not determine. Indeed, it must be said, to the praise of every Methodist subscriber, that he fulfils that apostolic injunction,—'If thine enemy hunger, feed him; if he thirst, give him drink; for in so doing, thou shalt heap coals of fire on his head.'—That the fire may melt every particle of the dross of malevolence, and fully imbue your heart with Christian charity, is the worst wish for you, in the heart of
                    Yours, &c.,—A METHODIST."

Some time after this—though anticipating the period of his personal history. Mr. Dawson observed to the biographer,—"You have been suspending Mr.———, I understand, for attending public meetings of a political character." "Such," it was replied, "has been the decision of the District Committee." Mr. Dawson returned,—"There is great sympathy excited for him in the country." "That may be," it was answered; "in all cases of *suspension*, the greater the offender, the greater the sympathy. Witness the still more serious *suspension* of Fountleroy!" "Honest men," he subjoined, "are not treated in that way." Then, whirling round his finger, like a person suspended from the fatal tree, he said,—"It is sure to affect the crowd. When we suspended Mr.——— at Leeds, about seventy local-preachers espoused his cause, and went off with him. A gentleman came to me, and asked,—'What is the matter with you at Leeds?' I replied,—We have had a riot,—have laid hold of the ringleader,—and *suspended* him; and having exercised discipline upon him, there are about seventy others of the local brethren, who are determined to *hang*, —or, if you please, *suspend* themselves, in consequence of it."

Subsequent to this again, he observed to the writer somewhat playfully, when speaking of the Protestant Methodists, as they were denominated,—"Every man has his own interpretation of St. Paul's *thorn in the flesh*. I have mine. It appears to me, that it was some restless person who wished to rule in the Corinthian church; and who, by his conduct, pierced like a *thorn*—acting, at the same time, the character of a *messenger of Satan*, being *sent* with a view to *buffet*.

At Leeds, Mr.—— seems to be Pauls's *thorn in the flesh.*" After a formal separation took place, he rarely made any enquiry respecting the dissentients, and only noticed the subject when casually drawn into it in the course of conversation. War was not his element; and besides this, he possessed a portion of the wisdom embodied in a sentiment of Plutarch, when he observes, —" It is of use to a man to understand not only how to overcome, but also, how to give ground when to conquer would rather turn to his disadvantage : for there is such a thing sometimes as a Cadmean victory; to which the wise Euripides attesteth, when he saith :—

> ' Where two discourse, if the one's anger rise,
> The man who lets the contest fall is wise. ' "

He knew, too, in the language of a wit, that—" It is in disputes, as in armies; where the weaker side sets up false lights, and makes a great noise, to make the enemy believe them more numerous and stronger than they really are. " In all disputes, it would be well to observe the moderation recommended by Hierocles ; —" When we are in a condition to overthrow false-hood and error, we ought not to do it with vehemence, nor insultingly, and with an air of contempt; but to lay open the truth, and with answers full of mildness, to refute the falsehood. " Still, as much depends upon the temper of the sword in the scabbard on the one side, as on the other, it may be necessary to enquire, whether the case does not warrant the exercise of the apostolic injunction,—" rebuke them sharply. "

The organ in Brunswick chapel, respecting which there had been so much angry feeling, was opened

September 12th, 1828 ; on which occasion, Mr. Dawson was present. He preached sermons on special occasions, in the course of the year, at Stokesley, Manchester, Salford, Rothwell, Burslem, Knaresbro', Bacup, Derby, Ashley, Burton-on-Trent, Belper, Sheffield, Norton, Yarm, Appleton, Bedale, Gatenby, Pickering, Hull, Beverley, Newport, Briestfield, Hapton, Barnsley, Skipton, Pateley-Bridge, Gloucester, Birmingham, Birstal, Nottingham, Burrow Ash, Macclesfield; Harrogate, Pontefract, Ashbourne, Masham, Middleham, Bradford, Great Horton, Retford, Newcastle-on-Tyne, Carville, Sunderland, Rochdale, Longholme, York, Acaster, Staley Bridge, Ashton-under-Lyne, Newcastle-under-Lyne, Bingley, &c. To some of these places, as Manchester and Burslem, his visits were repeated in the course of the twelve months. In addition to this extra toil, he assisted at the opening of chapels at Wakefield, High Town, Wighill, Gomersal, Stamford Bridge, Tadcaster, Ryther, Wesley chapel— Leeds, and Langton-Street—Bristol. The latter was opened June 19th ; the Revds. Richard Watson and Robert Wood, were also engaged on the occasion. Some of these journies, when one engagement was in the train of another, occupied a week. These taxes upon his time, imposed heavy agricultural toil upon him, when he reached home. But still, he was never behind with his work ; taking care to say to his servants, " *come,* " instead of " *go ;* " — the difference between which two words, according to a well-known anecdote, occasioned the transfer of an *estate* from a *master* to his *steward.* He not only inspected, but put his hand to the work. Sixty places may be enumerated, as above. Several of the journies would require three or more days to accomplish them, and most of them two ; and if we include his Sabbaths at home, we may consider this excellent man—with no other temporal reward than his travelling expenses, —and not always these,—as devoting upwards of the one-half of his time to the public service of God.

In one of his excursions, a lady of great gravity was desirous of being introduced to his society. Supper was on the table ; and the lady sat opposite him, conning him with an apparently curious eye, and lending deep attention to every remark he made. He was served with fowl, &c. The plate by some mishap, got to the edge of the table, and lost its balance, when the contents fell upon his drapery. The lady was now doubly attentive to see how he felt in this predicament ; and it is with a view to shew the man, that the somewhat ludicrous and trivial circumstance is introduced. The mifortune was not generally perceived ; but a lady,—a friend of the biographer, concluding from the expression of two or three fair faces, that something had occurred to provoke a smile, and not being able to ascertain the occasion by the dim candle-light, glided from her seat, and asked in an under tone,—"What is the matter?"   Mr. Dawson coolly replied, while scooping up the contents with his hand, till a towel was brought,—"Only a small mishap."   No difference was perceptible in his spirit or manner, though his clothes were spoiled by the accident ; and he pleasantly remarked to the lady who made the enquiry,—"Do not look at my clothes on the platform to-morrow ; attend to what is said, not to what is seen."   But it was too visible to an eye acquainted with the fact, not to be seen when he presented himself in front of the platform. Very unlike the "bashful man," it seemed to be no concern of his; and the lady of demure look was as much delighted with his philosophy as his Christianity. The tables were generally crowded at the houses of the friends where he was entertained, — the parties knowing the general anxiety which existed to enjoy his society. Being seated at the corner of a well-crowded table one day, he pleasantly observed,—"I love the corner; for here I have elbow-room." And this position he generally had by common consent; so that the honour conferred upon him, by being placed on the right or the left of the heads of the house, came to the relief of his more masculine form, which would otherwise often have been inconveniently crowded.

One circumstance ought not to be omitted. He often requested the friends with whom he was on terms of intimacy, and when there was sufficient time to prevent it, not to invite persons to meet him on the Lord's day; being desirous of securing as much of the day as possible for private devotion and pulpit preparation. How far this will be serviceable as a hint to others, will depend upon the use they are disposed to make of it.

One of the speakers, when out on a missionary occasion, appearing on the platform with a bundle of papers in his hand, Mr. Dawson, suspicious of an attempt to inflict punishment on the patience of the people, enquired—"What are you going to do with all them papers?" "To read them, to be sure," was the reply. "What, the whole of them?" he repeated. "Yes," returned the intended reader; subjoining, "such documents constitute the *life-blood* of

a speech." "Let me tell you, then," said Mr.
Dawson, who looked upon reading on a platform as
producing the same effect upon a congregation, that
the damper produces when put into the oven; and
who knew well the difference between the exercise
of the intellect upon written documents, and matter
bubbling up from the heart, — "Let me tell you,
that your speech will die of *apoplexy*, for the *blood*
has all gone up to the *head*."

His aversion to everything that tended to produce
weariness in a congregation, rendered him solicitous
to keep the affections on the move with the mind.
Though strictly a *revivalist*, he employed great discretion in timing the meetings; watched with narrow-
ness the influence of the Spirit upon the mind, and
rejoiced over the smallest indications of good. In a
prayer-meeting, in Oldham-Street, Manchester, after
a very impressive sermon, a person came up to him,
while the Rev. Jonathan Crowther was standing by his
side. Turning to Mr. Crowther, "This is Moses,"
said Mr. Dawson. Mr. Crowther not having either
seen or heard of the person before, was rather amused
with his introduction to him under the simple name of
the Jewish Lawgiver. Mr. Dawson added,—"He
met in my class, but fell away:" then, suddenly
wheeling round to the man, he said,—"Moses, pray
—and begin afresh." The man, as quickly dropped
upon his knees. Impressed with the loss he had
sustained in his spirit, while early days rushed upon
his mind with all their hallowed associations, he
seemed to pray in the Holy Ghost. "Aye," said
Mr. Dawson,—"hear him; he knows the way; he has
not forgotten it." After a brief space, while he was

yet on his knees, Mr. Dawson, again, at intervals, continued to encourage his wrestlings, with—"There, Moses, pray on;—bless the Lord!—Hear him, O God." Poor Moses at length rose from his knees professing to have found peace.

The morning following one of those meetings, a young person came to him, and stated with great simplicity, the good feeling that continued in the prayer-meeting, after he, (Mr. D.), had retired. "There was one man," said the informant, naming him, "who was under a concern for his soul the night before. But he did not obtain the blessing; and I was certain he would never obtain it, till he acted differently." Mr. Dawson enquired, "How so?" "Why," it was replied with great artlessness, but with a good knowledge of outward signs, "he was down only o' *ya knee*. But last night," it was continued, "he was down o' *both knees*; and then, I said to *mysen*, when I saw this, he will get the blessing. Yes, and he did get it *tu!*" This was appended in a tone of triumph. Mr. Dawson sometimes employed this little circumstance with good effect, when shewing that prostration of person generally accompanies prostration of spirit. The best of men know, that they are but recipients, and that to be indebted to another, and yet to be too high to show it, by a becoming carriage to the donor, "is but the old solecism of pride and beggary, which, though they often meet, yet ever make but an absurd society."

Being at Brunswick chapel, Leeds, two or three friends followed him into the vestry, where he stood by the fire a few seconds, while others were carrying on a prayer-meeting in another part, after public service. Looking at the Rev. R. A., he pleasantly, yet significantly remarked, while pulling down his wig on either side,—under a deep sense of the Divine presence,—" I may as well go home ; there is nothing for me to do here, or indeed for any of us ; God seems to have taken the whole into his own hand." And yet, on other occasions, under a similar overpowering influence of God upon the mind, he both spoke and acted in a reverse way. Preaching at Ancoats, Manchester, on Judges viii. 4,—" Faint, yet pursuing," every eye seemed at one time suffused with tears ; and when people and preacher were craned up to the highest pitch of feeling, a momentary pause ensued, during which the clock struck *twelve*, and broke the stillness that reigned, like the hammer on the bell at a watch-night, on the departure of the old year. In an instant, he darted his eye to the front of the gallery, and personifying the time-piece, said,—" You may speak—clock, but I am not done yet." Though no apparent expectation existed on the part of the auditory, that he would close his discourse with the hour, yet it had all the effect of reviving disappointed hope, and threw a gleam of sunshine into every countenance.

When preaching in Irwell-Street chapel, Salford, he adverted to the subject of *restitution* in his sermon, and drew the harrow across the consciences of some of his hearers. Such were his appeals, that a person sent him a letter after the service, enclosing a sum of money ; stating that he had been abroad,—that with others, he had committed a theft,—that the persons, if not dead, were out of reach, to whom restitution should be made,—and that, as he had no likely way of restoring to them the value of the plunder, he enclosed the amount, requesting him to dispose of it, as he might judge proper for the further-ance of the cause of God.   It was not only Christian, to permit conscience to speak out, but highly honour-able ; much more so than those who retain the property of others till the near approach of death, when they secretly endeavour—after all the advantage derived from its use, and all the injury sustained by its rightful owner, in consequence of being deprived of it, to make amends by their will, subsequent to their decease. But such persons, in the esteem of a popular Essayist, " had as well do nothing, as delude themselves both in taking so much time in so pressing an affair, and also, in going about to repair an injury with so little demonstration of resentment and concern.   They owe, over and above, something of their own ; and by how much their payment is more strict and incom-modious to themselves, by so much is their restitution more perfect, just, and meritorious ; for penitency requires penance."

It may be readily supposed, that Mr. Dawson ex-perienced great variety in his travels, as to accommo-dation, both in the way of lodging and conveyance. He was at the house of a friend, in a part of his own county, where he was put into a bed which was the worse for wear, and which was used occasionally by a gentleman of more slender make than himself. On lying down, away went the sacking, when he was immediately placed heels up.   His invention was never at fault ; and turning the pillows to the foot of the bed, he lay, as on an inclined sofa, till morning. Even this, amusing as it may seem, shews the character of the man. Some persons would not only have been disturbed themselves, but would, perhaps, have disturbed the family, already retired to rest ; and would have either hazarded an exchange of beds to the inconvenience of some of the members of the family, or rendered them uncomfortable by a knowledge of the peculiar situation of their guests. There is a moral here. The fountain of content springs up in the mind ; and the trouble it would have given to the family, would have disturbed Mr. Dawson's repose much more than any inconvenience experienced by himself.

Another point to which reference may be made, in connection with his delicacy in avoiding unnecessary trouble, was, his noble spirit of independence. He would never allow others to help him in anything, when it was within the range of possibility of aiding himself ; and, therefore, avoided, — considering even friendship itself unentitled to such claims, laying contributions on the horses and vehicles of his friends, to convey him to different places. He felt the full force of the sentiment of a writer, whom it would be heresy to name,—though Satan himself has been quoted—that all " Obligation is thraldom, and thraldom is hateful. " Nor would he press persons to accompany him to different places, with the selfish view of protecting his person and hushing his fears to repose, on his return at night. He knew that persons might be unwilling to give a denial, who could ill spare the time ; and that he had no more right to expend the time of another—time which might be demanded by the family, the business, and the friends of the individual, than he had a right to institute unnecessary claims upon his money. Time, in many cases, is much more valuable than gold; and the man that values his own time, like Mr. Dawson, will be sure to value the time of others. And besides, when he was going to exercise in public, he preferred quiet to conversation. When a man lays himself under obligation to another to accompany him, he but ill requites him by imposing silence upon him; and on the other hand, in proportion as conversation is indulged, the mind is abstracted from the subject intended for the pulpit, while inroads are made on the calm, prayerful spirit of devotion, by a variety of desultory topics,—one leading to another, till the place is reached, when the family, to whose house the *workman* repairs, have two guests quartered upon them instead of one. Company has impoverished many a spirit,—made many an insipid sermon,—and inconvenienced many a family. It is a difficult thing to disengage the mind from subjects on which it has been employed in conversation. Experience tells us, that "the thoughts will be rising of themselves from time to time, though we give them no encouragement, as the tossings and fluctuations of the sea continue several hours after the winds are laid."

Glancing over his outgoings for 1829, he appears to have lent himself out as freely, and to have gone as far from home as in the year preceding. He opened new chapels at Farnsfield and Batchworth. As many of his engagements were on the week-day, it must still be borne in remembrance, that he regularly fulfilled his Sabbath appointments, according to the plan, when at home.

His time was trenched upon also, in various valuations, and in having to attend to the executorship of the

Q

wills of some of his friends. Aware of his influence
with the people, he had often to engage too in the
" drudgery of begging ; " into the work of which
he was drawn by others. His friend, Mr. Sumner
of Cowick, having been deputed to solicit subscriptions for a chapel at Goole, concluded if he could
obtain the aid of Mr. Dawson, he would be able to
assist his object in the town of Leeds. Accordingly,
he set off for Barnbow, where he found Mr. Dawson
ready for every " good work ; " and, in company with
him, proceeded the next day to Leeds, in the cold
month of February, at the expense of several other
engagements demanding his attention. Mr. Dawson
was generally the spokesman ; and accosting the first
friend they visited, he jocosely observed,—" I have
often appeared before you in my own person, in
the character of a beggar ; but to-day, I am begging
for a beggar : " next stating the case. In the space
of about two hours, he obtained the sum of £20 for
his friend. There was a cheerfulness in his manner,
which would have disarmed the churl ; a cheerfulness, however, which bore no affinity to mirth ;—
the latter, to a prudent man, being merely accidental,
and never—to be effective, premeditated. Cheerfulness with him, was in the temper of the mind ; and
it is a fact, that " The most manifest sign of wisdom
is continued cheerfulness : her estate is like that of
things in the regions above the moon, always clear
and serene. " Besides its being natural, it was improved by grace ; and, with a heart brimmed with
love, he was the better equipped for errands of charity.
Importunity, in his case, was unnecessary. His own
warm sun thawed the ice wherever it was found. There

was no occasion for a man to purchase his own quiet, and so to relieve himself, by getting rid of rude, eager importunity and vexatious noise; the subject of these pages had too much delicacy to push any case beyond a certain point, and was too much beloved, not to excite a readiness and pleasure in the donor, to impart of his abundance.

A painful occurrence took place in one of his "begging excursions." He was invited to preach occasional sermons, and make collections at Heckmondwike, Sunday, April 12. Some person, during the service, either inadvertently rested upon a stove-pipe, which did not fit exactly, or was pressed against it in consequence of the crowded state of the place, when it suddenly gave way, and raised an alarm. Persons who were not aware of the cause, rushed to the door, under the impression that some part of the chapel was giving way. The shrieks and tumult cannot be described; and the effects were fatal. In a memorandum, left by Mr. Dawson, he has penned, within a broad black border, somewhat in the shape of a coffin,— "Heckmondwike: a panic in the chapel; five persons killed; one died next day." Besides these, many were seriously hurt. It left such a painful impression on Mr. Dawson's mind, that, though much importuned, he could not be induced to revisit the place till Oct. 3rd, 1837.

In the course of the spring, he met with the Rev. Gideon Ousely, brother of Major-General Sir Ralph Ousely, and heard him preach. He was much pleased with the old veteran, who, as a protestant, had been so often in the field against popery in Ireland. Gideon was not one of those "theological knight-errants"

who converted controversy into a species of quixotism;
nor was he one of those testy and quarrelsome persons, who have been contemplated in the light of a
loaded gun, which may by accident go off, and kill
the bystander. He seemed to have looked upon the
ignorance and superstition of the people, and the
"illiterate presumption" of the priests, like Milton in
another case, as the disease of the Roman Catholic
peasantry,—a disease that had entered into the very
constitution, and proved "the hectic evil" of Ireland.
He was, in general, of the opinion of Sir W. Temple,
that it "is best to take words as they are most commonly spoken and meant, like coin, as it most cur-
rently passes, without raising scruples upon the weight
of the alloy:" but then, he took the advantage of
Sir William's exception, which renders it more than
admissible in a man,—even praiseworthy, to test the
metal, when the "cheat or defect is gross and evident."
The conflict between Popery and Protestantism, is a
conflict between darkness and light, truth and error,
gold and dross. Gideon, though far from elegant,
was generally convincing. He tested every doctrine
by the word of God, and every absurdity in argument by the light of reason. Not so the papists.
With them, remarks Addison, "The most notable way
of managing a controversy, is that which we may call
arguing by torture. These disputants convince their
adversaries with a sorites, commonly called a pile of
faggots. The rack is also a kind of syllogism which
has been used with good effect, and has made multitudes of converts. Men were formerly disputed out
of their doubts, reconciled to truth by force of reason,
and won over to opinions by the candour, sense, and

ingenuity of those who had the right on their side; but this method of conviction operated too slowly. Pain was found to be much more enlightening than reason. Every scruple was looked upon as obstinacy; and not to be removed but by several engines invented for that purpose. In a word, the application of whips, racks, gibbets, gallies, dungeons, fire and faggot, in a dispute, may be looked upon as popish refinements upon the old heathen logic." This is a fine piece of irony, and not out of place, it is hoped, in the present connection. Mr. Dawson was not more delighted with Mr. Ousely, than Mr. Ousely was delighted with the flashes of Mr. Dawson's genius, elicited by the introduction of the corruptions of the Romish Church.

Towards the close of July, Mr. Dawson had an attack of rheumatism, which prevented him from fulfilling an engagement at Otley. Though sharp, it was short in its stay, and he was soon in the work again. In September, he preached a sermon on occasion of the death of Mrs. Martha Tarboton of Thorner, the wife of a nephew of the venerable John Pawson, and sent an account of her to the Editor of the Wesleyan Methodist Magazine, which was published in the obituary of 1820, p. 568. But another case, touched him still more tenderly. Samuel Hick, "The Village Blacksmith," was in his last sickness; and in the month of November, Mr. Dawson visited him, settled his temporal concerns, and attended his remains to the grave. He preached two funeral sermons on the occasion, one at Aberford, in the open air, with snow on the ground, and another at Rothwell.* A

* There are rare things respecting honest Samuel yet untold. Calling upon his sister one day, at Tadcaster, he said, " Thou hast a poor fire." She

Memoir of Samuel appeared from Mr. Dawson's pen in the Wesleyan Methodist Magazine, for 1831, p. 217, which he wrote at the time of his death.

Mr. Dawson's farm was at this time a losing concern. He lost, also, through distemper, three horses at once, and found it difficult to replace them. His friend, Mr. Reay, of Carville, who had bought a farm in the neighbourhood of Newcastle, knowing his circumstances, offered it to him,—generously proposing to take any rent Mr. Dawson might judge proper to give. But there was equal nobility on the side of Mr. Dawson, not to take advantage of the kindness of a friend, while there remained the slightest hope of improvement; and besides, he knew not how far he might be in the way of providence, in removing from the neighbourhood in which he had so long resided.

Having been at Stokesly, he crossed the country in the gig of a friend, and proceeded within a few miles of Stockton, where he had to wait an hour at the station, to catch the train for Darlington. The good woman belonging to the station, had to go to Stockton,

returned,—" We are not so near the pit as you." He made no reply,—went home,—rose early next morning,—proceeded to the pit,—loaded his cart,—and before eight o'clock, poured the coals down before her door,—and returned home without looking into the house,—being a distance of about 20 miles there and back. The neighbours, as the coals lay undisturbed, said to her,—" Why do you not get the coals in ? " She looked surprised, and could not be persuaded that she had any claim to them, till she was informed her brother had placed them there.

A grave man on a missionary platform, knowing that Samuel had to speak, whispered to him,—" Let us have no levity to-day, Sammy." When he arose, he observed,—" Mr. I., sitting there,"—pointing to him, " says, ' let us have no levity to-day.' Why, bless him, as to himself, he can *nother mak* folk laugh nor cry." To another gentleman, who said,—" Be short, Sammy," as he ascended the platform steps, he smartly returned,—" Stop a bit, I have not begun yet."

for which purpose she borrowed the gig, hoping to regain her own residence before the train arrived. She left Mr. Dawson in charge of the house, and gave directions as to matters of business. During her absence, he felt the smell of something burning in the oven; but as he had received no commands respecting the cooking department,—the oven not being specified among the items to which he had to attend, he left it, together with its contents, to itself. On her return, she found a spice-cake reduced to a cinder; leaving, however, her guest much more innocent than Alfred, who permitted the peasants cakes to burn while stringing his bow,—a subject admirably portrayed by Sir David Wilkie. Had his curiosity been strong, he might have saved the cake; but he acted in the absence of persons, as in their presence,—erring on the side of too little, rather than too great a curiosity; with a conviction, in all probability, of the general truth of the remark, that the " person who is too nice an observer of the business of others, like one who is too curious in observing the labour of the bees, will often be stung for his curiosity."

The year 1830 brought much more foreign labour than the year preceding. In addition to the opening of Cawood, Summerseat, Budsworth, and Bradmore chapels, he visited, on special occasions, Barton, Hutton Rudby, Stokesley, Malton, Marston, Sheffield, Belper, Wirksworth, Wensley, Salford, Selby, Bolton, Market Weighton, Beverley, York, Sowerby Bridge, Ripponden, Tadcaster, Rochdale, Littleborough, Halifax, Wakefield, Otley, Derby, Elland, Bradford, Chesterfield, Wimeswould, Loughborough, Leicester, Darlington, Barnard Castle, Bishop Auckland, Howden, Stillington,

Helmsley Black Moor, Doncaster, Lincoln, Sleaford,
Billingbro', Grantham, Brierley, Wragley, Yarm, Denby
Dale, Seamour, Harrogate, Birstal, Longholme, Stock-
port, Bullock Smithy, Manchester, Osset, High Town,
Great Horton, Newcastle-upon-Tyne, Wall's End, Shi-
ney Row, Monkwearmouth, Snaith, Tockwith, Rothwell,
Nottingham, Barrowford, Colne, Steeton, Bradford.
Some of these places having been visited twice in the
course of the year, his journies out of his own cir-
cuit could be little short of a hundred.

A short account of Alice Manchester of Thorner,
proceeded from his pen, and was published in the
Wesleyan Methodist Magazine for the year, p. 716.
These Memoirs are noticed the more readily in their
succession, to shew the esteem in which he was held,
as proofs of his industry, and because of the vein of
piety which runs through them,—all shewing the high
value he set upon the " excellent of the earth," and
his readiness to perpetuate the remembrance of them
in the Christian church.   He never wrote for persons
" of a nice and foppish gusto ;"—not even remotely
for fame : he was too sensible of his defects in composition, to aspire after the honours of authorship.
There is encouragement, however, for men of his own
stamp, if there is any truth in the remark of a popular
writer, who, by the way, might have been securing
an apology for himself ;—" The way to acquire lasting
esteem, is not by the fewness of a writer's faults,
but by the greatness of his beauties ;" further observing, that " our noblest works are generally replete
with both. "

CHAPTER XIII.

It is disputed by some writers, whether a vigorous friendship can strike root in a bosom chilled by years. Though this sentiment comprehends a general truth, and the most lasting friendships are usually the produce of early life, when persons are susceptible of warm and affectionate impressions, there are exceptions,— —and Mr. Dawson was one. The fire of nature never ceased to burn ;—he had a deep and ready insight into real worth, and never failed to affix his own approving stamp upon what he valued. There is a great deal of difference too in the character of real friendship, when

q 2

Divine grace enters into companionship with the finer feelings of the heart.   Friendship is not a thing that a person can "regularly *undertake* to cultivate," but seems to be born with some persons, as they may be born poets.   Two men may meet, as Goldsmith observes, and may imperceptibly find their hearts filled with good nature for each other, when they were at first only in the pursuit of pleasure or relaxation : then the current of tenderness widens as it proceeds.   Mere speculators in friendship expect too much ;   and by drawing the bands too closely, they at length break them, and so dissolve the connection.   Catharine Phillips seems to have had a just, and therefore, an exalted notion of friendship.   It is—to reduce her verse into prose, an abstract of the truly noble flame of love—love, purified from all its dross—love refined— next to angelic for its strength,—that which antedates the joys of eternity—and is an epitome of heaven : or, to return to her poetry ;—

> " Thick waters shew no images of things ;
>   Friends are each other's mirrors, and should be
>   Clearer than crystal, or the mountain springs,
>   And free from cloud, design, or flattery."

Such was Mr. Dawson, as a friend ; and such was the friendship he enjoyed with the Rev. John Storry while he travelled in the Leeds circuit, and to which friendship he refers in a note, dated 1831—the year before the demise of that excellent man, and useful minister of God.   Wesleyan ministers did not occupy an ordinary place in his esteem ; and it was his delight when he could avail himself of an opportunity, on visiting Leeds, of returning into the country with them, when their labour lay at Barwick or the neighbourhood, for the evening : nor was it less an enjoyment on their part to be in his society. He refers to the Rev. R. Treffry, sen., and others, in this way.

In the month of February, of this year,—1831, Mr. Dawson paid a visit to the widow of Samuel Hick, and presented her with a copy of the Memoir of her husband. Though like her *careful* namesake—Martha, her true nobility of soul never forsook her. On Mr. Dawson presenting her with the first-fruits of the profits of the first edition, she observed,—" I cannot think of taking anything, till I know that Mr.——shall suffer no loss by it ; " and it was not till she was satisfied on this point, that she could be induced to accept the offering. With all the prudence and care which characterized her proceedings, proper occasions were all that was necessary to draw out the fine independant spirit which she possessed, and of the credit of which she had—though not intentionally, been partly deprived, from the heedless exuberance of her husband's givings. Her faculties were now somewhat impaired ; and the year following, she left the world, if not with Samuel's triumph, yet in Christian peace.

Though this year, like its predecessors, was distinguished for little short of a hundred journies, exclusive of his regular work, and some of them long, there were two or three months in the spring which exceeded anything he had before accomplished in travelling, and which could only have been performed by another minister besides himself in the Wesleyan Connexion —the Rev. Robert Newton, whose Herculean ministerial labours are unequalled, perhaps, in ancient or modern history. In the months of *April* and *May,* including a few days in *June,* he either occupied the pulpits or was on the platforms, engaged often in double, and sometimes treble services, at Tadcaster, Huddersfield, Old Chapel—Leeds, Liverpool, Chester, Micklefield, Aberford, Armley, Weeton, Barnsley, Doncaster, Epworth, Leicester, Long Eaton, Nottingham, Alfreton, Mansfield, Brunswick—Leeds, Pudsey, Farnley, York, Newark, Boston, Sibsy, Wainfleet, Spilsby, Raithby, Horncastle, Lincoln, Seacroft, Chapel Town, Barwick, Albion-Street—Leeds, Stamford Bridge, Dewsbury, Darlington, Wakefield, Barnard Castle, Bramham, Burnley, Todmordon, Sowerby, London, &c. And yet, mixed up with these, as heretofore, we find during the intervals, when at home a day, or a few hours, the following items in his memorandum book,—"Oat Stack got in."—"Finished sowing at Ashole."—"Sowed barley on the Car."—"Sowed Well Close."—"Finished a survey."—"Winnowed oats in top granary."—"Settled accounts in different places." —"At Barwick Court."—"Made a duck-pond."— "At Leeds market."—"At Collieries."—"Measuring malt."—"Cutting potatoes to set."—"Thatched the holm."—"Set potatoes."—"Sowing Sweed turnip seed in Quarry Close."—"Clipping sheep," &c.—"Winnowing wheat," &c. These things were not barely superintended by him, but as has been intimated elsewhere, it was work in which he often took a share. Idleness would have been a heavy affliction to him, as it must be to all who are subject to it; for man must be always either doing or suffering. Well he knew, with Franklin, that "Sloth makes all things difficult, but industry all easy; and he that rises late must trot all day, and shall scarce overtake his business at night; while laziness travels so slow, that poverty soon overtakes him." He was a living comment on that text, as his biography hitherto attests,—"Not slothful in business; fervent in spirit; serving the Lord."

As an agriculturist, he was considered one of the best in the neighbourhood; and, as a workman, few men who entered the field could compete with him. He had a way of doing every thing peculiar to himself. Mr. J. Agar, of York, stated, that even in catching a horse in the field, there was a peculiarity. He gained the confidence of animals the most shy, and would have caught them after others had failed in the attempt. His brother Richard informed the biographer, that, for firmness, expedition, and neatness, in binding sheaves, he never saw his equal: the same in making a stack. Mr. Outhwaite of Leeds, also observed, that he could generally obtain a shilling per load more for his corn in the market, than other farmers. This partly arose from the confidence people reposed in him—his knowledge of the markets—and his selling at the commencement of business. He rarely overstood the market, but despatched business at once, and was at liberty while others were hanging on to the last.

The chapels opened or re-opened by him in the course of the year, were those of Long Eaton, Hensal, Colton, Gateshead Fell, Oakham, and the Park—Sheffield. He observed to the biographer, in reference to the Oakham chapel, that he was obliged to take the mail coach, in consequence of the line of road he had to travel, and to engage a seat in the inside, because of the night and the state of the weather, and that when his expenses were deducted from the collections, he felt exquisite pain. In this way, it may be remarked, he was often rewarded by his sensibilities for the toil, risk, inconvenience, wear and tear of travelling—in the midst of dust and mud, the heats of summer and the colds of winter, storms and calms, sunshine and rain. While he was honest to a fraction to others, he exacted with severity upon himself.

In the midst of his exertions, he rarely ever lost his elasticity of mind; and when even slightly chafed, he had the good sense to conceal it, and not disturb the minds of others with it. Follow him whithersoever we might, there was always something interesting connected with his society. Speaking of a clergyman in his own neighbourhood, who read a sermon in the forenoon, and attempted extempore preaching in the afternoon, but who found less freedom in the latter case than is witnessed among some other Christian communities, it was remarked by the biographer, — "He should have commenced his work by meeting in class. That is the foundation of extempore speaking among the Wesleyans. People give expression to two or three sentiments,—these accumulate,—they grow up to exhorters,—and then into preachers." With this Mr. Dawson coincided, as the secret of successful extempore preaching, in connection with the love of God in the heart, and then gave his own enlightened views of the subject.

A person being named, one day, possessed of learning and sense, but who was often blundering in practical matters, and therefore without the art of using the knowledge he had acquired, Mr. Dawson observed,— "*Common sense* is a very good thing when it is used; but it is like a five-hundred pound bill,—it is good for nothing till it is cashed." This remark will pair admirably with a couplet of Young,—

"Of plain sound sense life's current coin is made ;
With that we drive the most substantial trade."

Conversation turning upon criticism,—"A critic," said
he, "sitting in judgment on a sermon, is like a fly,
which selects the sore part of a horse's back to revel
on, to the neglect of the sound, unbroken flesh."
Adverting to a passage in Young's Night Thoughts,
where the poet exclaims,—"Bound every heart, and
every bosom burn," and where he represents Mercy,
or Love's "lowest round, high planted in the skies,"
he said,—"I beg leave to differ from the poet. If
its 'lowest round' were in heaven, we should be unable
to reach it. Thank God! its 'lowest round' is on
earth, and encircles the globe."—Passing from the subject of criticism to the Christian, and seizing on the
expression of the apostle,—"epistles seen and read of
all men," he observed,—"Some EPISTLES are neither
fit to be *seen* nor *read;* they are *blotted* and *blurred*
with *sin;* the sight is grievous. But the *finger* of
God has *written* the Epistles which are created anew
in Christ Jesus; they are seen and read of all men,
—worthy of being posted at the corner of every street,
—may be read in time, and to all eternity!"—
"*Shadow* of death!" he exclaimed on another occasion, when encouraging the timid at the approach
of death,—"what Christian's *bones* didst thou ever
break? A *shadow* cannot break bones!"

When in conversation, he sometimes rolled his body
in a kind of circle—next inclining it forward—and
then, in that position, would turn up his face and
his eye, sidelingly, to see the effect of an anecdote
upon the person he was immediately addressing,—
and when wishful to impress the mind with it,—would

again raise his person, twitch up his nose, and rub his face with both hands, unable to restrain the motion of the more risible faculties, particularly when the subject closed with anything of a stirring character, a keen stroke of wit, or a little humour. He was sometimes playful, but never imbecile ; and therefore, an exception to the reflection couched in a remark of Addison, when he affirms, that " in private conversation between intimate friends, the wisest men very often talk like the weakest ; for the talking with a friend is nothing else but thinking aloud." It is by no means intimated, that he was either a sage, or that he delivered oracles : no more is intended by it, than that his good sense never forsook him. Some of his loud thinkings, however, even when softened with a little playfulness, told with unusual power. A person of penurious habits, possessed of property, but of whom he stood in doubt, said to him one day,—either from an aversion to be examined too closely, or a wish to leave an impression on the mind that he was one of those persons who prevented the right hand from knowing what the left did.——"What I *gives* is *nought* to *ony* body." Mr. Dawson quickly and pointedly returned,—though not the version wished by the speaker,—"You are right there, friend, for I believe you give nothing to any body."

As he never lost the spirit of his work, God never ceased to use him in the conversion of sinners. A person writing to the Rev. Daniel Isaac, requesting him to use his influence with Mr. Dawson to induce him to pay a visit to Malton, observed in a letter, —"He (Mr. Dawson), will have the pleasure of seeing a very respectable man here, when he comes, who was—till he heard him when last at this place, a poor degraded, drunken backslider, and had been for years. He confesses that Mr. Dawson was the instrument in the Lord's hand of his conversion." This was by no means a solitary case. He combined, in his addresses to backsliders, the tender and the severe, and was more than ordinarily successful in his appeals to their consciences.

He was at a public breakfast, and attended a public meeting of "The Teachers and Friends of Sunday-Schools, assembled in the Music-Hall, Leeds, to celebrate the SUNDAY-SCHOOL JUBILEE, *and to commemorate the* CORONATION *of His Majesty King* WILLIAM IV., September 8th." A speech which he delivered on the occasion, was "Published by request," and had an extensive circulation in Leeds and its vicinity. The day following, he attended the funeral of an old friend, Mr. Thomas Pawson of Farnley, and afterwards preached his funeral sermon. There is a Memoir of this Christian man, (whose son is now, 1842, mayor of Leeds), from the pen of Mr. Scarth, published in the Wesleyan Methodist Magazine, 1834, p. 489.

Some notice has been taken of the use Mr. Dawson made of the hymns, when giving them out during divine service; and he was equally striking when he referred to them, either in whole, or in part, in the course of his sermons. Adverting to the 4th verse of Hymn 599, p. 553 of the "Supplement," he observed, that a boy, weak in mind, was asked, while rubbing a brass plate on a door, what he was doing? when he replied, " I am rubbing out the name." " Little," said Mr. Dawson, " was the poor boy aware, that the more he rubbed, the brighter it shone. So

it is with Satan, who wishes to obliterate the word
of God from the memory, as well as every impression
of its internal evidence from the understanding and
from the heart. But,"—continued he, in holy triumph,—

> " Engraved as in eternal brass,
> The mighty promise shines ;
> Nor can the powers of darkness rase
> Those everlasting lines : ' "

then shouting amain, as if the chief fiend of hell were
as idiotish as the poor boy, and engaged in the same
useful employment,—" Rub, devil,—rub ! but all is
vain ; the evidence only brightens by the attempt ;
for the Lord,—yes, of the Lord it may be said,—

> ' His hand hath writ the sacred word,
> With an immortal pen. ' "

Citing another verse, on another occasion, which had
the Bible for its theme, he took the sacred volume
in his hand, and held it up to the congregation,
turning to the right and the left, above and below,
as if exhibiting an article which he could safely recommend for sale ; closing the exhibition with some
striking sentiments on the value of the sacred writings,
and the deep interest man has in acquiring a knowledge of their contents. At one place, the gravity of
the people, as well as his own, was in danger of
being disturbed, while announcing,—

> " Oh that it now from heaven might fall ! "

some plaster falling from the ceiling at the moment.
The singularity of the coincidence was felt the more,
as no harm ensued to soften the lighter feelings. But
the solemn subject invoked, soon returned upon the
soul with all its impressive weight.

Some of his actions and attitudes, however, placed certain parts of his adornments in jeopardy. His head was singularly formed, being rather long from back to front,—the forehead high,—abrupt,—and almost inclined to jut. This rendered it as difficult to fit him with a head-dress, as it was impossible to keep it always properly adjusted, when highly impassioned. Being on the platform at Scarbro' once,—and fortunately it was the platform instead of the pulpit, he slipped his hands, in the height of his zeal, beneath his wig, and unintentionally placed the sides where the back and front should have been. Though not particularly unseemly, from the peculiarity of its construction, it occasioned a momentary smile, till it was adjusted, which was instantly done. A friend or two in Manchester, confounding the peculiarity of its form with what they deemed a state of decay, sent a new wig for him to the biographer, in the month of January, 1832, with a respectful message, that it should be delivered to him, as from those who valued him as a man and a Christian minister. Mr. Dawson, aware of the trouble he had experienced in such matters before, enquired, when it was presented to him,— "Who has taken the measure? For a wig, without first gauging the head for it, is one of the worst things in the world to guess at; and my head, among all heads, is one of the most difficult to hit, and therefore to please. There are heads of all sizes and shapes; and mine," proceeded he, smiling, "which belongs to the second class, is the largest that is made of the kind:"—thus humorously giving the notion of a number of human heads turned off by some mechanical process, and fitted on the trunk by the artist.

Mr. Dawson was the staunch friend of the poor; and the "FACTORY QUESTION," so called, being agitated at this time,—a question which had for its object, the "shortening of the hours of labour in factories," he addressed a letter to his friend M. T. Sadler, Esq., M.P., who, with himself, felt deeply interested on the subject; stating his readiness "to throw into the scale the weight of his humble influence, to cast the beam on the side of justice and mercy." The letter was dated from "Barnbow, Jan. 27, 1832," and was published, not only in the Leeds and other papers, but in a separate form. He was invited by the Secretary of the operatives to attend a public meeting, and being prevented from acceding to the request, in consequence of public engagements in another part of the county, he addressed a letter also "To the Chairman of the Meeting assembled at Halifax, to petition Parliament for restricting the hours of labour in various Factories through the United Kingdom, appointed to be held March 6, 1832," in which he apologized for his unavoidable absence, expressed how cordially he sympathized with the chairman and others in the object proposed; and laid before them more fully his general views of the subject. Messrs. Wood and Walker of Bradford, Mr. G. R. Chappell of Manchester, and other gentlemen belonging to the manufacturing interests, have felt deeply on this subject, and laboured hard in what may be denominated, the cause of humanity. The Athenians, who were the politest and best natured people of their day, were the kindest to their slaves. What would be their opinion of the hearts of some of the "Millocrats" of the present day? The "long hour" system is admirably adapted to a race of beings without souls,—children who have no mind to cultivate,— families regardless of domestic comfort. No wonder it should rouse the indignation of Mr. Dawson—not a man, be it observed, who ever either sympathized with idleness in others, or shrank from labour himself, but a man who had a *head* and a *heart*, and permitted reason, justice, humanity, and religion, to speak for the servant as well as the master.

Between the first and second of these letters, he had a correspondence with some persons in Canada, which was resumed in June, highly honourable to himself, but respecting the complimentary part of which his modesty maintained a general reserve. Amidst all his popularity, such was his approachableness, and such his fine temper of mind, that those who knew him, felt they could make free with him without giving offence. "We have been looking for a preacher," said a friend at Holbeck to him, "to preach our charity sermons; but we have met with so many disappointments, that I believe we shall be driven to come to *you* at last." "We want not," observed another, in a letter to him, "men of the first order for our sermons; we shall be quite content with the Dawsons of the day." They knew well, that they could not only secure larger congregations, but larger collections through him, than almost any other man.

His friend, E. Brookes, Esq., paid him a visit in the month of March, and they both proceeded to York and Malton, where they engaged in different religious services, to the edification of the people. In addition to his regular appointments, parish meetings, and the cares of the society and chapel at Barwick, such as attending to the seat-rents, &c., he had an unusual press of business this year connected with his colliery agency, both at home and abroad: and yet he contrived to open, and re-open chapels at Hoby, Headingley, Garforth, Beeston in Bedfordshire, and Bedford, and to take scores of other separate journies, east, west, north, and south, for the purpose of attending missionary meetings, and preaching occasional sermons.

He was twice in London in the course of the year, once in April, and another time in December. During his first visit, he examined, in connection with other places of public interest, the West India Docks. He preached in the Wesleyan chapels at Kensington, Lambeth, Walworth, and Southwark. The morning sermon, founded on Mark v. 36,—"Be not afraid, only believe," was taken down by a short-hand writer, and published in "The Wesleyan Preacher," Vol. II., part 3, p. 52. *The object of his services at Lambeth, was to make a collection towards the reduction of a debt incurred by

* In addition to another sermon published in the same work, and obtained in the same way, p. 148; on John ix. 4, preached in Southwark Chapel, April 17, 1832; several are to be found in another periodical, entitled "The Pulpit. Sermons by Eminent Living Ministers." See

Vol. xxiii. p. 17, on Gal. vi. 7, 8. "Sowing in Time and Reaping in Eternity." Preached in Great Queen Street Chapel, Sunday Morning, November 10th, 1833.

Vol. xxv. p. 47, on Matthew xvi. 26, 27. "The Inestimable Value of the Soul." Preached on behalf of the Radnor Street Sunday Schools, at the City Road Chapel, November 9th, 1834.

Vol. xxvi. p. 193, on Psalm cxliv. 11, 12. "A Warning to Youth." Preached in Great Queen Street Chapel, June 14th, 1835.

Vol. xxvii. p. 231, on John iii. 16. "The Infinite and Everlasting Love of God to Man." Preached at Lambeth Chapel, December 13th, 1835.

Vol. xxix. p. 169, on Acts xiii. 38, 39. "Full and Free Pardon to every Penitent Believer." Preached in City Road Chapel, November 13th, 1836.

Vol. xxxi. p. 409, on Luke xii. 47. "The Enlightened, yet Disobedient Servant, beaten with many Stripes." Preached in City Road Chapel, on the behalf of the City Road Sunday and Day Schools, Nov. 12, 1837.

exertions to maintain and spread the preaching of the gospel in various villages and hamlets of that populous district. The monies collected on the occasion amounted to £140. The object of his second visit,—to connect them by way of dismissing the subject, was to diminish the debt of the circuit belonging to Queen-Street, in which chapel and on which occasion, the collections amounted to £90. Here, for the first time, he was apprehensive of diabetes, and had symptoms of it till the March following. The Rev. George Marsden, adverting to his extra work, enquired of him, by what name he was to be designated, when he replied, in Hibernian mood,—" A TRAVELLING *local* Preacher." And certainly, some of his feats, were rarely equalled, previously to the introduction of rail-roads. During *six days* in the course of summer, aided only by the regular heavy coaches, it appears from a note in his own hand-writing, that " from the 27th of June, till the 3rd of July," he " travelled 340 miles—preached 10 sermons,—was *only* three nights in bed,—and during the whole of those three nights, the time allowed for repose, occupied only a space of 10 hours,—not averaging quite three hours and a half.

Some of his popular speeches at this time, on the missionary platform, were denominated by his hearers, owing to the parallelisms, metaphors, and allegories employed,—" The Telescope,"—" The Rail-Road,"—"The Musical Clock,"—" The Enclosure Act,"—" The Reform Bill,"—" The Transportation of Religion,"—" The Silent Man,"—" The British Lion,"—" The Slave Speech,"—" The Openings of Providence,"—" The Cause of Christ our own,"—" Arguments in favour of Christian Missions," &c.

He attended a missionary meeting at Bristol during the interregnum of Earl Grey's ministry, when the nation was anxious for reform, and popular feeling ran strong against the Duke of Wellington. It was a time of peril. James Montgomery, Esq., the bard of Christianity, was in the chair; who, adverting to the spirit that was abroad, observed to the biographer, when giving an account of the meeting, that, in politics, the nation seemed to be placed as on a mine— ready to spring at any moment; and that, at such a time,—in such a city,—a city that had witnessed its populace in a state of riot, and its buildings in flames, it was hazardous to introduce the subject of politics in any shape. He called one speaker to order in the morning, and cautioned others against even political allusions. Mr. Dawson had to come on at night, and Mr. Montgomery, who well knew the daring character of his genius, was afraid lest anything should escape from his lips, capable of a political construction. What should his speech be, but the "REFORM BILL," that had just been thrown out!—the Bill,— the whole Bill,—and nothing but the Bill! Well, observed Mr. Montgomery,—"I concluded to say nothing, but let him—as he appeared to have come primed and loaded, have his full sweep. It was a piece with twelve barrels, and every barrel had its contents." The bard's continued description of the speaker, and of the speech, was truly characteristic. He represented him as proceeding to the front of the platform— bowing with respect to himself and the audience,—and then placing his broad shoulders before the chair, after which he was never once able to see even the tip of his nose, as if half afraid of meeting a rebuking eye, because of the line of remark adopted. He run a parallel in the allegorical way for which he was so remarkable, and went, according to Mr. Montgomery's account, over the whole Bill—taking up clause after clause,—frequently running as along the verge of a precipice, yet never—though often in danger of it, falling over—nicely cautious—often wild, but with a great deal of that which was excellent, and of which he was never any length of time without exemplifying. The whole was so dexterously managed, that the auditory would have found it difficult to determine at the close, whether, in politics, the speaker was Whig or Tory.

August 24, the cholera first made its appearance at Barwick, and a person of the name of Eliza Bean died of it in the evening. For several successive days, its victims were carried to the tomb, and the class was removed from a private dwelling to the chapel, in consequence. Mr. Dawson preached a sermon on Wednesday the 29th, to improve the awful visitation, taking for his text, Ecclesiastes vii. 2. In addition to this, the weather was such, as to lead him to exclaim,—" A dark appearance for harvest ! " Yet, in the midst of all exposures, he acted the part of a guardian angel to those who escaped the contagion, as well as an angel of mercy to the poor families that suffered, by collecting money for their relief. At the commencement, there were seven deaths out of nine cases, and afterwards, fifteen out of twenty.

War with Holland being the subject of conversation, towards the close of autumn, a person in a half jocose and half serious mood, observed,—" It is now seventeen years since we had a war ; many of

R

the sons of the nobility who were then young, have grown up to manhood in the interim,—these are in want of employment; there are others among the poor, who are lazy and profligate; in both cases, they constitute the surplus stock of society, and are often taken off by war." Another gentleman remarked, that Lord Hill had a great number on his list, soliciting commissions, some of whom had waited for years, and were in want of that kind of employment. Mr. Dawson, without entering into the subject, observed, when connecting with it the *wickedness* of man, and the *providence* of God,—"It is an awful way of skimming the pot." So thought an old author, when he said,—"For a king to engage his people in war, to carry off every little humour of state, is like a physician's ordering his patient a flux for every pimple." Equally correct was another writer about the same period, when he remarked, that in all cases of war, "Very much of the man must be put off, that there may be enough of the beast."

When in some of the southern counties, in the months of October and November, he rode in company with two friends in a gig, on one of the cross-roads, which was not quite in Macadamised order. A good man and his wife passed them on the road, in a tax-cart, drawn by an active pony, the shaking, setting, and jolting of which, made them forget their own tossings, and excited the smile. Their gig, however, was soon disabled by an accident, and Mr. Dawson was obliged to leave his more respectable conveyance for the tax-cart, which was so well packed, that the owner, who acted as charioteer, was obliged to stand. He took his position in the front, which not only shaded the view from the company, but the jolting of the vehicle threw him occasionally against them, giving an extra double to the hat and the bonnet. Mr. Dawson, for the two-fold purpose of relieving both the driver and his companions, got the latter to compress themselves into as small a space as possible; requesting the good man at the same time, to sit down on the part they contrived to make vacant for him. He, on the other hand, disposed to be polite, and to give the party the full benefit of the seats, told Mr. Dawson to be perfectly at rest in his mind, repeating,—"Don't mind me, don't mind me;" appending to it, for further satisfaction, and by way of at once settling the business, —"this is the way I always *stands*, when I *drives* calves." Such a remark was too much for Mr. Dawson's gravity; but the worthy man, unconscious at the moment of the bearing of it upon the *stock* he was then driving, again touched the flank of the pony and stood to his work to the end of his journey. Time being short, expedition was required. Against this, however, the rough road was in constant operation; and when Mr. Dawson narrated the journey to the writer, combining with it the action of the driver, —the crack of the whip,—the laugh of the persons they passed on the road,—now rolling from side to side, occasioned by the cart roots,—then bouncing from their seats in consequence of the loose stones, it was as much for the writer to sustain with anything like sober feeling, as was the driver's reply respecting the *calves*, to Mr. Dawson.

Till Mr. Dawson was forty years of age, he had never, except when he went to Hull, been forty miles from home. It was well for the Christian church, that travelling was conducive to health. He observed to the writer, that he was of opinion, if he were to retire, and indulge in a sedentary life, he would soon die. Numerous, however, as the invitations were to which he acceded, he could by no means meet the one-third of the demands made upon him. This year he had one for nearly every day included in it—no less than *three hundred and ten* for occasional sermons in different parts of the kingdom.

The calls of the year 1833, were no less numerous than those of the year preceding, embracing—exclusive of his own county, and without enumerating the distinct places, journies into the counties of Northumberland, Durham, Cheshire, Lancashire, Derbyshire, Staffordshire, Leicestershire, Nottinghamshire, Lincolnshire, Warwickshire, Cambridgeshire, Gloucestershire, Bedfordshire, Northamptonshire, Norfolk, &c. He visited Sheffield twice in the course of the year, Nottingham twice, and Manchester four times; and in the course of some of his journies, opened new chapels at Howden, Bishopthorpe, Peterborough, and Bristol.

Mr. Dawson, who venerated Dr. Adam Clarke, and sincerely lamented his death the year preceding, had now to sympathize with the friends of Christian Missions and of humanity, in the demise of the Rev. Richard Watson; both great men, but differing from each other, as one star differeth from another star in glory. "The worth of some men," it has been stated, "lies in their mighty names; upon a closer inspection, what we took for merit, disappears. It was only the distance which imposed upon us before." Not so here: the men could bear inspection while living, and their works speak for them now that they are dead. Even in their last hour, like all great men, they "bore a countenance more princely than they were wont." And why? "It is the temper of the highest hearts, like the palm tree, to strive most upwards, when it is most burthened." Can anything be more simple and touching to a truly devout mind, than the remark of Mr. Hobbs to Dr. Clarke, and the Doctor's mono-syllabic reply to it,—so characteristic of his trustful, unadorned, simple, yet truly Christian mind,—"My dear Doctor, you must put your soul into the hands of your God, and your trust in the merits of your Saviour." —"I do, I do." After this declaration of the work of faith being perfected, then follows Richard Watson with his dying testimony,—the testimony itself being not only Christian, but bearing the stamp of real genius,— "When I come before God, I feel myself like a worm that has crawled out of its hole in the earth, and meets the glory of the meridian sun. It behoves me to lie low in the dust before him." There is no glorying here,—none in either case. How true it is, that "He only is great who has the habits of greatness; who after performing what none in ten thousand could accomplish, passes on like Sampson, and 'tells neither father nor mother of it!'"

Actively engaged as Mr. Dawson had hitherto been, the extinction of these two great "revolving lights" rendered it still more imperious in him to replenish his lamp with fresh oil, and to hold himself, if possible, in still greater readiness to obey additional calls to hold forth the word of life in places yet personally unvisited. And what was not a little extraordinary—and in this he was on a par with Dr. Clarke, if not in the amount, at least in the principle,—the collections of one year almost invariably exceeded those of the year preceding. He obtained about £90 for Wesley Chapel, Manchester, this year; and the sum of £81 8s. 2¾d. at Oldham, for the Sunday Schools,—the largest amount that had ever been collected on the occasion.

The writer having had repeated opportunities of hearing him in the course of this year, availed himself of them; as well as enjoyed much of his private society. Meeting him at the coach, on one of these occasions, he was accosted by a friend, who was unperceived, till his hand was felt upon the shoulder, and the words were uttered—" You are my prisoner." Mr. Dawson turned round, and smiled. But he was scarcely seated in the house of Mr. Braik, before he was beset by suppliants from different places, soliciting the benefit of his services. This was no unusual thing. He observed to the friends —not ostentatiously, but to shew the impossibility of complying in every case with their wishes,—" Out of twenty-six Sundays in the last plan, I have been only six at home, exclusive of week-day services; the remainder having been devoted to extra work. I only reached home last night at twelve o'clock, having been at a missionary meeting in York, and had to start for Manchester this morning."

Speaking in the morning on—" We would see Jesus," in Oldham-Street chapel, he observed,—" He is to be seen in the Bible; " then suiting the action to the expression, he placed the Bible on its edge, which was unfolded about the middle, and, turning it to each part of the congregation, with his head inclined towards it, and his eye fixed upon its page, he pointed his finger to its sacred contents, as to a mirror, into which every one might look, and perceive the image of the divine personage referred to,—repeating, "You may see him here; 'see' him in the Old Testament, in prophesies, types, and figures;—'see' him in the New, in his life, miracles, doctrines, promises, precepts, death, resurrection, and ascension;—'see' him in the beginning, middle, and end:—yes, seen *here* —not at the dance, not at the card table, not at the theatre, not at the horse-race;— to such as attend *these*, if seen at all, it is in the distance;—and the more such amusements are indulged, and such places are frequented, the further he recedes from view—further —and further—and further, till he becomes invisible." Having thus fixed attention, he then unfolded and applied his subject. Without adverting to his plan, a reminiscence or two forces itself upon the mind, which may be preserved, as many of his fillings up were never committed to paper. The backslider, whom he depicted as having lost sight of Jesus, after having seen him by faith, and enjoyed him in fellowship of spirit, was further portrayed as conquered, and laid prostrate on the ground, while Satan, in the character of a victor, was brandishing his sword over him, and shouting in triumph, with his foot upon his neck, —"Ah, so would we have it; so would we have it!" adapting the intonations of the voice to the subject, and producing a living image on the imagination.

In the evening, while dwelling on Luke xii. 41— 48, he was somewhat trite in the former part of his discourse. He shewed that all were the servants of God by creation, preservation, and redemption, whether slothful, disobedient, or faithful; and that the congregation especially, knew his will and owed him

obedience. Passing over the intermediate parts of the
sermon, when he came to apportion to each offender
his "few" or his "many stripes," according to the
nature and magnitude of the offences committed, the
sinewy, athletic body of his thoughts seemed to burst
their scanty apparel : he was like a person who had
just had a vision of the misery of lapsed intelligences,
but unable to tell the whole of what he had seen
and heard. He illustrated the enormity of sin, by
shewing its several degrees of aggravation in offences
against civil authority,—passing from the private subject
to the constable, from the constable to the magistrate,
and from the magistrate to the monarch, when it
reached its climax in treason. Sin, he observed, was
an offence against the Majesty of heaven,—in sight
of the atonement of Christ,—against a positive law,
—and in defiance of the strivings of the Holy Ghost.
" Such," said he,—and this is only a faint image of
his terrific power, " shall be beaten with ' many stripes.'
The sinner, in this country, in this day, in this congregation, has not the plea of the Jews, who crucified Christ *ignorantly ;* nor yet of Saul of Tarsus,
who also ' did it ignorantly." He has no plea to offer.
Bring him forth, and let him see himself, as a lost
spirit, tied, like a soldier, to the halberts—receiving
his '*stripes*.' The *devil* comes forward, and commences
with his ' stripes ; ' and every stroke makes him cringe,
while his misery is enhanced, by hearing his tormentor
say,—' *We* had no Bible, no Saviour, no remedy,—
but *you* had. ' Next comes the *Law*, issuing, as of
old, from Mount Sinai, enveloped in fire and smoke,
and gives its round of lashes. After that, comes
Conscience, which applies the lash, with its internal

upbraidings. Then comes *Jesus*, with the aggravation of rejection. In the rear of Jesus comes *Justice*, whose every stroke is like the cut of a whip upon a sheet of water, which instantly closes on the lash being taken out, and is ready for another gash ;—an eternity of healing and wounding ! " He next changed the imagery, and represented each lost spirit under the notion of a flame of fire, lighted up, and preserved burning by the wrath of God,—the separate flames differing from each other in force, width, and fierceness ;—and each flame with its own distinct lamp or vehicle,—the congregated mass being ' vessels of wrath, '—some large, some small,—yet all *full* of *misery*. To follow him,—except in short-hand, in his lightning flashes and thunder peals, is next to impossible. On applying the subject to backsliders, to the children of praying parents, and to formal professors, he was equally tremendous ; especially in reference to the second class. "The prayers of thy father," said he, "will be like breath to fan up the flames of hell ; and the tears of thy praying mother, which had been deposited in the Lord's bottle for thee, will be constantly dropping, like oil, on the fire of hell, to feed it. " The sinner was depicted in all his odiousness,—"enough to startle the devil himself ; " and as met in the "regions of woe," by companions "whose eyes shot lightning at him,"—piercing the inmost soul with the very essence of mental agony. Several persons were convinced of sin under the sermon, and some obtained a sense of mercy in the prayer-meeting, at the close of the service.

Anything like sober, sedate feeling, through the whole of even a solemn discourse, was very often

R 2

out of the question; and in his more tempestuous moods, he was dangerous as a model, and never to be imitated. He stood alone, and ought to remain alone; but in that individual form, as in all unique cases, he was rather to be prized than diminished in value. He paid a visit to Sheffield about the same time, as above, and preached in Carver-Street chapel. The congregation was large, and the feeling was intense. He exhorted his hearers, in the course of his sermon, to give their hearts to the Lord, and added, —laying his hand upon his own, with a fine gush of feeling, and his eyes lifted up to heaven,—"Here's mine!" when a voice from the gallery cried out,— "Here's mine too, Billy!" Nor was this the only audible token of the effect of his preaching; such exclamations as,—"That's right,"—"True,"—"Glory be to God," &c., being frequently repeated during the service.

It was at the peril of the more decorous behaviour of persons of uneducated minds and warm feelings, to hear him on some of those occasions. He was preaching on the conquest of David over Goliah, in his own circuit, when he had his friend Samuel Hick for a hearer. The feeling was so powerful, the imagery so vivid and expressive, that Samuel was unable to check the emotions of his heart. His eyes twinkled,—his lips were in motion,—and joy was flickering over the whole countenance,—during which he manifested considerable restlessness, and made several essays to rise from his seat. Unable to contain himself any longer,—and just at the moment the stone was represented as whizzing through the air, penetrating the forehead, and Goliah was seen staggering, falling, and stretched upon the ground, he started from his seat, and exclaimed,—as if the actual scene were before him,—having taken such hold on the imagination,—"Well done, Willy,—off with his *yed*."

Having had occasion to advert to Providence, he remarked, that its inequalities argued the necessity of a general judgment; while providence itself was illustrated, in connection with the assertion,—"The ways of the Lord are not equal," by a straight stick put into a vessel of water, which, in consequence of the medium through which it was viewed, appeared crooked; and by the wheels of a piece of mechanism, moving in opposite directions, yet guiding the fingers aright, and directing them to the proper hour.

His friend, Mr. Reinhardt of Leeds, died early in the spring, whose funeral sermon he preached March 1st, and to whose will he administered April 9th. Mr. Reinhardt had been a member of the Wesleyan Society thirty years, and had filled, for several years, the offices of class-leader, steward, and trustee.

In the summer of the same year he was called to improve the death of Mrs. Turton, the wife of the Rev. Isaac Turton, who was awakened to a sense of her guilt and danger as a sinner, in the eighteenth year of her age, under a sermon which he preached in her native place, the village of Harewood, near Leeds, in 1809. Mournful as it is, yet it is satisfactory for a Christian minister to see the fruit of his labour safely housed;—not only first to place the sapling in the nursery, but to see it finally transplanted to another soil, where it is to bloom forever; and of all the fruit of Mr. Dawson's ministerial toil, he never saw a more lovely Christian in person and character grow up,—flourish,—bend,—and fall before him than Mrs. T.; closing life with,—" All is well." A few weeks after this, he observes,—" I called at the house of William Thompson of Barnber, and, to my great surprise and grief, found him dead." A funeral tribute was paid to the memory of this person also.

His labours were not always confined to the places he visited, according to previous arrangement; but he was sometimes drawn into_ work of which he had no anticipation when he set out on his journey. Thus, the friends at Rudham, in Norfolk, finding that he was to be at Lynn, waited upon him, to ask him to give them an extra sermon in aid of their chapel. Never backward to labour, when a door was thrown open, and time and physical strength would allow, he preached twice at Lynn, on the Sabbath,—proceeded to Rudham, and preached there at 11 o'clock in the forenoon,—returned to Lynn, where he preached in the evening,—and went forward the next day to preach at Wisbeach. Being the first time of his appearance at Rudham, &c., some dissenting ministers were drawn to hear him, who intimated that it was a style of preaching they had never heard before, and could not fail to awaken the attention of the people to sacred subjects. In consequence of his pulpit labours, and conversation with friends at Wisbeach, the latter were led to commence a plan for the enlargement of their chapel, which he afterwards re-opened, and the anniversaries of which he subsequently attended.

Having succeeded so well in stealing a march upon his time and toil for Rudham, the good friends at Fakenham, in the Walsingham circuit, were equally successful on the occasion of a subsequent visit to the county of Norfolk, in securing a few of his "Spare Minutes." The chapel, though large enough for ordinary occasions, was too small for the congregation; in the evening, therefore,—being in the height of summer, he proposed to conduct the service in a field adjoining the place. An *auctioneer* obligingly furnished him with his "*stand*" as a substitute for the pulpit; —a fine incident in connection with the peculiarities of his playful fancy. Behind this, with a very different *company* before him to that with which the knight of the hammer was generally indulged—a company in whom were in operation widely different *views, feelings,* and *expectations,*—and with an *article,* which he could not only conscientiously recommend, but in the praise of which he could not be too high, he could safely say to each, to all,—"Buy the truth." But as this was not his text, the elevation—in open air, furnished him with an equally favourable opportunity of enquiring with Moses, who, while he "stood in the gate of the camp," asked,—"Who is on the Lord's side?" a question, involving a subject, which he pressed in no ordinary way upon the conscience. The good effect of this sermon is noticed in the "Cottager's Friend" for 1840, p. 35, in a Memoir of Abraham Jacob.

In the month of November, he acceded to a pressing invitation to the Metropolis, when he preached in Great Queen-Street chapel, at Islington, Southwark, and City Road. From thence he proceeded to Bristol, where he opened the chapel noticed in a preceding page. At the close of this journey, he exclaimed, on entering his own house, under a deep sense of his obligations to Divine goodness,—"Praise the Lord, O my soul, and all that is within me praise his holy name!"

Travelling, which is but too often the case, never seemed to dissipate his mind. He returned home,— not poorer in spirit,—but more enriched in grace; he resembled the bee loaded with honey. The mind was rarely so intensely employed on particular subjects as to lose its vigour in the exercise ; and when it did flag, being impatient of ease, it soon recovered itself again, not by continuing inactive, but by varying its applications. He was thrown only into such society as kept up the flame of devotion in himself; while his habits of piety, and his love to souls, led him to augment the flame in others. His happiness was derived from God, and therefore, beyond the power of circumstances to change. This world was beheld only as a kind of stepping-stone to a better. While such a state of mind,—simply referring to its bias respecting the future, adds a double relish to every enjoyment, it blunts also, in the language of Dugald Stewart, the edge of every suffering. Even in cases where human life presents to a man no object upon which his hopes can rest, religion invites the imagination beyond the dark and troubled horizon which terminates every earthly prospect, to wander unconfined in the regions of futurity. While memory soothed the mind of Mr. Dawson, by storing it with the recollection of past mercies, hope overjoyed it with "pleasant pictures" of the future.

1834—an eventful year in the history of Methodism, brought still heavier labour to Mr. Dawson than that to which he had been accustomed, and which the reader will perceive had been gradually growing upon him.

The Rev. Robert Aitkin, a clergyman of the Established Church, had preached some time in the Wesleyan chapels, in different places, and had been extensively useful in the awakening of sinners; and persons, like him, with more than ordinary zeal, were sure to find their way to the subject of these Memoirs. Mr. Aitkin paid him a visit at Barnbow; Mr. Dawson heard him preach in the month of January,—some letters passed between them,—and they met on different public occasions. His friend Mr. Brookes, also paid him a visit in the course of the same month, and preached in the neighbourhood. Bachelor as Mr. Dawson was, he was a social being;—he loved society, and was loved by society: not because of the fineness or intensity of his feelings, or the display of a little amiable sensibility,—which only requires a little acting, but because of his experience, his talents, the value of his character, and his ability and willingness to benefit the church and the world.

In the month of February he rejoiced in symptoms of public good at Barwick, while the Rev. Robert Bond was preaching, saying,—"Praise the Lord! His presence was with us; souls were enquiring their way to Zion, and some found the road." The Rev. Francis West was noticed by him also, as succeeding Mr. Bond, and whose ministry was useful to the society. In consequence of this spring of feeling given to the people, the missionary meeting produced £16. 15s. 4d. While God was enlarging his boundaries in the country, he was also extending his work in the town. Hence, says Mr. Dawson,—"I was at Leeds, Wednesday, Feb. 19, at the laying of the first stone on the premises adjoining the Old Chapel. On my return home in the evening, I preached at Barwick."

Lady Hertford, under whom he had an agency,
died in the month of April; but her demise effected
no immediate change with him; and he seems, about
this time, in addition to his farm and executorships, to
have had the business of two or three collieries in
charge.   But in the midst of his secular engagements,
which his business qualities would never suffer him to
mistime or neglect, he was found within the space of
four brief days, proceeding with his relative, Mr.
Edward Phillips, to Colne and Cornshaw, in Lancashire,
and instantly on his return, attending the Leeds market,
from thence to Aberford, and, without returning home,
proceeding, as by express, with his friend, Mr. J.
Peart, to Pocklington, to engage in the work of the
sanctuary there.   And yet this was but trifling compared with one of his feats in the month of June,
when, in different kinds of conveyances, in one route,
he embraced,—including intermediate places, Newark,
Wisbeach, Downham, Wireton, Swaffham, Northampton,
Thetford, Kilbro' Mills, Falkenham, Norwich, Marsh,
and Peterboro', closing his account, after giving the
milage from place to place, with—"Returned home.
Travelled, by cross-roads, in *nine* days, upwards of *two
hundred* miles, and exercised *sixteen* times.   As was
my day, so was my strength.   Halleluia, praise the
Lord!"
In all his journies, he avoided giving the respective
families with whom he domiciled, any unnecessary
trouble, and took such fare as was placed before him
with cheerfulness.   Even at an inn, where the traveller
may assume the airs of a gentleman, and issue his
commands to the master and mistress of the house, as
to his own servants, Mr. Dawson was as unobtrusive

and untroublesome, as in a gentleman's family. He reached Market Harborough at twelve o'clock one evening, towards the latter part of September, when the weather was setting in cold. There was no time for bed between the leaving of one coach, and the arrival of another by which he hoped to be forwarded ; and yet such was his feeling for the servants, whom he considered as having had fatigue enough with the toil of the day, and little enough time allowed for refreshing repose, that he allowed them to close the doors, and retire to rest, under the impression that he was going to take up his residence somewhere in the town, while, in fact, he stepped quietly into one of the stables in the yard, where he remained with the horses as his companions, till half-past two o'clock in the morning, when he left for home. He might, while there, have trilled one of the madrigals of Wilbye, of 1598 :—

> " There is a jewel which no Indian mine can buy,
> No chemic art can counterfeit ;
> It makes men rich in greatest poverty,
> Makes water wine, turns wooden cups to gold,
> The homely whistle to sweet music's strain ;
> Seldom it comes, to few from heaven sent,
> That much in little—all in nought,—*Content.*"

In the course of four days after this, he was in Newcastle-upon-Tyne, with the Rev. Robert Aitkin. The visit was well-timed, there being a division just then in the Gateshead Society. Both preached, and both attended the quarterly love-feast in Brunswick chapel. Poor Crister, the " Wall's End Miner," was present, and spoke with great interest. Mr. Aitkin also gave a narrative of the dealings of God with his soul,—clear,—striking,—artless,—and attended with a divine unction. Whatever might be his subsequent doctrinal or merely notional wanderings, it would be as difficult to get rid of the genuineness of such experience, as it would have been for Robinson of Cambridge, in later life, to answer his own arguments in favour of the Divinity of Christ, as embodied in his " Plea." Several souls were saved in the course of the Sabbath. The writer was present on the occasion, and was in the chapel from half-past ten o'clock in the morning, till five in the afternoon. One young man may be noticed, of the name of Robert Combey, who was awakened to a sense of his moral wretchedness, and who, in the space of nine months, was swept into eternity, with upwards of a hundred more, men and boys, by a blast in one of the pits.

Shortly after this, Mr. Dawson was at Hull, preaching occasional sermons, and addressing the seamen,— shewing them " the difference between a pious and an ungodly sailor." The next forenoon he was in Leeds market, by half-past eleven o'clock. So mild was the weather, that on the second of November, the larks, to the joy of his soul,—for he was a close observer and lover of nature, were singing their morning carols; and in the same month, he sent up his own carols to heaven, on his return from a journey of hazard, saying, " I came by railway to Lazencroft. Adored be Divine Providence, for returning me without the slightest injury, and finding all right and well at home!"

The dissension occasioned by the establishment of the " Theological Institution," had arrived at a considerable height at the close of the year. Scores of pamphlets and letters were published, *pro* and *con*, comprising, when bound together, four thick octavo volumes, exclusive of the " Illuminator," &c. Mr.

Dawson was at first a dissentient; and so also was the biographer,—the latter strongly so. Some of their reasonings and objections paired with each other,—though neither were averse to the abstract question of ministerial improvement. When, however, they found men passing over from the Theological Institution to the Wesleyan Constitution, and trying to sap its foundation, they perceived it was high time to sacrifice mere *opinion* for the sake of *essentials*,—to give up an *outwork* or two for the sake of the *citadel*. Hence, Mr. Dawson addressed a letter, December 16th, to Dr. Warren, entitled,—" More Work for Dr. Warren;" and his name stands in the subscription list of the first " Report of the Wesleyan Theological Institution," as a subscriber of £5. 1s. As his primary opposition had more the character of a *fear* of consequences, than actual hostility ; so his subscription was given in *hope*, rather than *confidence*—and not without prayer.

Without entering into the merits of the question, which may now be considered as settled, one great good resulting from the whole, in the trial which ensued, and the decision of the Lord Chancellor Lyndhurst on the case, is the act of legalizing the discipline of the Wesleyan Conference in reference to the preachers, during the intervals of its sittings, and, to a certain extent, making the Wesleyan Constitution a part and parcel of the law of the land. The removal of a few factious spirits from the body, who were dissatisfied with the system, was merely temporary ; but this boon will go down to the latest posterity with British law ; and in this invaluable boon Mr. Dawson rejoiced,—nor less the biographer. During the conflict, the language of Sir T. Brown could not but impress the minds of those persons who were familiar with it ; —" Scholars are men of peace ; they bear no arms, but their tongues are sharper than Actius' razor ; their pens carry further, and give a louder report than thunder. I had rather stand in the shock of a basilisk, than in the fury of a merciless pen." Though the times cannot be contemplated without painful feeling, the subject is now capable of a much more dispassionate consideration. Selden was not far wrong, when he said,—" In troubled water you can scarce see your face ; so in troubled times you can see little of truth. When they are settled and quiet, then truth appears."

The year 1834 has been stated to have been a laborious one for Mr. Dawson ; and as another little memento for the friends in the respective places he visited, as well as a memorial of Christian zeal, it may be remarked, that he either attended in the course of the year, public meetings, or preached occasional sermons, or both, at Clayton Heights, Grantham, Wansford, Yeadon, Ripon, Sheffield, Stokesly, Guisbro', Whitby, Robin Hood's Bay, Manchester, Salford, Almondsbury, Wansley, Kendal, Addingham, Acaster, Tadcaster, Stockport, Wakefield, Dewsbury, Huddersfield, Birmingham, Bradwell, Colne, Cornshaw, York, Pocklington, Nottingham, Borrow Ash, Draycolt, Derby, Sandiacre, New Basford, Skipton, Keighley, Doncaster, Lincoln, Sleaford, Gainsbro', Chesterfield, Macclesfield, Bacup, Cheadle, New Mills, Stamford, Wrotten, Topham, Downham, Swaffham, Thetford, Kilbro' Mill, Fakenham, Norwich, Marsh, Peterboro', Doncaster, Malton, High Town, Wetherby, Otley, Minsten, Leek, Barton, Ashby de la Zouch, Cromford, Wensley, Belper,

Brotherton, Addingham, Bradford, Higham Ferrars, Bedford, Rowell near Kettering, Newcastle-on-Tyne, Carville, Shields, Blyth, Retford, Hull, Gildersome, Loughbro', Bramcote, Beeston, Granby, Broomsgrove, Tockwith, London, Luton, Wednesbury, Stoke-upon-Trent, Rochdale, Congleton, Middlewich, Stokesley, Selby, Darlington, and Gainford. To half a dozen of these places, he paid two visits in the course of the twelve months; besides opening chapels at Biggleswade, Granby, Hull, and also St. Peter's, Leeds.

CHAPTER XIV.

SPECIAL attention having been paid to the operations of the Spirit of God upon the mind of Mr.
Dawson in the early part of these pages, and subsequently to his excessive labours, it may be proper to
observe, that while those labours rose out of a continued
growth in grace, his advancement in the Divine life
was, in the way of re-action, augmented by his labours.
God alone was permitted to occupy the chief place in
his heart. He knew, and he felt, that to put him in

a second place, was to treat him opprobriously; that
even to equal another object with him, was to
insult him. With him, it was a fixed principle,
that wherever God is, he must possess the throne;
and that, if a holy heart is an image of heaven,
—as in effect it is, he must reign there, and
everything must submit to his authority. The
love of God in his soul was an immense fire; and
like the fire of the vestal virgins at Rome, which
was lit up by no common flame, and never suffered
to go out; or more sacredly, like the fire in the
temple at Jerusalem, which the priests were bound
to preserve alive on the altar, he continued to fan the
flame with earnest, constant, faithful prayer. While
God was loved, not barely supremely,—a slight degree
above other things, but with all the heart, he found
that such love would admit of love to man: but then,
to man—with his good alone for its object, it was only
like the emission of a few sparks, or faint emotions,
compared with the body of flame that mounted upward; just as a king is said to collect in his own
person all the honours of his kingdom, and communi-
cates some lucid titles to inferior objects. Hence, with
even the love of God brimming the soul, the parent
loves his child, the husband his wife, and man his
fellow. But then, agreeably to what has been stated,
divine love will neither admit of any other love *contrary*
to itself, nor yet any other object, except God himself, to occupy the chief seat in the soul. It is in
the heart, amidst all the other affections, what
a prince is among the officers of his army; or
in still stronger language, what God himself is
among all the creatures of the universe— giving

to all life, and motion, and power, and efficiency.
This was the case with Mr. Dawson. His love to
God was without measure, as well as without subordination,—without bounds, as well as without par-
tition.   The reason of this will be found in the object,
which it resembles, and which is infinite. It is true,
in one view of the subject, it is impossible for finite
creatures to perform infinite acts.   But still they are
in a manner infinite ; and this comparative infinity
has been argued as consisting in two things : first,
the good man's emotions go to the utmost extent
of his power without coolness or caution ; and secondly,
when he has stretched his soul to the utmost of his
power, he is never content with himself, but acknow-
ledges his duty goes infinitely beyond his emotions
and actions.   Thus it was, that the soul of Mr. Dawson was continually running out after God in all the
ardour of divine love ; and to promote his glory, in
the salvation of man, in connection with all the energies of both body and mind, he devoted every hour
he could spare from his farm.

In the commencement of 1835, he was engaged at
"Thorp Hall in surveying the boundaries of Lady
Gordon's property, in order to the opening of a new
winning ; " and was much employed in other secular
affairs. His correspondence was also becoming more
and more heavy ; and was such as, in other cases,
would have justified a secretary or an amanuensis.
To one of his early correspondents,—the Rev. Samuel
Settle, he wrote on the 30th of January ; to whom
a special reference is here made, with a view to
revive early associations, and to shew the endeared
friendship still subsisting between them.

The uneasiness manifested in different societies, towards the close of 1834, was carried into 1835. Serious as was the subject, a somewhat amusing conversation took place upon it between Mr. Dawson and John Patrick, *—the latter, an excellent man, who met a class near Kirkstal Abbey.

Mr. Dawson.—"Well, John, how is your class succeeding?"

John Patrick.—(In a pensive mood.)—"We are doing very well; but the disturbance existing in some of the societies affects me a good deal."

Mr. D.—"Nothing has occurred recently I hope?"

J. P.—"Why, perhaps not. But I was with a person the other day, who asked me, whether I was not going to leave the Old Connexion?"

Mr. D.—"What reply did you make?"

J. P.—"I said,—No; I am resolved to abide by the *old ship.*"

Mr. D.—"What then?"

J. P.—"He said,—'She is not sea-worthy.'"

Mr. D.—Amused with the simile, though familiar to him, and desirous of hearing the result,—"How did you meet that?"

J. P.—"I considered the Wesleyans as forming a part of the Church of God; and in reference to that Church, I said,—She carried all the Old Testament saints to heaven; and when he, who, by way of derision, was called the carpenter's son, appeared upon earth, she was new bottomed, and I think she will now carry the New Testament saints into the same port."

* J. Patrick was in the Bramley circuit when the writer travelled in it in 1813—14. An account of him, by the Rev. Thomas Galland, A.M., is published in the Wesleyan Meth. Mag., 1841, p. 634. He died, Friday, Feb. 22, 1839, aged 82 years—full of grace.

S

Mr. D.—" What was his answer? "

J. P.—" He asked,—' Why all the mischief at Manchester, Leeds, and elsewhere, if the vessel were not in a sinking condition? ' "

Mr. D.—Pleasantly,—" How did you surmount that difficulty? "

J. P.—" I said,—Oh, the vessel is as good and safe as it ever was : a few of the *crew* are only striving for the *mastery.* "

Mr. Dawson relished this not a little ; and the last stroke the most, as he was aware that John knew the character of the person he was addressing.

The Rev. Robert Aitkin, who was impressed with it being his duty to leave the Established Church, wrote to Mr. Dawson on the subject. Not long after, he published a pamphlet on the existing dissensions, which shewed,—however well meant, that he was unacquainted with the system of Methodism. Mr. Dawson being asked his opinion of the pamphlet, returned,—" Mr. A. was never designed for a legislator ; at most, he is only intended for a bellows to blow the dust from the embers, and then to kindle the embers into a flame. "

Being in the metropolis in the course of the year, preaching occasional sermons at Great Queen-Street, and at Chelsea, he visited the "Theological Institution." He informed the biographer, that the students expressed a wish to receive an address from him, and that the Rev. Samuel Jones, the classical tutor, urged him to write his address, and read it to them. To the latter he objected, while he acceded to the wishes of the former ; and as in early days, at Barwick, when he occupied the chair in the place of

the Rev. John Graham, so now, he occupied the
office of a Professor of Theology, telling the students,
in playful terms, that they were about to be addressed
by "*Bishop Dawson.*"   Among other observations,
he told them,—that it was their duty, in the outset, to convince the people that they wished to do
them good,—that he at first, with some others, had
his fears and prejudices respecting the "Institution,"
—and that it remained with them, by improving their
talents, and turning out well, to shew the groundless-
ness of such fears.   The several topics to which he
adverted, and the force and point which accompanied
several of his remarks, diverted attention from his
rural appearance, and a few of his provincialisms,
and rendered them much less singular,—the home-
training of some of the students being taken into
account, than they would have been at either our
English or Scotch universities : and besides, there
was a soul in all he said.   On his return home from
this journey, he exclaimed,—"Praise the Lord ! all
is well in body, soul, and circumstances."

It was not always that he could exclaim, "all is
well in *circumstances.*"   For on one occasion, he
found himself minus a top-coat, after preaching in
Brunswick chapel, Newcastle-on-Tyne ; some miscreant
having gone into the vestry during divine service,
and stolen it.   Though soon replaced with another,
by the friends, it is a hint to chapel-keepers,—and
it is for this purpose that the subject is introduced,
to prevent access to the vestry by strangers, in time
of service.

But even under untoward circumstances of importance, and not those of a trivial character like the

preceding, his argumentative resources for gratitude, patience, and contentment, in the midst of them, were endless; nor less so, when consoling and encouraging others. His introductions, however, to some of his pathetic addresses, were sometimes characterized with a buoyancy and eccentricity, which, while they yielded no immediate promise, were nevertheless sure to find their way to the heart, and were rendered the more welcome, the moment they were recognized as the means leading to that end. He was at Colne, during a period of great commercial distress, when the spirits of the people were depressed, and but slender hopes were entertained respecting the collections for the day. On commencing the service, by opening the Hymn-book, he said,—"When I am engaged in preaching occasional sermons, I am often presented with a number of notes, containing different announcements. After reading them, I put them into my pocket, where they sometimes inconveniently accumulate, till I reach home. Going into the fields, I occasionally take them out, and look at them, to see whether any of them are worth preserving. I read one,—not being worth any-thing, I tear it into fragments;—up comes a breeze,—and away the shreds fly;—I look at a second, a third, a fourth, and a fifth,—tear them,—and scatter them in the same way." While he was narrating this little incident, imitating himself, by putting his hand into his waistcoat pocket,—as if reading,—tearing,—and scattering, the congregation meanwhile on their feet, waiting for the hymn,—and wondering what the relation might mean,—with the shreds of paper drifting like flakes of snow in the imagination across the field, he suddenly adverted to the depressed state

of the trade of the place,—directed his hearers to
an overruling providence,—exhorted them to exercise
confidence in God,—gliding into the hymn in his
peculiar way, as noticed in other cases, announcing,
with the number of the hymn and page,—

> " Give to the winds thy fears ;
>   Hope, and be undismay'd :
> God hears thy sighs, and counts thy tears ;
>   God shall lift up thy head.

> " Through waves, and clouds, and storms,
>   He gently clears thy way :
> Wait thou his time, so shall this night
>   Soon end in joyous day, " &c.

The effect was overpowering ; and the sermon being
of an encouraging character, the whole had a per-
manently soothing influence on the minds of devout
persons, who were exhorted—as he had done the flying
shreds, to "give to the winds *their* fears."

Preaching one day on John iii. 16, he laboured
hard to remove every impression of fear from the
hearts of the timid and the desponding. "Here
is one," said he, "whose language is,—'There is
no mercy for me ;—God does not love me ;—I have
neither part nor lot in the matter.'" On this, he
paused,—inclined himself over the front of the pulpit,
—assumed an inquisitive, significant, yet pleasant air
—just such a look as a person puts on, who is wishful
to draw an answer from one whom he is disposed to
embarrass,—though for personal benefit, asking,—
"*Where do you live ?*" and turning his head aside,
like a gentleman at the bar, after proposing a question
to a witness. Then, helping the mourner to an answer,
he said,—"You live in the *world*, do you?" If so,
then there is love for you ;—yes, God loves you ;—

the text embraces the *world ;*—and you will have
to run out of it, before you can escape from the
love of God."

He was present at the ceremony of laying the "first
stone" for a new chapel in the Leeds West circuit,
Wednesday, Feb. 4th ; and on Wednesday, April 8th,
he had the pleasure of laying the foundation-stone of
a new Sabbath-School, at Barwick, where he had
laboured so long, and so effectually, and relative to
which erection, he devoutly prayed, that it might
"be a blessing to the village and the neighbourhood."

He generally adapted his prayers to circumstances,
and to the occasion ; and was often, on momentous
subjects, exceedingly touching. During a period of
continued rain once, in time of harvest, he employed
among others, the following expressions :—" Lord,
hadst thou seen our tears—our tears of penitence,
our tears of sorrow for sin, thou wouldst not have
commanded thy clouds to mourn and weep ; but,
because we have not wept—not wept for our sins,
thou hast bid thy heavens weep—weep even for this
nation. "

In the midst of his various other engagements, he
continued to preach occasionally at Barwick on the
week-day. Here we have an association not often to
be met with ; — " Rent-day,—and preached in the
evening on—' One thing is needful. ' " Nor was this
a solitary case. It was the same the year succeeding.
Any of the other tenants, who might be disposed
to linger behind, to hear the sermon, would find that
their own vineyard required cultivation, as well as
the ground they rented of their landlord ; that, in
the language of Young, — " No man is blest by

accident;" but, in order to be holy and happy, he must "Redeem the time," and, to his "funds and acres, join his sense." A sentiment of Cowley may be worked out with considerable effect, in its bearing upon the immortal interests of man; — "The first minister of state has not so much business in public, as a wise man has in private; if the one have little leisure to be alone, the other has little leisure to be in company; the one has but part of the affairs of one nation, the other all the works of God and nature under his consideration." What is the cultivation of even some thousands of acres of land, when compared with the cultivation of the mind, and the improvement of the heart? The "One thing needful," combines with it—"This one thing I do."

The Connexion at home being still in a perplexed state, and the annual Conference being about to commence its sittings, Mr. Dawson wrote to the Rev. Joseph Taylor, the President, July 21, and still lived in anticipation of peace and prosperity. No state of things, however, caused him for a moment to relax his exertions to promote the welfare of his fellow-creatures. He felt the labour hard, but never complained. Between the close of September and the beginning of October, he exclaimed, on reaching home, — "A laborious week; but praise the Lord! my strength has been equal to my work." No wonder that he should feel. He had been engaged the whole of the Friday in "leading oats out of the Marlpit Field," after which he went to Leeds, where he took the mail at nine o'clock the same evening, and did not arrive at Bedford till one o'clock the next day. On the Sunday, he preached three sermons in Bedford;—three more at Ridgemount on the Monday ;—one at St. Ives on the Tuesday, and attended a missionary meeting ;—delivered two more at Littleport on the Wednesday ;—the same number at Upwell, in Norfolk, on the Thursday ;—thence to Wisbeach ; — from Wisbeach to Newark on the Friday ;—from the last of which places, he set off at half-past eleven o'clock at night, and reached home on the Saturday. The next day, he was again in the pulpit, preaching twice in his regular appointment. Though the repetition of these extraordinary exertions may be in danger of palling, in some instances, yet it is in their continuity that we see the man; and in that continued toil, the marvel is, how human nature bore up under it so long; for, in his ardour of spirit, and through his vehemence, he put as much physical strength into the delivery of one of his sermons, as the ordinary run of preachers put into half a dozen. It was not here, as stated by Tillotson, in other cases,—"What men want of reason for their opinions, they usually supply and make up in rage." He never substituted sound for sense,—mere noisy declamation and rant for argument : nor was he ever vehement, but when most burthened with strength of thought. In the esteem of some persons, "Great turns are not always given by strong hands; but by lucky adaptation and at proper seasons;" and with these, "it is of no import where the fire was kindled, if the vapour has once got up into the brain." But there was no "vapour" here; nor was it unimportant either, where "the fire was kindled,"—to accommodate the simile to the present case; for fire, like the lights on a stage, may be lit up from *beneath;* and it was of prime "import" with Mr. Dawson, that his fire should proceed from the *heart*, and that the altar there should receive its warmth from *above*. And others than Wesleyan Methodists, had no objection to warm themselves at such fires. Hence, at Wisbeach, Nov. 5th, after preaching in the Wesleyan chapel, he remarks, that in the evening he "preached in the Calvinistic chapel, on 'Wherefore the rather, brethren, give diligence to make your calling and election sure,'" &c., 2 Pet. i. 10; a perilous text for an Arminian to take in a Calvinistic pulpit! But Mr. Dawson had the good sense to waive all minor matters on debateable ground, and to deal out the essentials of religion in which all agreed.

It is not to be omitted, however, that, on another occasion, he was on the point of a breach of religious courtesy, in a chapel belonging to the particular Baptists, when assisting at a missionary meeting. He took up the subject of the "Sower," scattering his seed —quoting appropriate passages of Scripture for his purpose—and imitating the sower in his action. On coming to that text—" He is the propitiation for our sins, and not for ours only, but also for the sins of"—he suddenly turned round to the Baptist minister, who sat behind him, and repeated, hesitatingly, but with an expressive, cheerful look,—" of—of—of—of;" then wheeling again to the congregation, who perceived where he was, and smiled at his manner, he added, with another evolution of the body, while bending his eye once more on the worthy pastor,—" of the whole world;" further observing, "It is there; I cannot help it; do with it what you like." Being asked the reason of his conduct in the evening, he replied, that he felt completely imbued with the spirit of his subject, and being

s 2

accustomed to congregations of his own people, in chapels
of all forms and sizes, he forgot everything but his work,
and just at the moment he had proceeded half way
with the passage in question, he recollected where he
was, and immediately drew up—hesitated—but found
he had gone too far to recede without being perceived,
and of either laying himself open to the charge of
cowardice in defending his creed, or of incurring the
displeasure of the good people, who might construe it
into a designed insult ; and therefore it was, that he
had recourse in his haste to the expedient, which he
was happy to find, from the expression of the meeting,
produced pleasure rather than pain. Though he escaped
censure, there is great truth in the remark of an elegant
writer, that "the greatest parts, without discretion,
may be fatal to their owners ; a Polyphemus, deprived
of his eye, was only the more exposed on account of his
enormous strength and stature."

As he often manifested great dexterity in extricating
himself out of a difficulty, he was no less adroit in
taking the edge from off a disappointment ; though
no man had less occasion to do it than himself, in the
case to be introduced, owing to his popularity. Having
to supply the place of the Rev. R. N. at Lofthouse, near
Guisborough, he opened his sermon with—"In looking
over the Bankrupt Gazette, we find that failures are
very common now-a-days. If people pay ten shillings
in the pound, it is considered very fair ; fifteen is
deemed handsome. You expected Mr. N. ; he, though
altogether unavoidable on his part, has *failed* you.
Never mind ; let us look up to heaven for the presence
of the Lord, and we shall have twenty shillings in the
pound, notwithstanding."   This not only gave him

ready access to the good feelings of his hearers, generally, but at once arrested attention, and furnished him with a fine opportunity of enforcing the advice of Sir Matthew Hale; "Run not into debt, either for wares sold or money borrowed; be content to want things that are not of absolute necessity, rather than to run up the score: such a man pays at the latter end a third part more than the principal comes to, and is in perpetual servitude to his creditors; lives uncomfortably; is necessitated to encrease his debts, to stop his creditors' mouths; and many times falls into desperate courses."

Exclusive of opening Dringholm, West Bromwich, Kirkstall, Ruddington, Hemmingbrough, Yeadon, and Guiseley Chapels, together with that of Oxford-place, Leeds, he preached occasional sermons in nearly a hundred other places, including Whitby, Beverley, Broomsgrove, Shrewsbury, Kidderminster, Birmingham, Leicester, Darlington, Macclesfield, Huddersfield, Lincoln, Halifax, Birstal, Doncaster, Leek, Newcastle-on-Tyne, Grantham, Leighton Buzzard, Cambridge, Woolwich, Burslem, &c., &c., repeating his visits to Nottingham, Manchester, and London, in the course of the year. At the close of his last Metropolitan journey, in connection with which were several other places, requiring a succession of hard labour, his heart was filled with "melody to the Lord," saying, "Praise the Lord! he hath done all things well."

On Christmas Eve, which was two days after his return, an interesting Tea Meeting was held, in the vestry of Brunswick Chapel, Leeds, of the Committees and friends of the Juvenile Missionary Society for the Leeds East Circuit. The room was tastefully decorated with evergreens, and the tables were amply furnished

with provisions suited for the season. Tea being
finished, the Rev. Robert Newton was called to the
chair, who introduced the business of the evening in a
very appropriate speech, distinguished for its manly
eloquence. He stated that the object of the meeting
was to present Mr. Dawson with a copy of Dr. Adam
Clarke's *Commentary*, as a testimony of their regard for
his exertions in the missionary cause. He alluded to
Mr. Dawson's unremitted exertions in the service of the
Leeds Juvenile Missionary Society, and stated that, with
one exception, he had every year attended its anniversary
since its establishment in 1816. Mr. Newton concluded
by calling upon Mr. Alfred Brigg, the Treasurer, who,
after a few short but appropriate remarks, formally
presented Mr. Dawson with the *Commentary*, on behalf
of the Committees. Mr. Dawson then rose, and in a
very suitable manner, acknowledged the reception of
the gift. He adverted at considerable length, to the
advantages resulting from an early cultivation of religion — and strongly deprecated the conduct of those
who slighted the ordinances, and were ashamed of the
practice of the religion of their parents. The Rev. W.
Vevers, R. Young, and W. Barton, together with
Messrs. T. Denham, J. H. Gibson, M. H. Davis,
and D. C. Roadhouse, severally addressed the meeting.
Thanks were given to Mr. Newton, the chairman, and
after singing the doxology, Mr. Dawson concluded the
meeting with prayer. In order to avoid crowd and
confusion at the meeting, the number of tickets issued
was limited to 250, but so great was the interest excited
that double the number could have been disposed of.
Several friends actually offered five times their price,
but were unable to be accommodated. The Commentary

was the last edition, published by Tegg and Son, in six volumes 4to. It was handsomely bound in Russia leather, gilt lettered, and with gilt edges. Within the back of the first volume was the following inscription, in gilt letters ;—"Presented to Mr. William Dawson, of Barnbow, by the Committees of the Juvenile Missionary Society, Leeds East Circuit, as a testimony of their regard for his indefatigable, disinterested, and successful exertions in the cause of Missions. Decr. 24th, 1835."

Having attended the Bradford Juvenile Missionary Society for a series of years, he was presented by the Committee of that Society with the Works of Arminius, as a similar token of respect for character, and a grateful remembrance of his services. His friend, the Rev. Thomas Galland, A. M., sent him the Rev Richard Watson's Exposition, as far as the revered author had proceeded with it. His language on the first of these occasions, in a private memorandum, is—"O my Lord, thou knowest, I am an unprofitable servant. I would render all back to thee." These humbling views of his services were evident indications of his increasing piety, and are the more to be relied upon for their sincerity, from the circumstance of their not having been addressed to the ear of any one,—and so exposed to the charge of "voluntary humility," or penned for the sake of inspection, but uttered in his communings with God, and not expected to proceed beyond his own notice ; and thus illustrative of the fact, that—"The best way to prove the clearness of our mind, is by shewing its faults ; as when a stream discovers the dirt at the bottom, it convinces us of the transparency and purity of the water."

Two days after the presentation of Dr. Clarke's
Commentary he called upon Mr. Scarth, who communicated to him an "outline" of what himself
denominated,—"the Sheffield Scheme;" a plan for
rendering his labours still more generally available to
the missionary cause, by raising a fund for the purpose
of enabling him to devote himself exclusively to the
interests of the Wesleyan Connexion, and in reference
to which his prayer to God was,—"Thy will be done."
A Meeting of several of the friends was held in Leeds,
Feb. 5, 1836; and a circular, containing a list of subscribers of one guinea each, was issued Feb. 20,
embracing a view of the object, together with certain
Resolutions to forward it, and so constituting a new
era in his personal history.*   The circular was afterwards inserted in the Wesleyan Methodist Magazine,
1836, pp. 296, 311.

"*Leeds, February 20th,* 1836.

• "DEAR SIR.—I beg to submit to your kind consideration the subjoined
Statement and Resolutions; and most respectfully suggest, that, if you approve
of our object, you will kindly aid us in its accomplishment.
I am, Dear Sir, (on behalf of the Committee)
Your's very respectfully,
W. G. SCARTH.

"At the suggestion of many Preachers and Gentlemen of various Circuits,
(particularly of the two Sheffield Circuits,) who have long thought it desirable
that such arrangements should be made in reference to Mr. WILLIAM DAW-
SON, of Barnbow, as would enable him to spend the evening of his life
unencumbered with temporal anxiety, and entirely at liberty for those occasional religious services, to which he is so frequently called,—in which he so
much delights,—and which, under the Divine blessing, have been rendered so
efficient in the support of the WESLEYAN METHODIST CHAPELS, SABBATH
SCHOOLS, and FOREIGN MISSIONS;—services which have been long continued,—at great personal sacrifice and inconvenience—and for which, any
thing that can be done to promote his comfort, will form but a very inadequate
remuneration:—A Meeting of a few friends of the two Leeds Circuits was
held in the vestry of Brunswick Chapel, in the Leeds East Circuit, February
5th, 1836:—

Adverting to the subject, in a conversation with the biographer, he observed,—"I am as comfortable at present on my farm as I need to be. Home has many endearments. The house was built by my father; the family have lived in it for a period of

ALDERMAN SCARTH IN THE CHAIR.

"IT WAS UNANIMOUSLY RESOLVED.—1st. That to promote the object contemplated by the friends of Mr. Dawson, it would be highly creditable to the Wesleyan Connexion, to raise by voluntary subscriptions not less than the Sum of *Four Thousand Guineas*, to be invested with the General Treasurers of the Wesleyan Missionary Society, on condition that they allowed to Mr. Dawson, an annuity of *Two Hundred Pounds*, during the term of his natural life; and at his decease, an annuity of *Fifty Pounds* to his brother, Thomas Dawson, should he be the survivor, (who is fifty years of age, and from peculiar circumstances dependant on his brother,) during the term of his natural life.—The said sum of Four Thousand Guineas to be at the disposal of the said Treasurers for the time being, for the purchase or erection of suitable premises for a Mission House, Offices, &c., for the transaction of the general business of the Society, in London; or for the general purposes of the Wesleyan Missionary Society, as the Committee may deem expedient.

"2nd. That in order to allow the numerous friends of Mr. Dawson to unite in this testimony of affection for him, and express their estimation of his valuable services, no single subscription is expected to exceed One Guinea, but any smaller sum will be thankfully received.

"3rd. That these Resolutions be addressed (by circular) to every Superintendent preacher in England; and that he be requested to adopt such measures in his Circuit, as he judges most likely to promote the object proposed.

"4th. That William Gilyard Scarth, Esq , be appointed General Treasurer. It is desirable that such Subscriptions should be forwarded by the 1st of June, 1836, at the latest.

"5th. That the following persons form a Committee (with power to add to their number) to carry these Resolutions into effect, *viz*:—all the Itinerant Preachers in the two Leeds Circuits, with W. G. Scarth, Esq., F. Marris, Esq., J. Hargrave, Esq., John Burton, Esq., Joshua Burton, Esq., J. Sykes, Esq., W. Smith, Esq., J. Ogle, Esq., Messrs. C. Turkington, B. Stocks, C. Smith, T. Bell, M. Outhwaite, S. Tarbotton, B. R. Vickers, T. Mawson, R. Scarth, B. Stocks, jun., W. D. Bootham, D. Underwood, and T. Simpson, of the *Leeds East Circuit*: and J. Musgrave, Esq., B. Beverley, Esq., Messrs. J. Howard, C. Dove, W. Dove, C. Waton, J. Ramsden, J. Patrick, E. Joy, S. Watson, H. Spink, J. Raynar, G. Reinhardt, J N. Brigg, J. Walton, T. Holt, J. Thackrah, C. Bowes, W. Haley, J. Richardson, S. Holmes, R. Dewsbury, J. Johnson. R. Ripley, S. Whalley, and E. Heaton, of the *Leeds West Circuit*.—W. G. SCARTH, CHAIRMAN."

sixty years; and I shall have to give up my classes, to the members of which I feel strongly attached. With me, it is a hard struggle. I only wish to know the will of God;—that once known, I can make any sacrifice. The question has come to this,—In which of the two situations shall I be able most to honour God, and unreservedly consecrate myself to his service? But the scheme begun at Sheffield, seems likely to be spoiled at Leeds, by confining the subscription within a guinea, and so depriving the missionary cause of the advantage of higher sums."

One of his friends informed him, that the fund proceeded but slowly in his neighbourhood, and pleasantly added,—" If you cannot obtain £200 per annum, you must be content to sit down, like a supernumerary, with £100." Mr. Dawson, who did not altogether relish the jocularity, returned—as he stated to the writer,—"There is a difference between my case and that of a supernumerary. The latter receives £100 for *sitting down;* whereas I am to receive £100 for *rising up.* At present, I am in a state of independence; then, I shall be at the call of every one. Besides, I may now be considered in the decline of life, and shall soon work myself out." For a considerable time, he was in great suspense respecting the propriety of giving up his farm, as proper notice was requisite, and some time would have to elapse before he could sell his stock, &c.;—such a measure being exceedingly impolitic, should the "scheme" not succeed; and yet much time would be lost in the event of its success, on leaving the whole till then.

After some time elapsed, another circular was issued,

to awaken the attention of the friends to the subject ; *
but this second appeal was still not equal, in effect,
to what might have been anticipated, especially when
it is considered, that it was made to a people imbued
with a missionary spirit, and that the prime object
of the measure was to promote the interest of the
missionary cause.

In observing to his friend, as in the preceding paragraph, that he was " now in the decline of life,"
he was reminded of this, by certain symptoms of

* DEAR SIR.—I beg to submit to your kind consideration our renewed
appeal, with the subjoined statement and Resolutions, respecting the Dawsonian Fund ; and as this measure has received the sanction of the Conference,
we hope that you will make such arrangements in your circuit, as you may
deem necessary to the accomplishment of our object.

I am, dear Sir, (on behalf of the Committee,)
Yours very respectfully,
W. G. SCARTH, TREASURER.

Leeds, Nov. 1st, 1836.

DAWSONIAN FUND.—"The Committee for securing an Annuity for Mr.
DAWSON, deem it expedient to renew their application to their friends, with a
view to the immediate accomplishment of their object. They gladly embrace
this opportunity to present their thanks to those Preachers and friends who
have kindly co-operated with them ; and are happy to state that the Subscriptions already received by their Treasurer amount to the sum of £1,500.

"While the Committee have pleasure in stating this fact—they regret to find
that the ultimate appropriation of the total amount of the Subscriptions, ' for
the purchase or erection of suitable premises for a MISSION HOUSE, OFFICES,
&c.; or for the *general purposes of the Wesleyan Missionary Society, as the
Committee may deem expedient,*' as stated in their original Resolutions, a copy
of which they subjoin, has been in some cases overlooked : they must therefore remind their friends, that though their first object is to secure for Mr.
Dawson such a provision as they deem desirable, and thus to secure the
Methodist Connexion the entire services of one who has already rendered such
efficient aid, by his labours in the pulpit and on the platform, to Sabbath
Schools, embarassed Chapels, and Wesleyan Missions; yet their ultimate
object is to secure to the WESLEYAN MISSIONARY SOCIETY the entire amount
of the sum to be raised. This part of the Plan they find it necessary to bring
in the most prominent manner before the attention of their friends.

" The Committee have also reason to believe that some friends have not
contributed to this Fund, from an apprehension that to institute a subscription
of a connexional character, without previously obtaining the approbation of

physical decay. He had lost some of his front teeth, which slightly affected his articulation, particularly in moments of rapidity, and when highly impassioned. His sight also was now such as to compel him to resort to the occasional use of glasses. Looking across the table at the writer one day, during dinner, he smiled, and said, in reference to the first defect,—— "My grindstones do not fit each other." And in reference to the last, he said,——"The first time I

the Conference, was establishing a precedent which might be very objectionable : they are, however, happy to state that the sueject was considered at the last Conference,—and they now renew their appeal with the sanction of that Body: and without any wish to institute any inviduous comparison between Mr Dawson and any other member of the Methodist Connexion, they hesitate not to avow it as their deliberate conviction, that Mr. Dawson, during the last twenty years, has served the interests of the whole Wesleyan Connexion by his labours for SCHOOLS, CHAPELS, and MISSIONS, at an expense of time, personal convenience, and even of pecuniary sacrifice, to which no other lay gentleman can make the slightest pretensions. But while the Committee unequivocally express their opinion, that Mr. Dawson is legitimately entitled to consideration for his past services, yet they ground their present appeal chiefly upon the increased facilities of usefulness which will be given to their esteemed friend, by relieving him from the care and attention connected with the management of his farm,—and enabling him to devote the residue of his days to the best interests of humanity, and the welfare of the Methodist Connexion.

"The Committee in their first appeal, thought it expedient to limit the Subscription to One Guinea, anticipating that many of their friends would subscribe for the members of their families, which in many instances has been the case ; but they now withdraw that limitation, and will be happy to receive Subscriptions to any amount, which the services of Mr. Dawson, and the ultimate application of the money to Missionary purposes, may induce them to contribute.

"In again submitting this subject to the consideration of the friends of Mr. Dawson and of Wesleyan Missions, the Committee are only influenced by a desire to extend his usefulnes: and place at the disposal of the Missionary Committee, the sum of Four Thousand Guineas, for the general objects of the Wesleyan Missionary Society.

"As it is the intention of the Committee to print an entire List of Subscriptions with as little delay as possible, they respectfully request, that any money received for this fund, may be forwarded to the Treasurer, W. G. SCARTH, Esq., Leeds, by December 21st, at the latest ; by whom, and also by the Itinerant Preachers, in their respective circuits, Subscriptions will be received.

detected a failure in my sight, was when I was attempting to mend a pen."

Yet no sympton of decay, whatever might be its nature, was ever rendered available as an excuse for him to abridge his labours ; and hence——for it is a matter of curiosity, as well as personal history, to recur to such things, we find him in the course of the year at Darlington, Stokesly, Sheffield, New Basford, Nottingham, Congleton, Heywood, Salford, Ripon, Belper, Derby, Clifford, Malton, High Town, Almonbury, Colne, Conningby, Middleton, Oldham, Dudley Hill, Tadcaster, Coventry, Wellington, Walsal, Broomsgrove, Birmingham, Barnsley, Gainsbro', Cawthorne, Skipton, Towcester, Northampton, Leicester, Sandiacre, Yarm, Middleham, Newton, Bolton, Burnley, Tanfield, Northallerton, Woodhouse Grove, Rawcliffe, Macclesfield, Manchester, Norfolk, Downham, Thelford, Little Port, Spalding, Boston, Ashley, Draycott, Keyworth, Greetland, Rothwell, Killinghall, Brompton, Whitby, Swinefleet, Birstal, Thorne, Doncaster, Leek, Yeadon, Cheadle, Wensley, Otley, Wetherby, Gotham, Bedford, Dunstable, St. Ives, Daventry, Banbury, Newcastle-on-Tyne, Blakely, Carville, Carlisle, Tockwith, Glass Houghton, Louth, North Sumercote, Grimsby, Loughbro', Markfield, Biggleswade, London, Brentford, Colchester, Lambeth, Stoke, Pontefract, Longholme, Rochdale, Burslem, Newcastle-under-Lyne, and Bradford : and at some of these places, two or three times, as usual. In the course of one of these journies, which occupied *seven* of the hottest days of the year, he was engaged in *ten* public services, in *five* different places, wide apart from each other, and travelled 242 miles. And yet, this is not equal to another journey,

in autumn, when, in *eight* days, in *six* places still
more remote from each other, he engaged in *thirteen*
services, and travelled 432 miles, and nearly the whole
by the regular coaches.   But, in a general way, however arduous his duties, he returned home more like
a person who had been indulging himself with the
recreation of a morning walk, than one who had been
engaged in Herculean toil ; giving utterance to such
sentiments as these ;——" Travelling is meat and drink
to me."——" Left Carlisle a quarter before eight o'clock,
(Oct. 12), by the Glasgow mail ; on the outside ; a
tremendous wet night ; but blessed be God, I took
no harm.   Hallelujah."——" Returned home ; all well,
and in health.   Praise the Lord, for all his benefits ! "
Here was spirit in its most buoyant state ; not in the
perverted sense in which the term is employed in the
fashionable world, when it is said, that a man acts
with spirit, when acting rashly and indiscreetly ; but
the man who shews his spirit by words of love, and
resolute actions,——who burns without consuming, and
knows nothing of timidity, while there is work to
perform, and strength to accomplish it.

An extract from Mr. R. M. Beverley's "Letters
on the present state of the visible Church of Christ, "
——referring to an "itinerant revivalist" having at this
time been so arranged in juxta-position with editorial
remarks, in the columns of one of the public journals, as to lead to a supposition that it "referred
to Mr. Dawson, the well known preacher of the
Wesleyan Methodists ; " Mr. Beverley, to prevent such
a mistake, addressed a letter to the Editor, in which
he observed,——" I beg to state, that my remarks in
that extract have no reference to Mr. Dawson, whose

character I much esteem, and whose talents as a preacher, both in natural eloquence, powers of pathos, and originality of thought, do, in my judgment, entitle him to a high station among pulpit orators."

He assisted in the services of opening a chapel at Wellington, at Glass-Houghton, and a new school-room at Garforth, with a few extra journies,—one of them to Hull and Lincolnshire, with his endeared friend, the Rev. Thomas Galland, which closed the year.

Like the good man, who is not only *devising* liberal things, but *doing* them, Mr. Dawson started the year 1837, by going "to Parlington, to solicit Mr. Gascoigne to give a little ground for a chapel at Saxton." But not finding him at home, he wrote a letter to him on the subject the next day,—not omitting to pray,—"Lord, give success." The application was successful ; for soon after, he had to remark, on a second visit,—"I went to Parlington respecting ground for Saxton chapel, when Mr. Gascoigne, in the most gentlemanly manner, gave leave for ground to be selected for the purpose. Hallelujah." His notes, however, were on a less elevated key the day following ; observing,—"I went by Parlington to Saxton, with Mr. Fox, when he made such propositions, and started such objections, as sunk our hopes. Lord, help ! " By the resistless force of perseverance, he at length completed his object.

Returning from a journey to Derby, West Bromwich, Coventry, and Tipton Green, in the month of February, he had immediately to set to work, and with "the hand of a ready writer," to answer nineteen letters with which he was greeted on entering the house.

Between two and three weeks after this, he went

to Haslingdon, in connection with some other places, and was there during the " Hoppings." *   But taking the " Horrible pit " for one of his subjects, and " Escape for thy life, " for another, he spoiled the *hoppings* of some who had repaired to the place for amusement.   May 3rd, he preached two sermons in the Independant chapel, at St. Albans, and made collections for the benefit of the Wesleyan Trust in that place ;— another instance of liberality to be added to those which have preceded.   On the 14th of the same month, he opened a new chapel at Mirfield, near Dewsbury.

During the summer months of this year, he preached more frequently out of doors than usual, owing to the crowded state of the chapels, particularly in Norfolk, Suffolk, &c.   Five of these open air services occurred in the month of June.   In the same month he preached in the Calvinist chapel at Wellingboro', in Northamptonshire.   We are reminded here, in connection with the case at St. Albans, of a saying of Tillotson : — " A good word is an easy obligation ; but not to speak ill, requires only our silence, which costs us nothing. "   These interchanges go further ; they require the sacrifice of party feeling ; and when such kindly interchanges take place in a town, they are not only creditable to the spirit that dictates them, but they invariably benefit the individuals concerned, by promoting the growth of Christian charity.

* This term is derived from the Anglo-Saxon *hoppan*, which signifies to leap or dance. Hence, dancings in the country, are called hops.   The word, in its original meaning, is preserved in grasshopper.   Both were indulged in by the Grecian youth.   One was called *akinetinda*, which was a struggle between the competitors, who should stand longest motionless on the sole of his foot.   The other, denominated *ascoliasmos*, was dancing or hopping upon one foot ; the conqueror being he who could hop the most frequently, and continue the performance longer than any of his comrades.

Mr. Dawson himself found his soul much enriched by the journey, chanting his usual notes, on his return home,—" Praise the Lord, O my soul, and forget not all his benefits !"

The biographer having had different interviews with him in the course of the year, was, as usual, much delighted with his society. The following are a few miscellaneous remarks, made on different occasions, and drawn forth either by particular circumstances, or the introduction of certain topics by others. Fictitious feeling being the subject ;—" It is easy to detect it," said he. "The Spirit of God can no more be mimicked, than the sun in the firmament. The works of God's fingers, too, are always to be distinguished from the works of man's hands. So, in the soul :—the finger of God leaves a *shine*,—the finger of man a *soil*." Speaking of the dissensions of 1834, he remarked,—" We never had a *doctor* but once ; and what was the result? The first year we had a storm,—the second a dead calm, —and now the third year, a few breezes are springing up here and there." He here made a distinction between warding off what might be deemed by some of the best men, as well as by himself at the first, the *introduction* of either a *real* or an *imaginary* evil *into* the *body*, and that of *tampering* with the *system*, and so endangering the general health, by an actual prostration of strength. To *ward off* is one thing ; to *preserve* what we *have* is another. There is no occasion for a man to destroy a valuable and extensive estate, because of an attempt to add an odd patch of land to it, of which he may not exactly approve, in consequence of it requiring a different mode of cultivation from that of which he is already in possession, and which he may

still enjoy,—secured to him by law, and sufficient for
all the purposes of social and public life.

The race of eternal life being adverted to, he said,
—"Abraham, Moses, Peter, Paul, and John, were all
found in the course.   And for what did they run?
Abraham was running out of the obscurity in which
he was shrouded, to see the 'day' of Christ, and was
glad to have a glimpse of it in the distance;—Moses
ran for a 'recompense of reward;'—Peter for an 'inheritance, incorruptible, undefiled, and that fadeth not
away;'—Paul for an 'eternal weight of glory;'—and
John, that he might be 'like' Jesus.   In an earthly
race, people *tire;* but here, they *renew* their *strength.*
The man noticed in the seventh chapter of the Epistle
to the Romans, was unable to run with 'the law of sin'
in his 'members,' and a 'body of death' at his heels.
But as the first verse of the eighth chapter necessarily
connects itself with the last of the seventh, he had
nothing to do but to step across, and then he was
ready for the race."   Directing attention to the "bruised
reed" and "smoking flax," he observed, by way of
encouraging the drooping spirit;—"There is some *fire,*
because there is *smoke.*   The *fire* cannot be *seen;* but
the *smoke* has got into the *eyes,*—the eyes begin to
smart,— and the penitent thus sheds *tears* of *sorrow*
before the Lord.   Fear not.   He who has lit up the
spark, will kindle the *flame.*"

"Teetotalism" being introduced, he observed:—
"Some of the friends have abused me, for not confining myself to *water;* though when I take anything
stronger, I take it *medicinally.*   They insist upon
sober persons setting the *example* of total abstinence
to others.   But this is absurd:—here are some men,

who will not behave themselves,—who will not keep
their hands from picking and stealing ; the consequence
is, that they are *handcuffed*, to prevent further *depreda-
tions :* but here are others, who not only know how
to behave well, but having no *temptation* or *inclination*
to behave ill, conduct themselves with *propriety.* For
the sake of *example,* however, and to *deter* others,
they must wear *handcuffs* too.   Is there, I ask, any
reason why I should become a *teetotaller,* because
another man gets *drunk ?* "   An enquiry having been
made respecting the work of God at Leeds, he replied,
—" Our numbers do not increase in the way we had
a right to expect, after the erection of our new chapels.
Some persons attribute this to one cause, and some
to another.   *My* opinion is, that we have the ' Reform
Bill ' chiefly to blame for it.   It introduced several
of our friends into office ; they next began to dabble
in politics ; attention was soon divided ; and muni-
cipal business put in its claim for the time and care
they formerly gave to the Church."   Here is, at least,
an *opinion* ; but if it should be founded on *fact,* then
a retreat becomes necessary.   At all events, it is worth
an enquiry with such as may feel interested in it as
a question.   It is scarcely possible to pay undue
attention to minor matters, without doing positive
injury to things of greater moment : and all that
know anything of politics, are aware, according to
the definition of an eminent statesman, that—"Political
reason is a computing principle ; adding, subtracting,
multiplying, and dividing, morally, and not meta-
physically or mathematically, true moral denominations,"—furnishing the mind when improperly indulged,
with everlasting employment and vexation.

T

Though Mr. Dawson did not permit politics to engross his attention, he is not to be considered as totally indifferent to public affairs, or to his privileges as a subject. No; Aug. 3rd, he is heard stating,— "I went to Leeds to vote for Mr. Wortley." However difficult it might be to discover his political bias at Bristol, when Mr. Montgomery was in the chair, it is easy to perceive his creed in this instance. But religion was the atmosphere in which he loved to breathe: and he expressed himself with greater pleasure, when, the day before, he said,—"I went into Leeds in the evening to witness the ordination of the young men." About the same time, he preached at Halton, a funeral sermon occasioned by the death of his excellent friend Mrs. Bywater, of Temple Newsam. *

The criminal in the condemned cell, was a favourite simile with him when addressing the penitent. But he varied it, as will be perceived in the following instance; and this was the case when he was the most impassioned, as it was then he was most in the habit of extemporizing. Thus combining the pictorial with the pathetic, in brief broken sentences, to animate the hopes of "the contrite," he exclaimed, while addressing such,—"The gospel is just adapted to the state of a sinner. The penitent says he is

---

* Mrs. B. resided with old Mrs. Dean, of Whitkirk, in early life; and as Mrs. D. was often visited by the nobility, who resorted to Temple Newsam, she generally availed herself of an opportunity of introducing religion to them, in some form or other. On a visit of Lord William Gordon to her house, she proposed prayer before they parted, when "Kitty," afterwards Mrs. Bywater, was requested to exercise her gift on the occasion. Her gift in this hallowed duty was extraordinary; her voice was soft—her manner was unassuming —and her language correct; she was timid—wept—and prayed: but such was the effect upon his Lordship's mind, that he not only seemed to engage in the exercise, but went up to her afterwards, and shook her respectfully by the hand.

unworthy,—that it would be presumption in him to look for pardon. What! presumption to do what God commands,—to take what he offers! In the *suitableness* of the gospel to thy state,—for I address myself to thee, poor penitent, thou hast only to advert to the case of the criminal in his cell, for an illustration. The criminal is visited,—he is told that a person has left him a thousand pounds;—he feels the kindness, but it avails him nothing,—' *to be hanged to-morrow !* ' It is added, he has become heir to an estate, —is shewn the title deeds,—but no comfort,—' *to be hanged to-morrow !* ' The king's coronation robe is thrown around him,—but this is only solemn mockery, —' *to be hanged to-morrow !* ' At length his Majesty's pardon arrives;—but ' *it is too good news to be true !* ' When once persuaded of the fact,—then, ' *Oh, what a sovereign !* Oh, what a sovereign! I will bless him all the days of my life!' Yes, penitent spirit, though guilty, the Gospel offers thee pardon through a Saviour." In this way, by some sudden turn of thought, he often depicted the despondings and the rejoicings of man in separate states, and in peculiar moods.

At a meeting of the SPECIAL MISSIONARY COMMITTEE, during the Conference, W. G. Scarth, Esq., who was a member of that Committee, adverted to the arrangement which had been proposed, in order to secure the entire services of Mr. Dawson, both to the missionary cause and to the connexion generally. He observed, that it would be impossible for him to say anything in reference to the excellent character of Mr. Dawson, which would make a deeper impression than had been already made on the minds of the committee. "His past life," said he, "especially during the last

twenty years, had been devoted—most disinterestedly
devoted—to the service of the Missionary Society :
however it had been thought by many of his personal
friends, and the friends of Missions, that if the remainder of his life could be separated from all secular cares
and concerns, he would be still more able to continue
those services which had been so acceptable to the
connexion at large, and so owned and blessed of God,
in raising the supplies which the missionary cause
required."   Mr. S. then detailed the measure which
had been adopted by the committee of the Dawsonian
Fund in Leeds.   It appeared that the sum originally
proposed had not been realized, and that not more than
£2,000 had been raised, though a few hundreds more
might probably be received, in consequence of the
appeal made to the connexion.   As it was somewhat
below the amount anticipated, he thought it reasonable,
in placing it at the general disposal of the committee,
to suggest that a smaller annuity than was originally
proposed, should be secured, both to Mr. Dawson and
his brother, in case the latter should be the survivor.
With the amount named, Mr. Dawson was perfectly
satisfied.   He (Mr. S.) thought it right to state, that
this matter had not been taken up under the idea of
remunerating Mr. Dawson for his past services.   Mr.
Dawson was not the man to urge the slightest claim in
reference to those services ; he himself would say, the
society was welcome to them ; he *had* his reward in the
testimony of a good conscience, the approbation of God,
and the success with which his endeavours had been
blessed.   Neither was Mr. Dawson under any circumstances of necessity whatever to require any aid of the
kind at the hands of the society ; on the contrary, he

considered himself in the hands of Providence, comfortably circumstanced, as to all things needful for this life. The great object of the committee was to benefit the missionary cause, both in reference to the sum to be raised, and the future services of Mr. Dawson. He did not mean to say, that the committee wished Mr. Dawson's labours to be devoted exclusively to missionary objects, but they did wish them mainly and principally to be employed for that cause; while he occasionally, as at present, served trustees by preaching at chapel anniversaries, or pleaded the cause of education. In conclusion, Mr. S. stated, that as treasurer, he offered them the money, upon the condition he had specified. It was remarked by other members, that independent of Mr. Dawson's valuable services, the proposition, merely as a matter of finance, ought to be accepted. The proposition was accepted by the special committee, and was forwarded for the sanction of the general committee.

Mr. Dawson wrote to the missionary committee, August 14th, and the following is a copy of a rough draught of the letter, found among his papers:

"To the Missionary Committee.—Dear Brethren.— Last Saturday the Watchman* fell into my hands, when I received the first information of the Conference discussion respecting the Dawsonian Fund, so-called; and though I cannot give expression to my gratitude for the unmerited and liberal intention of my friends, yet one subject gives me some little pain, and that is, that the sum of £3,000 has not been raised to meet the offer of £150 towards my living and expenses. It is on *this subject* that I feel the most sensible regret,

* The account was published in the number for Wednesday, August 2nd.

because it was the *benefit* of the *missionary cause* that conquered my will, and obtained my consent to leave a comfortable *home*—though with its cares, labours, and forbearances, to promote the glory of God in the advancement of the Redeemer's kingdom in the earth : and my views and feelings oblige me to confess, that I shall reluctantly embark in the plans of the Conference, until at least some attempt is made to raise the sum to £3,000. I feel the greatest objection to have the deficiency *made up* from the missionary collections. To make it up from these, would open the mouths of our enemies, and would grieve the hearts of some of our best friends. If some of our respectable friends were apprised of my views on this point, they would, I am inclined to think, be ready to remove my scruples respecting it. This point once settled, I should think it my duty to obey the call of the church ; and yielding to the generosity of God's people, should put body and soul into the work, so long as health and strength might be afforded. I am not unreasonable, I hope, in my wishes, that this sum should be raised, as I have no present interest in it, and the annuity would be given— at least so I suppose, whether the amount were raised or not. Do, my brethren, endeavour to meet my request, by some sort of appeal or statement, such as may be judged best by yourselves. This alone will relieve my feelings, and make my way more plain to acquiesce in the wishes of the friends.

"I was surprised when I read Mr. R. W's. suggestion, which went to confine my labours to the missionary work. Had a resolution been grounded on it, and that resolution been carried, it would have effectually barred me out from engaging in the enter-

prize at all, as I could never have suffered my liberty
to be so palpably infringed upon by such a measure. I
consider myself the servant of the *Connexion*, and not
of any *committee* for any distinct and separate fund;
and therefore, to have excluded me from serving the
Chapels, Sunday-schools, &c., according to my ability,
would never have met with my consent. I think even
the modification of my friend Scarth goes full far
enough, which states that my labours shall be 'mainly
and principally' directed to the missionary interest. I
perfectly agree that the missionary cause should have
the preference, both as to time and place; but I should
be sorry to be deprived of the pleasure of assisting the
Trustees of chapels, and the friends of Sunday-schools,
through my time being taken up by the missionary
cause, for which I sensibly feel I am but ill qualified.
It would be impossible for me to go with deputation
after deputation on this important business. For such
employment, I have neither mental variety, nor yet
physical energy; and should, therefore, shrink from
the task. But I know the members of the missionary
committee are 'Men and Brethren,' and would not
think of laying more upon me than I am able to bear.
I have deemed it proper to open my heart to you, and
leave you to take those steps which you think will best
meet the wishes of the heart of——Dear Brethren,

"Yours, &c., W. DAWSON.

"P. S. The suspense in which I have long been
kept, must painfully continue, as you are aware, until
something definite is settled. I can neither properly
manage my farm, nor yet give legal notice to quit; and
I hope the time is not far distant, when I shall be able
to say, 'Yea,' or 'Nay,' to my landlord."

On the arrangements being brought to a termination, which were to fix Mr. Dawson for life as the servant of the public, he received the following communication from the Missionary Committee, through the medium of one of the Secretaries :—

"London, 28th Sep., 1837.

" MY DEAR MR. DAWSON.—The Committee of the Wesleyan Missionary Society have desired me to convey to you their decision on your letter of the 14th of August, which was laid before them yesterday, together with one on the same subject, from Mr. Scarth of Leeds.

" The committee rightly appreciate your motives for wishing that means should be taken to increase the sum which has been raised for the purpose of securing your valuable services to the cause of Christ, without interruption or embarrassment from secular engagements : but on the fullest consideration, they are of opinion, they cannot with propriety, for various reasons, take any step, or make any appeal for that purpose. There are, at present, two special objects before the friends of the Society, — the Stockholm Chapel, and the Negro Schools,—and it is not improbable that another may be presented before long. At the same time, I am directed to assure you, that the committee most cheerfully adopt the recommendation of the Conference committee of review. They will take the amount which has been collected, and secure to you an annuity of £150; and £30 annually to your brother, in case he should survive you. The committee are also anxious that such arrangements should be made with you as would leave you, as much as possible, consistent with the claims of the

Society, at liberty to follow your own judgment and inclinations. They have, therefore, resolved to propose to you, that for six months in the year, not continuous, but to be specified by mutual agreement, as the interests of the Society may appear to require, you shall be considered under the direction of the Society, to attend such anniversaries as they may think best: and that for the remaining months you shall be at liberty to gratify your friends, and your own kind heart, by attending such other missionary, chapel, and school anniversaries, &c., as you may please. And they hope the arrangement will meet your wishes. If agreeable to you, you may, therefore, consider yourself an annuitant of the Society from the 29th of September, 1837; and you will please to signify to us your acceptance of this plan; or if any practicable modification occurs to you, you will suggest it.

"I am desired to say, that your valuable services have been promised to the Cornwall District. Their anniversaries are held in the end of March and beginning of April,—but you shall hear farther, when we receive your approval of the plan."

On receiving this letter from the Missionary Committee, which came to hand just as he was setting out on a tour to the north, he exclaimed,—"Father, thy will be done!" And on Monday, Oct. 23, he observes,—"I went to Parlington, and finally settled to give up the farm;" to which he again appended, —"Lord, thy will be done!"

His extra journies this year amounted to nearly one hundred; and the chapels which he assisted in opening, were those of Wath, Shaw Green, Micklefield, and Buxton Road, Huddersfield. The collections

T 2

at the village of Wath, amounted to £110. In the opening of Huddersfield chapel, which is capable of accommodating 2000 people, he was associated with the Rev. R. Newton, G. B. Mc Donald, Dr. Beaumont, &c., among the Wesleyans; and the Rev. James Parsons of York, and the Rev. J. Harris, the celebrated author of "Mammon," the "Great Teacher," &c., among the Dissenters. The sermons were stated by the public journals to be of the highest order of excellence, the attendance uncommonly numerous, and the collections munificent; the latter assertion being borne out by the fact, that they amounted to £1578. 18s. 3¾d.

Instances of usefulness were constantly stealing into public notice, as effected under the ministry of Mr. Dawson. Mr. Edward Jennings Olley was noticed among the "Recent Deaths" of the Wesleyan Methodist Magazine for the year, as one who had been both convinced of sin, and received a sense of pardon, while the subject of these Memoirs was officiating. An interesting account, too, is given in the same periodical of Mr. W. J. Brown, who was convinced of sin some time prior to this. He was in the establishment of Mr. Wilton of Doncaster, where he had been about six months, and from which Mr. Wilton was about to dismiss him, in consequence of his infidel principles. In his own account of himself, he observes, that when Mr. Wilton was on the point of sending him home, "at Mrs. Wilton's solicitation, he consented to try me a little longer, that I might have an opportunity of hearing a celebrated local-preacher, *of the name of Dawson;* who, it was said, had been instrumental in awakening some of the most desperate sinners in the land. He was going to open a new chapel at Thorne; and, though I knew it not, the religious members of the family agreed to make it matter of earnest prayer, that God would bless the opening services to my conversion. The day arrived, and I was easily persuaded to make one of a large party, who went from Doncaster. Mr. Dawson's text in the morning was Matt. xiv. 31. The subject was much more applicable to timid Christians, than to hardened sinners; and as I had gone merely to have a little fun, I was not greatly affected; but though my affections were not much moved, my understanding was enlightened. In the evening, his text was Heb. iii. 15, — 'To-day if ye will hear his voice, harden not your hearts, as in the provocation.' The sermon was expressly to the ungodly and unawakened. His language was powerful and glowing; and there was an overwhelming influence with it, which seemed to carry every sentence into the inmost recesses of my soul. I left the chapel with views and feelings of the most distressing kind, arising from a piercing sense of my awful state and condition as a sinner before God. I felt a burden on my conscience which I could neither bear nor remove. My sins had been great; consequently my convictions were deep." Mr. Dawson had spoiled the "fun" of many a sinner in this way.

CHAPTER XV.

MR. DAWSON being now in a position in which he
had not been placed before, and the people, in various
places, taking it for granted that he was more at liberty
than he really was, petitions poured into the Mission
House from different quarters, requesting a share of
his public service. In consequence of this, the following advertisement appeared on the cover of the
"Missionary Notice" for January, 1838 :—" In answer
to the numerous applications to the general Secretaries
of the Wesleyan Missionary Society, for the attendance
of Mr. Dawson at missionary anniversaries, &c.; the

Secretaries beg to state, that, for several months, Mr. Dawson's engagements with the Society will not come under their cognizance. When Mr. Dawson's engagements with the Society commence, a plan will be made, with Mr. Dawson's concurrence, embracing that portion of his time, during certain specified months in the year, which may be at the disposal of the Missionary Society ; and the places included in that plan will have due notice at what time they may expect Mr. Dawson's valuable services."

He continued to proceed in his usual way till he quitted his farm, and entered upon his engagements with the Missionary Society ; after which he went to reside at No. 6, Springfield Terrace, Burmantofts, Leeds, where his niece, Miss M. Dawson, kept his house,—his brother Thomas residing with them. In his niece, he had everything he could wish in reference to domestic happiness ;—prudence, piety, good sense, industry, order, and affection. He himself was a man of order, especially in the arrangement of his papers, and anything which belonged exclusively to his own department. It was his custom also, to write out a list of his engagements during a given period, and give it to Miss Dawson, that she might know in what part of the kingdom he was, and how to answer enquiries. He opened a new chapel at Tingley, March 11, and another at Batley Car, April 24 ; both in the Dewsbury circuit.

His work now became sometimes excessive. The good friends, in different places, attended chiefly to their own wants and wishes, without considering the claims of others ; and to have complied with the wishes of all, would have required the compression of two years into one. "Uncle," said Miss Dawson, "your labour is too oppressive; you should contrive, in your arrangements, to secure two or three days to yourself occasionally, for rest." "Mary," he returned, "I shall *rest* in my grave. I must work while it is day; the night cometh when no man can work." This reminds us of Arnauld's remarkable reply to Nicole, when they were hunted from place to place, the latter refusing to assist him in a new literary work, observing, "We are now old, is it not time to rest?" "Rest!" returned Arnauld, "have we not all eternity to rest in?" Mr Dawson had never seen this; but the sentiments pair admirably.

At the Conference, held in Bristol, July and August, several resolutions were entered into on a proposition of the preceding Conference respecting the celebration of the "CENTENARY OF WESLEYAN METHODISM." Minutes, pp. 115—119. On the morning of Nov. 7th, 1838, pursuant to these resolutions and directions of the Conference, a meeting of ministers and gentlemen, convened by the President from different parts of the United Kingdom, was held in Oldham-Street chapel, Manchester, in order to devise a proper plan for its celebration the ensuing year. This meeting the biographer had the pleasure of attending; at which were present the President and Secretary of the Conference, seven Ex-Presidents, and about two hundred and fifty other ministers and gentlemen connected with the Wesleyan-Methodist Societies and congregations in London, Manchester, Salford, Liverpool, Leeds, Bramley, Birmingham, Bristol, Sheffield, Bolton, Stockport, Halifax, Bradford, Wolverhampton West Bromwich, Macclesfield, Bury, Wakefield, Newcastle-upon-Tyne, Sun-

derland, Chester, Rochdale, Oldham, Huddersfield, Sowerby-Bridge, Birstal, Hull, Whitby, York, Louth, Haslingdon, Dublin, Bandon, and elsewhere. The resolutions and speeches delivered at the meeting, were published in a "Supplement to the Watchman" of Nov. 21st, and also in the Wesleyan Methodist Magazine for December, pp. 932—944. On this occasion, and at subsequent meetings, the members of the Methodist Society, and the friends of Methodism, poured into the Centenary Fund, for various connexional purposes, upwards of £220,000.

At the adjourned Meeting of the Centenary Committee held in Brunswick Chapel, Leeds, in the month of December, Mr. Dawson took a share in the proceedings. He observed on the occasion, that he was a stranger at home ; and that having been so much engaged elsewhere, and with other matters, he had had no time to direct his attention to the subject of the Centenary. He expressed the pleasure he experienced in seeing his brethren dwell together in unity ; and he was sure the feeling connected with the meeting would not disturb a dying hour. He remembered meetings in the circuit of a very different description,—meetings that occasioned pain,—that occasioned the separation of hearts and minds. He even then felt for some, and wished them present to behold their joy. He stated, that he once made a speech at a meeting,—referring to the division, when forty of them left their brethren. But after they left, God was evidently with both himself and his brethren ; and now, they seemed to be tied together with a band, like a sheaf,—not only united, but full of good fruit. As to himself, he further observed, he had always been a nondescript, and he

remained so up to that period,—an itinerant Local
Preacher,—or, according to others, a middle link between the travelling and Local Preachers; something
like the Acts of the Apostles between the Gospels and
the Epistles, which united the two. Taking hold of
the latter comparison, he said,—"If I could, I would
take hold of the Travelling Preachers with the one
hand, and of the Local Preachers with the other, and
would draw them still closer to the body. A friend of
mine once observed to me, that when Matthew Henry
died, he was in the Acts of the Apostles. That, I
replied, is where I should like to be when I die,—in the
Acts of the Apostles. I exercised a sort of preach-
ment some years before I became a decided Methodist;
but I found it would not do to be halting between the
Established Church and the Methodists, and gave myself to the latter,—soul and body,—head, heart, and
hand. On Mr. Pawson sending me a class-paper and
a plan, I entered at once upon the work." After giving
a sketch of the characteristic peculiarities of Methodism
and its founder, he then adverted to the Theological
Institution, and expressed a hope, that "the lads
would come out like flaming torches." There were
two meetings in Leeds on the same day; and the
"day's receipts" were announced in the evening to
amount to £10,590, which, added to £6,130, previously received, amounted to £16,720 for the Leeds
Centenary District, independent of what was afterwards
contributed.

Exclusive of finance, there were several other important beneficial results arising out of the celebration
of the Centenary of Wesleyan Methodism. It brought
both preachers and people back to *first principles.*

Upon those, the whole Wesleyan body seemed to fall, and found in them both footing and repose. Methodism was ascertained to be the very same then, in all the *essentials* of religion, that it was when it first came out of the hand of its Founder : and although, like Christianity itself, it had passed through various gloomy and turbulent periods, it always came out of the cloud and out of the storm, the same in substance as it entered. The waves had sometimes been heard to roar, but when they reached a certain point, a voice had been heard,—" Hitherto shalt thou go, but no further." The sun had been occasionally overcast, but never totally eclipsed. The Wesleyans had witnessed a few volcanic eruptions, but their Pompeii still stood, —their Herculaneum had not been permitted to disappear beneath a superincumbent mass of ashes and burning lava. The members of the body could still say,—" Beautiful for situation is Mount Zion ; " and although they could not affirm her to be the " joy of the whole earth ; " yet they could invite the gaze of the crowd, and say,—" Walk about Zion, go round about her ; tell the towers thereof ; mark well her bulwarks, consider her palaces, and tell it to the generation following ; "—tell them that Methodism was, at the *close* of the century,—as to the essentials of Christianity, what it was in the *beginning*.—A second result was, that it brought together a number of *facts* and *incidents,* as well as a great deal of Methodistical lore to light, which otherwise, in all probability, would have sunk into oblivion. These, together with *local* histories, were calculated to form the ground-work of a general ecclesiastical history of the Wesleyan body, which is still a *desideratum* in Methodism.—It produced, as a third result, a stronger bond of union among the members of Society. There had not been an *era* in Methodism, in which the people were more united ; nor was there a circumstance in the history of Methodism, that had imparted equal pleasure ;—never a measure that had been better supported. Rich and poor, young and old, seemed to vie with each other in paying a tribute of respect to a system, which, under God, had placed them among the princes of his people.—In addition to others, it was the means, as a fourth result, of reclaiming several *wanderers*, if not in life, at least in *feeling, sentiment*, and *expression*. Children, grand-children, great grand-children, nephews, nieces, distant relatives, and friends, who seemed to have forgotten for a season, that such a thing as Methodism existed, and that even they themselves owed their wealth and respectability to the habits induced by it in those that had gone before, threw the mind back upon *early days*, and brought the past to bear upon what was then passing in review before them. Hence, in the list of Centenary contributions, were tributes of respect for a revered grandfather, —a beloved father or mother,—friend or relative, of the first, second, or third generation of Wesleyan Methodists. These things afforded proofs, that if they were not *with* the body, they were in the way of being *of* it ; —that a latent spark of affection still existed in the soul, which might burst forth, and not only become a burning, but a shining light.

During part of the winter, and the whole of the spring of 1839, Mr. Dawson was employed in fulfilling such engagements as he had entered into prior to those which were immediately connected with the arrangements of the Missionary Committee ; which engagements were

not completed till the month of July. A list of the
places, commencing with July 25, 1839, and ending January 23, 1840, as constituting the labours
of the *half year* claimed by the Missionary Committee—being, during that time, obliged to preach
twice a day very often, and to attend missionary
meetings,—at a period of life when he was fast verging
towards seventy years of age,—somewhat stiff and
unwieldy in bulk, will abundantly shew, while it exhibits a constitution of brass, and the most ardent
zeal in the cause of Christianity, that the office upon
which he thus entered, after leaving all secular employment, was no sinecure.* On one occasion, in addition
to the instances of excessive labour, already mentioned,
he preached twenty-five sermons, delivered fifteen addresses at missionary meetings, and travelled 886
miles, in less than a month.

Some of his outdoor scenes were exceedingly picturesque. When on a visit to Wheatley, near Retford, in

* The plan given to him, and which he fulfilled to the letter, is as follows:—
1839.

July 25........Beal	Aug. 13........St. Albans
26 ....Snaith	14........Thrussington, near
28 (Sund) Doncaster	Leicester
29........Misterton	15........Broughton, ditto
30........Goole	18........Scarborough
31 ....Ancoats	19... ....Ditto
Aug. 1........Kelfield	20..... ..Ditto
2........Acaster	23........Chickingly, near
4 (Sund.) Leeds	Dewsbury
5........Worksop	25 (Sund.) Cross Hills, nr. Skipton
6 ....Grundle on the Hill	26........Otley
8........Ferry	27........Manchester
8........Proceed to Nottingham	28 ....Swanlow-Lane, near
9........Radcliffe, near ditto	Nantwich
11 (Sund.) Leicester	29........Etruria, Potteries
12 ....Through Coventry to	Sep. 1 (Sund.) Riddings, nr. Belper
St. Albans	2........Critch, Derbyshire

Nottinghamshire, he was compelled to leave the chapel, in consequence of the multitude of persons anxious to hear him, but unable to gain admission. He took his stand near a stack-yard ; and soon, boys, girls, men, and women, were perched on walls, carts, stacks of stubble, and any little eminence that would admit of a sight of the preacher, apart from the dense mass of human beings before him, collected from the neighbouring places. A few smiled at first, at the novelty of the scene ; but every eye was speedily fixed, and a death-like silence prevailed, except in cases where persons were wrought upon by the force of truth. The rustic simplicity of the major part of his hearers, and the rural

Sep.   4........Armley, near Leeds
       5........Middleton
       6........Horsley, Woodhouse
       8 (Sund.) Burton-on-Trent
       9........Tamworth, near Bir-
                mingham
      10........Ticknale, nr. Ashby
      11........Heanor, near Derby
      12........Ilkestone, near Not-
                tingham
      13........Breedon, near Ashby
      15 (Sund.) Loughborough
      16........Thurmanstone
      17........Anisty
      18........Ecton, nr. Northampton
      19........Finedon,   ditto
      20........Higham Ferrers
      22 (Sund.) Bedford
      23........Perhaps Newport-
                Pagnell
      24........Aylesbury
      25........Oakham
      26........Grimsby, Lincolnshire
      27........Ditto,   ditto
      28........Caister,   ditto
      29 (Sund.) Scumthorp, ditto
      30........Minterton, ditto
Several engagements are omitted here

Oct. 31........Set off for Birmingham
Nov. 1........Newport-Pagnell
      2........Gate, St. Albans
      3 (Sund.) St. Albans and Watford
      4....-...St. Albans
      5........Watford
      6 ....A wish for me to preach
                in the neighbourhood
      7........City Road, Missionary
                Meeting
      8........In London
      9........Go to Ipswich
     10 (Sund.) Ditto
     11........Ipswich Miss. Meet.
     12........Woodbridge
     13........Manningtree
     14, 15....Unengaged
     16........Travel to Brighton
     17 (Sund.) Preach   ditto
     18........Ditto   ditto
     19........Lewis
     20........Worthing
     21........Walworth
     22........In London
     23........Travel to Windsor
     24 (Sund.) Preach at ditto
     25........Meeting, ditto
     26 ...... Maidenhead

objects around, furnished a fine picture of primitive times,—not of those when "Paul stood in the midst of Mars-hill,", with the splendid temples of Greece, and the polished and philosophical orators of Athens before him, but when he "went out of the city by a river side, and sat down, and spake unto the women that resorted thither." It is no wonder that Dr. Southey, with his fine genius, should have fastened on such scenes as these, in his Life of Mr. Wesley, and have expatiated —abstracted from religion, on their poetic effect on the human mind. But visible things had fewer attractions than the voice of truth ; and not a few were impressed with the subject, which was selected from that

Dec. 27........Stanhope-Street
28........Chelsea
29, 30....Unengaged
Dec. 1 (Sund.) City Road & Lambeth
2........Spital Fields
3........Westminster
4........Southwark
5, 6.....Unengaged
7........Go to Brentford
8 (Sund.) Brentford
9........Hinde-Street
10........Go to Stainford
12........I hope to see home
13........Home
14........Set off for York
15 (Sund.) Preach at York
16........Missionary Meeting
17........Water
18........Acaster
19........Foggathorpe and Holme
20........Home
21........Set off for Congleton
22 (Sund.) Preach at ditto
23........Middlewich, Cheshire
24........Return to Bradford
25........Bradford Juvenile Miss. Meeting

Dec. 26........Preach near Bradford
27........Home
28........Go to Oldham
29 (Sund.) Preach at Oldham
30........Goto Winsford, Cheshire
1840. 31........Burslem
Jan. 4........Go to Stokesley, Cleveland
5........Stokesley
6........Return
This week is not yet filled up
12 (Sund.) Ripon
15........Sheffield
16........Ecclesfield
19 (Sund.) Bilston
20........Kidderminster
21........Uttoxeter
26 (Sund.) Rochdale
This week not yet filled up
Feb. 2 (Sund.) Hull
4........Driffield
5........Crowle
9 (Sund.) Derby
10........Belper Potteries
11........Buxton
16 (Sund.) Nantwich
This week not yet filled up
23........Near Manchester

portion of Scripture which relates to the worth of the soul.

His sermons were always of a character that might be understood ; and being occasionally interwoven with "COTTAGE STORIES" and "COTTAGE SCENES," particularly in the rural districts, they never failed to rivet attention, and affect the heart. The author of "The Wanderer of Switzerland," has been heard to express his admiration of Mr. Dawson's tact for relating "Cottage Stories," being distinguished for so much simplicity, ease, character, and pure nature ; combined with point, and good moral and religious improvements ; and often so beautifully illustrative withal, either of the general subject, or some particular point arising out of it, as well as admirably adapted to the occasion.

On the platform, when in a state of high-wrought feeling, he sometimes proceeded to extreme lengths. This was the case at S———. He had been rolling on in all his strength for some time ; and, in the esteem of most, even seemed to surpass himself for freedom of expression, power of thought, and splendour of imagery ; when, all on a sudden, some freak of fancy shot across the mind, and he took his seat. He had borne the people onward with himself, who seemed like persons transported into a strange country, when their leader suddenly disappears, and they are left in silent astonishment. After a short pause, he sprang from his seat again, with the elasticity of youth, and directing his eye to the chairman, said,— " With your permission, Sir, I should like to sing a little ; " and immediately pitched a tune to—

> " We are soldiers fighting for our God,
> Let trembling cowards fly," &c.,

assuming, at the same time, a martial air, as he crossed the platform,—bidding defiance to all the powers of earth and hell, and representing the missionary cause as towering above all opposition. The effects of this eccentric movement were various, but such as would scarcely warrant a repetition; nor could the thing itself apparently have been premeditated; as under such circumstances it must have been an evident failure.

At the same place, on another occasion, he was interrupted in his speech by an unusal commotion, in which every eye was directed towards the door, accompanied with loud peals of approbation; on which he coolly and mildly turned to the chairman, saying,—"I'll stop a little, Sir;" adding, with a sudden turn of pleasurable feeling—"There he is—there he comes—all are glad to see him,—fresh as a *roe* from the mountains of Israel, and leaping with all the agility of a *buck* over his neighbour's fences." This only heightened the feeling of gladness, as the Rev. George Roebuck, who had travelled in the circuit, and just then unexpectedly appeared, making his way over the backs of the seats to the platform, being unable to gain access to it by any other mode, owing to the crowded state of the aisles. In this way, he often laid hold of little incidents, to relieve attention,—incidents which would prove the death of mere *rehearsals*, but which were life to him, as they were the occasion of life in others.

Several remarks escaped from him in different social parties, in the course of the year, when the biographer was present, some of which, though separate from their connexion, may be useful to others, and also serve as a key to the character of his mind. "Without the SPIRIT, the promises of God are ineffectual. You may lay promise upon promise, like plaster upon plaster, to staunch the bleeding wounds of the soul ; but all is vain, till the Holy Ghost presses his hand upon them. With the *letter* we must have the *Spirit.*   Look at Adam ; one of the fairest creatures of God ; perfect in all his limbs and features.   God breathes into him a living soul, and he instantly starts on his feet.   So much for *forms* without the *Spirit.*   There is yet a little wreck of divinity in man ; but he must be *in* Christ before he can live ; and thus, in Christ divinity meets divinity."   He met in his travels, one of the descendants of Oliver Heywood ; and referring to this, he observed,—" I regret to find, that most of the descendants of that excellent man are Socinians."   Then glancing at the history of the Church, he said,—" Mohammedanism arose at an early period, and the Arab thief from hell tried to rob Christ of his honours. Popery, though long working, came next in its grosser form ; and required paintings, vestments, and other adornings, to hide its hideous features.   But we, as Methodists, preach Christ the MEDIATOR, and have no need to go to the virgin Mary to mediate for us. We preach forgiveness, through faith in his blood, and have no need to go to the priest for absolution ; we receive it from our Great High Priest.   We preach the sanctification of the Spirit, and have no need to go to purgatory to be purified ;—no, we shall glide past it without feeling the heat.   After the Reformation, the Church again relapsed. The Nonconformists,—some of whom were among the best men that ever lived, were expelled from the English Church: then came Socinianism, into which most of the Presbyterians fell ; and chapels, erected by orthodox men, were consecrated to error."

"The Letters of Joseph Alleine," said he, "are equal to those of Fletcher for piety ; but he cannot stoop like the latter." Directing attention to preaching, he observed,—"Ministers cannot be too plain and striking provided they are not vulgar and absurd. Let Mr. E. read a page out of Bishop Butler's Analogy of Religion, Natural and Revealed, to a Christian congregation, and another out of Bunyan's Pilgrim's Progress, and it will soon be seen which strikes the most, and with which they will feel most interested."

At the Leeds borough parliamentary revision, before Mr. Kaye, Mr. Dawson was objected to by the liberals, when some rather amusing questions were proposed, arising from the station he occupied in the Wesleyan body ; but the "objection was disallowed." *

* The following account appeared in the Leeds "Mercury," among other cases.

Mr. *William Dawson*, house, Springfield Terrace, Burmantofts.—Objected to by the Liberals.

Mr. BOND called a person named Hargreave, who proved the occupancy of the house in question by Mr. Dawson, the sufficiency of value for the purpose of conferring a vote, and also the period of possession by the voter.

Mr. PREST.—What is Mr. Dawson?

Witness.— He's a Methodist preacher.

Mr. PREST.—Don't you know he occupies the house under trustees?

Witness.—He is not a travelling preacher, unless he has become so very lately.

Mr PREST.—Why, you anticipate the question.

Mr. BOND.—I believe Mr. Dawson is not called 'Reverend.'

Mr. MORGAN.—He is as much ordained as any other Methodist preacher.

Mr. PREST.—Don't you know that gentlemen of Mr. Dawson's calling are removeable at pleasure?

Witness.—I believe he is considered a local-preacher, and not a regular minister.

Mr Thomas Simpson, painter, said, that he had a notion—

Mr. PREST.—We don't want any of your notions here unless you can swear to them.

Mr. Simpson.—I have known Mr. Dawson for thirty years.

MR. KAYE.—Then what is he?

Mr. Simpson.—He is a local-preacher, and nothing more. He takes the

U

At the time the liberals were disputing his civil rights, he received marked attention from the Mayor; to whose polite note he returned the following answer :

" The right worshipful the Mayor of the borough of Leeds.

" Honoured Sir,—Your kind invitation to dine with you on Wednesday the 16th instant, came to my house in due season. But not being at home at the time, I was unable to do myself the honour and the pleasure of

house himself, pays the rent, and no one has any control over him. I am a local-preacher, same as he is.

Mr. PREST.—How do you know that?

Mr. Simpson.—I know it as well as I know my own brother's affairs.

Mr. PREST.—Can you give us the definition of a local-preacher?

Mr. Simpson.—If the Barrister wishes it I will give him one, but I don't see that it is requisite.

Mr. KAYE.—Does Mr. Dawson occupy this house under trustees?

Mr. Simpson.—No: he has nothing to do with trustees.

Mr. KAYE.—Does he preach in any particular chapel.

Mr. Simpson.—No; he travels from one part of the country to another, and preaches to any congregation who may send for him.

Mr. KAYE.—Then he takes the house, and the furniture is his own?

Mr. Simpson.—Yes.

Mr. BOND.—Is he removeable by Conference?

Mr. Simpson.—No.

Mr. KAYE.—If you shew me that this house belongs to certain trustees, then the occupation is a permissive one, and there is an end of the case : but if, to use a familiar expression, he takes it in his own private right, why then he stands unconnected with trustees.

Mr. PREST.—He may be removed.

Mr. KAYE.—Show me the difference between an officer in the army or navy, sent on foreign service, and the case of Mr. Dawson. You don't mean to contend that an officer sent abroad is not entitled to have a vote. I think there is nothing in the objection.

Mr. PREST.—My objection is, that Mr. Dawson may be removed at any time from this house by the Conference, and sent to a distant part of the country.

Mr. KAYE.—Exactly: he may be sent from Leeds to attend a congregation in some other part ; but can you, as I said before, distinguish him in any way from an officer in her Majesty's service. You might as well say that I have no vote in London, because her Majesty's Judge of Assize sends me here for so many days in a year. I think there is no validity in your objection. *Objection disallowed.*

complying with your wishes : the honour, so far as
being under your roof as the chief magistrate of the
borough of Leeds goes ; and the pleasure of being in
your presence, as a friend,—not omitting, a friend and
relative of old and dear friends.   To have been with
you, would have afforded a gratification, which few, if
any, of your respectable company would equally have
felt.   So speaks the heart of—Honoured Sir,
   " Yours, most respectfully,—W. DAWSON."
   Being in the house of a friend about the same time,
and looking at a bust, he said to the biographer,—" I
never like to see a bust.   There is no soul in the eye ;
it always appears ghastly, and reminds me of death in
a coffin. "   Painting had rather more charms than
sculpture ; but here too—more perhaps from a want of
knowledge than a want of taste, he felt comparatively
little interest.   " If I have any taste," said he, " it
belongs more immediately to the ear than the eye.
When I visited Windsor Castle, I was struck with the
antiquity, the grandeur, and the majesty of the place,
In passing from room to room, I saw paintings, which,
I take for granted, were by the first masters ; but they
were all lost upon me.   I was pleased with the group-
ing, colouring, &c., but could not tell why.   I was
grieved at myself, and said inwardly, ' I wish I had my
friend Mr.—— here ; he would be able to point out
the peculiarities and excellences of each.'   This itself
was a drawback upon my pleasure."   The truth is, in
all art there is more or less deception ; and hence, the
artist is advised to "put a generous deceit on the
spectators, and effect the noblest designs by easy
methods."   Another authority—Sir Joshua Reynolds,
tells us,—" What has pleased, and continues to please,

is likely to please again ; from whence are derived the rules of art." The more perfect the deception, therefore, the more likely it is to please. Mr. Dawson was a pure child of nature, and hence it was, that nature had always more charms than art. In the mean time, " it must be a great mortification to the vanity of man, that his utmost art and industry can never equal the meanest of nature's productions, either for beauty or value. Art is only the under-workman; and is employed to give a few strokes of embellishment to those pieces which come from the hand of the master. Some of which may be of his drawing, but he is not allowed to touch the principal figure. Art may make a man a suit of clothes, but nature must produce a man." The "Mountain Daisy," or the cowslip, possessed more attractions for such a man as Mr. Dawson, than the *chef-d'-œuvre* of the most eminent master of either the chisel or the pencil.

When speaking of the tour, in the course of which he visited Windsor, he observed to the biographer,— "My heart was wrung with grief during the six weeks. With only one reluctant exception, the speakers were never cheered when Popery was referred to with disapprobation. The people seemed absolutely afraid of giving the smallest countenance to any discussion on the subject. So much for popish influence in the cabinet and elsewhere."

In the course of this journey also, he met with his venerable friend, the Rev. H. Moor. Speaking of the leader of a certain party, and the dissension occasioned by him ; " Yes, " said Mr. M., "the devil took it into his head once to set up for himself; but he soon found, he had better have been quiet."

Mr. Dawson himself made a good remark, when speaking of two persons who were often striving for the mastery,—"The English [language] will never admit of two great I Is together." Referring to Mr. M's attack of paralysis, he related the following characteristic anecdote :—"When he began to rally in mind, he expressed a wish to be taken down stairs. There were none but females in the house at the time. He was impatient to be removed, unable to assist himself, and the females were unequal to the effort. One of them going out for aid, saw a gentleman passing, and requested his assistance. When they got him down stairs, and matters adjusted, Mr. M. thanked the gentleman, who, as he was about to retire, politely put his card into his hand. Mr. M. looking at it, and seeing 'UNDERTAKER' upon it, returned it, and coolly observed,—'Thank you, Sir, for your kind attentions; but it has not come to that yet.'" With the exception of physical debility, Mr. Dawson thought the mind of Mr. M. very little impaired.

Mr. Dawson having been advised, in a certain transaction in which an equivalent was not given for value received, and which would admit of certain claims of justice and mercy, in the event of success, called upon the biographer, and said,—"I was at——, in the course of my journey, and recollecting your hint, I called on Mr.——, who handed me £10, as part profit on——; I therefore made up my mind, the first time I should meet with you, to thank you for £10. This I shall devote to the two orphan children." These were the children of a friend. Friendship, with Mr. Dawson, was not merely, as La Rochefoucauld defines it,—an exchange of good offices, a reciprocal management of faults and virtues,—a commerce in which self-love finds something to gain. To lower thus the principle of human actions, may serve the cause of infidelity, but not that of disinterested Christianity ; and the worst of consequences may be deduced from such theories. These orphans would have lost £10 on reducing such principles to practice : and say —What would be the loss to the poor in particular, and to the world at large !

He was at Swanlow-Lane, in Cheshire, about the same time. His friend, Mr. Russom, drove him to the house of Mr. Stones, where he was to lodge. Having perspired profusely while preaching, and forgotten his top-coat, he felt chilled by the evening air. While his friend was urging on the horse, he said, " Friend R., a prudent man foreseeth the evil, and hideth himself, but the simple pass on, and are punished." He was providentially preserved, however, from receiving any material injury.

Occasion being taken, in the course of this journey, to point out to him a passage in Philip's Life of Whitfield, in which he was noticed, and to which the reader's attention will, in due time, be invited, he significantly closed the volume, on reading it, exclaiming, in prayerful mood,—" Lord help me ! " accompanying it with the act of putting his spectacles into his pocket.

After much hard labour in the course of the winter, and in the early part of the year succeeding, he left Leeds, March 30th, 1840, for Liverpool, and set sail for Ireland, April 1st, the day on which the Rev. R. Newton embarked for America. He had not been in Ireland before. While there, he travelled from place to place, preaching, and attending missionary meetings. His fire and his genius were admirably adapted to gain the attention and the hearts of the inhabitants of the Emerald Isle; and his conversations, on his return, afforded no small proof of close observation, and shewed, that if he had been so disposed, and had had sufficient time at command, to have gone forth for the purpose, he might have produced a good article,—not in an offensive sense, on the "Lights and Shadows of Irish Life;" omitting, of course, the farce of brogue and humour, the *gusto* and buoyancy, and the finish of touch displayed by some authors that might be named. The productions of his pen would have been more adapted to the closet than the drawing-room table,— his "Lights" arising from the wholesome effects of Protestant instruction and piety, and his "Shadows" from Popish ignorance and superstition. Some hundreds of volumes and pamphlets have been published on the evils of Ireland, and the remedies for those evils; but it has been affirmed, and affirmed with truth too, that scarcely any three of the doctors are agreed as to the nature of the disease; and there is still a greater discrepancy as to the mode of cure. Two or three valuable aphorisms, however, may be selected from some of these *brochures.* "The evils of Ireland," says a sound thinker, "are high rents and low wages;" and he is perfectly correct. "The evils of Ireland," says another, "are its book-makers and its speech-makers;" and he is not very far wrong; especially if the latter be coupled with Daniel O'Connel, who, by the way, has made as much in hard cash by his speeches, as some of the greatest landed proprietors in Ireland have made by their estates. Here comes a

third: "Give me," said the celebrated Mr. Stephens
—and the saying contains volumes,—"Give me," said
he, when the Government was about to send an armed
force into Ireland,—" Give me an army of schoolmasters, and I will conquer Ireland." Aye, there it is ;
—WHOLESOME INSTRUCTION ! The evils of Ireland
must be traced, in a great measure, to the important
fact, which, with the exception of Mr. Taylor in his
"Civil Wars of Ireland," both Protestant and Catholic
writers have been careful to suppress,—the fatal gift
of the island by the Pope to Henry II. To this
atrocious act may be attributed most of the misery
of Ireland. It armed the conquerors with a right
divine, and it unnerved many of the wisest Irish
chieftains, who imagined that opposing the will of
one, whom other nations regarded as the infallible
head of the Church, was at once fruitless and impious.
Popery is at the root of all : its crimes and follies
have disorganized Irish society, rendered the fertility
of the Irish soil a curse, and derived misery from
the very bounties of heaven.

Few men, with the exception of the author of
"Traits and Stories of the Irish Peasantry,"—who
has been justly denominated a Crabbe in prose, would
have been better able to depict the state of the peasantry, than Mr. Dawson. Like the author in question,
he would have delineated with sternness, but with
fidelity ; with inexorable severity, when a vicious system
was to be portrayed, yet ready to shed the tear of
sympathy over those whom that system had made
its miserable victims. He possessed the power of
giving reality to humble life, and the consistency of
his narratives never failed to convince those who

attended to them, of his fidelity; constantly reminding a person acquainted with them, of some of the Dutch painters; possessing like them, minute fidelity, even in the circumstances which are apparently the most trifling, and depicting matters often slurred over by mere narrators of fiction.

Mr. Dawson saw enough of the Irish character, during his brief stay, to produce a love of it; every peasant with whom he met—and this is the general feeling pervading society, considering his visit more as a compliment paid to himself, than a general love to the cause of Missions, and deemed it a direct duty to pay him every possible respect.

Not long after his return from the green isle, he re-opened a chapel in Gloucester; and soon after this, again improved the death of his beloved friend, Mr. Thomas Stoner, the father of the Rev. David Stoner, with whom he had been intimately acquainted for a period of forty years. He died, Friday, May 22nd, 1840, aged 75 years. Mr. Stoner, as well as himself, was brought to God under the ministry of the Rev. Thomas Dikes; and afterwards, he received the sanctification of the Spirit, Friday, April 12th, 1806, under Mr. Dawson's own ministry. He was a man of slow speech, of great tenderness, timidity, and modesty; uniform in his Christian character, powerful in prayer, faithful and persevering in the discharge of religious duty. When he joined society, the Wesleyans in Barwick had only one sermon in the month from the local-preachers, on the Sabbath afternoon: but the few members who were competent to exercise in prayer, and in this Mr. Dawson joined, "went two and two, on a Sabbath evening, to hold prayer

u 2

meetings in the neighbouring places." On the alternate Sabbath, he threw open the best room in his
house, for a "fellowship meeting;" and it was here
that Mr. Dawson received so many baptisms of the
Spirit. Mr. Dawson, in a manuscript account of this
good man, observes, in reference to this room; "This
was the birth-place of many souls. This *room* was, for
years, the study of the preachers. They felt, when
within its walls, that it was like the 'holy of holies,'
in which the glory shone from between the cherubim
upon the High Priest, while worshipping within the
veil. If the figure may be allowed, it was always kept
well warmed, well aired, and well perfumed with the
'odour of sweet smell,'—emanating from the presence
of God, who appeared to take up its abode within its
sacred walls."*—Mr. Stoner established a class of young
boys and girls, and was eminently useful in the Sunday-
school. Before he died, instead of a room, preaching
once a month, and only one class, he lived to see a
chapel, preaching twice every Sabbath, and once on
the week day, and four classes. Though called to pass
through deep waters in the course of a few of the last
years of his life, "the bitters of his cup," observes
Mr. Dawson, "were softened and sweetened by the ex-
emplary, and truly praiseworthy affection of his beloved
daughter, and her no less worthy husband; added to

* It may be useful here, to recur to two or three particulars in Mr. Dawson's
own personal history and labours, in connection with the efforts of this good
man, to diffuse the spirit of piety through the neighbourhood. Though reference has been made to the number of members in Mr. D's. classes at a time when
the work was low, one of them had 31 members in 1808,—32 in 1819,—and 30
in 1832. There were also three revivals of religion at Barnbow, at different
periods; during which—Barnbow being a short distance from his residence,
Mr. D. was in the habit of sending his horse home in the evening, by a boy,
while he himself,—after long rides, and hard pulpit labour, remained behind
to assist in carrying on the prayer-meetings.

which was the love and care of his youngest son, who was to him a JOSEPH." Mr. Stoner left Tadcaster on the 7th of May, to visit his son, resident at Barwick. There he was taken ill, and finished his earthly, where he commenced his Christian course. During his last illness, the family wished to know what message he had to deliver to his daughter, the wife of the Rev. George Croft, a Missionary in the West Indies, when he said,—" Heaven! heaven!" Some of his last words were,—" I am ready! I am ready!

> ' For me my elder brethren stay,
> And angels beckon me away,
> And Jesus bids me come.' "

Mr. Dawson preached the same sermon on the occasion, both at Tadcaster and Barwick. His friend John Batty, heard him at both places; and named the circumstance. "I had forgotten you were there," said Mr. Dawson; "and it is as well I did, or it would have been a snare to me." John replied, "I liked it better the second time than the first." This was not a solitary case; for as he often extemporized, and always left room for the inspirations of the Spirit in the pulpit, his sermons, by the occasional introduction of episodical matter,—though substantially unaltered, carried a freshness with them, resembling the breath of spring, and the balm of summer. Hence, when his sermons were published by short-hand writers, he met occasionally with passages which he had forgotten, being struck off at the moment, and possessed of amazing force and beauty.

Prior to the Newcastle Conference, the "Gown" question, which was settled the Conference following, became a subject of conversation. "My prejudices," said Mr. Dawson, "are in favour of a gown; but my reason, in the present state of affairs, is against it. When young, I could not bear to hear a person preach without a gown; and hence I feel strong objections to the use of one in the Sheffield Proprietary School. The boys will, like myself, imbibe a prejudice in favour of the gown; and it will have a tendency to alienate the mind of the boys, on their return home, to find Wesleyan Ministers denuded of what they have been practically taught to value."

In one of his excursions, in the course of summer, he was in the neighbourhood of Chatsworth, and availed himself of the opportunity of going over the house and grounds belonging to his Grace the Duke of Devonshire. What he was especially struck with was, the "CON-SERVATORY;" * from which he came to Acaster, fresh

* This is stated, by Dr. Granville, in his "Midland and Southern Spas of England," to be perfectly original and unique, so far as it was proceeded with, when his work was published. It would, by modern Parisians, receive the title of "Terre Monstre." It stands at a short distance from the great water-work or cascades in the park. Here a spot of ground was cleared of trees and shrubs to the extent of two acres, one of which is covered over with glass. The glazed surface contains seventy thousand square feet of glass, divided into slips, each two feet long, and six inches wide; arranged in perpendicular rows, and so that the angles upwards and downwards, give to the whole the appearance of a series of horizontal zig-zag lines of panes of glass, one above another. Under this enormous dome, some of the best garden soil is strewed on the levelled ground, to the extent of seventy thousand square feet, including both wings; and in it is planted, sown, and transplanted, every vegetable production that requires a permanent atmospheric heat, higher than what is peculiar to our own climate,—a temperature for which a suitable provision is made under the Conservatory, by means of boilers and pipes, conveying hot water along corridors some hundreds of feet in length, and high enough for a man to walk upright in them from one to another. The various plants, shrubs, and flowers, of the two tropics, and Australia, are reared in this artificial southern hemisphere, arranged in groves and parterres, as if growing naturally on the spot, without the appearance of pot or box of any kind; streamlets of running water, or standing pools, giving freshness to the sultry atmosphere; and meandering paths through these bowers, and a carriage-way, across every part of this conservatory.

as from paradise, where the biographer met him at the house of his brother, Mr. Richard Dawson. He took up the subject at a missionary meeting, which was held in a large barn, and with a fine play of rich imagination, and gorgeous colouring, represented the Christian Church as the conservatory of Jesus Christ, adorned with every variety of character, like flowers of various hues, and enriched with "the fruit of the Spirit."

After this, he went into the north, and though not in full strength, yet he had, on reaching Carville, travelled four hundred miles, and preached twenty-nine times, within the space of eighteen days.

On completing this tour, and returning home, he visited the Rev. Alexander Bell, Superintendent of Leeds first circuit, and, making a low bow, pleasantly said,—"I am a poor man, and have been out of work four days; will you be kind enough to give me a job?" Such were his habits of industry, that he could not endure the thought of being out of employment. He had never eaten the bread of idleness; and even with his limited annual stipend from the Missionary Fund, he never thought he could do enough for the sacred cause. When he went to John Burton, Esq., of Roundhay, who was commissioned by the Missionary Committee to pay him his quarterly instalment, which was little more than an acknowledgment for labour so great, he would say, "You had better take ten pounds of this for the Missions; I have no use for the whole." Mr. Burton replied, "I am commissioned to pay the whole, and the whole you shall have from me. Do with it what you please, when you receive it."

A solitary individual here and there, to whom Mr. Dawson's charities and pecuniary circumstances were unknown, might be induced, from his habits of economy, to conclude that he was defective in benevolence. But he has been known to refuse his travelling expenses, when in justice to himself, he ought to have taken them, and when he had the example of others for his encouragement. On a Friday morning, during his residence at Burmantofts, which was the day when he often returned from one journey to be ready for another on the Saturday, his house was beset with a number of poor persons out of employment, soliciting charity; and the fact of their not applying to others in the neighbourhood, and the regularity of their visits on that particular day, may be adduced in favour of his charities. His means were but limited, though sufficient. He was a rigid economist both from habit and necessity, and his *savings* had an invariable reference to his *givings*. Economy has been considered as an excellent lure, in some instances, to betray people into expense; but it has been more frequently employed as a cloak for covetousness. In neither of these cases was Mr. Dawson implicated. He had a heart always superior, with economy suitable to his circumstances.

Adverting to his physical state at this time, he remarked to one who wished to engage his service, "You must not trust to such a broken reed, as your old friend." He was troubled with cough and shortness of breath.

Having to go into the north again, he wrote to his friend Mr. Longden, of Sheffield, from North Shields.

"DEAR SIR,—God willing, I hope to set off on Saturday evening, by the train which leaves Leeds at five o'clock in the evening, and professes to arrive at Sheffield about half-past six, when I expect to enjoy the mental, social, and spiritual pleasures of your society, and that of your worthy partner and family. So be it, says the heart of, Yours truly,—W. DAWSON.

" P. S. I write this note in the house of Mr. Bramwell. Mr. and Mrs. B. desire to be affectionately remembered to you and yours."

On reaching Sheffield, he was a good deal indisposed. Mr. and Mrs. L. urged him to seek medical advice; but to this he objected, owing, it was supposed, to his having been so seldom in the hands of the gentlemen of the profession. This passed over; and Mrs. L. having to make a call or two the day following his pulpit services, asked him to accompany her, with which request he readily complied, supposing a morning ride might be serviceable to him. Alighting at the door of a friend, he was soon introduced to the good lady of the house. Not long after, the gentleman of the house stepped out of an adjoining room. Combined with the object of Mrs. L. seeing her friends, was the welfare of Mr. Dawson. The plan was complete. The gentleman belonged to the medical profession. Mrs. L. told him Mr. Dawson had been complaining a little, and wished to know whether he could prescribe anything to afford relief. Mr. Dawson found where he was, and saw no way of escape. He, therefore, entered frankly into the state of his health, when the doctor told him, that there was water in the chest. "That," said Mr. Dawson, without any emotion of fear, "is the complaint of which my mother died." The doctor advised him to relax his pulpit exertions; stating, that if he did not, it would be perilous, if not fatal.

No advice, however, of this kind, seemed at the time to be availing, in consequence of the engagements into which he had entered, and his anxiety to fulfil them.

While at Sheffield, the following account on "the power of conscience," was written, which pairs well with another case mentioned in the preceding pages. "It is always pleasing," says he, "to a pious mind, to observe the workings of Divine grace in the soul, as it manifests itself in appropriate fruits ; but seldom do we witness such a remarkable instance of its power on the conscience as in the following case, which lately came under my observation :—About seventeen years ago, a young man in this town was sent to get change at a neighbouring shop for a ten-pound note, when, by mistake, he was paid ten guineas, which he received, and said nothing on the subject. Of late he has been converted to God ; and, having an uneasy conscience on account of this transaction, felt desirous of making restitution. But the person from whom he received the money being dead, he was unable for sometime to obtain any information concerning the family. At length he discovered where the son resided ; and having ascertained that neither of the parents was living, during the last week, he sent a person to inform him of the circumstance, and to pay him the extra ten shillings which had been received of his father at the time stated, with interest, if required ; adding, that he could not be happy until he had paid the same. The son expressed pleasure in witnessing such an instance of the grace of God ; but said he would not take the interest, and that the ten shillings should be given to the cause of Christ. He has since presented it to the Wesleyan Missionary Society as God's own peculiar property. I understand the same person has made restitution in several other cases of a like nature."

This account appeared in the Wesleyan Methodist Magazine, 1841, p. 123, signed, "William Dawson." The Rev. B. Clough appends to it, "The ten shillings referred to in this interesting note, have been paid to me on the behalf of the Missions, and accounted for accordingly."

He visited the city of York in December, where the biographer had much of his society, and where he could not but observe a change for the worse in his physical energies. While accompanying him to the houses of a few old friends, Messrs. Peart, Rocliffe, Lyth, and Agar, he observed to the writer on passing along the street, "I believe I shall die of diabetes at last." He lodged at the house, as usual, of Mr. Isaac Taylor, while in the city ; and when the son of his friend was parting with him at the railway station, he said, "Farewell, John ; this is perhaps the last time I shall see you upon earth ; I have a presentiment that I shall go off suddenly, and you must not be surprised if you hear tell of me being found dead somewhere."

In addition to his regular missionary work, which, as already intimated, included one-half of his time, he had no less than four hundred and twenty letters of invitation to different places in the course of the year : not from small insignificant places leading him hither and thither, and giving the notion of a mendicant, by accepting them with hungry anxiety, as though "the smallest offering would be thankfully received." His popularity was of a higher order ; it partook of the character of that of some of the "mighty dead,"—not forgetting a few of the living, to whom the connexion is so deeply indebted.

The London "Times," relying on the report and

comments of the York *Herald*—a paper not to be trusted for too much candour where Methodism is concerned, nor yet for too little where Popery is in question, passed some strictures on Mr. Dawson's speech at the York Missionary Meeting, stating, that railway travelling and steam-engines were *improved* in a style which, though common two centuries ago, and not unknown to the early ages of the Church, bordered too closely on the ludicrous to be properly applied to sacred subjects. It was admitted that the speaker's meaning was good, and that the speech was well received; but that they seldom had read anything which gave them a lower opinion of the taste of orator or audience. In this, there is as severe a reflection on the Wesleyans, for being pleased with such an orator, as on the speaker himself. But Mr. Dawson, with all his eccentricities, was too high for the pages of the York Herald, which it would be much more easy to burlesque, than the subject in question.

A few days after Mr. Dawson left York, he preached a funeral sermon at Barwick, occasioned by the death of his friend Mr. Thomas Lumb, a local-preacher, who died suddenly, on the 15th of December, in the fortieth year of his age, just after he had been engaged in private prayer. A few sentiments at the close of Mr. Dawson's address, will show the views he entertained of " sudden death; " and these taken in connexion with his own presentiment, expressed at the York station to Mr. Taylor only a few days before, cannot but awaken in the mind some powerful emotions;—the preacher living in daily expectation of the sudden transit on which he was descanting, in reference to the subject of his discourse!—" Blessed is that servant whom when his Lord cometh shall find watching; so he found our beloved brother. O the delightful, the important change! Now bowing before the throne of grace, and in a few minutes worshipping before the throne of glory; one minute surrounded by his fellow creatures, clad in the garments of mortality, and another minute, surrounded by angels, and archangels, and the spirits of just men made perfect,—one minute holding communion with the presence of his adorable Saviour by faith, and in another minute, beholding him face to face. Farewell! may we meet thee in glory!" A manuscript account of this excellent man was found among Mr. Dawson's papers. His demise is noticed among the "Recent Deaths," in the Methodist Magazine, 1841, p. 152.

Immediately on this, Mr. Dawson appears to have paid a visit to the Isle of Wight, where he was put into a bed, which was too thinly clothed for the season of the year, and of which the family do not appear to have been sufficiently aware. The consequence was, that he took cold, and became much indisposed. Ill as he was, he had to preach. In this state also he proceeded to London, where other public services awaited him. Having fulfilled these engagements, he returned to Leeds, where he instantly entered an omnibus, went first to Mr. Reinhardt's, and then proceeded to the house of Mr. Morley, who, perceiving his state, requested him to drive home with all possible speed. On reaching his own house, Mr. Morley bled him, till, in his own language, he was "almost drained," when he fainted. Mr. Morley was apprehensive of pleurisy following; but by precautionary measures, it was prevented, and Mr. Dawson began to recover. Although he had experienced a few slight illnesses, yet till this period, he had never been confined to the house one whole week through indisposition.

His state of mind will be perceived, as well as his views, under this affliction, in an extract from a letter to his nephew, the Rev. W. Dawson, dated "Leeds, Dec. 24, 1840.—It has been occasion of serious pain to me," he remarks, "that I shall be obliged to disappoint upwards of ten places; and some of them of a rather important character. But I am not left destitute of subjects of thankfulness, with those of regret. My friends have rallied round me, and sympathized with me, as well as prayed for, and with me. Mary Dawson has nursed me, as if she had been my own child. I have a good home,—a good bed to lie on;—and, what is best of all, sweet heart-cheering tokens of the Divine presence. This promise has again and again presented itself to me,—'Fear not, I am with thee; be not dismayed, I am thy God.' Shut out of my pulpit work, and shut up in the parlour, is a new cross to me. My Master Jesus is so excellent, that I always feel my soul in its element, when engaged in his service. I may say, he is the circle in which my passions move, 'the centre of my soul!' So I could always wish to find him; for He is 'worthy.' In a review of life, I cannot see one thing on which to depend for salvation on my own account. Recollection of sins committed, and especially of duties omitted, impose silence on every plea, except 'God be merciful to me!' In preaching the truth, I can say, it has been my greatest desire, that God should be glorified in the salvation of souls; and though conscience itself has always approved of the *object*, yet I cannot say, that I have always had a single eye in the use of the *means* in coming to that object. I have sometimes felt *self* in the *expression*, and in the *manner* of repeating that expression : and if I am able to see this, what must the eye of God have seen ? From the depth of my heart, — so far as my own studies, labours, travels, and preachments go, I would say,—

> ' Excluded is my every boast,
>   My glory swallowed up in shame. '

But, then,—glory be to God in the highest! I feel the tear of gratitude, wonder, and love, rising, when I add,—

> ' Jesus, the Lamb of God, hath bled,
>   He bore our sins upon the tree ;
>   Beneath my curse he bowed his head,
>   ' 'Tis finished ! ' he hath died for me ! '

Hallelujah! Praise ye the Lord. "

CHAPTER XVI.

The King's Daughter.—The Will of God.—Proverbial Sayings.—
Indisposition.—Acaster.—Plan of Labour.—Mr. I. Wild.—
Missionary Meeting at Weeton.—Dover.—Letter to Mrs. Ince.
— Croydon.—Birkhamstead.—Last Sermon.—Return Home.—
Colne.—Sudden death.—Reflections. — Processions. — Funeral
Obsequies.—Tokens of Respect.

MR. DAWSON commenced the labours of 1841 with
his accustomed spirit, but not with his usual physical
strength.

Being at Nottingham, he took for his text, Psalm
xlv. 13, &c.,—" The King's daughter is all glorious
within; her clothing is of wrought gold," &c.;—a
part of the imagery according as much with the
net, lace, and needle-work of the place, as it was suited
to the peculiar character of his genius.   His manner of
handling the subject was peculiar to himself; and in
consequence of making everything tell on the conscience
and the understanding, the sermon, connected with an
extraordinary influence of God upon the people, was
rendered extensively useful.   A friend, who had heard
him in different parts of the country, enquired afterwards,—" How is it, we have not had this sermon
before?"   Mr. Dawson replied,—" It is not altogether
new; for I took it at Manchester, in Oldham-Street

chapel, on the evening of **Dr. W's.** return from his Chancery trial in London, when the Society was balancing, and when it was unknown a short time before, whether I should be allowed to occupy the pulpit. Since then, I have had her, in true oriental style,— though the daughter of a king, locked up, and have not once suffered her to go abroad till to-night." And with his touchings and embroiderings, she was, indeed, on the testimony of those who heard him, made "glorious" to the auditory,—being arrayed in the "beauties of holiness."

When speaking of subjects for the pulpit, he observed to the writer,—"I never preached on *the will of God* but once." This was owing to the comprehensive character of the subject, the nicety required in its management, and to what he conceived to be the prerequisites of the speaker,—whose own will, should, in everything, be swallowed up in the will of God : and though few men could, with greater sincerity, say,— "Thy will be done," yet such were the views he had of his many imperfections, that they awed him away from the subject. Glancing at Acts xiii. 36,—"For David, after he had served his own generation, by the will of God fell on sleep, and was laid unto his fathers," he said,—"I have long viewed this passage as David's epitaph, endited by the Holy Ghost, written by the pen of an apostle, and placed, as it were, over his tomb, to be read by the Church and by the world to the end of time."

In his *tête-à-têtes* with his private friends, he often introduced the proverbial expressions of rural and humble life ; and even seemed to delight in them. "Allow me to help you to a little more, Mr. Dawson," said a friend at a social meal, where plain colloquy was in use. "No more, I thank you," was returned; hitching in,—"if there have been shameful eatings, there shall not be shameful leavings:"—a gentle hint, by the way, for the more saucy part of the community, who pay more attention to the desire of the eye, than the wants of nature and the feelings of the provider of the repast, by turning aside what, perhaps, they have previously solicited. To waste, sauciness, and extravagance, he was a determined enemy.

He was down in Lincolnshire, preaching occasional sermons in connection with Mr. Charles Welch of Hull, author of "Wesleyan Polity," and some other excellent publications; on which occasion, he stated, that he felt the work too laborious for him; further adding,—"I purpose going on till July; and then I shall state to the committee, that I must become a supernumerary." It was not the feeling of a trifling ailment, that induced him to make this remark; and it is only to be regretted, that it had not been made earlier, and made also to the committee, as his labours would have been instantly diminished.

In the month of March, he spent three days with his brother, Mr. Richard Dawson, at Acaster, one of which was his *birth-day* ;—the longest period the family had enjoyed his society for many years; and even then, he was engaged part of the time in preaching in the neighbourhood. He complained of indisposition; and said to Mrs. Dawson, who was previously painfully impressed with what she had observed, that he was "troubled with a wheezing, tickling cough, accompanied with difficulty of breathing; and believed he was labouring under the complaint of which his mother died." He manifested on this, as on a former occasion, no painful apprehensions, but was cheerful, as usual, and under a sweet religious influence.

He left Acaster for Leeds, on the 1st of April; and on his arrival at his own house, he had almost immediately to set out on his missionary tour. * This he undertook with the fortitude of a martyr going to the stake ; and with as full a persuasion apparently, that his adherence to the good cause was hastening his dissolution, as the sufferers for Christianity were

* The following is his route.

1841.

April	4 (Sund.) Burslem and Tunstal	May	11........Bristol
	5........Uttoxeter, Staffordsh.		16 (Sund.) Pontefract
	6........Newcastle-under-Lyne		17........Ditto
	7........Burslem, ditto		19........Bramley
	8........Tunstal, ditto		23 (Sund.) Northampton
	9 (Good Friday) Leek		24........Ditto
	10........Return home		25........Daventry, Northamp.
	11 (Sund.) Hunslet & St Peter's		26........Towcester
	12........Aberford		28........Leighton Buzzard
	13........Vacant		30........(Sun.) Dudley
	14........Barwick S. School	June	1........Perhaps Burton circuit
	15........Vacant		4........Melbourne
	16........Ditto		6 (Sund.) Borrowash, near Derby
	17........Go to Birmingham		7........HysonGreen,nearNott.
	18........Birmingham		8........Long Eaton, ditto
	19........Ditto		13 (Sund.) Richmond
	20........Ditto		14........Brompton nearNorthal.
	21........Redditch, Worcestersh.		15........Perhaps Masham
	22........Tewksbury, ditto		16........Weeton, nr. Harewood
	23........Evesham, ditto		20........Queen-Street, London
	24........Go to Oxford		25........Tunbridge Wells
	25 (Sund.) Oxford		27 (Sund.) Perhaps Canterbury
	26........Return to Birmingham	July	4........Colne
	27........Denby Potteries		5........Haworth
	28........Riddings, Derbyshire		6........Steeton
	29........Rotherham		11 (Sund.) New Mills
May	2 (Sund.) Cheltenham		18 (Sund.) Knaresbro'
	9 (Sund.) Bristol		25 (Sund.) Doncaster
	10........Bath		26........Worksop

x

assured, that their creed was the cause of their premature death.   But it was a cause in which he gloried,
—to advance the interests of which he laboured,—
for which he felt he was ready to die ;—and, to the
memory of such a man, everything is due, in the
shape of honour, from the Wesleyan body.

In the course of his peregrinations, he preached
the funeral sermon of his old friend, Mr. John Wild
of Armley, of whom there is a brief account in the
Wesleyan Methodist Magazine for 1841, p. 620.   From
a nearly thirty years acquaintance with this man of
worth, the biographer does not say too much, when
he affirms from his personal knowledge, that the religion of Mr. Wild bore the character of Seneca's
description of virtue, which, like fire, turned everything into itself ; his actions and his friendships being
tinctured with it, and whatever it touched was improved.   He died at the age of between eighty and
ninety ; and in advanced life had the ruddy hue of
youth.   He suffered long and much, before he died ;
but his religion, like precious odours, became the
sweeter, the more he seemed to be crushed by affliction
in its exercise.

Though the introduction of Letters from Mr. Dawson himself, has been studiously avoided, for reasons
stated in the preface, yet it may be proper here to

July 27........Hayton	Aug. 22 (Sund.) Scarbro'	
28.. .....Tuxford	29 (Sund.) Ashton-under-Lyne	
Aug. 1........Birstal	Sep. 5 (Sund.) Farnley	
3........Acaster	6........Armley	
8 (Sund.) Cullingworth	12 (Sund) Perhaps Camileo	
9........Bradford Low Moor	19 (Sund) Liverpool	
10........Wibsey perhaps	21........Winsford, Cheshire	
11........Wilsden	26 (Sund) Selby	
15 (Sund) Loughborough	30........At Workington, Cumb.	
17........Draycott		

give an extract from one to Mrs. Ince, 21, Bedford-Street, Covent Garden, London, dated June 11, 1841. "I thank God," he remarks, "that my health is considerably restored, though I still feel a little difficulty in breathing, when going up stairs, or walking quick up hill. But I must not expect to be exempt from the failings of mortality. The pins of my tabernacle must loosen, and the canvass must have its rents and holes, as well as others; and, therefore, the leading wish of my heart is, as strikingly expressed in those words of the German Hymn, translated by Mr. Charles Wesley,—and which I often say and sing:

> ' Let me in life, in death,
> Thy steadfast truth declare ;
> And publish with my latest breath,
> Thy love and guardian care. ' "

When in the metropolis, in the latter part of June, he domiciled several days in the house of his friend, Mr. William Ince; and proceeded from thence to Tunbridge Wells, and some other places.

It will be perceived by the plan, in the foot-note, that he was at Weeton, Wednesday, June 16th. He proceeded thither with his friend, Mr. Charles Turkington, to assist in a missionary meeting. They took up their residence at the house of Mrs. Mallorie, where they had often enjoyed each other's society on similar occasions. After taking a little refreshment, conversation turned upon the missionary cause, and passing events; among the latter, the approaching election, and the dissolution of Parliament, when he expressed his mind strongly on some of the candidates in the field. Being left alone by the party after dinner, with the exception of Mr. Turkington, he said,—"Well, Charles, you have long been one of my most intimate friends; and it was in your father's house I was first entertained in Leeds. We have had uninterrupted friendship, but our work will soon be done; we must work the works of Him who has sent us into this state of being, while it is day." They proceeded to the missionary meeting at two o'clock, over which Mr. Turkington presided. Mr. Dawson was evidently labouring under great indisposition. He had assisted others freely at the table, in the spirit of kindness, but partook of little himself; and now, through the heat of the weather and the place, together with a lethargic feeling, he fell asleep on the platform, and remained unconscious of everything around him for the space of a quarter of an hour. Before it was his turn to speak, he was roused; and when called upon to address the meeting, he commenced in a somewhat playful strain; then suddenly checking himself, he paused, and gave vent to a deep sigh, when, turning to the chairman, he said,—"We have both been in the habit of coming here for the last forty years. I have been looking round, and I cannot see one of our early friends in this assembly." With a view to improve the fact, he remarked with great solemnity,—"The consideration is a serious one; those with whom we associated, are now numbered with the dead;—they have seen corruption; and it is a thousand to one whether you and I shall meet here again on the like occasion." After this, he gave a serious exhortation, saying,— "I am much pleased in seeing so many young persons present." Then, addressing them more immediately, he said,—"You will be called to put off the tabernacle, as our Lord Jesus Christ has shewn us, and as I also shortly expect to do. I wish you, however, to bear in remembrance one thing,—it is my last, and, perhaps, dying legacy." Here, a solemn stillness pervaded the whole congregation ; when he added,—"This is what I wish to leave with you, and for you to have always in remembrance,—MAKE GOD'S CAUSE YOUR OWN, AND HE WILL MAKE YOU HIS OWN." The assembly departed under deep and solemn feeling ; taking away with them his best blessing.

Mr. Geden observed, in correspondence with a friend, that Mr. Dawson had been at Dover, where he preached on Psalm xl. 1—3, and Luke xv. 11 —to the end ; and also, that he had preached at Canterbury on Acts xiii. 38, 39, and Matt. xvi. 26 ; and that at Dover especially, his ministry was made a great blessing, while his private conversation was truly spiritual and impressive. The Rev. Jonathan Cadman took part of the services at Dover, (June 27) and remarked to Mr. Dawson, in the forenoon, just before he entered the pulpit—"THEY work you well, Sir !" "No" he returned, "*I* work *myself*. It is all voluntary. *My day cannot be long.* I must do all I can." In the evening, he interceded with great earnestness for his native country, exclaiming in prayer, "A kingdom divided against itself cannot stand ;" adding in an interrogatory strain, "and shall England fall ? fall by her own hands too ? Forbid it, Lord !" There was in this, a reference to the approaching elections ; and some of the friends considered his appeals to the people, as exceedingly salutary and seasonable ; for notwithstanding the unusual excitement, the friends of truth, with only one exception, maintained their integrity.

On leaving the house of Mr. Geden, he laid his hand upon the head of his son, who was just entering upon the work of the ministry, and said, with great affection and solemnity,—"Live, when I am dead;—live better than I have lived!" This was truly Dawsonian; urging others to duty, while he attended to it himself,—but with his glory swallowed up in shame.

The following notice in the "Watchman," of July 7th, shews that he was at Croydon on the 30th of June. "On Wednesday last, the friends of this place were favoured with the services of Mr. W. Dawson, who preached two sermons in aid of the Sabbath School. The congregations were excellent, particularly in the evening. The use of a meadow, adjoining the chapel, was kindly granted by W. Taylor, Esq., where a spacious booth was erected, in which about 250 persons sat down to tea; after which the friends reassembled in the chapel, and were gratified with appropriate addresses from the chairman, E. Corderoy, Esq., — Haynes, Esq., (Independent), Mr. Dawson, J. Corderoy, Esq., and the Rev. H. Castle."

According to previous promise, having a little time to spare for more extra work, he proceeded the next day to Great Birkhamstead, in the St. Albans circuit, to engage in the services connected with the opening of a place for divine worship. These services he closed on Thursday, July 1st, by preaching in the afternoon and evening. On commencing the afternoon service, he remarked, in reference to the hymn he was about to give out,—"This is a solemn and remarkable hymn;—unlike most of those we sing. It is neither a hymn of praise, of adoration, nor yet of prayer: it is a soliloquy; and represents a person talking to himself. Let each person in the congregation, then, talk to *himself*, as I purpose talking to *myself*, while singing these solemn words:—

> ' And am I only born to die ?
> And must I suddenly comply
> With nature's stern decree?'" &c.

He then joined in the singing, with a loud and clear voice, and manifested great depth of feeling. On offering up a deeply interesting and ardent prayer, and reading the thirty-second chapter of the book of Exodus, he selected part of the 26th verse of the same chapter as his text,—"Who is on the Lord's side?" In introducing the subject, he observed,— "This is a most remarkable chapter, respecting a most remarkable people, by a most remarkable man;" and afterwards, in his peculiar and impressive manner, pointed out the base ingratitude of the children of Israel to Moses. At the close of the afternoon service, he took tea with about one hundred friends; immediately after which, he delivered an appropriate and interesting address, in reference to the infant cause in the place, and exhorted the friends, tenderly, watchfully, and perseveringly, to care for the *infant*, with which they had thus been entrusted. At the evening service, the congregation was exceedingly large, —many of the people having journeyed several miles to the place. He took for his text,—"And now also the axe is laid unto the root of the trees: therefore, every tree which bringeth not forth good fruit, is hewn down, and cast into the fire;" Matt. iii. 10. In preaching on this text, his familiar acquaintance with rural life, furnished him with various observations, which, proceeding from some ministers, might have been deemed not sufficiently dignified for the pulpit; but which,—with the Baptist before him as a model,—a plain, pointed preacher, homely in costume, and with a "wilderness" for his sanctuary, were rendered strikingly illustrative of the subject. He made, in the course of his sermon, some interesting and touching references to the doctrine of divine Providence; and, in support of it, noticed the particular providence of God towards himself and his family connexions. After this, he offered up a devout and suitable prayer for the salvation of souls, and thus closed the public service.

The last text was mixed up with several affecting circumstances in the mind of Mr. Dawson. He preached on it at Horseforth, near Leeds, in the year 1819, when much good resulted from it. Mr. J. Verity, having to wait upon him some time afterwards, told him, that Thomas Jackson, who had heard him on the occasion, retired to rest in health, about nine o'clock in the evening, after taking his supper, and was found dead, by the side of his son, at eleven. Mr. Dawson clasped his hands; and, after a brief pause, said—"It is very strange! I never feel my mind impressed to preach upon that text, but it is almost invariably followed by a sudden death."

Having completed his southern tour, which, with journies in other directions, had occupied a period of some months, and during which he had been engaged in almost incessant pulpit and platform labour, he returned home, where he arrived on the Friday,—having travelled all night. On his arrival, by railway, at Leeds, he was about to engage a cab, to convey himself and his luggage to his own house.

Two of the cab-men, each asserting his right to the conveyance of his person to the destined place, quarrelled,—both maintaining the priority of addressing him. Mr. Dawson, in order to settle the dispute, having been frequently annoyed by such officiousness, dismissed them both, and resolved upon carrying his own luggage. It was heavy, and fatigued him so much, that he was compelled to leave it at a friend's house on the road. He felt the effects of the exertion; but concluded, that a little rest would enable him to regain his wonted state of feeling and strength. Accordingly, after a few hours repose, he felt improved; set to work, and wrote sixteen letters, in answer to a number he found lying in the house, and which required immediate attention. One of the shorter, to the Rev. P. Wilkinson, being among the last letters he wrote, may be here introduced.

"Burmantofts, Leeds, July 2nd, 1841.

"DEAR SIR.—Returning home this morning, after a fortnight's absence, I found your letter. My arrangements at present are as follow:—Newcastle-upon-Tyne, Sunday, July 18th; Wall's End Colliery, 19th; Middlesbro', 21st; and Dishforth, 22nd. I thought I could get from Middlesbro' on Wednesday, and then by railway to Thirsk on Thursday, and from thence to Dishforth that day, and return next day. But as I am not yet sufficiently acquainted with the railway communication, I cannot speak positively upon the subject. I have received no intelligence from Middlesbro' yet; but I think of writing to-day to Mr. Jackson, to know his mind upon the subject.

"Could I meet every case, it would highly delight, Dear Sir, yours affectionately—W. DAWSON."

x 2

After this, he went into the town to see the members chaired, who passed the house of his friend, Mr. Reinhardt, where he enjoyed himself with a social religious party; and was Tory enough to express his satisfaction in the non-election of Mr. Joseph Hume. While in the shop of Mr. Reinhardt, druggist, a friend enquired into the state of his health, when he replied, laying his hand on his breast, and gently patting it,—"I am not right here;" subjoining, "my work is too hard for me." The propriety of medical advice was suggested, and the Rev. Edward Walker, with his accustomed kindness, proposed to attend to his appointment, provided he would tarry at home. He returned, that he was always best when in the open air and travelling, and hoped that the journey would be conducive, rather than prejudicial, to health. On his return home with Mrs. Phillips, he paused, and said,—"I am short of breath;" and reclined himself against a wall. Mrs. Phillips, on their reaching Spring Field, again urged the propriety of medical aid, coupled with the advice of a few days' rest from labour. But he still clung to the hope that the journey would be advantageous to health. He, therefore, rose about six o'clock on Saturday morning, July 3rd, and left Leeds for Colne, in Lancashire, in company with his relative, Mr. Phillips, at which place they arrived in safety, and took up their residence at the house of Mr. John Phillips, the brother of Mr. Edward.

Though his appearance seemed to indicate that he was not quite well, when he arrived at Colne, yet he did not complain, but conversed on various subjects in his usual cheerful manner with the friends, in whose society he spent the afternoon. He also joined in singing several hymns, and selected the tunes which he wished to have sung in the chapel on the ensuing day. At eight o'clock, he took a Bible, and went to his apartment, where he remained for some time. On his return, after a light supper, he prayed with the family in a very comprehensive manner, for the nation, the Church, and particularly the inhabitants of Colne,—that the Lord would assist, and crown with his blessing, the services of the approaching Sabbath. He retired to his chamber about eleven o'clock, and was soon after followed by Mr. E. Phillips, with a floating light, in order to leave it in the room, stating, that as he had not been very well, it would be better to have a light at hand; to which Mr. Dawson replied,—"O child, I am much better; there is no need of it,—blow it out." It would seem, that he soon sunk into a state of rest, on his friend leaving the room, as nothing was heard of him till two o'clock in the morning, when he awoke Mr. Phillips, saying,—"Edward, get up, I am very poorly." Mr. Phillips was instantly at his side; and, in a few minutes, several members of the family and a medical gentleman were present, to render all the assistance in their power. But it was unavailing.

While sitting in a chair, and labouring for breath, he spoke a little to those around him. His walking-stick, (which is preserved as a little memento of private friendship by the biographer,) was reached to him by Mr. Phillips, to grasp, while the medical attendant endeavoured to open a vein. But the hand had nearly become powerless. He slightly pressed the "staff" between his finger and thumb, upon which, like another Jacob, he had so often

leaned,—an incident not beneath the pen of inspiration, and fell back in the chair on which he sat. The
increasing difficulty experienced in respiration, soon
rendered speaking next to impracticable. The few
sentences, however, which fell from his lips, attested
that all was right within, and his last words were,—

> "Let us in life, in death,
> Thy steadfast truth declare."

In attempting to repeat the other lines of the verse,—

> "And publish with our latest breath,
> Thy love and guardian care,"

utterance failed; and in his inclined position, he
crossed his hands upon his breast,—as occasionally
in the pulpit, and expired without a struggle; thus
giving reality to poetic expression,—he "ceased at
once to work and live."

His sudden departure from the present state of existence—itself but transitory, reminds us of the sentiments
to which he gave utterance in the sermon he preached,
occasioned by the sudden death of the Rev. William
Bramwell. "Mr. Bramwell," said he to the listening
multitude, who, in the open air, stood near the spot where
he had expired—"Mr. Bramwell was unusually favoured in this respect. His health was seldom interrupted
by sickness; and he tasted little of the bitter cup of
indisposition, of which many take large draughts. In
the time of his removal from this world, he was also
peculiarly indulged. Never was Jordan's current
smoother than when he embarked, and along its banks
was never seen a narrower place than that which he was
privileged to cross. He was not, as some have been,
five or six weeks, or even a longer period, in passing

over the river, 'tossed with tempests and not comforted.' No : in a few minutes he was wafted across the
stream : so that we may justly adopt the language of
the Rev. Henry Moor, who emphatically remarked, upon
the suddenness of Mr. Bramwell's removal,—' We can
scarcely call it DEATH. It is almost a TRANSLATION.' "
In this brief statement, he might have been describing
his own general state of good health ; nor could he, if,
with the eye of a seer he had beeen capable of glancing
at his own exit, have portrayed it more correctly.   It
was, indeed, a narrow place, occupying only a few
minutes in crossing,—from ten to twenty ! All was like
the sudden dropping of a curtain ; and when over, and
once awakened from the hurried surprise, left upon those
around the impression of a dream.   In his own house
at Leeds, in Yorkshire, on Saturday, and at Colne,
in Lancanshire, the same evening.   In Time, when the
clock struck twelve on Saturday night ; in Eternity
a few minutes after two on the Sabbath morning !
leaving the dawn of one Sabbath for the brighter day of
another—and one whose day should never have a close.
The body animated by its active spirit, and in its home,
at the close of one week ; and after a sudden transit
from one county to another, coffin'd within the walls of
that home, at the beginning of another week ; and in
the space of two brief days more, conveyed to the
church in which he had sat as a hearer, when a boy,
and laid in the ground over which his boyish feet had
often strayed ! It brings to recollection also, some of
the expressions he employed in his sermon a few months
before at Barwick, on the equally sudden death of
Thomas Lumb, to which the reader will be able to
advert.

Another reminiscence may be here indulged, relative to a previous visit to Colne, in company with his friend Mr. Phillips. It will be recollected that the two lines of the hymn which he falteringly quoted, form a part of the eighth verse of the hymn which he gave out with his accustomed energy and animation, in the pulpit of the Wesleyan Chapel, in the same place, on a public occasion, at the time to which reference is made. It was, as has been already observed, during a period of considerable commercial depression, when the spirits of many serious persons were bending beneath the load, and when he laboured to elevate their spirits by singing—

> " Give to the wind thy fears ;
> Hope, and be undismayed," &c.

Little was he aware, that part of the *last* verse of that hymn would be the *last* words that should escape from his lips—that they should be uttered in the town to which he was then on a visit—that they should be addressed to the ear of the friend who was with him on both occasions, and in the house he had just left—and that the *last* "night" on which he closed his eyes, should so

> " Soon end in joyous day."

Equally remote was it from his apprehension, on the Thursday previous to his death, when giving out the hymn at the commencement of the service at Great Birkhamstead, that he was, on that day, closing his public services,—that " nature's stern decree " was to be fulfilled within the space of little more than two days from the close of the one on which he was preaching,—that the text and sermon which had been so often the forerunners of the sudden death of others, should immediately precede his own,—and that he was

not only unconsciously sounding the requiem of his
ministerial labours, but that he was, as if in prophetic
strains, singing, in mournful yet in fearless notes, his
own funeral dirge. But, being "on the Lord's side,"
the "axe" was "laid at the root of the tree" of mortality, only for the purpose of fixing him by the side of
the "Tree of Life" for ever.

The tidings of his death soon spread through the
town and neighbourhood, and the house was beset with
a crowd of people by five o'clock in the morning. After
Mr. Phillips had given orders for a lead coffin to be
made, and entered into other necessary arrangements,
he hastened into Yorkshire, to communicate the melancholy intelligence of his death to his friends ; and in
the afternoon of the same day, the tidings reached
Acaster, near York, the residence of Mr. Richard
Dawson.

On Mr. Phillips leaving Colne, the itinerant and local
preachers, and other officers in the Society, with the
members and friends, assembled in the chapel, to pay
their last tribute of respect to the memory of the deceased. The Rev. T. Powell, of Burnley, it may be
observed, very obligingly preached the sermons on the
Sabbath day. Mr. Charles Smith, co-executor with
Mr. E. Phillips, left Leeds at four o'clock on the Monday morning, from whence a hearse had also been forwarded, to convey the corpse to its place of rest. On
the coffin being placed in the hearse, it was preceded by
travelling and local-preachers, stewards, trustees, and
leaders ; and these were followed by a crowd of Wesleyans and others. Some of the factories having been
stopped, in order to give the members of society an
opportunity of joining the procession, the crowd of

attendants became the greater.   In passing slowly
through the town, the people sung one of Mr. Dawson's
favourite hymns; and when the procession had proceeded about a mile, the people divided themselves into
two companies, one on each side of the road, where
they stood—men and boys, with their heads uncovered,
while the hearse passed between; when, as a last farewell, they again united in singing the verse which he
had attempted to repeat the morning before—carrying
it out for him, as it were, and wafting it with becoming
reverence to heaven :—

> " Let us in life, in death,
>   Thy steadfast truth declare;
> And publish with our latest breath
>   Thy love and guardian care."

Before the hearse reached Keighly, it was again met by
Wesleyans and others, when another procession was
formed, accompanying it some distance through the
town; where, as the friends had done at Colne, they
halted, bared the head, gazed sorrowfully on the moving vehicle as it passed between the lines, and then
sung,—

> " Oh that without a lingering groan,
>   I may the welcome word receive;
> My body with my charge lay down,
>   And cease at once to work and live."

The same respect and deep feeling appeared in every
place which the hearse had to pass through.   The
remains arrived in Leeds on the same day.   It was intended that the funeral should take place on the
Friday; but circumstances rendered it necessary to fix
upon Wednesday the 7th, as the day of interment; so
that little more than twenty-four hours could be secured
to give notice to the friends, and make other arrange-

ments. But short as the time was, the feeling of respect was such, that the hour had only to be announced, for public homage to be paid.

The Trustees of the principal Wesleyan Chapels in Leeds, expressed a wish that the remains should be interred in connexion with one of the places of worship belonging to the body, and kindly offered a vault, and proposed a tablet to his memory. But the family burying ground was preferred by the surviving relatives.

One o'clock was the time fixed for removal; and on the corpse being brought out, an interesting service took place in the open air. The Rev. Edward Walker commenced by giving out an appropriate hymn; after this, the Rev. Alexander Bell, engaged in prayer; he was followed by the Rev. Thomas Galland, A.M., who delivered an interesting address, combining with it the character and talents of the deceased; then the Rev. J. Cusworth concluded with prayer. At the close of the service, the procession formed, composed of the travelling and local-preachers, together with the leaders, &c., of the four circuits belonging to Leeds; these preceded the hearse, six abreast. A long train of people followed the hearse and mourning coaches. The streets, and public road out of Leeds, for the space of about a mile and a half, presented one congregated mass of people, though the weather was rather unfavourable, and the funeral had thus taken place earlier than was at first anticipated by the populace at large; and multitudes of these followed to the distance of a mile and a mile and half. The distance from Leeds to Barwick-in-Elmet is seven miles, and the funeral did not reach the village till six o'clock. The hearse, drawn by four horses, was preceded by the singers, and followed by three mourning coaches. Besides many persons on foot, who proceeded the full length of the journey, it was calculated that there were not less than a hundred persons on horseback, while sixty-eight carriages were counted in the train, multiplying to eighty-six when the remains reached the village, containing friends of various ranks, who thus paid their voluntary respects to one whom they loved in life, and by the effects of whose ministry they were likely to be benefited for ever. Hymns were sung in passing through Seacroft, Scholes, and Barwick, while the old family residence of Barnbow appeared on the brow of a hill to the left, reviving many recollections, in the minds of the mourners. The church was crowded, and those who were unable to gain admission stood in the church-yard amidst heavy rain. The service was impressively read by the Rector, the Rev. W. H. Bathurst, nephew of Earl Bathurst, in the midst of deep feeling; and the 50th Hymn, on page 52, of the Wesleyan Collection, was sung,—the son of John Batty, the early friend of the deceased, officiating as clerk. Another hymn was sung at the grave. The grave itself was very deep, penetrating through the rock, lined at the bottom with brick, and at least a couple of yards deeper than the remains of his mother, part of whose coffin was visible to the eye. On seeing the multitudes, hearing the sighs, and witnessing the tears that were shed, the writer could not but recur again and again to that portion of holy writ,—" Them that honour me, I will honour." But even "THIS honour have" NOT "all his saints." Thus lived—thus died—and thus was honoured WILLIAM DAWSON, who departed this life, July 4th, 1841, in the 69th year of his age.

In his Will, dated April 15th, 1841, written by himself,

we find the following bequests :—To the Wesleyan
Missionary Society, 50 guineas ; to the Methodist
Preachers' Annuitant Society, 30 guineas ; and to
Kingswood and Woodhouse Grove Schools, 30 guineas.

Funeral sermons were preached in different places,
on the occasion of his death. The Rev. R. Newton
preached on the occasion at St. Peter's, Leeds, on
2 Sam. xiv. 14,—the circuit in which Mr. Dawson
had resided. The biographer preached sermons on
the same occasion at Barwick, Bradford, Tadcaster,
Bramley, in Wesley Chapel,—Leeds, and in York. In
the last place, the collectors of the Juvenile Missionary Society were all arranged in front of the
gallery of the Centenary Chapel, some of whom were
Mr. Dawson's children in the gospel, and at the formation of which Society he preached the sermons,
as well as generally aided the young friends for a
period of upwards of twenty years.

Several touching tributes of respect were paid to
his memory, at missionary meetings. The day after
his death, a missionary meeting was held at Thorparch, in the Tadcaster circuit, at which W. G. Scarth,
Esq., presided. On the forenoon of the same day,
a trustee meeting was held at Tadcaster, and when
Mr. Dawson's name was called over, which stood at
the head of the list, the mournful intelligence of his
sudden death was communicated. At the missionary
meeting, in the afternoon, Mr. Scarth, to whom Mr.
Dawson had been endeared by an intimate friendship
of forty years, adverted to his character and labours.
Several of the speakers also referred to his services,
and their value to the missionary cause ; and at the
evening meeting, a substantial proof of a feeling of

gratitude to God, and affectionate regard for his departed servant, was furnished by the presentation, through the Rev. Alexander Bell, of a purse of gold, containing £11 10s., privately offered in the course of the meeting by various friends in the chapel, and announced as—"A token of affectionate esteem, presented by a few mourning friends of the late Mr. William Dawson, in support of the mission cause, which lay so near to his heart, and which he so zealously laboured to promote." Mr. Bell was much affected while presenting this appropriate expression of truly Christian feeling; and ventured to express a hope, that the example set in this—probably the first missionary meeting held after Mr. Dawson's death, would be followed by his numerous friends through the Connexion.

Two or three friends at the small village of Buckland, in the Aylesbury circuit, who heard Mr. Dawson preach his last sermon at Berkhamstead, were deeply affected by the intelligence of his death so soon after, and felt an earnest desire to offer some memorial of their attachment to him, and of the high estimation in which they held his services. In reading an account of the above meeting at Thorparch, which appeared in the "Watchman," and especially that part of it which stated that the sum specified had been presented to the meeting, by certain friends, in grateful remembrance of Mr. Dawson's services, it was thought something might be done at Buckland for the same noble cause. The subject was named to the Society and other friends, and the sum of £4 was raised for the mission fund, as a thank-offering to God for raising up a man so eminently distinguished for his Christian virtues, ministerial abilities and great usefulness ; and in mournful, but submissive remembrance of that Providence by which the Church was so suddenly deprived of his valuable services. A donation also, of £10, was given by Jacob Harrison, Esq., of the St. Albans circuit, to the mission cause, in memory of his labours. In none of these instances are we to look so much at the *sum*, as at the *principle*;—in each we recognize a principle recommended by our Lord,—"She hath done what she could;—verily I say unto you, Wheresoever this gospel shall be preached throughout the whole world, this also that she hath done shall be spoken of for a memorial of her."

The Rev. Louis Rees, it may be added, composed a "Funeral Anthem" on the occasion of his death, to "Servant of God! well done;" a piece entitled, —"The Christian Soldier," by the Author of the "World before the Flood," &c.

In "The Annual Address of the Conference to the Methodist Societies," is the following tribute to his memory, "Valuable members of the Connexion have likewise been removed by death; among whom we feel it right to mention the venerable William Dawson; who, after many years of useful and acceptable labour as a Local-Preacher, has this year died in the Lord. Few men were ever more extensively known in the Wesleyan Connexion in Great Britain, or more highly esteemed wherever known : it is, therefore, unnecessary that we should speak to you at any length of either his character, talents, or labours. Earnestly desirous of promoting the prosperity of the work of God, especially in its missionary department, he devoted his very popular talents to its advocacy. His numerous sermons and addresses, delivered with all that sanctified energy which belonged to his character, were highly acceptable, and often produced the most important results. His removal was sudden, and he was engaged in his valuable labours to the last. During the brief interval between his final seizure and death, he was enabled to express his unfailing trust in the Saviour who had died for him, and had been his guide through life. While he lived, he had always been ready to attend to the voice of Providence when it called him to labour : by the grace of God he was not less ready when suddenly called to die. The calmness which he manifested on experiencing what he felt to be the stroke of death, and the holy joy with which he at once commended his spirit to his Redeemer, proved that while he had long and extensively lived what may be termed *a public life*, he had yet maintained all the *inward power* of religion, and had walked humbly with God. His happy death was a suitable close to his holy and useful life." Minutes, 1841, pp. 137—8.

———

To such as were personally acquainted with Mr. Dawson, any description of his external appearance will be unnecessary, as a correct portrait of him—in full length, will be found suspended in the inner chambers of the soul, touched off to the life with all the colourings of the imagination, and will there hang for the eye of the inner man to repose upon till its own outward form shall crumble into dust, and mingle with the clods of the valley; for, with such, his image will ever live. It was that of a man,—a man in the most manly sense of the term. He was strong of bone,— muscular,—well built,—well rounded,—proportionate, —standing about five feet nine inches,—had hair of a deep auburne,—and a complexion approaching the em- browned rather than the dark. The eye, of a lightish grey, and with a dark pupil, was round,—keen,—full of fire,—and well set in the head, mounted with slightly overhanging eyebrows. The face too, was round, some- what full;—the ears small, thick, and closely attached to the head;—a good mouth, with a somewhat biting expression, similar to what is found in some of the portraits of Sir Walter Scott;—and an excellent fore- head, covered in later life, as was that of the Rev. Daniel Isaac with false hair, but hair much worse in construction, ill adapted to the head, and overhanging the fine sinciput like an eave of thatch,—an article on which the writer did not fail to rally him, though perhaps indispensable to comfort. The features might be pronounced regular, but expressive,—inclining to the fierce, on the eye being fixed,—full of meaning,—and conveying the impression of thought;—that thought which is brilliant, active, penetrating,—which only himself could seize, and which others could neither tame nor break,—fertile in a fruitfulness which only died with himself. Three or four years prior to his death, he shrunk a little,—walked with a stick,— and complained of being more timid in pointing the foot at night, than formerly, lest he should fall. Still, his general health was unbroken, and he soon regained more than he had lost in actual corpulence.

In social life, there was an agreeableness which

ingratiated Mr. Dawson into the good feelings of the
heart, and made him a general favourite.   It was not
that, however, which connects itself with softness, and
with a something bordering upon harmlessness and
insipidity, turned off with a smile ; but that which
partakes of cheerfulness ;—that which proceeds from
the heart rather than the will, and is innate rather
than acquired.   When his wit was the most sparkling
and penetrating, he never assumed any ostentatious
airs ; and when his thoughts appeared a little high in
their bearing, they were still perceived to be seated in a
heart of tenderness and of courtesy.   Though free to
converse, he was never forward or loquacious,—always
leaving the company with a relish for more, rather than
producing satiety ; and though void of polish, possessed
of a fine sense of propriety ;—that kind of behaviour
which is destitute of all squeamishness and fastidious-
ness, and which, in the higher walks of life, in properly
constituted minds, "gives beauty to pomp, and majesty
to adversity."   This is not too much to claim for Mr.
Dawson, and would only be denied by "puppets led
about by wires," and who would reverse the order of
things, by converting the cottage into a drawing-room,
and who confound good behaviour with affectation.
    Though he loved society, yet he was not one of
those persons, who can only live in its bustle.   He
took society in his way to more important work, and
enjoyed it as a relaxation from severer mental toil.
His popularity was not merely the result of certain
peculiarities, combined with great native genius ; but
added to good soil to work upon, there was more
than ordinary persevering industry.   For want of this,
—even talented men,—men popular in early life, have

become formal and insipid before they have more
than reached their prime. They have settled down
upon a few years' industry, at the commencement of
their ministerial career; and by attending to anything,
but *the thing* itself, for which God called them into
the work of the MINISTRY, have lost the freshness
which they once had for the pulpit,—have starved
the spirit of preaching out of their souls,—and at
length have found the sacred work of calling sinners
to repentance irksome, and have shunned it;—moving
in the church of God with a decent morality, the occasional cant of better things upon their lips, in full
orders, and in full pay, and yet living monuments of
indolence, as to pulpit reading and pulpit thought.
It is melancholy, when men outlive the spirit of their
office. Not so with the apostles of Christ, who improved as they proceeded; nor yet with the subject
of this sketch. He earned his notoriety with hard
toil, though he might have flourished a little without
it; and candidates for the Christian ministry should
be deeply impressed with the fact, that the industry
which is necessary to raise a man to a high point
of elevation, is equally necessary to keep him there;
for, like a growth in grace, not to proceed, is to draw
back, and a man often loses the past for want of perseverance. Mr. Dawson's studies and reading could
not be denominated systematic; but still he thought,
—and thought intensely too; and he also read to
purpose,—not absorbing the mind in the newspapers
of the day, and giving a political hue to everything
he touched,—but works that assisted his piety and his
preaching. He was far from being extensively read, as
to the actual number of volumes which passed through

Y

his hands,—though extensive when taken in connexion
with the small portion of time he had at command for
the purpose : but when we advert to the authors that
have incidentally occurred in the course of the Memoir,
such as Dr. Walls, Flavel, Drelincourt, Sherlock, Luther,
Dr. Owen, Romaine, Burgess, Scougal, Dr. Bates, Saurin,
Dr. Manton, Dr. Goodwin, Baxter, Cotton Mather,
Alleine, Showers, Law, Fletcher, Brainard, Young,
Venn, Benson, Bishop Newton, Bishop Butler, Bunyan,
Rogers, Ambrose, Doddridge, Wesley, Whitfield, Cennick, Henry, Preston, Watson, Clarke, &c., and others
that might be noticed, a familiarity with the theological
writers of his own country may be fairly inferred ; and
when the manuscripts he has left, are taken into the
account, comprising at least four hundred sermons,
mostly full, and others in outline, exclusive of essays,
diaries, speeches, and other public addresses, and an
extensive correspondence,—he may,—all his secular engagements, travels, and pulpit labours being preserved
in remembrance, be exhibited as an unusual type, or
model of industry ;—a son in whom the Founder of
Methodism—himself one of the most laborious men
that ever lived, would have gloried.   A sentiment found
in Ischomachus, will apply either in a civil or ecclesiastical sense,—" He who will not apply himself to business, evidently discovers that he means to get his bread
by cheating, stealing, or begging, or is wholly void of
reason."   In Methodism, however, there are, perhaps,
fewer opportunities for the indulgence of indolent
habits than in almost any other religious system ; and
if a man's zeal is not tempered with knowledge, he
may soon abridge life, and bring it into much less compass than the portion of time allotted to humanity.

Such a habit, in connection with talent, was sure to raise a man above the common-place characters of which society is often composed. In passing from his private, to what more immediately connects itself with his public character, his manner might not, in every instance, be prepossessing when in the pulpit; but it was rarely offensive,—though sometimes strange to strangers. He did not uniformly commence his sermon by announcing his text; and then proceed with his introduction; but very often made two or three remarks before, by way of awakening attention, and then by an easy transition glided into it. When the text was rousing, and the materials he had to bring to it, by way of enforcing and applying it, partook of the same character, he sometimes employed too much vehemence in the outset, and conveyed the notion of a general resolved to storm and fire a city, rather than to take it by tact and stratagem. On these occasions, while grappling with a subject, and battling with the vices and follies of men, there was generally fixed attention and deep feeling in the hearers; but through continued excitement, a degree of fatigue ensued. This, however, was only the case when he missed his way in the commencement, which was but seldom. His more general manner was not subject to this charge; and if brought to bear upon the energy displayed by the celebrated Dr. Chalmers, the difference would be found to exist in the circumstance of the latter giving out in greater lengths, that which the former usually let out at intervals. In Mr. Dawson, the disturbed air, so to speak, came in more frequent and unexpected gusts; in the doctor, the tempest,—when he himself was in the heyday of health, was of longer continuance;—yet both moving the leaf, the twig, the branch, the stem, and the trees of the human forest, over which the voice was permitted to pass.

Though very far indeed from being a finished speaker, yet there was that about him, as there has been already occasion to remark, which at once disarmed criticism, and disposed persons to apologize rather than find fault. The energy which he displayed, often trenched, as has been seen, on violence ; but it was not energy *throughout*, as in the comparison of his manner with that of Dr. Chalmers ;—it was not the torrent over the wide and inclined champaign, which sweeps on with one continued force ;—it belonged more to the flood upon the mountains, rolling over tremendous heights ; and in proportion to the depth of its falls, again tossing its spray upward, —with breaks and pauses among the rocks,—then murmuring along the plainer portions of the country,— and rarely ever, in its loudest roar, its boldest dashes, distracting the ear of the bystander.   The secret of this is, that he was never vehement, never impassioned, except in cases where truth—from its strength, and sin —from its atrocity and other peculiar characteristics, required it ; then, and then only, was he energetic,— powerful,—overwhelmning,—almost oppressive.   He seemed to set persons before him, in danger of drowning or burning.   Every turn bore on the point of rescue ; and invention was the most rife when trying to succeed in desperate and difficult cases.   To *save* was his object.

One point, touched by the Rev. R. Philip, in his Life of the celebrated George Whitfield, chimes in here, and is distinguished for its justice, so far as the moving principle by which Mr. Dawson was actuated goes ;

when he says,—"I studied Whitfield until I understood him; and therefore, I have instinctively recognized whatever resembled him, in all the popular preachers of my time. James, of Birmingham, has occasionally reminded me of his alternate bursts of tenderness and terror, in all but rapidity; Rowland Hill of his *off-hand* strokes of power; and Spring, of New York, his *off-heart* unction, when it fell like dew, copiously and calmly. Baptist Noel, also, has reminded me of this. Robert Newton has some of Whitfield's oratory, but none of his high passion. Irving had nothing of him but his voice. Cooper, of Dublin, when in his prime, and preaching in the open air, has enabled me to conceive how Whitfield commanded the multitude in Moorfields. I must add,—although I shall not be generally understood,—that Williams of the Wern, and my friend Christmas Evans, of Wales, and Billy Dawson, of Yorkshire, have oftener realized Whitfield to me, than any other preacher of my time : and yet, these three men do not resemble him, nor each other, in mind or body; but they can *lose* themselves entirely as he did, in tender and intense love to souls. This is what is wanted;—and it will *tell* by any voice or style, and from any eye or stature." Mr. Philip's either did not know Mr. Dawson personally, or had ceased distinctly to remember him, when he states him not to have resembled Mr. C. Evans " in mind or body ; " for in both of these there was a striking resemblance. Both were corpulent,—each had a strongly marked countenance,—and there was a similarity in the formation of the head. Mr. Evans was taller than Mr. Dawson. With regard to mind, a friend well acquainted with both, observes,—" If originality of thought—a luxuriant

imagination—a peculiarity of voice—a singularity of
style—and influence over their hearers, beyond precedent, possessed by both, will not identify likeness, I
am at a loss to imagine what will." Admitting Mr.
Philips to have seen and heard Mr. Dawson, he must
only have glanced at him, while he studied Mr. Evans.
On intense love to souls, Mr. Philips is correct ; and it
was this that influenced Mr. Dawson's manner, as well
as his matter. Never, never did man, in modern times,
take captive an audience sooner or more effectually, in
consequence of the ardour of his love. He bore his
hearers along with him, after first drawing them to him,
—relieved them every now and then from an intensity
of feeling, under which was manifested the stillness of
the tomb, by some lighter, but more graphic picture
presented to the imagination, and coming upon them
as unexpectedly as a beautiful, yet picturesque scene, in
a lovely valley, invisible to the tourist, till he is brought
in his rambles to the verge of the elevated ground in
the vicinity.

Instances have occured in the course of the Memoir,
to shew, that there was as little formality in his mode
of commencing the general service, as in commencing
his sermon ; but his usual manner was, to glance at the
hymn, after announcing the number and page, and to
give out the first and second line, with his eyes closed,
—engaging in the singing himself, and often beating
time with his hand, which rose and fell either on the
Bible, or the open pages of the hymn-book, accompanied with an occasional graceful sweep, like a half
circle, and a pendulum kind of motion, with the palm
spread downwards. The eyes were often closed, too,
when delivering a sentence or two during sermon.

This was chiefly the case, when through impetuosity of feeling, he struggled for expression ; and it was too rapid for distinct enunciation. His features then became distorted,—the nose was partially drawn up,—the eye-brows were knit together,—the eyelids compressed,—and the forehead was thrown into conflicting curves, shewing the struggle within. The face, meanwhile, was flushed? and the veins, full and throbbing, seemed like snakes writhing their way up the temples. These, to persons unacquainted with him, were moments of peril,—being half afraid of the rupture of a blood-vessel. But he was no sooner relieved by expression, than—though crippled and halting before, away he went,—the curves retiring like dying waves, leaving the face open,—the eyes piercing through the unruffled countenance, like planets breaking forth from a serene sky. He had amazing flexibility of muscle : and could have accommodated the whine, the wooing, the smirk, the comic, the sneer, the tender, the terrific ; and, with a little more refinement, would—had he been disposed to indulge in them, have made as great a noise in the world, as the most noted for such qualifications. When he was in his gayer moods, he was a little extravagant in this way, not being in every instance well-timed, and bordering upon the ludicrous, though mostly tolerated, and always within the pale of forgiveness.

When very vehement, there was often a sway of the whole person from side to side, like a vessel yielding to the rocking of the waves ; and the hand occasionally placed on the top of the head, as if a little anxious respecting the proper adjustment of his upper adornment, which, owing to its form, was apt to shift its position with his violence,—sometimes requiring the thumb and finger of each hand to draw it over the ear. His hand was inclined to the thick and short,—was sometimes laid upon the breast, as if suddenly smiting it, and at other times,—according to the subject in hand, as if gently patting it. On other occasions, when extremely emphatic, it was suddenly driven down by his side, as if giving a sudden stroke to a stake, with a view to fix it in the earth ; during which the shoulders were slightly raised, —the chin partially lowered on the breast,—the eyebrows rising and falling like curtains,—and the eyes flashing from beneath them. His actions were occasionally a little heavy towards the close of life, but never, strictly speaking, awkward ;—almost invariably comporting with his person, his matter, and the expression of his face. There was generally ease, if not in every instance, grace ; and, till latterly, they corresponded with his eye,—varied and quick ; and though sometimes slightly redundant, not offensive. In his more colloquial moods, when he had a rest for the hand, or the arm, he often planted one leg across the other ; but when impassioned, the union was instantly dissolved, and there was an occasional stamp with the foot.

He had a tolerable ear, but not a correct one : and here, as in the case of certain provincialisms, persons are much more alive to the defects of others, than their own. Hence, Mr. Dawson has sometimes remarked to the writer, on the monotonous manner in which the late excellent Rev. Daniel Isaac gave out the hymns ; and yet, when he brought his own imitative powers to bear on some exquisitely tender subjects, or those of a bolder character, such as pro-

clamations, &c., the subjects were occasionally over-
wrought by the manner.* Like all others, he was most
natural when without design. When he set his heart
on the manner, he often failed. His voice was not
adapted to all circumstances, subjects, and occasions;
and yet he tried all with it, when it would gladly
have yielded, but could not, for want of flexibility.
It was not, like some, equally adapted to the sar-
castic, the ironical, the colloquial, the pleasant, and
the oratorical; but excelled in the three latter,—in
which it sometimes yielded the same variety to the
ear, that a tolerable landscape affords to the eye.

In reading the Lessons, he was sometimes running
and monotonous; leaving the impression, that there
was not only a defect in taste, but in the ear;—for
though he delighted in music, he had not the nice
discrimination requisite to enable him to form a judgment in every case;—being pleased, without the ability
critically to examine it. Hence, in imitating the persons supposed to speak, which he often did while
reading and preaching, he sometimes failed to hit to
a nicety the intonations required, as just noticed,—
being either underdone, or overdone, but most frequently,
in consequence of the strength of his own feelings,
the latter. At other times, he was extremely happy;
though generally more natural in extempore speaking
than reading. His expositions of the Lessons, when
he indulged in this way, were mostly brief sentences
on some particular verse or turn of expression; rarely
entering comprehensively into the design of the sacred

---

* He sometimes doubled his hand on the platform, and at other times the
Resolution, in the form of a tube, to imitate a trumpet, and spoke through the
one or the other, as through a speaking-trumpet, in a kind of trumpet tone.

Y 2

penman, connecting one part with another, or bringing one part to bear upon another. His forte was not exposition; and therefore, he generally, and wisely avoided any formal attempt to elucidate Scripture in that way.

But though he failed in real effectiveness occasionally in reading, he amply made up for it in his sermon. His voice was not clear, nor yet sweet and musical, and rarely varied beyond three or four notes; but amazingly effective in its higher and bolder tones. In its middle tone, there was occasionally the apparent effect of a slight hoarseness, after hard labour and out-door exposure, accompanied with something like roughness, but not unpleasantly so; perhaps, rather a want of sharpness, than otherwise. Its ordinary tone could be given out with great fulness,—then screwed up to a height, till it became shrill,—narrowing the mouth, and pouring it out from a smaller aperture,—still rising, till the key differed, and there was a pause for want of breath,—the last note quitting the ear, like the last shrill blast of a bugle horn among the mountains,—which was as much felt in the sensations produced, as the other is heard in its echoes. He would next,—according to the subject, move the more tender feelings, or rouse the stronger passions,—sometimes roaring it out, like the lion in the forest, while his eyes seemed to flash fire upon all that looked upon them. At a moment, when perception was clear, but recollection was faulty as to expression, in not bringing up words for the occasion, he became rapid,—stuttered,—and would have run on three or four times, with "*there, there, there,*" &c.,—but seemed to feel no pain on that account; or if any were felt, it instantly died on the sentiment being delivered, pleased with its anticipated beneficial effect upon the audience. On some of these occasions, he exhibited some of the finest and most sublime strains of natural oratory. One of his sermons, on "the fields are already white unto the harvest," which he preached at Hull, on a missionary anniversary, in 1818, which the writer heard, was in the highest style of sacred action; especially when, like an ancient priest under the law, he waved his hand over his head, as if filled with stalks of precious grain, and with a heart teeming with the finest emotions,—his prophetic eye, meanwhile, darting forth its rays to the grand millenium, when God shall have gathered into his church all nations,—and the reapers shall be seen returning, and heard shouting,—"Harvest home! harvest home! harvest home!" The voice and manner being adapted to the occasion,—and for which they were admirably fitted, nothing but the "joy of harvest" was felt by an electrified auditory. The same fine intonations were heard also in his appeals to sinners, hastening to destruction, and whom he was urging to enter the Christian race;—"Stop, stop,—strip, strip,—start, start, sinner!"

Often at the close of an impressive passage, he would offer up a petition in prayer, as "The Lord grant it! The Lord apply it," &c., during which, the hands were either clasped or spread, the face turned up to heaven, and the piercing eye, like a wedge, seemed as if it would cleave the heaven towards which it was directed.

In singing, his voice was much sweeter than in speaking; he could humour it more; and it seemed

as if it had acquired additional flexibility in the exercise. His voice was, upon the whole, sound and full,
though not richly varied. He had much more eloquence of feeling, than correctness of ear. His feelings
were right, when his intonations and emphasis were
not always properly placed,—but always most correct
when loud, or rising to a climax. His, in short,
was not among the "airy tongues that syllable men's
names," but which put forth things, and dealt them
out with tremendous force.

As to his language and pronunciation, there were
several defects to a merely critical ear; the one, in
some instances, being homely from preference, and the
other provincial from habit and localization. It was, in
some cases, expressively *Yorkshire ;* as *nou, shou,
nou-en, shou-en,* for know, show, known, shown,—
giving the two latter the effect of words of two syllables.
Wouldn't, shouldn't, &c., were often employed, and
earthen had the sound of *earthern.* Yet, like most
persons, he was unconscious of some of his defects, and
could occasionally smile at those of others, when tried
upon his own ear. His accentuation very often partook
of the same character as his pronunciation. When in
a homely vein, he would—as to language, have selected
"black hole" instead of prison or cell; and would
have represented, in true "Pilgrim Progress" style,
the devil as the "goaler" of the "prison house of
sin," and the sinner with the chains of his unforgiven
crimes "clanking around him" Then in a moment,
like a sudden gleam of sunshine, he would have stolen
over the spirit, with—"But even, in this state, there
is, while on this side the gulf, encouragement for the
poor sinner. If angels sung, 'Glory to God in the

highest,' when Jesus was in a manger, we may well sing it now, that he is upon a throne." There was a negligence about him now and then,—a want of neatness in his style; but still, in the general, his language was respectable,—sometimes rough, or rather plain,—but never vulgar. Its leading characters were strength and perspicuity. Though occasionally undignified, it was never distorted, laboured, or inharmonious. He was not among the defilers of the pure "well of English," but preserved the idiosyncracy which it possesses independent of mere grammatical rules. He was never harsh, crude, dissonant, or obscure,—but might have been understood by a child. "Style" has been properly denominated "the envelope of the inner thoughts;" and his perceptions being invariably clear, his language was in harmony with his ideas. There was nothing misty and undefined. It was not difficult, as just stated, to detect occasional inaccuracies, and to perceive a want of early classical training—sometimes, in his impetuosity, substituting *were* for *was*. But even here, there were no blemishes of thought, through the weight of which he sometimes broke down. Independent, however, of his own style, and also of the style of those men, he united in himself the allegory and tenderness of two of the most famous of the Italian poets; and he would have excelled in language,—in its strength, if not in its ease, if polite literature, instead of the world's business, had engaged his time and attention. "He sought," in his own words, "to impress truth upon the heart in living characters of light."

In his writings, as in his public speaking, are to be found some fine touches, and some passages of great brilliancy and strength. He published a sermon, as already adverted to, on occasion of the death of the Rev. William Bramwell, several short memoirs, a few letters, and some addresses on passing events; and some of his sermons were taken down in short-hand, and published in the "Wesleyan Preacher." But he was not equally happy in writing as in speaking. The *reader* loses the fire and the unction enjoyed by the *hearer*. And besides,—except in his private letters to his friends, many of which are exquisitely tender, faithful, forcible, and graceful, he generally wrote under restraint, when the press and the public stood before him, owing to a consciousness that he wanted the prerequisites for the niceties of English composition. Proceeding in fear, a degree of stiffness was the result; the fountain of his thoughts sent forth its streams with less copiousness, and the affections of the heart were but partially unsluiced. Yet, in this case, *his* poverty would have been another man's wealth; and it was only the poverty of a rich man, under less felicitous circumstances. He always paid for perusal, and imparted to the reader what he could not obtain elsewhere, though somewhat less than might have been obtained from himself under more auspicious circumstances. He frequently interlined his manuscript sermons with large emendations—introduced whole paragraphs—wrote out new plans, and prefixed them to the old materials,—and sometimes re-wrote the greater part, and intermixed the new with the old, in such a way as to confound any one besides himself; and in such a way too, as would have even distracted his own attention, had he been a mere memoriter preacher. But he dwelt on things, not on mere verbiage; the thought was there, and the drapery followed.

Perhaps, in prayer, he was less acceptable to the fastidious, than in preaching and writing. By some persons, who knew but little of his sincerity, and could make no allowance for the peculiar cast of his mind, he would have been deemed too colloquial at a throne of grace, and more desirous of producing an effect upon the hearer, than of obtaining a blessing from God; more busily engaged with man than with his Maker; more disposed to strike the one, than to produce reverence towards the other;—in short, too quaint, figurative, and familiar—giving the notion of a person working out, and working up a thought, with a view to impress the creature, rather than interest the Supreme Being. Not only the fastidious, but pious, candid, and intelligent persons, have demurred here. Hence, the Rev. J. A. James, of Birmingham, in a letter to the biographer, observes, "It occurred to me, that with occasional real pathos, there was blended, as in the case of my venerated friend, Rowland Hill, too much of the humorous : and, in prayer, I thought there was a too great familiarity in his style of address to God." This defect was sometimes felt by his best friends; and both matter and manner might give rise to an impression of this kind; but it was generally more at the commencement, than in the body of his prayer. As an example; he commenced his prayer, on a particular occasion, by telling his Maker, that he is the *centre* and *element* of man; that man had wandered from his proper centre, and must now address himself in the language of the Psalmist,—"Return unto thy rest, O my soul;" and that he could no more be happy out of his element, than "the fish of the sea could be satisfied to live in green fields." Than this, not anything

can be more naturally or theologically correct. The
last expression was the result of the previous train of
thought ; and though few men, besides himself, would
have employed the simile in prayer, yet the intonations
of the voice which followed—his earnestness of spirit—
his evident hold of God—and the thorough Christian
feeling of his heart, instantly swallowed up the first
impression of the ludicrous ; and nothing but the sober,
deep, devout, yet fervid emotions of the soul, were felt
by all present. These were the general impressions
left upon the minds of religious characters, who united
with him in devout addresses to heaven, with the exception of the drawback to which reference has been
made.

Being familiar with the liturgy of the Church of
England, he not unfrequently interwove a part of its
sentiments and phraseology into his prayers ; which,
with his earnest pleadings, had an amazing effect upon
the heart, and drew forth the deep response from the
audience. On other occasions, he would lay hold of
some text of Scripture, such as,—" I will sing of
mercy," or, "His mercy endureth for ever," and
would apply it to the various states in which persons
might be found, or the circumstances in which they
might be placed, and then plead with God for mercy,
in connection with his promises to man.

He was always most in danger when he indulged his
fancy, which led him to the verge of the wild and
ludicrous. This faculty, when restrained, has been
aptly compared to a fountain, which plays the highest
by diminishing the aperture. But though he occasionally,— apart from prayer, indulged in the arabesque,
and the picturesque ; and was fond,—especially on the

platform, of bewitching fancies; and though he abounded in carelessnesses, yet he rarely dealt in the superficial, and scarcely—beyond a few moments, ever lacked vigorous variety. There was such glowing imagery, such strength of expression, such fine strokes of wisdom, such tenderness; that the turns of humour, and the sportings of fancy, were soon lost, "like the splendid but unsubstantial creations which rise in the mists of the morning, but are dissolved in the noon-day sun." He knew, to change the metaphor adopted by another, that sand often contains gold, but that sand would make a very sorry foundation; and therefore, never failed to dig till he reached the rock.

Imagination, which is less airy in its character, and somewhat more sedate in its movements, as well as more correct in its delineations, was still more conspicuous. This was always at his command; and through the influence of the grace of God upon his heart, he rarely failed to mirror things to the life. Every man could see himself in the glass held up, and the particular truth in which he was most interested. The likeness was not always finished, but it was invariably strong; and no one could mistake the object or character portrayed. He had the power, in a high degree, of representing even sentiments and abstract ideas, — such as justice, mercy, and truth, and of putting appropriate speeches into their mouths, as in the "Sacred Dramas" of Mrs. H. More, and other moral dramatic pieces; and these impersonated ideas, had very often an extaordinary effect upon his auditors. Had he not been under the influence of religion, and had he belonged to the reigns of JAMES and CHARLES, or to the seventeenth century, he would have excelled Daniel in his *masques*—a species of writing consisting chiefly of dialogues, and supported by allegorical characters.

On subjects where all was gay and brilliant, fancy would sometimes steal a march upon him; as when representing the church under the similitude of a building. "There," he would say, "every stone is polished—each fitted to its place; and on one square is written—sparkling, not in letters of gold, but in living letters of light,—'Him that cometh unto me, I will in no wise cast out;' on another,—'Wherefore he is able also to save them to the uttermost that come unto God by him;' and on the top-stone,—'Glory to God in the highest.'" Yet, for the spiritually-minded class of hearers before him, the whole was sufficiently intelligible, and his other matter amply atoned for any little freak of imagination in which he might indulge,—the object and motive tolerating, if not justifying, the thing itself, when even at issue with good taste and rigid criticism.

His descriptions were sometimes mixed up with pictorial remarks, referring to moral and religious ideas, while his moral and religious sketches and personifications were now and then as quaint as Quarles;—at one moment horrid and unearthly, and at another, gay;—thus rendering them occasionally repulsive to persons of refined taste, but accordant with the feelings of the uncultivated mass.

He seemed to have the faculty for representing what are called the "Miracle Plays," whose object was to present the principal supernatural events of the Old and New Testament,—not with their proofs of divine authority by argument, but in their proper character, and the incidents attendant on them. This remark is of course made with a view to shew the character of his mind, and is not to be understood as expressive of regret, that it was not employed in that peculiar way on divine subjects. Like Bunyan, he stood in a class by himself. He exhibited some of the darker and more violent passions of human nature, often beautifully relieved and contrasted with the sorrows of an unoffending and virtuous mind, as to the characters he drew. He spoke as a traveller writes, who has seen the object, and designs—not neatly, but boldly, touchingly, and sometimes minutely, as by the pencil of an artist ; and he felt like a man who believes what he says. His descriptive powers were such, as to enable him to throw off what might be deemed faithful portraits : they were exact and living, and often rapid in their succession,—for he had amazing quickness ; and such, — though often explored in their hidden depths, as were not always brought to view. Others often *referred* to what he *described;* and the descriptions, as already observed, in reference to himself, were hung up in the chambers of the heart like a portrait, — but sometimes in the reverse way to his own, for the portraits, as noticed in the commencement of this article, were such, that the possessors, —when they themselves were represented, would have gladly exchanged for others, but could not get rid of them, and memory would not permit their destruction ; and though sometimes a little caricatured, still the likeness,—even under these seldom occurring circumstances, might be seen, and the portrait fastened on its rightful owner. He never attempted, however, to caricature, but with a view to induce the sinner to fall out of love with his sins and with himself. He seemed now and then to have the singular faculty, which is said to have been possessed by an eminent German poet, of divesting himself of intellectual identity,—of becoming that which he contemplated or described,—of feeling the sensations, of thinking the thoughts, of other persons. He would have become the mother, the child, the penitent, the joyous Christian,—the horror-stricken sinner, and his hearers seemed to see and hear the person, and sympathize with him.

Distinct from imagination, and from his descriptive powers, there was the faculty of invention, and that too, in an eminent degree. This may be distinguished from the creative power which he possessed, and which will not be overlooked, by applying the one to the act of bringing a world of thought, so to speak, into existence, in the mass ; and the other, to the power of eliciting from that mass, things in detail, in an almost endless diversity of form. Not that his inventive faculty was equal to his creative powers. He had his divisions and subdivisions ; but still his sermons were not branched out into various puritanical particulars. Multiplicity would have embarassed him ; a settled plan of this kind would have destroyed his freedom. It was the inspiration of the moment that awakened his inventive faculty. He could have taken up a single thought or figure, which flashed upon his mind,— could have turned it round and round in a cylindrical way, both in prayer and preaching,—constantly exhibiting, as it revolved, some new point,—some new appearance on the surface, producing on the minds of others the same effect that is experienced by panoramic exhibitions upon the eye. On other occasions, to employ the still less sanctified allusion to the chase, which almost demands an apology for its use, because of other more serious associations, he would start a thought,—pursue it for some length of time,—keep pressing upon it,—loose sight for a few seconds,—then branch off in another direction, in consequence of other conceptions,—suddenly, and, in an unexpected moment, springing upon the old thought again, in another part of the field,—then re-pursuing it for a brief space, till, like an animal, taking shelter among the brushwood, it no less suddenly disappeared. When he broke away thus, they were moments of intense interest with the hearers, who were all fixed in palpitating pleasure in the pursuit. He never,—in any of his chasings,—any of his revolvings, failed to rouse and instruct : and on other occasions, he would have conjured up enemies to the truth, of all sorts, and would have knocked them down like " nine pins."

When not on particularly touching subjects, his wit would sometimes unexpectedly escape ; and though not always refined, yet always helpful to the point in question, and never indulged merely with a view to produce amusement. He invariably gave greater latitude to his devious, roaming, and abrupt imagination on the platform, than in the pulpit ;—a proof of his discretion.

As is generally the case with highly imaginative characters, he never shone as a logician ; and would,—from his want of ability to enter consecutively into subjects of a profound, subtle, and abstract nature, have been soon baffled by a metaphysician. Yet, notwithstanding this, there was great shrewdness and quickness of perception : but with him, it was the blade that made an entrance at once,—the logic of a single stroke ; a few sentences grasping the general

argument, but specially, and, as by instinct, finding
their way to a vulnerable part,—laying it bare,—and
producing such conviction as to effect, and to render
suspicious, if not to demolish, the whole, in the esteem
of his unsophisticated hearers. He frequently employed
the terms *therefore* and *consequently*, which shewed
that the mind was exercising its reasoning powers.
But while he admitted with Fuller, that "Reasons
are the pillars of the fabric of a sermon," he knew
with him at the same time, that "similitudes are
the windows which give the best light." Hence, he
dismissed argumentation the moment he found he had
established his point, and gave scope to his imagination.

But though it was not a mind that could delight itself
with entering into the various subtleties and niceties
of an argument,—pursuing it through all its intricacies,
doublings, and bearings,—ferreting the designs of an
opponent out of all their lurking places, and keeping
close to the heels to the very last ; yet he possessed
what was infinitely better for his purpose and for
his work,—and this, by the way, is no bad proof
of the sagacity of the friends and members of the
missionary committee, in the selection they made,—a
ready perception of truth, took a masculine grasp of
his subject, and had a bold, persuasive, effective oratory. The facts of man's fall were too glaring, and
the truths of the gospel too clear, for a profuse
expenditure of logic. In thus speaking of his argumentative powers, it is by no means insinuated, that
there was any essential defect in the manner, the
process, or the result of his reasonings. He sustains
no injury, when it is affirmed, that he was not a
Locke, nor a Reid, nor a Beattie, nor a Dugald Stewart.

There are many gradations of intellect between a person of respectable talents, and the first of these masters. He might not have reached any of these, and yet have surpassed millions of the human species. Mr. Dawson's was not the long even thread of the finest spun silk, but a logic of points and angles, shooting out in unexpected directions, and excessively annoying to the persons against whom it might be directed; scattering, to change the metaphor, his shafts, like a shower of barbed arrows, which were left rankling in the conscience of the sinner,—compelling him to flee to the spiritual physician for healing and strength. It was the logic, not of the study, but of the market, of the exchange, and of the counting-house; the logic, not of the few, but of the multitude; the logic which the least cultivated could understand. It was, in short, the logic of the lightning, whose stroke was death to the subterfuge of every sinner, and whose flash was conviction to the lukewarm professor.

He proceeded to work with an argument, like the eagle, on perceiving its prey, never for a moment busying itself in the examination of the plumage or the form of the bird upon which it is about to pounce, but viewing it as a whole,—making one fell swoop,—clutching it at once,—and bearing it up, writhing in very agony, till lost for ever to the gaze of the spectators. There was no delicacy in the handling; —it was prey he had to deal with,— prey to be destroyed,—not for its value, but because of its odiousness, having been hurtful to the life of the sinner, himself, and his associates, and in the destruction of which angels might rejoice. This was the man for the work of the ministry. If there was a naked point, it was seen; and though visible before to the sinner, it was laid still more bare to the public eye, so that he began to suspect he was as well known to the preacher and others, as to himself. One thing which rendered him so effective was, that his characters, when connected with any particular vice, were almost invariably taken from real life; and as the depraved nature of man is the same in every place,—with the exception of a few circumstantial differences, the person was certain to recognize his own image: the face, the form, and the features were all there,—the principal difference resting in the drapery which covered the more odious parts of the vice, there was an anxiety to conceal. As an example selected from many others, a person of property, who lived at H—l—n, remarkable for covetousness and oppression, "beholding his natural face in a glass," and feeling himself speared in the presence of the congregation, accosted Mr. Dawson the next time he met him, with—"You were too personal when I last heard you;" to which he replied,—"I candidly confess I intended it for the class of characters to which you belong; and therefore, as one of them, I embraced that opportunity of warning you of your danger." As there was no possibility of escape, on the part of the hearer, there was no evasion on the part of the preacher. If deception had been resorted to, it was exposed; if the sinner persevered, the branding iron was applied. If he had been in the hands of others,—had been tampered with,—and his case had become desperate, he was dealt with like a person whose life was at stake. There was no ceremony,—rank never occurred to the mind,—health was the object,—a few twinges and writhings in the patient were unheeded, so intensely was the eye fixed upon the grand object to be attended to,—health, perfect health. He boldly lashed the vices and follies both of individuals and whole classes, sometimes with bluntness, but always with fidelity : and when he found persons ministering to the grovelling tastes, and unreasonable prejudices of the multitude, he never failed to launch a bolt at them, regardless of consequences.

Everything was done and said, whether in the pulpit or the social circle, with such honesty of purpose and manner, that his very failings commended him to confidence. There were no suspicious pretensions to credit. When speaking of himself, though he might excite a quiet smile now and then at his own expense, it was unmixed with anything offensive ; and at no time did he ever attempt to raise himself by sinking others. All his remarks upon himself were good-natured, not selfish,—somewhat gregarious ; and he felt a pleasure in extolling others whenever praise was due. The fact is, that in the minutest circumstances, and in all his transactions with men, he permitted an enlightened conscience to tell its own tale ; and trivial things,—things unavoidable in themselves, produced the greatest sensibility, when they would have been passed off by others as matters of course.

He never sought to occupy the first position in company ;—a line of conduct which often springs from vanity ; and, than which, not anything,—except that which is flagrantly vicious, will more speedily let character descend from its real eminence. Persons of this class, have been represented by a writer—

z

and not unjustly, as robbing the mountebank of his livelihood ; and have been recommended to lock themselves in their closets, and take out their vauntings in soliloquy, under the impression, that if they are partial to their own praises there, and can reconcile themselves to the belief of them, it will then be time enough to try them upon other people. It is an undoubted truth, fixed on the page of another writer, that "every man has just as much vanity as he wants understanding." But in proportion as he is under the influence of the former, he is to be avoided ; because, in such a character, the smallest spark may kindle into the greatest flame,—the materials being always prepared for it. Now, though vanity and affectation are nearly allied — and some persons, not remarkable for the opposite perfection, have deemed the subject in review as possessed of a touch of the one, yet no man was ever more free from the other,—from affectation, than he was : he verily loathed it ; and his loathings of the latter, would never subject him to a state of vassalage to the former. Saville, speaking of their alliance, says, —"I will not call vanity and affectation twins ; because, more properly, vanity is the mother, and affectation is the darling daughter ; vanity is the sin, and affectation is the punishment ; the first may be called the root of self-love, the other, the fruit. Vanity is never at its full growth, till it spreadeth into affectation ; and then it is complete." If the "daughter" was never seen, there is reason to dispute the existence of the "mother ;" if the "fruit" was not perceptible, the "root"—as most roots are, must have lain deeply concealed in the heart ;—and if *concealed*, how came it to be *known?* "Extinguish vanity in the mind," says Steele, " and you naturally retrench the little superfluities of garniture and equipage. The blossoms will fall of themselves, when the root that nourishes them is destroyed." Divine grace had destroyed the "root" in the heart of Mr. Dawson; and his homely, unassuming—though agreeable, manners, were at variance with the "little superfluities of garniture and equipage," whether physically or mentally understood.

Generally speaking, he had a consummate knowledge of man,—a shrewd insight into business transactions,—and good judgment and experience in the leading truths of the Bible. This, with his rich imagination, which aided him in drawing out and illustrating the general doctrines of the gospel, in his peculiar way, formed a good ground-work for his appeals to the conscience. In some very rare cases, the love of novelty, and the desire of producing effect, gave a momentary bias to the judgment; particularly when grappling with some great subject, or employed in the work of *illustration,* and at the moment that thoughts appeared to be teeming in upon him,—returning to them again and again,—then, throwing out his feelers for expression,—but still in love with the conceit or novelty,—and trying to justify it, with a disposition to maintain it, from a pure love of its being new, till the judgment rose up in rebellion against it. Thus, in an attempt to encourage the desponding sinner, he observed on one occasion,— "There are two *Infinite Loves;* one in the Deity, and another in the humanity of Christ;—two infinite oceans meeting in one." Now, the idea of two infinities, and one of those infinities in a *finite* humanity,

involves an absurdity which would soon be detected
by the mind, though capable of administering encouragement to the feelings of an uninstructed awakened
sinner. Besides, an attempt to augment the infinite
love of God by *dividing* it,—for it could never increase it, will admit of but little support in the way of
argument. This, however, was urged by the excellent
subject of the Memoir; and when, in his amplification,
he found the love of novelty fetter him, he endeavoured
to qualify it, by asserting an *infinite* love in the God-
head, and a *perfect* love in the manhood. The same
consequence resulted from his desire to produce effect,
which was generally mixed up with his love of novelty,
—the one originating chiefly in his creative powers,
and the other in his deep feeling. The latter sometimes led him to mar his best thoughts, by overshooting
them. His mouth was generally, in the language of
the apostle, full of "strong meat" from ˉGod to the
people. His thoughts resembled his physical frame;
they were solid,—full,—strong. It was not unfrequently the sledge-hammer,—the battering ram,—the
thunder,—the lightning. In some instances, he would
be heard by persons of no religious feeling, but of
refined taste and classical attainments, for amusement,
owing to his light, daring, terrific singularities.

If he ever failed, it was when fancy was indulged
in the *illustration* of a subject: in his *deductions* from
scriptural truth, he was remarkable for soundness of
judgment; always clear and condensed in his defini-
tions, and convincing in his conclusions. He had a
quick and clear insight into the Word of God; and
the truths there, like certain propositions noticed by
Reid on the "Intellectual Powers," were no sooner

understood than believed. The judgment followed the apprehension of them necessarily; and both were equally the work of nature, and the result of his original powers. There was no searching for evidence, no weighing of arguments; no inference drawn from other things. He saw the light of truth in itself; and with the same clearness, and force, and correctness, he imparted it to others. There is but too much truth in the remark, that "it is with our judgments as our watches; none go just alike, yet each believes his own." But if a man wish to keep his watch right, he will take care to regulate it by the sun, as the good man takes care to regulate his creed by the Bible. This was the case with Mr. Dawson, who read and examined the Sacred Records for himself, and would never rely on "visual beams refracted through another's eye."

In directing still further attention to the mind, his originality seemed at once to invite observation;—a talent by which things and qualities not previously described, are discovered and exhibited, or, if familiar, are shown in new lights. It is only occasionally,—as it was in his case, united with power,—for it is a slow and studious faculty; and when combined with genius, is often mistaken as the peculiar element of that remarkable energy. His creations were numerous and varied, and of a character peculiar to themselves—but never finished. They resembled a bold, rich, well-wooded country,—not the gay, lined, systematized pleasure-ground, in which art is stealing upon the gaze of the spectator at every turn : but though rich, always in want of a certain portion of cultivation, the veriest trifle of which would amply compensate for the labour bestowed, and which stood more in need of the hoe, the knife, and the mattock, than the shower, the sun, and the manure. When most unfinished, they still bore the hand of a master,—the principal thing required to improve them being, not so much the general adjustment, as merely a little levelling here and there, for the sake of greater grace and ease, there being prominences sufficient,—even more than a due proportion, without it. Nor were they, it may be added, always beautiful, indeed rarely ; but they were invariably striking. He was never without original imagery, striking sentiment, fertility of expression, and happy combinations—though occasionally a century behind some of the modern sermonizers, associating more immediately with the most useful, the purest, and noblest of the Puritan divines.

The Rev. J. A. James, of Birmingham,—himself an excellent model, as well as an admirable judge of ministerial character and qualification, whose opinion has already been adverted to, observes in the same letter to the biographer,—"With respect to the opinion which I am alledged to have expressed of Mr. Dawson, I cannot take upon myself either to confirm or deny the report. If you had it from Mr.——himself, I have no doubt of its correctness : for if I did not *say* it, I thought it. Mr. Dawson was in every respect a man *sui generis*, and must not be tried as a public speaker by the rules which are applied to other men." Mr. James then, in allusion to what the classical reader will find in one of the most admired Italian Poets—one of those thoughts which could only proceed from a great mind, and only occur once to the same mind,—

" Natura lo fece, e poi ruppe la stampa ; "

"Nature formed him, and then broke up the mould ;"

further observes,—"The mould in which his mind and manner were cast, was exclusively his own, and was broken up when his character was formed. No one *should*—none I believe *did*, for none *could* imitate him. I never heard him preach but once, nor did I ever hear more than one speech from him ; but both the sermon and the oration displayed a force of genius, and command of striking illustration, such as I had scarcely ever heard. The taste of some of his most splendid corruscations of mental brilliance might be questioned, but their power over a certain class of minds was irresistible." Mr. James, in stating that "none *could* imitate" Mr. Dawson, is correct ; and the biographer, in coinciding with the reverend gentleman, entertains the opinion of Villegas, a Spanish poet, in another case, who says, "Thou art so great that thou canst only imitate thyself with thy own greatness ; " which approaches an expression of our own—"None but himself can be his parallel. " In a conversation which the biographer had, about the same time, with the author of "The World before the Flood," the latter remarked, when speaking of Mr. Dawson, that he often employed beautiful figures,—not figures for the occasion, introduced for the sake of embellishment, as in a poem, but woven into the very texture of his language, and forming a part of it. He admitted that he occasionally bordered on the absurd, when he gave scope to his fancy, but that he sometimes rose into sublimity, and into the highest style of natural eloquence ; added to which,—and it was here that he admired him most, there was often uncommon power of thought, and unusual pathos ; though he always preferred him in the pulpit to the platform. He considered him a good subject for biography, though not equal to Samuel Hick for simplicity and unexpected variety; being much more varied in his *discourse* than in his *character*, —and so constituting one difference, with many others, between Hick's originality and his own. In matter, he pronounced him to be exceedingly varied — having height and depth, with all the shades between.

It will be easy to perceive the kind of matter in which it was likely he would deal, from the peculiarity of his genius, and the strength of his feelings. His thoughts, both in prayer and preaching, were like masses of ore —and often of the most valuable kind, like ingots of pure gold, from which the most beautiful current coin might be struck into form and size, and without which, though devoid of polish, a realm might have been without a currency;—at least, without a currency but for similar minds; as it is not likely that the "coinage of the brain," would have received the same sort of die —if die at all, except taken up from such minds, by others of inferior intellectual grade. Throughout the whole, there was an evident want of refinement, which a thorough discipline might have produced. It is doubtful, however, whether the exuberance of his fancy and genius, would have ever allowed him to be pinioned down to order. The question proposed to the Rev. J. A. James, of Birmingham,—" What would he have been had he been favoured with an academical education?" and the reply given to it,—" He would have been spoiled," comprehends much more of truth —without at all interfering with the general question which involves the propriety of a wholesome early training—than will at first be admitted; for it is not improbable, that the buoyancy of his native genius, whatever might have been the polish bestowed, would have turned up the surface, and have rendered it occasionally a little rough to the eye. He was one of the patriarchs of Methodism—not in years—but for being hale both in body and mind—unsmitten by effeminacy ;—a diamond in the rough, who received sufficient polish from the station which he was destined to adorn, as he rolled on with the tide of labour that carried him forward—precious for his value, and dazzling for his brilliancy, without being indebted to the hand of the lapidary. His value was seen and known through his coating; as much so, as was that of John the Baptist through his "leathern girdle," and his garment of "camel's hair." He thought strongly, and he spoke strongly. The thoughts, however, which he bolted forth, were not mere huge, shapeless masses, but were often worked up with considerable skill.

Love and fear were the two passions on which he principally laid hold; and these had a corresponding influence upon his matter. No congregation could resist his appeals, when addressing the maternal, filial, or fraternal feelings. On all pathetic subjects, the people were like a piece of mechanism in his hand, which he could wind at will. In the same sermon, and within only a few seconds, the same persons, melted into tenderness, and like the wax, ready to receive the impression, or like the ore in a fluid state, ready for the mould, would have been suddenly awestruck,—the eyes fixed,—the lips apart,—the body motionless,—and within hearing of the beating of their own hearts. On the horrors of hell, the flame seemed to flash upon the eye,—representing, in terrific contrast, the rich, the titled, the gay, surrounded with everything

z 2

calculated to fascinate the eye, captivate the ear, and
minister to the taste,——tossed from a bed of feathers
into a bed of fire, exchanging the salubrious air for the
suffocating stench of brimstone, the salute of fondest
friends, for,——in his own language, the "grin of
demons," and where "the least and meanest fiend in
the regions of woe, was permitted to spit hell fire in
their face." It was, indeed, on such occasions, "the
reign of terror." But even here, he was very often
on his way to something exquisitely tender. He was
never remote from the cross ;——rarely out of sight of it,
——generally hovering round it,——and sometimes, like a
bird of heaven, would seem to alight upon it, and there
make his stay. He generally avoided long declamation ; and his style being highly impassioned, was
consequently metaphoric, and therefore, striking; for
all metaphor is the natural language of a raised
imagination and agitated heart : and his own heart
being affected with his subject, he found ready access
to the hearts of others. When he did declaim, he
was generally brief; though he was as powerful a
declaimer, as he was an excellent painter ; and always
had logic enough for the subject upon which he descanted.

In connexion with his matter, and uninjured by his
lighter moods, was a certain authority which he
invariably exercised over his respective auditories.
Whatever he might have felt, he appeared an utter
stranger to everything like fear in the pulpit. He
was there like "one having authority." Beside his
native courage, the immense crowds that attended
his ministry,——sometimes, as in Manchester and other
populous places, rendering the presence of the police

necessary, attested how much he was beloved by the people; and it was love in him which, in return, "cast out fear." He spoke, whether colloquially or oratorically,—acted,—and was as free, even with the most splendid, and most numerously attended audience in the city, as with the smaller and humbler in the rural districts. On entering the pulpit, and closing the door, he was like a man who had entered his own dwelling, where *he* only, of human beings, exercised the authority of a master, and those around were at his bidding, and under his influence, as dependants. The pulpit was his home, wherever it might stand. Yet, though master, there were no authoritative airs. With a becoming dignity, there was always that feeling of reverence present, that left the impression, that one was his *Master*—even CHRIST. In his fearlessness and authority, with other qualifications, he reminds us of the self-possession, and some other traits that were found in the character of Bridane, who, like himself, acted in the capacity of a Christian missionary. *

* The Abbe Maury has given us a striking exordium of Bridane's. Speaking of Cicero, and extolling his eloquence, he says,—

"If there remain any traces of this ancient and vigorous eloquence, which is no other than the voice of nature, it is among the missionaries, and we must go to the country for examples. These apostolic men, endued with an imagination vigorous and strong, know no other success than conversions, no other applause than tears. Often destitute of taste, they descend, I grant, to burlesque details; but they strongly strike the senses. Their threatenings impress terror; and the people hear them with concern. Yet many among them have sublime strokes; and an orator does not attend them without profit, when he knows how to distinguish the great effects of his art. Mr. Bridane, the man of this age the most justly celebrated of that order, was born with a popular eloquence, full of metaphors and fire; and no one possessed in a higher degree the talent of seizing on an assembled multitude. He had such a fine voice, as rendered credible all the prodigies that history recounts of the declamations of the ancients. He could be as easily heard by ten thousand people in the open air, as though he had spoken under the most sonorous arch. One could remark in all he said, natural turns of eloquence; very expressive

Associated with his authority, was his power, which
was still more perceptible, though often confounded by
less critical minds, with power altogether divine, as
attendant on his ministry.   This faculty was distinguished in him, not barely by bringing a creation of
the mind into existence, but by occasionally heaving up
the mighty mass — manufacturing materials already
brought into being, and shewing a Herculean power
in their use : hence it has been styled, and not unaptly, "a manufacturing faculty."   It is not in the
light, superficial, "namby pamby" way that it acts ;
but it shews itself by wielding the mace, or, like the
giants of old, by handling the weaver's beam ;—or,
perhaps, more appropriately still, like Samson shaking
pillars, temple, and all, but without expiring in the

metaphors; blunt, new, and striking thoughts, with all the characters of a
fertile imagination ; some extemporaneous stroke, and sometimes even whole
discourses, delivered with the correctest taste and warmth.   I remember to
have heard him preach his first sermon in the church of St. Sulpicius, in Paris,
in the year 1751.   The most brilliant circles of the capital, excited by curiosity,
came to hear him.   Bridane perceiving in the assembly many bishops and
persons of distinction, with an innumerable crowd of ecclesiastics, the sight,
far from intimidating, inspired him with the following exordium :—

"'At the sight of an audience so new to me, it might seem, my brethren, I
should not open my mouth, but only ask favour in behalf of a poor missionary,
destitute of those talents which you require when we address you on the concerns of your salvation   But I feel impressed to-day with a sentiment widely
different; and if I appear to humble myself, do not believe that I abase myself
to the miserable inquietudes of vanity, as though I were accustomed to preach
myself.   God forbid that a minister of heaven should think he has any need
of apologizing for himself to you !   For whosoever you are, you are no other
than sinners like myself.   It is before your God and mine, that I feel constrained
to smite upon my breast.   *Ave Maria !*

"'Till the present time, I have published the righteousness of the Most
High in temples covered with thatch ; I have announced the rigours of
penitence to the miserable who wanted bread ; I have proclaimed to the good
inhabitants of the country, the most terrific truths of my religion.   What have
I done—wretch that I am?   I have saddened the poor,—the best friends of
my God.   I have carried grief and dismay into those simple, faithful souls
whom I ought to have consoled, and with whom I should have sympathized.

"'But here my looks fall on the great, on the rich, on the oppressors of

struggle,—again and again rising with the same giant
might as before : and here was a peculiarity in the
subject before us ; for it was not with him, as with
a man, who puts forth all his energies on a solitary
occasion, and, by one single effort, exhausts his strength,
—requiring a lapse of time to recruit again, but it
was a regular succession of efforts,—without any apparent feebleness occasioned by exercise,—year after year,
and in place after place, manifesting the same power
in body and in intellect. He had a remote resemblance to one of our first poets,—whom to name
might be deemed a profanity by some, and a weakness
by others,—but so it is believed is the fact,—he had
a power of conceiving characters, and, after conceiving
them, a readiness of throwing himself into them, as

suffering humanity; or on sinners audacious and hardened. Ah! it is here
only I should make the holy word resound with all its strength and thunder;
and place with me in this pulpit, on the one hand, death, which threatens
you; and on the other, my great God, who is about to judge you. I hold
to-day your sentence in my hand. Tremble, then, before me, ye haughty and
disdainful men, who hear me. The necessity of salvation; the certainty of
death; the uncertainty of that hour so terrible to you ; final impenitence; the
last judgment; the small number who obtain salvation ; and, above all,
ETERNITY!—ETERNITY! These are the subjects with which I come to entertain you; and which I ought, without doubt, to have reserved for you alone.
Ah! what need have I of your applause, which might damn me without saving
you? God is going to affect you by his unworthy minister who addresses
you; for I have acquired a long experience of his mercies: then penetrated
with horror for your past sins, you shall come and cast yourselves into my
arms, pouring out tears of compunction and penitence ; and, by the force of
remorse, you will find me to be eloquent enough. Ah! upon what do you
found your hopes, my brethren, that your last moments are so distant? Is it
because you are young? *Yes, you say, I have as yet but twenty or thirty years.*
Ah! it is not you who have twenty or thirty years, but death who has twenty
or thirty years in advance upon you. Take heed. Eternity approaches. Do
you know what eternity is? It is a clock, the pendulum of which incessantly
says, ALWAYS! EVER! EVER! ALWAYS! ALWAYS! During these vibrations, a
damned soul cries out, *What o'clock is it?* And the same voice replies, *It is
ETERNITY!*"—*Dicours sur l' Eloquence de la Chaire*, page 45.

I am afraid we have no traces of this missionary eloquence in England,
unless it be among the itinerant missionaries.

has been shewn,—though a little too comic now and then, so as to bring from them a discourse which would generally be allowed, to be such as would be spoken under the supposed circumstances. It was the same with characters selected from Scripture, from personal observation, and general history. He seemed to have strong pleasure, when his subject led to it, in whatever was terrible, even though it bordered sometimes upon extravagance; and there were single passages in his sermons, which, as exhibitions of the more violent passions, were inferior to nothing in the whole range of modern pulpit oratory. He shewed extraordinary power also, as has been noticed, of managing argument in sentences,—of compressing his thoughts, like Pope, in his "Essay on Man," into clauses of the most energetic brevity, as well as of expanding them into passages glittering—though in the rough, with every ornament calculated to captivate the general hearer. Such a man, it would not be unnatural to conceive—when we connect with his native energy, the overwhelming power that attended his ministry, would have been a fine companion in open field with Luther; nor is it at all derogatory to either the birth or native character of Luther,—his learning of course unmixed with the comparison, to have another noble creation of God placed by his side.

There is a passage in the works of a popular author, on the least fascinating portion of Luther's character, which—as it contains some points of similarity, will produce the impression that the writer wishes to convey, and so form an apology for the subject in question, —an apology, be it observed, not so necessary because of any positive defect in the subject alluded to, as because of the mistaken views of others. "Hitherto," the author observes, "the too common idea of the great Reformer's character has been, that it was a mere compound of violence and ruggedness. These traits have been made so prominent, that the finer lines of the portrait have been completely shaded from the sight. If, in fact, we knew nothing of Dr. Johnson but his occasional bursts of savage and uncouth manners, we should not have a more erroneous impression of him than is generally entertained of Luther. Another reason of our misconception is, that we too often honour mere *daintiness* of mind with the name of delicacy, sensibility, humanity, and virtue ; whilst the rough exterior and the passionate expression, smack to the taste of drawing-room, fashionable society, whence opinions are usually circulated, only of brutality and ferocity. Perhaps, however, the finest, richest, and most generous species of character is that which presents to the *dainty* the most repulsive surface. Within the rough rind, the feelings are preserved unsophisticated, robust and healthy. The rough outside keeps off that insidious swarm of sensibilities, which taint, and adulterate, and finally expel all natural and vigorous emotions from within us. The idea of a perfect man has always been figured forth in our minds by the emblem of the lion coming out of the lamb, and the lamb coming out of the lion. Of this description of character was Luther. Nothing could exceed his submissiveness and humility when choice was left him whether to be humble or daring ; but when conscience spoke, no other consideration for the moment was attended to, and he certainly did then shake the forest in his magnificent ire. But if we behold him one moment, to use his own quotation from Scripture, *pouring contempt upon princes,* and highly raging against the highest upon earth, we see him the next in his familiar correspondence, a poor, humble, afflicted man, not puffed up with pride at the great things he had accomplished, but rather struck down at a sense of his unworthiness. As to his violence, it was part of his mission to be violent, and those who charge it as a fault, blame Divine Providence. Not to have been violent, would have been in him not to be in earnest. And here it may be observed, that his violence was not *verbal ;* it was merely the rousing *voice* to awaken Europe from the lethargy of ages. In his opinions and views, he was the most moderate of all reformers. In his coarseness, however, his low origin certainly speaks out ; yet there is something sublime in the peasant (the miner's son) dragging popes, and kings, into his wrestling ring, and handling them with as much roughness and as little ceremony as he would a hob-nailed clown from a country market-place. He was moulded by the hand that sent him. The accidents of this world had no power to change or modify his moral conformation. There was a oneness, a wholeness, an uncompoundedness of character in him. The Divine finger had chiselled on his moral frame but one idea—and that external to his earthly condition. Hence was begotten the simplicity and homeliness of Luther's walk and life. Had he acted the great man, he would have proved that he was not the apostle."

The similarity between the two men,—the son of the Isleben, or Saxon Miner, and the son of the Yorkshire Colliery Agent, is not, as already intimated, so much to be seen in the detail—in the filling up—as in the broad mass,—the masculine character sustained in the

seperate spheres in which they moved. The one had
the range of Germany,—the other, England, Ireland,
and Wales ; the one had to do with princes and ecclesiastical dignitaries,—the other with the humbler orders of
society ; the one had to uproot error in the church,—
the other to grapple with vice, in its various forms, in
the world ; the times of the one were of the most
sombre character,—those of the other, of religious light;
the one had few aids,—and public favour was on the
side of the other : but like Luther, from the colloquial
cognomen of "BILLY" in his own neighbourhood, and
the "YORKSHIRE FARMER" abroad, an air of rus-
ticity was thrown around his character which did not
belong to it ; and from the mistaken notions of others,
who never entered within the walls of a Wesleyan
chapel, and who received their impressions from the
statements of either the ignorant, the irreligious, or
from the burlesqued accounts of the profane, he
dwindled down into the character of a plain well-mean-
ing man,—with something of fancy,—with less of judgment,—whose popularity arose from his eccentricities,—
the thunder of whose power was merely in the strength
of his voice,—and whose religion was enthusiastic rant.
But combined with vast power, he possessed, beyond
all question, the greatest degree of originality of any
of his contemporaries in the ministry. His genius too,
was of a high order—the highest in the body ; but it
was by his power and originality that he was principally
distinguished. In Luther's day, and in Luther's circumstances, he would have been found, vested with a
Luther's prowess, and armed with the quailing power
comprised in some of the best and most condensed of
Luther's replies. Who, but a man of more than

ordinary mental capacity, could have given birth to the
conception, or would have been ready with the reply
which Mr. Dawson gave to the question respecting the
sublime and benevolent object of Christian Missions?
" Their object," he returned, " is no other than that
of blocking up the ' *broad way* '——of covering it over
with verdure—and of preventing the keen eye of an
archangel from seeing so much as the print of a human
foot upon it." This was reformation on a much more
magnificent scale, an object much more sublime, than
Luther ever contemplated, whose object was not so
much the conversion of the world, as the purification of
the church.

But in that which has been stated, we can scarcely
fail to perceive, in the late Mr William Dawson, the
MAN, the CHRISTIAN, and the MINISTER; the Man,
who was an honour to human nature,—the Christian,
who was an ornament to the Church,—and the Minister,
who, in Methodism, whether ancient or modern, stood
more apart from his brethren than almost any other
preacher for the peculiarity of his genius, and the
bold, original, and successful character of his ministry
—approaching the nearest of any man to the definition
given by the poor countryman of the celebrated George
Whitfield as a preacher, who, in reply to the interrogatory of his master on the subject, returned,——" Preach,
Sir! He preached like a lion; " a metaphor full of
life, full of fire, full of power, full of majesty. But
if Mr. Dawson preached like a lion, he lived like a
lamb; and has in this furnished posterity with another
example of a " perfect man "—as far as perfection can
be attached to the human character, in connexion with
its own peculiarities—" the Lion coming out of the

Lamb, and the Lamb coming out of the Lion "—bold, yet harmless, innocent, inoffensive ;—nay, more, a blessing to his species ;—thus terminating one of the most brilliant and extraordinary careers in the history of the lay ministry of Methodism, at the close of its first triumphant CENTENARY.

FINIS.

YORK :—J. COULTAS, PRINTER.

EXTRACTS FROM REVIEWS

OF

"THE WALL'S END MINER."

"Of the merits of this interesting and instructive volume, we must be understood to speak candidly — we are disposed to do justice — they are of an order which cannot fail to elicit commendation. The memoir of an orphan, from beginning to end, is well written—the characters introduced, fairly sustained,—and the interest kept up throughout." MONTHLY MAG., Feb., 1836.

"With how small a portion of the world is the most widely-travelled acquainted; in how narrow a circle of interests and feelings does the most liberal thinker live ! Want of time, want of opportunity, the pursuit of one or two engrossing objects confine him to his own orbit in spite of himself; but should any casuality lead him to tracts new and strange, he has the advantage over the narrow-minded of being, at least willing to contemplate, and to open his understanding and heart to things which may not heretofore have been comprehended in his philosophy. At least such we feel to be our case, in stumbling upon a book like 'The Wall's End Miner,'' a work which, in its own class, will have— probably has had already—both circulation and influence.—We can perceive that though there be only a hair's breadth between enthusiasm and fanaticism, still, the separation is clear and decisive: on one side of the boundary the morals and charities of life exist and flourish, though in an atmosphere strange to us." ATHENÆUM, Feb. 27, 1836.

"This work will be very acceptable to readers of the persuasion of the Wesleyan Methodists, and the various sects that have branched off from that vast stem. The narrative is, of itself, very interesting." METROPOLITAN MAG., March, 1836.

"William Crister's narrative, in the hands of Mr. Everett, is both interesting and instructive, and we shall be much mistaken if this small volume does not obtain a more extensive circulation, and make a deeper impression than the author has ventured to anticipate. It is well written; and we sincerely recommend it to those who wish to become acquainted with excellences of character which have been exemplified in humble circumstances." NEWCASTLE COURANT, Dec. 19, 1835.

SECOND EDITION.

"We need say no more in recommendation of this volume, than that, 'The Wall's End Miner' is an excellent companion to the 'Village Blacksmith." WATCHMAN, March 28, 1838.

" We are glad to see a second and improved edition of the Memoir. It abounds in very useful reflections and observations. Mr. Everett writes like one who well knows how to separate not only the chaff from the wheat, but the bran from the finer flour, and has furnished a very useful addition to the stock of Christian biography." WESLEYAN METHODIST MAGAZINE, April, 1838.

" This is a brief and novel Memoir of a singular, yet sincere disciple of Jesus, and a Northumberland collier. " NEW-YORK CHRISTIAN ADVOCATE AND JOURNAL, August 16th, 1839.

THE POLEMIC DIVINE:

OR

MEMOIRS OF THE LIFE, WRITINGS, AND OPINIONS,

OF THE

REV. DANIEL ISAAC.

" THESE are judicious and interesting Memoirs, illustrative of the upright, unaffected, and sound-minded subject of them. They will interest the reader of popular works, as well as afford some true and agreeable lights, whereby to study varieties of human nature, and when placed under peculiar circumstances. " MONTH-LY REVIEW, Sept., 1839, p. 145.

" It is not merely the scarcity in the article of biography, which makes us relish this life of Daniel Isaac. Were the memorials of departed worth, genius, and learning, ' plenty as blackberries,' we should still keep a corner for any fresh leaves from Everett's Book of Worthies. We know him of old, to be happy in the choice of his subjects, and skilful in the treatment of them. Enough to say, that we have read through this Life with pleasure, and cannot close it without recommending it to all such as love what is earnest and genuine, whether it go forth licensed by a bishop, or a synod of non-conformists. " ATHENÆUM, Aug. 24th 1839, p. 628.

" Of Daniel Isaac, we must speak with praise. He was simple, sincere, and temperate, with considerable humour, and with little temptation; but we have more to do with the subject, than with the man. " WEEKLY DESPATCH.

" This book will be of considerable interest to the Wesleyan Methodists, among whom Mr. Isaac, a man of strong character, was an eminent and influential preacher. It gives considerable insight into the domestic life of the lower and middle classes of England. Though not without some of the small blemishes, or rather distinctive marks of his sect and calling, Mr. Isaac was

both a good and an able man, full of life and energy ; possessing
and exercising the power of independent thought upon most
subjects. '' TAIT's EDINBURGH MAGAZINE. Nov., 1839, p. 758.
    " This is one of that class of works which appeal to a certain
exclusive, but very extensive order of readers, and to them it will
prove very acceptable.   The Polemic Divine is neither more nor
less than a memoir of the late Mr. Daniel Isaac, a Wesleyan
Preacher, and one of sufficient celebrity in his day and order to
justify a work of the kind devoted to his memory.   The work
is written with care and industry; and may, as a biography, be
read with interest by other persons than those devoted to the
extensive sect to which the writer and the subject belong. ''
NEW MONTHLY MAGAZINE, Nov. 1839, p. 431.